# AFRICAN AMERICAN

# POLITICAL THOUGHT

## 1890-1930

### Washington, DuBois, Garvey, and Randolph

# AFRICAN AMERICAN
# POLITICAL THOUGHT

## 1890-1930

### Washington, DuBois, Garvey, and Randolph

Edited by Cary D. Wintz

*M.E. Sharpe*
Armonk, New York
London, England

Selections 14–18 and 20–24 in part II are used with the permission of *The Crisis.*
Selection 25 in part II and selection 1 in part III are used with the permission
of Current History, Inc.
Selections 15 and 22 in part III are used with the permission
of the National Urban League, Inc.

Photograph of Booker T. Washington, front cover and p. 19,
courtesy, Library of Congress, LC-USZ62-49568.
Photograph of W.E.B. Du Bois, front cover and p. 83,
courtesy, Library of Congress, LC-USZ62-16767.
Photograph of Marcus Garvey, front cover and p. 167,
courtesy, Library of Congress, LC-USZ61-1854.
Photograph of A. Philip Randolph, front cover and p. 243,
courtesy, A. Philip Randolph Institute.

**Library of Congress Cataloging-in-Publication Data**

African American political thought, 1890–1930 : Washington, Du Bois, Garvey,
and Randolph / edited by Cary D. Wintz.
p.    cm.
Includes bibliographical references and index.
ISBN 1-56324-178-1 (alk. paper). — ISBN 1-56324-179-X (pbk. : alk. paper)
1. Afro-Americans—Politics and government—Sources.
2. Afro-Americans—History—1877–1964—Sources.
3. Political science—United States—History—Sources.
4. Du Bois, W. E. B. (William Edward Burghardt), 1868–1963.
5. Washington, Booker T., 1856–1915. 6. Garvey, Marcus, 1887–1940.
7. Randolph, A. Philip (Asa Philip), 1889–    . I. Wintz, Cary D., 1943–
E185.61.A239 1995
973′.0496073—dc20 95-33287
CIP

Printed in the United States of America

The paper used in this publication meets the minimum requirements of
American National Standard for Information Sciences—
Permanence of Paper for Printed Library Materials,
ANSI Z 39.48-1984.

∞

BM (c)   10   9   8   7   6   5   4   3   2   1
BM (p)   10   9   8   7   6   5   4

To my mother, Madge Mackey Wintz

# Contents

# Preface

This volume represents an effort to create a deeper understanding of the issue of race and the impact of race on the political thought of African Americans in the early twentieth century. It approaches the subject through the writings of four major figures in African American history—Booker T. Washington, W.E.B. Du Bois, Marcus Garvey, and A. Philip Randolph. Each of these figures grappled with the complex issue of race and worked to define the most effective way for African Americans to respond to the racial situation that confronted them in the United States at the beginning of the twentieth century. Each also approached the issue of race from a slightly different perspective and offered a range of strategies for confronting race and racial prejudice. Also, as the selections in this volume will underscore, not only did African Americans disagree (sometimes rather sharply) on the appropriate strategies and tactics for confronting racism in the United States, but each of the four men examined here modified his approach as circumstances changed and as his own interpretation of race and political power evolved.

Each of the four men encompassed in this collection represented a different approach to race in the United States in the early twentieth century. In each case, however, the complexity and evolving nature of their political thought undermine the generalizations usually made about their racial views. The result is that the lines dividing the racial thought of the four are not nearly as clear as many suppose.

Booker T. Washington is generally understood as an advocate of self-help and industrial education who avoided directly confronting the segregation and disfranchisement issues, while working quietly behind the scenes to combat the deteriorating racial situation at the turn of the century. Washington might be more accurately portrayed, however, as a pragmatic manipulator of political power who had a well-developed sense of the possibilities of the political and racial situation in the South, and used the power that he had to effect change in the context within which he operated. From this point of view, Washington's most serious miscalculations were his misunderstanding of how deeply entrenched racism was in America, and his belief that the future of African Americans was in the rural South. W.E.B. Du Bois is generally defined as an alternative to Washington, who rejected the Tuskegeean's moderate response to segregation and disfranchisement as defeatist, and Washington's commitment to industrial education as failing to prepare African Americans for either the political or the economic realities that they would face in the twentieth century. In reality, Du

Bois's views were more complex and more fluid. Initially he accepted much of the Washingtonian political philosophy, but the deterioration of the racial situation in the late 1890s and his dissatisfaction with Washington's exercise of political power caused him to side with the Tuskegeean's critics. Furthermore, Du Bois brought to bear on the African American experience a wide range of social, economic, political, and psychological theories. In the late nineteenth century, he became convinced of the duality of the African American experience—both African and American. In the years that followed, he would explore the implications that socialism (and Marxism), pan-Africanism, and racial nationalism brought to the racial debate. Du Bois also came to understand that racial integration carried a price—especially in a society that had not jettisoned its racial bigotry.

The political views of Marcus Garvey and A. Philip Randolph are equally complex. Garvey, on the one hand, is seen as the advocate of a black nationalism based on economic self-help (which drew inspiration from Washington), and a pan-Africanism (not dissimilar from that of Du Bois) that envisioned the liberation and union of the 400 million world inhabitants who were of African descent. In practice Garvey's nationalism brought him into conflict with advocates of desegregation, his iconoclasm and occasionally outrageous statements and actions brought him into conflict with most African American leaders, and his belief that African Americans must find their destiny in Africa ultimately isolated him from the African American masses. His flawed economic enterprises and his growing tendency to accuse his detractors from within the African American community with color prejudice further undermined his support and resulted in his ultimate failure. On the other hand, his vision of a self-sufficient African American community and his emphasis on the link between African Americans and Africa anticipated themes that Du Bois and other African American leaders would give voice to throughout the twentieth century.

A. Philip Randolph initially approached race from the perspective of class conflict. An advocate of radical socialism and a sympathizer with the Bolshevik revolution, Randolph represented the radical left within the African American community in the years during and immediately following World War I. He argued that all aspects of American racism, from lynching to economic poverty, had their roots in class warfare, and had their solution in the creation of a workers' political movement. Within this context Randolph was very critical of the "conservative" leadership of blacks like Du Bois, and sympathetic with many of the elements in the early Garvey movement. In the early 1920s, however, Randolph's views moderated as he embraced trade unionism and desegregation, and turned his back on communism. As Du Bois became more radical in the late 1920s and 1930s, Randolph would emerge as the mainstream advocate of civil rights.

The time frame encompassed by this volume is from the early 1890s to the mid-1930s. The collection begins with the early writings of Booker T. Washington that propelled him into the forefront of African American leadership in the 1890s, and it continues to trace the evolution of his political thought until his death in 1915. Du Bois is covered from his emergence as a major figure in the African American community in the late 1890s, until his separation from the NAACP and *The Crisis* in the mid-1930s. Garvey's work encompasses the period from his decision to come to the United States in 1916 until his deportation in 1927, while the A. Philip Randolph selections primarily cover the decade that he served as editor of *The Messenger,* from 1918 to 1928.

There are certain points about the text that I need to make. Except in rare cases (noted in the body of this work), all selections are reproduced exactly as they originally appeared. This means that errors in spelling and grammar, missing words, and typographical mistakes were not corrected. Word usage was also preserved. This means that terms such as "Negro," "negro," and on one or two occasions "nigger" appear exactly as they did when originally printed. The text remains unchanged, not to offend or cast aspersions on anyone, but to preserve the integrity of the historical document, as much as it can be preserved in a project like this, which strips the document out of its original context. Nevertheless, we have done as much as we can to reprint material as it was initially presented, warts and all.

For each selection I have included a very brief introduction, primarily to set the selection within a context. Also bibliographical information is provided for each selection, listing the location of the original, as well as the location of the most convenient reprints. In these references two abbreviations were used:

*BTW Papers*          *The Booker T. Washington Papers.* 13 vols. Ed. by Louis Harlan. Urbana, Ill.: University of Illinois Press, 1972.

*MG&UNIA Papers*   *The Marcus Garvey and Universal Negro Improvement Association Papers.* 7 vols. Ed. by Robert A. Hill. Berkeley: University of California Press, 1983.

This project, like all scholarly efforts, owes a debt of gratitude to all those whose previous work facilitated the work done here, as well as those who knowingly or unknowingly contributed to my work on this project. In the former category I acknowledge my debt to the hard work and scholarship that went into the collection and publication of the works of Booker T. Washington, W.E.B. Du Bois, and Marcus Garvey. Louis Harlan's work on the papers of Booker T. Washington serves as a model for all such scholarship; Robert Hill's work on Marcus Garvey and the Universal Negro Improvement Association matches the standards that Harlan set; I also appreciate the kind words of encouragement that Robert Hill gave me whenever I approached him with questions. Finally, anyone who begins to delve into the voluminous material that W.E.B. Du Bois produced during his extraordinary career appreciates the work Herbert Aptheker did in making so much of this material accessible in a well-organized manner.

My own research was greatly facilitated by the professional staffs of the many libraries that I visited during the course of this project. I want to give special thanks to the staffs at the Perry Casteñada Library of the University of Texas at Austin, the Fondren Library at Rice University, the M.D. Anderson Library of the University of Houston, and especially the Heartman Collection of the Robert J. Terry Library at Texas Southern University. They made the hours that I spent tracking down and copying articles from scores of magazines and periodicals productive. I also want to thank the staff at the A. Philip Randolph Institute in Washington, D.C., for their assistance in answering questions and helping me track down a photograph of the labor leader; as well as the staff at the NAACP library in Baltimore.

Finally, I want to show my appreciation to my colleagues in the History Department at Texas Southern University. At one time or another I used most of them for advice or as a sounding board for my ideas. Robert Baker, Merline Pitre, Gregory Maddox, Hunter Brooks, Robert Jackson, and Howard Beeth all provided advice and encouragement. Special thanks goes to my good friend and colleague W.M. Akalou for all the support he has given me. I also want to thank my friends Paul Finkelman and Michael Weber. They helped me conceptualize this project and kept me on task when other responsibilities threatened to side-track me. Of course, my wife, Celia, and my son, Jason, have my gratitude for their love, support, and patience.

# Introduction

By the end of the nineteenth century it was clear to any observer that emancipation and Reconstruction had not resolved the racial situation in the United States. During the first half of the nineteenth century, the existence of slavery in some ways obscured the fact that racism was deeply embedded in the United States. Reformers focused on emancipation, assuming that once they eradicated the evil of slavery, the resolution of other racial problems would be relatively simple, either through colonization or some gradual transition to full political and civil rights. Slavery would be abolished and political equality would be written into the Constitution, but the actual construction of a society that practiced racial equality remained remote. Furthermore, as the nineteenth century came to an end, all indicators pointed to the fact that racial lines were hardening in the United States as new restrictions were placed on the political and civil rights of blacks and as racial violence intensified.

In the years following Reconstruction, African American political ideology was dominated by two traditions. The first grew out of the remnants of the abolitionist movement and centered around both old abolitionists like Frederick Douglass and a new generation of militants like journalist T. Thomas Fortune of the New York *Age*. While Fortune and Douglass often disagreed on specifics, they both refused to accommodate themselves to segregation or political disfranchisement. Douglass, whose long career as an abolitionist made him the most prominent African American leader until his death in 1895, argued that the racial problem was not just a black problem, but an American one, and that the issue confronting the United States was whether justice applied equally to all citizens, or only to some. Fortune, who founded the Afro-American League in 1890, shared Douglass's commitment to agitation for civil rights, and his commitment to integration, and further asserted the right of blacks to resist those who would attempt to deny them their legal rights or subject them to mob violence. The second tradition in African American thought focused on community development and self-help. It was most closely associated with Alexander Crummell, rector of St. Luke's Episcopal Church in Washington, who was generally acknowledged to be the most prominent black intellectual of the nineteenth century. Crummell argued that, faced with racial hostility, African Americans should turn inward and construct a black community that would be a powerful economic force in the United States. Crummell, who advocated racial pride, solidarity, and self-help, believed that until racial justice prevailed, blacks had no option but to develop their own segregated institutions and communities, to develop a "nation within a nation."

These two traditions were not always exclusive of one another. Douglass, for example, was an advocate of racial pride, the economic development of the African American community, and self-help; he even sympathized with the need to develop a nation within a nation, given the racial antagonism that characterized the South in the late nineteenth century. However, he rejected the concept of self-help and community development as alternatives to agitation against segregation and disfranchisement, and he never endorsed the development of segregated schools or churches. He remained totally committed to integration and assimilation, even as the racial situation deteriorated in the last years of his life. Crummell, on the other hand, did not see the creation of African American institutions as an admission of racial inferiority. Rather, he argued from a black nationalistic perspective that the development of a black community within the United States would provide blacks with a power base that would eventually enable them to demand equal rights, and that blacks should maintain a sense of themselves as a distinctive people, even when the American caste system ultimately disappeared.

The death of Frederick Douglass in 1895 and the deteriorating racial situation in the late 1890s deprived African Americans of their most outspoken advocate of civil rights and strengthened the appeal of the self-help philosophy. The person who succeeded Douglass as the most prominent African American leader in the United States, and who succeeded Crummell as the most influential advocate of the self-help philosophy, was Booker T. Washington.

Booker T. Washington was born into slavery on a farm near Hales Ford, Virginia, in 1856. Following emancipation he received his education at Hampton Institute, where he fell under the influence of Samuel Chapman Armstrong's vision of self-help and industrial education. In 1881 he used the Armstrong model to found Tuskegee Institute, in Alabama, which became Washington's base of power as well as a center of industrial and agricultural education. At Tuskegee Washington stressed the belief that the practice of thrift, industry, and Christian morality would eventually earn blacks their rights. In preparation for this outcome, he said, blacks must learn trades so that they can transform themselves into a productive work force and begin accumulating capital and developing their community and their institutions. Washington believed that the future of blacks was tied to the South, especially the rural South, and that hard work and economic gain were more effective means of acquiring political and civil rights than were agitation and protest. However, Washington also used his growing influence as principal of Tuskegee to pressure, albeit rather gently, for fairness in suffrage laws and laws affecting public accommodations, and action against lynching and mob violence.

The event that symbolized Washington's rise to prominence as an African American leader, and also underscored the complexity of his political beliefs and his approach to racial problems, was his address to the opening of the Atlanta Exposition on September 18, 1895. This speech has come to symbolize Washington's acquiescence to segregation and the erosion of black rights—"In all things that are purely social we can be as separate as the five fingers, yet as the hand in all things essential to mutual progress"—as well as Washington's rejection of agitation—"The wisest among my race understand that the agitation of questions of social equality is the extremist folly. . . ." But both Washington's views and the Atlanta speech were more complex than this. First, while Washington did reject integration in all things "purely social" and "agitation of questions of social equality," he also warned his listeners that if white southerners did not involve their black neighbors in the economic progress of the South, then blacks would contribute to the destruction of the South. Second, while he rejected agitation for social equality, in that same sentence he asserted that "progress in the enjoyment of all the privileges that will come to us must be the result of severe and constant struggle rather than of artificial forcing." In other words, agitation alone will not gain civil rights, but a constant struggle combined with the preparation of the black community through hard work and education will bring blacks all the privileges enjoyed by whites. Finally, Washington urged blacks to "cast down your bucket where you are," to remain in the South and pursue their talents in agriculture, mechanics, industry, and the professions, rather than abandon the South. At the same time, though, Washington urged the leadership of the South to "cast down your bucket where you are" to build a new, prosperous South with the labor and skills of African Americans.[1]

The problem with Washington's Atlanta Exposition Address was that people read into it what they wanted to see. Most whites ignored Washington's warnings, and took comfort in the rejection of social equality; in other words, the tone of the address was acceptable, and there was enough in the content that was nonthreatening, or even supportive of white images of blacks, that Washington himself seemed to support the creation of a separate but equal southern society. This was not Washington's intent. While he believed in the value of self-help, industrial education, and the economic development of the black community, he rejected any political or social system that would place restrictions on black suffrage that whites did not face, or prevent blacks from acquiring access to equal public accommodations for their money, and he totally condemned lynching and mob violence. The problem was that Washington's public statements generally took such a nonconfrontational tone that he undermined the urgency of his message. Also, Washington placed too much confidence in the decency of southern leadership—even if this decency was based only on naked economic self-interest. The problem was that racial prejudice was not rational, and did not respond well to rational argument. It certainly was in the economic self-interest of the South to help develop a prosperous, well-educated, and productive African American population; yet few worked toward this end.

While some black leaders were critical of Washington's Atlanta speech, most applauded it, and Washington rode the wave of publicity generated by the speech to a position of leadership and power in the black community. Washington's true talents lay in political organization and the exercise of political power. As his biographer, Louis Harlan, observed, Washington "was not an intellectual, but a man of action. Ideas he cared little for. Power was his game."[2] In the years that followed Atlanta, Washington used every opportunity to speak about race and the role of African Americans in America; he participated in the creation of, or management of, black organizations such as the National Negro Business League (organized by Washington in 1900) and the Afro-American Council (which Washington supporters took control of in 1902); and he solidified his contacts with white philanthropists, civil rights advocates, and politicians. This latter activity increased his influence within the Republican Party, and gave him a great deal of control over the distribution of funds from white philanthropists to black institutions. The highlight of Washington's rise to prominence was the invitation extended to dine with President Theodore Roosevelt in the White House in 1901.

Even as his power and influence rose, Washington remained aware that African Americans were facing increasing attacks on their right to vote and their access to public accommodations and public education. Washington attempted to use his influence through open letters addressed to southern legislatures, and through editorials, interviews, and articles in white newspapers like the Atlanta *Constitution,* to publicize the injustice of suffrage laws that discriminated against blacks, and the unfairness of denying blacks equal accommodations on interstate carriers. Washington also spoke out sharply against lynching. In a remarkable public statement in the aftermath of the death of President William McKinley, Washington suggested that the anarchism behind the assassination of McKinley was connected to the lawlessness that had resulted in the deaths of several thousand African Americans at the hands of lynch mobs. Finally, Washington worked behind the scenes, often in concert with more militant black leaders like W.E.B. Du Bois, to undermine segregation on railroads and to counter other affronts to the civil rights of African Americans.

Despite these efforts to push forward a civil rights agenda, Washington came increasingly under attack by the more militant elements among black leadership. Initially Washington's critics represented the Frederick Douglass tradition in African American political ideology. The Tuskegeean was criticized as being too moderate in his dealings with white southerners, and for failing to adopt a more militant strategy and tone as the racial situation deteriorated in the years surrounding the turn of the century. Northerners such as William Monroe Trotter, Francis and Archibald Grimke, and—more and more in the early twentieth century —the young Atlanta University professor W.E.B. Du Bois stood at the center of the opposition to Washington. In truth the ideological difference between the two factions—the Bookerites and anti-Bookerites—was not that great. The Tuskegeean's supporters tended to be more moderate and accommodationist, and nonconfrontational in their campaign for racial justice, and they retained confidence in Washington's leadership. Washington's opponents were more strident in their demands for immediate and complete integration and restoration of full political rights, and they distrusted the leadership of the Tuskegeean. Both factions supported racial pride and self-help, but the anti-Bookerites increasingly were dissatisfied with the limitations of industrial education. There were two other sources of conflict. First, Washington and many of his supporters remained based in the South, and their program remained focused on the needs of African Americans in the South; the anti-Bookerites were either based in or had strong ties to the North, and had little sympathy or patience with the political restraints under which Washington and his supporters operated in the South. Second, Washington's critics became increasingly frustrated with the political and economic power that was concentrated in the Tuskegee machine. They attacked Washington severely for what they saw as his self-serving exercise of this power —especially his "takeover" of the Afro-American Council in 1902, his domination of the Committee of Twelve in 1904, and his use of patronage and distribution of white philanthropy to reward his friends and punish his enemies.

Faced with growing criticism in the early twentieth century, Washington did not dramatically alter his ideology or his approach to civil rights. He did address more and more the need for African Americans to remain in the South, and the need for white southerners to provide blacks with improved educational facilities, increased economic opportunity, and protection from mob violence if they wanted to head off the migration from rural areas to southern and northern cities. Washington also used his White House contacts (with Roosevelt and later Taft) in an effort to push his agenda for black voting rights and political rights. He was also more aggressive in using his political clout against his enemies, especially after the founding of the Niagara Movement in 1905. The strategy was simple. Washington excluded his critics from access to patronage—government jobs, university appointments, and access to philanthropic funds. In this way Washington effectively neutralized the Niagara Movement. By 1909 it was on the verge of economic collapse.

Washington's political domination of the African American community began to unravel after the establishment of the NAACP in 1910. Since the NAACP was established and primarily run by white liberals, it was relatively immune to the Tuskegeean control of political patronage and philanthropic purse strings; since it embraced the more militant civil rights philosophy of the anti-Bookerites, and made W.E.B. Du Bois an officer of the organization, it undermined Washington's political prestige, especially his reputation among whites as the preeminent spokesperson for his race. Washington responded to this threat to his leadership by moving slightly to the left. While he still maintained the basis of his beliefs, especially his commitment to economic development and self-help, and while he remained optimistic about the future of race relations, he began to place greater emphasis on his opposition to segregation. Even though, at the time of his death in 1915, Washington remained the most widely known and still the most respected black leader in the United States, it was also clear that power was shifting, and that the NAACP provided Du Bois with a power base as well as a forum from which to challenge the hegemony of the Tuskegeean.

During the first three decades of the twentieth century W.E.B. Du Bois represented several diverse themes in the ideology and politics of race. Initially he had been a disciple of Alexander Crummell and a supporter of the policies of Booker T. Washington; later he became one of the Tuskegeean's most important critics. However, Du Bois's ideology does not fit simply into the Bookerite/anti-Bookerite categories. To one degree or another, he advocated racial equality and desegregation; championed pan-Africanism, nationalism, and racial pride; and argued that economic and social justice could be attained only through what at the time was a poorly defined (and until the late 1920s, a non-Marxist) system of social democracy. In contrast to Washington, his strengths were as an intellectual—a theorist and a writer—not as a political organizer or power broker; he never attained the oratorical skills of either Washington or Marcus Garvey. Furthermore, Du Bois's political and social ideas continued to evolve throughout this period. By the mid-1930s his increasingly Marxist and nationalist ideology precipitated a rift with the more traditional leadership of the NAACP. In 1934 Du Bois resigned as editor of the NAACP journal, *The Crisis,* and his impact on American racial issues and politics diminished in the years that followed.

William Edward Burghardt Du Bois was born in Great Barrington, Massachusetts, on February 23, 1868. He attained about the best education available to an African American in the late nineteenth century. After attending public schools in Great Barrington, he went to Fisk and then did graduate work at Harvard and the University of Berlin. In 1895 he received his Ph.D. in history from Harvard University. After a brief stint on the faculty at Wilberforce University and as a researcher attached to the University of Pennsylvania, Du Bois joined the faculty at Atlanta University in 1897 as professor of history and economics.

It was during his years at Wilberforce and Pennsylvania that Du Bois first became involved in the politics of race. At Wilberforce Du Bois met Alexander Crummell, who had a significant impact on the young professor's early political thought. Then in March 1897 at the inaugural meeting of the American Negro Academy, an organization for black intellectuals created by Crummell, Du Bois presented a controversial and riveting paper that first publicly expressed his political and racial views. In this paper, "The Conservation of Races," Du Bois developed two themes. First, he argued that each race, including blacks, had specific and distinctive characteristics and must maintain its separate identity to fulfill its destiny. African American destiny was linked to that of the other peoples of Africa and the African diaspora, and could not be realized by assimilation or absorption into white culture. Secondly, Du Bois focused on the dualism of the African American identity. Blacks were American by birth, citizenship, political ideals, language, and religion, but they were also connected to the vast Negro race.³ At this time in his career, Du Bois embraced cultural dualism. This placed him in a political position between that of the nationalists and the integrationists; Du Bois supported community development and self-help and downplayed the need for immediate political or civil rights, and generally endorsed the Washington approach to race.

In the early twentieth century, Du Bois began to distance himself from the Tuskegee position. As racial violence, Jim Crow laws, and political disfranchisement of blacks spread in the early twentieth century, Du Bois began to have reservations about the policy of accommodation and cooperation with southern white leadership, and the effectiveness of the behind-the-scenes manipulation that Washington relied on so extensively; he also worried about Washington's emphasis on industrial education and he began to feel uncomfortable with the power that the Tuskegee machine wielded. Du Bois first expressed these reservations in "Of Mr. Booker T. Washington and Others," an essay published in *The Souls of Black Folk* in 1903. In 1904 he detailed his differences with Washington's conservative approach: "First, the scope of education; second, the necessity of the right of suffrage; third, the importance of civil rights; fourth, the conciliation of the South; fifth, the future of the race in this country."⁴ Specifically Du Bois argued that blacks needed a well-educated leadership—one that could not be created by institutions that focused exclusively on industrial education. He also rejected Washington's policy of accommodation, and insisted that protest, not conciliation with southern leaders, was the only way for blacks to secure their political and civil rights. Du Bois now repudiated segregation, even for the short term. Separate but equal was never equal; it was only a system designed to foster inequality and perpetuate the subordination of blacks. While Du Bois still endorsed racial pride and racial solidarity, he now viewed these not as ends in themselves, but as weapons to use to protest disfranchisement and segregation. Du Bois's new militancy not only contrasted with the more moderate Washington, it also contrasted with the philosophy and tone that he himself had used in the past.

The most tangible result of Du Bois's evolving political philosophy was the role he played in the organization of the Niagara Movement in the summer of 1905 and of the NAACP in 1910. In July 1905 Du Bois and twenty-eight other black leaders, impatient with accommodation, met in Fort Erie, Ontario, to organize a more militant civil rights organization. The resulting Niagara Movement selected Du Bois as its general secretary and dedicated itself to universal manhood suffrage, opposed all forms of discrimination based on race or color, and embraced protest, agitation, and confrontation as its weapons of choice. The major target of the movement was Booker T. Washington's domination of black America; in March 1905 Du Bois had charged the Tuskegee machine with buying the support of black newspaper editors by investing in their periodicals. In response to these attacks the Tuskegeean used his influence with the black press to discredit the Niagara Movement, and his political contacts and prestige to undermine the careers of the Niagaraites. Faced with Washington's relentless opposition, an inability to establish a broad base of support within even the black middle class, and divisions within its leadership, the Niagara Movement began to self-destruct in mid-1908. One reason for its failure was Du Bois's inexperience and ineffectiveness as a political leader; another was that the Tuskegee machine prevented the organization from acquiring much white support.

The failure of the Niagara Movement and the emergence of a small group of liberal-to-radical white progressives concerned about race in America provided the ingredients for the development of a biracial civil rights movement. The National Association for the Advancement of Colored People (NAACP) grew out of a series of meetings, primarily involving white liberals and former Niagaraites, in 1909 and 1910. Washington, perceiving the organization as simply the revival of the Niagara Movement, boycotted the organizational meetings. Du Bois was the most influential black involved in the new organization, and the only black selected as an officer and member of the board of directors. Although there was no formal merger of the defunct Niagara Movement and the NAACP, most of the Niagaraites joined the new organization, making that group the dominant black element in the NAACP from the outset. Most importantly, the NAACP succeeded where the Niagara Movement had failed. As a biracial organization that was actually dominated by whites during its first two decades, it was strong enough and sufficiently funded to withstand Washington's attacks and, after the Tuskegeean's death in 1915, successful in at least temporarily reconciling and uniting most of the factions in the black community.

The creation of the NAACP was a turning point in Du Bois's life. With some misgivings he resigned his faculty position at Atlanta University and moved to New York City in the summer of 1910 to begin working full-time as a political/civil rights activist in a new, poorly defined job for a new organization with an uncertain future. Du Bois's success was amazing. For once in his career he functioned effectively within a highly politicized setting. Without specific authority to do so, he founded *The Crisis,* the NAACP's monthly journal. Then he fought successfully with conservative members of the NAACP board to gain full authority over the editorial content of *The Crisis.* Du Bois's victory in this struggle meant that until he resigned from *The Crisis* in 1934 he had a forum from which he could express his ideas on the issues of the day. He used this position to push a fairly militant, somewhat radical civil rights agenda based largely on the program of the Niagara Movement, with a specific endorsement of political agitation. In the larger political context, however, most of the political positions that he took during his first decade as editor of *The Crisis* were fairly moderate. For example, in 1912 he resigned from the Socialist Party in order to endorse the presidential candidacy of Woodrow Wilson. Six years later he refused to join with other radicals in opposition to the world war. In one of his best known and most controversial editorials, he urged African Americans to "Close

Ranks," to put aside their racial grievances and stand "shoulder to shoulder with our white fellow citizens."[5]

At the end of World War I Du Bois was at the peak of his power and influence. He had just turned fifty years of age, he held a position of power in the most influential civil rights organization in the United States, and as editor of *The Crisis* he controlled a platform from which he could broadcast his political and racial philosophy to the country. However, the 1920s were not successful for Du Bois. Increasingly, his views and his leadership were challenged from both the left and the right—he was not radical enough for the new socialist/communist left of the African American community, or for the pan-Africanists who swarmed in support of Marcus Garvey, but he was too radical for the increasingly traditional leadership of the NAACP; furthermore he seemed stranded on the periphery as major developments swept through the black community.

Two issues, socialism and pan-Africanism, illustrate the problems Du Bois faced in the 1920s. In the early 1920s Du Bois became convinced that a reinvigorated American socialism might provide a viable political choice for African Americans. However, he distanced himself at this time from the radical socialism represented by the Bolshevik revolution and communism, opting instead for a moderate evolutionary socialism such as that practiced by the British Labour Party. This moderate socialism made him an object of scorn among black radicals. A. Philip Randolph of *The Messenger* led the attack on Du Bois and his conservative leadership; others such as poet and writer Claude McKay and Cyril V. Briggs, founder of the militant African Blood Brotherhood, echoed these attacks. Ironically, by the time Du Bois embraced Marxism and moved to the left in the late 1920s and early 1930s, Randolph and McKay had renounced communism and moved back to the mainstream. Du Bois's socialism now undermined his position at the NAACP.

At the end of World War I Du Bois also renewed his interest in pan-Africanism. This should have placed him in a position to influence the emerging Garvey movement, which focused so much of its energy on a vision of African–African American unity. Du Bois, however, was never able to sell his pan-Africanism to the black middle class, much less the black masses. And personal antagonisms prevented cooperation between Du Bois and Garvey. Even before he came to the United States, Garvey had been critical of Du Bois's leadership. Garvey unjustly accused Du Bois of selling out to the white leadership of the NAACP and of abandoning the interests of the black working classes. Du Bois, sensitive to this criticism, used the pages of *The Crisis* to launch an attack on Garvey and the operations of his Universal Negro Improvement Association (UNIA). When Garvey was convicted of mail fraud, Du Bois applauded the verdict.

In many ways Du Bois seemed out of step with the 1920s, challenged on all sides, and failing to react effectively to opportunities that presented themselves. In the early 1930s these failures combined with new problems that undermined his position at the NAACP. His renewed interest in socialism and pan-Africanism in the early 1920s and his enchantment with Marxism in the late 1920s distanced him from moderates in the NAACP. Also in the late 1920s, *The Crisis,* which previously had operated at a profit, began to lose money; the onset of the Great Depression intensified the financial problems of *The Crisis* and of the NAACP. With *The Crisis* no longer financially self-sufficient, Du Bois's autonomy as editor once again came under review by a board of directors that was already uncomfortable with his leftist politics.

Du Bois precipitated the final confrontation with the leadership of the NAACP when he wrote an editorial challenging the organization's anti-segregation position. Du Bois suggested that in a racist society it was necessary for black communities to develop their own segregated institutions. More specifically he argued that in a racist society it was better to have segregated schools and hospitals than no schools and hospitals at all, and that it was even preferable to have segregated facilities than to be discriminated against, mistreated, or given inferior service in an integrated facility. This position addressed the reality that most African Americans faced in the early 1930s, but it was a great departure from the position that Du Bois had championed since 1904, and from the position that had been the cornerstone of the NAACP's racial philosophy since its founding in 1910. In May 1934 Du Bois resigned.

In the second decade of the twentieth century, the political options available to African Americans broadened beyond those represented by the militant anti-segregationist/accommodationist self-help dichotomy. Anti-colonial energies unleashed by the world war fueled a resurgence of pan-Africanism, while the Bolshevik revolution underscored the potential of organized labor and socialism. In addition the rapid urbanization of African Americans created new political and organizational possibilities. While Du Bois's attempts to deal with these changes met with only limited success, other black leaders emerged to address these new options.

Marcus Garvey was born in 1887 in St. Ann's Bay, a small town on the northern coast of Jamaica. While still in primary school, Garvey was apprenticed to a printer. In 1906 he moved to Kingston, where he worked as a printer, became involved in labor activities, and, in 1909, briefly operated a newspaper, *Garvey's Watchman.* In 1910 Garvey left Jamaica, traveling first to Central America, and then to London. While in England he took courses at a college for working-class youth, observed British politics, from the debates in Parliament to the speeches in Hyde Park, and immersed himself in the life of the Commonwealth minorities that made up London's ethnic community. In this setting Garvey first encountered the philosophy of pan-Africanism.

Garvey returned to Kingston, Jamaica, in July 1914; on August 1, 1914, he established the Universal Negro Improvement Association and African Communities League (UNIA) with a platform that combined a traditional missionary program of caring for the needy of the race, civilizing backward African tribes, and developing schools and colleges for black youth with a pan-African commitment to establishing a universal confraternity among the race, establishing agencies around the world to protect the rights of all Negroes, and conducting worldwide commercial and industrial intercourse.[6] Interestingly, Booker T. Washington inspired much of Garvey's political thought at this time. Garvey corresponded with Washington in 1914 and 1915 about the possibility of traveling to Tuskegee and about his goal to establish an institution in Jamaica modeled after Tuskegee. Following Washington's death, Garvey wrote to Robert Russa Moton that he had adopted the "Washington platform" as the basis for the program of his organization.[7] What Garvey did was to combine the self-help, community development, industrial education aspects of Washington's philosophy with the internationalist pan-Africanism that he had picked up in London. However, this program did not enjoy much success in Jamaica. After two years of organizing, the UNIA had only about a hundred members. Garvey blamed his difficulties on the hostility of Jamaican blacks, especially those of light complexion; he said that most of his support came from whites.

In March 1916 Garvey came to the United States. His stated intention was to raise money for the school that he wanted to establish in Jamaica. He headquartered in Harlem and spent about fifteen months traveling around the country, delivering lectures, meeting with black leaders, and attempting without much success to raise funds. Initially Garvey was greatly impressed with the progress that blacks had made in the United States—especially in comparison to the lack of progress among Jamaican blacks. Garvey also was overwhelmed by what he encountered in the United States. The wealth of the country, the size and relative wealth of the African American community, the social and political turbulence (especially in the black community) unleashed by World War I and the accompanying black migration, and the divisions within African American leadership seemed a fertile ground for political organization. Sometime between his arrival in early 1916 and the end of 1917, Garvey made several important decisions. First, he concluded that the organization of black business and industry was far more essential for the development of the race than the establishment of a school for blacks. Second, he founded a branch of the UNIA in New York, effectively shifting the center of his movement from Jamaica to Harlem. More important, he decided that the wealth, business experience, and leadership skills of African Americans, if properly organized and directed, could stimulate the liberation of and economic development of African peoples everywhere.

The UNIA grew slowly in the United States. Initially its ideology was a fairly moderate blend of Booker T. Washington self-help and pan-Africanism. In 1919 several developments pushed Garvey toward a more radical ideology. The issues that he brought forward in 1919 would dominate his political thought through the mid-1920s. First, Garvey attempted to represent the interests of African peoples (especially those of the former German colonies) at the peace conference. In November 1918 he wrote that if future wars were to be avoided, the European control of Africa must end, and Africa must be left in the hands of the black people. Garvey also endorsed the idea that in the short term the former German colonies in Africa should be administered by committees of educated blacks from the United States, the Caribbean, and independent states in Africa. Garvey was also deeply affected by the racial violence in the United States in 1919, especially the riots in East St. Louis. These riots undermined his optimism about the United States and convinced him that ultimately the future of all people of African descent was in Africa. He also promised that violence would be met with violence. For a time he insisted that for every black lynched in the South, a white would be lynched in New York; and he predicted that unless colonialism ended, the next world war would be a race war, with the black and yellow people allied in a struggle against whites. Ultimately he would conclude that the United States was a white man's country and as such had no place for African Americans. Finally Garvey introduced his plan for the development of black business. In May 1919 Garvey announced the creation of the Black Star Line, a steamship company financed by shares sold to African Americans, which would carry freight and passengers between the centers of black population in the United States, the Caribbean, and Africa.

The announcement of the Black Star Line was a significant step for Garvey and the UNIA. It was, first of all, a dramatic response to his own call for the development of black-owned business. The UNIA had purchased its own building, Liberty Hall, in Harlem, and it had opened a restaurant and a newspaper, *Negro World*. The Black Star Line was a spectacular move that caught the attention and the imagination of the African American community. It would be the first phase of a program of economic development that envisioned a network of black-owned stores, factories, and other commercial establishments. Second, the Black Star Line fit well with the internationalist, pan-African aspect of Garvey's program. Garvey's black-owned, black-captained fleet of steamships would carry trade between the black ports of the world, stimulate the economic development of black peoples everywhere through commerce and trade, and carry millions of black immigrants back to their African homeland. Finally, the Black Star Line exposed Garvey's Achilles' heel. His vision exceeded his grasp. The Black Star Line revealed Garvey's weakness as a businessman and financier. It involved him in an enterprise about which he knew nothing, it undermined his credibility, it made him vulnerable to legal action, and it brought him down.

Regardless of his failures, Garvey's goals were ambitious. His vision was to unite under his leadership the 400 million black people of the world, liberate Africa from European colonialism, and develop a black economy that would coexist with the white capitalist economy. Toward those ends Garvey attempted to transform the UNIA into a mass-based international movement. In August 1920 the UNIA held its first international convention. Twenty-five thousand delegates crowded into Madison Square Garden for the month-long fete; they elected Garvey provisional president of Africa, and approved a fifty-four-article

Declaration of Negro Rights. Unfortunately the optimism of the 1920 convention was short-lived; 1921 was a bad year for the UNIA. The depression of 1920–1921 raised unemployment levels to 20 percent and precipitated a financial crisis for the UNIA; stock sales for the Black Star Line plummeted and although Garvey claimed 4 million UNIA members in 1921, the organization received only $4,000 in membership fees. Also, W.E.B. Du Bois published a somewhat critical two-part analysis of Garvey's activities in *The Crisis*. The situation did not improve in the following years. By 1922 a number of black leaders had serious questions about the viability of the Black Star Line and the legality of the financing of this enterprise, including former ally A. Philip Randolph, who compared Garvey's sale of Black Star Line shares to black workers with the activities of financial swindler Charles Ponzi.

In January 1922 Marcus Garvey was arrested and charged with mail fraud in connection with the marketing of Black Star Line shares. The legal problems connected with this case accelerated, but did not initiate the unraveling of Garvey's empire. Already in 1921 black leaders had begun to disassociate themselves from Garvey, and in 1921 and 1922 a number of officials resigned from positions in the UNIA. Garvey responded by blaming his problems on disloyal UNIA officers who had betrayed his trust, and on black leaders like Du Bois who did the bidding of his white enemies, and who were prejudiced against Garvey because of his darker skin color. In August 1922 Garvey reorganized the leadership of the UNIA and purged his critics. Garvey also gave fuel to his enemies in June 1922 when he met in Atlanta with Edward Clarke, second-in-command of the Ku Klux Klan. This meeting, together with Garvey's continued argument for racial separation and for recognizing the United States as the white man's country, convinced many of his critics that he had worked out a deal with the Klan. Squabbles within the ranks of the UNIA climaxed on January 1, 1923, with the murder in New Orleans of former UNIA officer and outspoken Garvey critic James Eason.

Garvey's trial for mail fraud began in federal court in New York City on May 21, 1923. On June 18 the jury found Garvey guilty, and the judge sentenced him to five years in prison, a $1,000 fine, and court costs. Garvey was jailed in The Tombs in New York City until September 10, 1923, when he was released on bond pending his appeal. Garvey spent his freedom attempting to revitalize the UNIA. In February 1925, Garvey's appeals were denied, his bail was revoked, and he was imprisoned in the federal penitentiary in Atlanta. Garvey approached prison with a sense of martyrdom and a determination that his movement would survive. Garvey was not martyred; he survived prison. On November 18, 1927, President Calvin Coolidge commuted Garvey's sentence; the Immigration Bureau arranged deportation papers, and on December 2, 1927, he was placed aboard the SS *Saramacca* in New Orleans, and shipped out of the country. The UNIA did not survive. Garvey's legal problems effectively destroyed the American movement, and his efforts to reestablish the movement in Jamaica never bore fruit. By the mid-1930s both Garvey and his movement had sunk into obscurity.

While Garvey gave voice to the ideology of black nationalism and pan-Africanism, his contemporary, A. Philip Randolph, emerged as the spokesperson for a socialist/labor approach to American racial injustice. Randolph was born on April 15, 1889, in Crescent City, Florida. His father was an itinerant AME minister who stressed the importance of education to his children. As a child Randolph's education was supplemented with tutors; as a young man he received his college education from Cookman Institute in Jacksonville, Florida. In 1911, at the age of twenty-two, Randolph moved to New York City, apparently hoping to pursue an acting career. There he held a series of menial jobs, dabbled at organizing his fellow workers, took classes at City College, and lectured occasionally on economics and black history at the Rand School of Economics, a socialist-sponsored institution. At City College and the Rand School, Randolph became interested in politics, embraced socialism, and fell under the influence of the writings of Karl Marx. He also met two people who had a significant impact on his life. In the spring of 1914 he met Lucille Green, a wealthy widow and former schoolteacher who was a business associate of the African American cosmetics tycoon, Madam C.J. Walker. Randolph and Green married in the summer of 1914. Green's wealth, and the income from the beauty shop that she owned, would help finance Randolph's political activities. In the summer of 1914 Randolph also met Chandler Owen, a student of political science and economics at Columbia University. Randolph and Owen would form a political partnership. Together they explored race and politics, and concluded that socialism, with its commitment to the working class, offered the best hope for blacks in the United States. American racism, they argued, was the product of capitalism; since virtually all African Americans were members of the working class, socialism was the obvious vehicle to liberate blacks and defeat capitalist-based racism.

During this period Randolph also was influenced by the street-corner speeches of black socialist Hubert Harrison as well as the work of white socialists Eugene Debs and "Big Bill" Haywood. He was especially impressed with the industrial radicalism represented by the Industrial Workers of the World (IWW); its effort to organize unskilled industrial and agricultural workers, as well as its radical politics, seemed to have great potential for the mass of African Americans. When the United States entered World War I, Randolph and Owen rejected Du Bois's call to "close ranks," and instead joined with radical socialists who opposed the war, and became spokespersons for the antiwar movement. As a result of these activities, Randolph and Owen were arrested and briefly detained at a socialist antiwar rally in Cleveland in 1918.

In 1917 Randolph and Owen became editors of *The Messenger*. Their foray into political journalism began when they were asked to edit *Hotel Messenger*, a monthly magazine for the New York Headwaiters Union. After several issues, Randolph and Owen severed their affiliation with the union (which they discovered was corrupt), and with financial backing from Lucille Randolph they launched *The Messenger* as an independent radical black journal of economics and politics. Proclaiming itself "The Only Radical Negro Magazine in America," the early issues of *The Messenger* championed industrial unionism, socialism, and an uncompromising commitment to racial equality in all forms, including racial intermarriage, while it castigated the NAACP and "conservative" leaders like Du Bois for supporting the war and opposing the radical political agenda of groups like the IWW. The antiwar activities of Randolph and Owen attracted the attention of the Justice Department, which attempted to shut down the magazine. However, except for a few issues that were delayed, *The Messenger* survived the hostility of Attorney General A. Mitchell Palmer and his special assistant, J. Edgar Hoover. Beginning in 1920 *The Messenger* began an analysis of American politics which concluded that neither the Republicans nor the Democrats offered anything to blacks, and urged black voters instead to support the Socialist Party. This advice corresponded with Randolph's brief incursion into electoral politics; in 1920 Randolph ran for New York State controller on the Socialist ticket, while Owen, Lucille Randolph, and two other black candidates ran for the state legislature.

In the early postwar period, Randolph confronted several problems that threatened to divide the left—especially the African American left. First, as an advocate of organized labor, Randolph had to contend with the fact that American labor unions historically discriminated against blacks and gave no evidence that this policy was about to change. Randolph was especially concerned about Samuel Gompers and the American Federation of Labor (AFL) and its record of excluding blacks from membership. In addition, American socialists did not have a very good record concerning race relations. Randolph's response was to castigate the AFL and focus on the organization of black unions, even though this ran counter to his belief in integration and the commonality of interests among all members of the working class. Randolph also had to deal with the fact that the black workers, who were the apparent target of *The Messenger*'s ideology, knew from experience that white unions had no interest in their needs and consequently were largely unconvinced by *The Messenger*'s message, while the white and black radicals who were the actual readers of and supporters of the magazine expected a prolabor, prosocialist message. The second problem that Randolph faced concerned Marcus Garvey. Randolph initially supported Garvey—in fact, he had been one of the first to introduce the Jamaican to Harlem audiences. He also participated with Garvey in efforts to influence the Versailles conference on the subject of colonialism in Africa, and he agreed with Garvey's commitment to racial pride. On the other hand, Garvey's race consciousness and racial separatism conflicted with Randolph's belief in interracial working-class consciousness and his commitment to integration. By the summer of 1922, Randolph was one of Garvey's harshest critics. Finally, Randolph was affected by the split in American socialism triggered by the Bolshevik revolution. Initially Randolph had been sympathetic to the Bolsheviks. However, when the American Socialist

Party split over efforts to create an American communist party under the control of the Third International, Randolph sided with the conservative faction that rejected Moscow control of an American political party. This division especially affected black radicals, who tended to divide along national lines, with West Indians supporting the communists and most American-born black socialists supporting the conservative, Randolph faction.

The schism in the socialist movement had a direct impact on Randolph's political ideology. Blaming the communists for the split, he became increasingly anti-communist; as he lost readers and staff to the communist left, and especially as financial support from socialists declined, Randolph and *The Messenger* began to drift toward the political center in the early 1920s. As late as 1923 Randolph would still urge blacks to support socialist and labor candidates instead of Republicans and Democrats, but in the essay "State of the Race" he focused on the confusion created by competing leftist ideologies, and urged black leaders and intellectuals to meet together to redefine political and racial strategies.[8] By 1924 Randolph was promoting the growth of black business along with supporting the cause of black labor, and he changed the masthead of *The Messenger* from "The Only Radical Negro Magazine in America" to "The World's Greatest Negro Monthly." The most significant change, however, came in August 1925 when Randolph accepted the invitation to become the head of a new African American labor union, the Brotherhood of Sleeping Car Porters; *The Messenger* became the official magazine of the union.

As a labor leader Randolph moved into the mainstream of American politics. Although *The Messenger* championed the cause of unionism in general and the Brotherhood of Sleeping Car Porters in particular, Randolph continued to use the magazine to express his political views—political views that rapidly were moderating. After 1925 Randolph became openly anti-communist, and ceased writing about socialism as the answer to the problems of race in the United States. Instead he steadfastly endorsed racial equality and desegregation, and he urged the election of black candidates to Congress—through the Republican Party; he continued to promote the development of black business, and he warned that black business would have to compete with white business as segregation lessened. Randolph also ended his feud with Du Bois and the NAACP; indeed, by the end of the 1920s Randolph and Du Bois would both call for the development of black cooperatives to strengthen the economic clout of black communities. Perhaps most indicative of Randolph's new status as a moderate African American leader, in 1926 he was invited to address the opening session of the Philadelphia Sesquicentennial Exposition. Conscious of the connection between this event and Booker T. Washington's address at the Atlanta Exposition in 1895, Randolph used the occasion to emphasize the importance of the contribution of African Americans to the development of the United States, and he tried to define the role they would play in the future. Randolph insisted that blacks wanted equality rather than separation, and he called for desegregation and mutual understanding so that the conflicts between races might one day be obsolete.[9]

In 1928 *The Messenger,* beset with financial difficulties, ceased publication. Randolph would focus most of his energies for the next decade on the development of the Brotherhood of Sleeping Car Porters. He won two major victories in this struggle. First, in 1929 he engineered the affiliation of the Brotherhood of Sleeping Car Porters with the AFL. This affiliation gave the brotherhood the support they needed to continue their struggle with the Pullman Company for recognition of the union. The second victory occurred in August 1937, when the Pullman Company finally signed a labor contract with the brotherhood, ending a twelve-year struggle. Randolph's success as a labor organizer, together with the decline in influence in the 1930s of other African American leaders, brought him to the forefront, and gave him the prestige and influence that first Washington and then Du Bois had held in the African American community. By the time Randolph organized the March on Washington in 1941 to protest job discrimination in the defense industry, he was the most significant civil rights leader in the United States.

Neither Booker T. Washington, W.E.B. Du Bois, Marcus Garvey, or A. Philip Randolph ever fully understood the complexity of race or found a solution to race in America. Nor were these four the only ones who explored this question in the early twentieth century. However, to a large degree they defined the parameters of the debate over race and politics in twentieth-century America, and their explorations provided the intellectual basis for the civil rights movement and the struggle for racial justice that has dominated so much of U.S. history in the second half of the century.

## Notes

1. See Booker T. Washington, Atlanta Exposition Address, pp. 23–26 below. There is some question about exactly what Washington meant by the term "social equality." In a letter to President Theodore Roosevelt on December 26, 1904 (pp. 58–60 below), Washington argued that southern whites interpreted social equality as meaning social intercourse, and he implied that they consequently feared that social equality was a code word for racial amalgamation, or miscegenation. If this is correct, Washington's rejection of social equality did not mean that he was rejecting civil rights or even equal access to public accommodations.

2. Louis R. Harlan, *Booker T. Washington,* viii.

3. Du Bois developed these thoughts more fully in "Strivings of the Negro People," *Atlantic Monthly: A Magazine of Literature, Science, Art, and Politics* 80 (August 1897): 194–98. See pp. 85–90 below.

4. W.E.B. Du Bois, "The Parting of the Ways," *World Today* 6 (April 1904): 521–32. See pp. 95–98 below.

5. W.E.B. Du Bois, "Close Ranks," *The Crisis* 16 (July 1918): 111. See p. 116 below.

6. Judith Stein, *The World of Marcus Garvey,* 30.

7. Marcus Garvey to Robert Russa Moton, February 29, 1916. See pp. 178–84 below.

8. A. Philip Randolph, "The State of the Race," *The Messenger* 5 (April 1923): 662. See pp. 286–91 below.

9. A. Philip Randolph, "The Negro Faces the Future," *The Messenger* 8 (July 1926): 203. See pp. 309–16 below.

## Selected Bibliography

The following materials represent the most recent biographical works on the four men whose political thought is featured in this volume.

Harlan, Louis R. *Booker T. Washington: The Making of a Black Leader, 1865–1901.* New York: Oxford University Press, 1972.

———. *Booker T. Washington: The Wizard of Tuskegee, 1901–1915.* New York: Oxford University Press, 1983.

Harris, William H. *Keeping the Faith: A. Philip Randolph, Milton P. Webster, and the Brotherhood of Sleeping Car Porters, 1925–1937.* Urbana: University of Illinois Press, 1991.

Lewis, David Levering. *W.E.B. Du Bois: Biography of a Race, 1868–1919.* New York: Henry Holt and Company, 1993.

Marable, Manning. *W.E.B. Du Bois: Black Radical Democrat.* Boston: Twayne Publishers, 1986.

Pfeffer, Paula F. *A. Philip Randolph, Pioneer of the Civil Rights Movement.* Baton Rouge: Louisiana State University Press, 1990.

Stein, Judith. *The World of Marcus Garvey: Race and Class in Modern Society.* Baton Rouge: Louisiana State University Press, 1986.

# I. Booker T. Washington

# 1
## Letter to the Editor, *Montgomery Advertiser,* April 30, 1885

*This letter sent by Booker T. Washington to the editor of the* Montgomery Advertiser *was published on April 30, 1885. Over the course of his career Washington
would express his views on a number of race-related issues in letters to the
editor of a number of southern newspapers. In this letter Washington establishes
his technique of criticizing the treatment of blacks without directly challenging
the core beliefs of southern bigots, or directly criticizing the South. The letter
also foreshadows the Atlanta speech. This letter was reprinted in* The Booker T.
Washington Papers, *13 vols., ed. by Louis Harlan (Urbana, Ill.: University of
Illinois Press, 1972), 2: 270–73 (hereafter cited as* BTW Papers*).*

Tuskegee, Ala., April 24, 1885

Editor *Advertiser:* Judging from some of your past utterances that you are in
favor of justice being shown the colored man on railroads, I am encouraged to
write the following for insertion in your paper. Having to some extent noticed
the position of many of the county papers relative to the subject, I am glad to
know that they, too, are outspoken in condemnation of the wrong which colored
railroad passengers are made to suffer. In fact, I have not conversed with a single
intelligent, progressive white man who has not shown the right spirit in the
matter.

I wish to say a few words from a purely business standpoint. It is not a subject
with which to mix social equality or anything bordering on it. To the negro it is a
matter of dollars and cents. I claim that the railroads in Alabama do not provide
as good accommodations for the colored passengers as those furnished white
passengers for the same money and that the fare is not first class as claimed on
the face of the ticket.

My reasons for the above assertions are (a) that in most cases the smoking car
and that in which colored people are put are the same; (b) when not put directly
into the smoking car they are crammed into one end of a smoking car with a door
between that is as much open as closed, making little difference between this and
the smoking car; (c) on some of the roads the colored passengers are carried in
one end of the baggage car, there being a partition between them and the baggage or express; (d) only a half coach is given to the colored people and this one
is almost invariably an old one with low ceiling and it soon becomes crowded
almost to suffocation and is misery to one knowing the effects of impure air. The
seats in the coach given to colored people are always greatly inferior to those

given the whites. The car is usually very filthy. There is no carpet as in the first class coach. White men are permitted in the car for colored people. Whenever a poorly dressed, slovenly white man boards the train he is shown into the colored half coach. When a white man gets drunk or wants to lounge around in an indecent position he finds his way into the colored department.

Plainly this treatment is not an equivalent for value received. Why should the railroads be allowed to make a discrimination that no other business man or business corporation makes? I enter a dry goods store in Tuskegee, buy a yard of calico, I am shown to just as good a counter, am treated just as politely by the clerk and for the same money receive just as good (though a separate) piece of calico as the white man. I subscribe for the *Advertiser.* For the same money you send me a paper printed just as nicely, done up as well and that costs you just as much in every way as the one sent a white subscriber. A lawyer is engaged to take a case for me. For the same money he seats me in his office, talks to me just as pleasantly and works for me just as hard before the courts as for a white client. Why should the railroads be an exception to these rules.

This unjust practice toward the negro cuts off thousands of dollars worth of negro travel every year, while just treatment of the negro would stop no white travel. There are ten times when I would take my wife or a lady friend on the railroad that I only do so once, and then am compelled to, because I shudder at the mere thought of the accommodations. Numbers of other colored men have expressed the same feeling. The mere thought of a trip on a railroad brings to me a feeling of intense dread and I never enter a railroad coach unless compelled to do so. On account of these discriminations the New Orleans Exposition has lost many dollars. Since the Exposition opened I have asked many colored people in Northern States if they were going to attend, but in almost every case the answer came that they would like to do so, but feared the railroads.

If the railroad officials do not want to let us enter the first-class car occupied by white passengers, let them give us a separate one just as good in every particular and just as exclusive, and there will be no complaint. We have no desire to mix. Even in Philadelphia and other Northern cities where there are no social barriers, the colored people have their own churches, schools, hotels, &c., showing that there is no disposition on the part of the colored to obtrude themselves on the whites when they can receive equal, separate accommodations. I have in mind the railroad running between Selma & Marion, which furnishes a coach of the same length and height and just as good in every detail as that furnished the whites. Running in one direction the whites use one of the coaches and running in the opposite direction the colored passengers use the one previously used by the whites. There is never any discrimination on this road. A party of colored people recently travelling over it were so well pleased with this feature, and the gentlemanly bearing of the conductor, that they passed a resolution of thanks to be sent to the controllers of the road. There are a few other roads in the South whose treatment of colored passengers can be commended.

If the railroads will not give us first class accommodations, let them sell us tickets at reduced rates. This will be somewhat in keeping with the laws of honest trade.

The railroad officers make the mistake of supposing because many of the colored people are untidy, careless of their habits and contented to ride in a car with chain gang convicts that all are to be thus classed.

The writer is in favor of assortment and discrimination, for there are many colored people with whom he does not care to ride, but let assortment be made on the ground of dress and behavior.

In Virginia, where colored people are not prohibited from riding in a first-class car, I have always noticed that colored passengers when not well dressed, voluntarily take the second class car.

I have written thus plainly because I love the South, had rather live here than in the North, and expect to remain here. My faith is that the influences which are going to permanently right such wrongs are going to come from within the South and from the Southern people. National legislation and other outside attempts fail.

I appreciate the fact that customs that were years in forming cannot be blotted out in a day, and I am willing to exercise a wise patience, but on this subject I believe that Southern public opinion is ripe for the righting of this wrong.

Regardless of the opinions of wild theorists, the negro and the white man are to remain in the South side by side. Under God I believe we can do so without these jars in our business relations. We can be as separate as the fingers, yet one as the hand for maintaining the right.

# 2
## Atlanta Exposition Address

*The Atlanta Exposition Address was given on September 18, 1895. There are several versions of this speech. The one reproduced here is the "standard printed version" that was printed in its entirety in* Up from Slavery. *While Washington is frequently criticized for being too accommodating, a close look at the entire speech will reveal that it is more complex and not as weak as its reputation implies. The very fact that the directors of the exposition invited Washington to deliver this speech during the opening ceremonies of the exposition is noteworthy. No such gesture to African Americans had been made during the Philadelphia or Columbian expositions.*

[Atlanta, Ga., September 18, 1895]

Mr. President and Gentlemen of the Board of Directors and Citizens: One-third of the population of the South is of the Negro race. No enterprise seeking the material, civil, or moral welfare of this section can disregard this element of our population and reach the highest success. I but convey to you, Mr. President and Directors, the sentiment of the masses of my race when I say that in no way have the value and manhood of the American Negro been more fittingly and generously recognized than by the managers of this magnificent Exposition at every stage of its progress. It is a recognition that will do more to cement the friendship of the two races than any occurrence since the dawn of our freedom.

Not only this, but the opportunity here afforded will awaken among us a new era of industrial progress. Ignorant and inexperienced, it is not strange that in the first years of our new life we began at the top instead of at the bottom; that a seat in Congress or the state legislature was more sought than real estate or industrial skill; that the political convention or stump speaking had more attractions than starting a dairy farm or truck garden.

A ship lost at sea for many days suddenly sighted a friendly vessel. From the mast of the unfortunate vessel was seen a signal, "Water, water; we die of thirst!" The answer from the friendly vessel at once came back, "Cast down your bucket where you are." A second time the signal, "Water, water; send us water!" ran up from the distressed vessel, and was answered, "Cast down your bucket where you are." And a third and fourth signal for water was answered, "Cast down your bucket where you are." The captain of the distressed vessel, at last heeding the injunction, cast down his bucket, and it came up full of fresh, sparkling water from the mouth of the Amazon River. To those of my race who depend on bettering their condition in a foreign land or who underestimate the importance of cultivating friendly relations with the Southern white man, who is their next-door neighbour, I would say: "Cast down your bucket where you are"—cast it down in making friends in every manly way of the people of all races by whom we are surrounded.

Cast it down in agriculture, mechanics, in commerce, in domestic service, and in the professions. And in this connection it is well to bear in mind that whatever other sins the South may be called to bear, when it comes to business, pure and simple, it is in the South that the Negro is given a man's chance in the commercial world, and in nothing is this Exposition more eloquent than in emphasizing this chance. Our greatest danger is that in the great leap from slavery to freedom we may overlook the fact that the masses of us are to live by the productions of our hands, and fail to keep in mind that we shall prosper in proportion as we learn to dignify and glorify common labour, and put brains and skill into the common occupations of life; shall prosper in proportion as we learn to draw the line between the superficial and the substantial, the ornamental gewgaws of life and the useful. No race can prosper till it learns that there is as much dignity in tilling a field as in writing a poem. It is at the bottom of life we must begin, and not at the top. Nor should we permit our grievances to overshadow our opportunities.

To those of the white race who look to the incoming of those of foreign birth and strange tongue and habits for the prosperity of the South, were I permitted I would repeat what I say to my own race, "Cast down your bucket where you are." Cast it down among the eight millions of Negroes whose habits you know, whose fidelity and love you have tested in days when to have proved treacherous meant the ruin of your firesides. Cast down your bucket among these people who have, without strikes and labour wars, tilled your fields, cleared your forests, builded your railroads and cities, and brought forth treasures from the bowels of the earth, and helped make possible this magnificent representation of the progress of the South. Casting down your bucket among my people, helping and encouraging them as you are doing on these grounds, and to education of head, hand, and heart, you will find that they will buy your surplus land, make blossom the waste places in your fields, and run your factories. While doing this, you can be sure in the future, as in the past, that you and your families will be surrounded by the most patient, faithful, law-abiding, and unresentful people that the world has seen. As we have proved our loyalty to you in the past, in nursing your children, watching by the sick-bed of your mothers and fathers, and often following them with tear-dimmed eyes to their graves, so in the future, in our humble way, we shall stand by you with a devotion that no foreigner can approach, ready to lay down our lives, if need be, in defense of yours, interlacing our industrial, commercial, civil, and religious life with yours in a way that shall make the interests of both races one. In all things that are purely social we can be as separate as the fingers, yet one as the hand in all things essential to mutual progress.

There is no defense or security for any of us except in the highest intelligence and development of all. If anywhere there are efforts tending to curtail the fullest growth of the Negro, let these efforts be turned into stimulating, encouraging, and making him the most useful and intelligent citizen. Effort or means so invested will pay a thousand per cent interest. These efforts will be twice blessed —"blessing him that gives and him that takes."

There is no escape through law of man or God from the inevitable:—

The laws of changeless justice bind
   Oppressor with oppressed;
And close as sin and suffering joined
   We march to fate abreast.

Nearly sixteen millions of hands will aid you in pulling the load upward, or they will pull against you the load downward. We shall constitute one-third and more of the ignorance and crime of the South, or one-third its intelligence and progress; we shall contribute one-third to the business and industrial prosperity of the South, or we shall prove a veritable body of death, stagnating, depressing, retarding every effort to advance the body politic.

Gentlemen of the Exposition, as we present to you our humble effort at an exhibition of our progress, you must not expect overmuch. Starting thirty years ago with ownership here and there in a few quilts and pumpkins and chickens (gathered from miscellaneous sources), remember the path that has led from these to the inventions and production of agricultural implements, buggies, steam-engines, newspapers, books, statuary, carving, paintings, the management of drug stores and banks, has not been trodden without contact with thorns and thistles. While we take pride in what we exhibit as a result of our independent efforts, we do not for a moment forget that our part in this exhibition would fall far short of your expectations but for the constant help that has come to our educational life, not only from the Southern states, but especially from Northern philanthropists, who have made their gifts a constant stream of blessing and encouragement.

The wisest among my race understand that the agitation of questions of social equality is the extremest folly, and that progress in the enjoyment of all the privileges that will come to us must be the result of severe and constant struggle rather than of artificial forcing. No race that has anything to contribute to the markets of the world is long in any degree ostracized. It is important and right that all privileges of the law be ours, but it is vastly more important that we be prepared for the exercise of these privileges. The opportunity to earn a dollar in a factory just now is worth infinitely more than the opportunity to spend a dollar in an opera-house.

In conclusion, may I repeat that nothing in thirty years has given us more hope and encouragement, and drawn us so near to you of the white race, as this opportunity offered by the Exposition; and here bending, as it were, over the altar that represents the results of the struggles of your race and mine, both starting practically empty-handed three decades ago, I pledge that in your effort to work out the great and intricate problem which God has laid at the doors of the South, you shall have at all times the patient, sympathetic help of my race; only let this be constantly in mind, that, while from representations in these buildings of the product of field, of forest, of mine, of factory, letters, and art, much good will come, yet far above and beyond material benefits will be that higher good, that, let us pray God, will come, in a blotting out of sectional differences and racial animosities and suspicions, in a determination to administer absolute justice, in a willing obedience among all classes to the mandates of law. This, coupled with our material prosperity, will bring into our beloved South a new heaven and a new earth.

# 3
## Address at the Unveiling of the Monument to Robert Gould Shaw

*This speech was presented at the unveiling of the Robert Gould Shaw Monument in Boston on May 31, 1897. Following the success of the Atlanta Exposition address, Washington received countless invitations to speak at a variety of occasions. This one honored the commanding officer of the Massachusetts 54th Regiment. This speech, like many of Washington's addresses, was reprinted in* Tuskegee Student *11 (July 1897): 1, 4; it was also reprinted in* BTW Papers *4: 270–88.*

Mr. Chairman and Fellow-Citizens: In this presence, and on this sacred and memorable day, in the deeds and death of our hero, we recall the old, old story, ever old, yet ever new, that when it was the will of the Father to lift humanity out of wretchedness and bondage, the precious task was delegated to Him who, among ten thousand, was altogether lovely, and was willing to make himself of no reputation that he might save and lift up others.

If that heart could throb and if those lips could speak, what would be the sentiment and words that Robert Gould Shaw would have us feel and speak at this hour? He would not have us dwell long on the mistakes, the injustice, the criticisms of the days

> "Of storm and cloud, of doubt and fears,
> Across the eternal sky must lower;
> Before the glorious noon appears."

He would have us bind up with his own undying fame and memory and retain by the side of his monument, the name of John A. Andrew, who, with prophetic vision and strong arm, helped to make the existence of the 54th regiment possible; and that of George L. Stearns, who, with hidden generosity and a great sweet heart, helped to turn the darkest hour into day, and in doing so, freely gave service, fortune and life itself to the cause which this day commemorates. Nor would he have us forget those brother officers, living and dead, who by their baptism in blood and fire, in defence of union and freedom, gave us an example of the highest and purest patriotism.

To you who fought so valiantly in the ranks, the scarred and scattered remnant of the 54th regiment, who with empty sleeve and wanting leg, have honored this occasion with your presence, to you, your commander is not dead. Though

Boston erected no monument and history recorded no story, in you and the loyal race which you represent, Robert Gould Shaw would have a monument which time could not wear away.

But an occasion like this is too great, too sacred for mere individual eulogy. The individual is the instrument, national virtue the end. That which was 300 years being woven into the warp and woof of our democratic institutions, could not be effaced by a single battle, as magnificent as was that battle; that which for three centuries had bound master and slave, yea, North and South, to a body of death, could not be blotted out by four years of war, could not be atoned for by shot and sword, nor by blood and tears.

Not many days ago in the heart of the South, in a large gathering of the people of my race, there were heard from many lips praises and thanksgiving to God for His goodness in setting them free from physical slavery. In the midst of that assembly, a Southern white man arose, with gray hair and trembling hands, the former owner of many slaves, and from his quivering lips, there came the words: "My friends, you forget in your rejoicing that in setting you free, God was also good to me and my race in setting us free." But there is a higher and deeper sense in which both races must be free than that represented by the bill of sale. The black man, who cannot let love and sympathy go out to the white man, is but half free. The white man, who would close the shop or factory against a black man seeking an opportunity to earn an honest living, is but half free. The white man, who retards his own development by opposing a black man, is but half free. The full measure of the fruit of Fort Wagner and all that this monument stands for will not be realized until every man covered with a black skin, shall, by patience and natural effort, grow to that height in industry, property, intelligence and moral responsibility, where no man in all our land will be tempted to degrade himself by withholding from his black brother any opportunity which he himself would possess.

Until that time comes this monument will stand for effort, not victory complete. What these heroic souls of the 54th regiment began, we must complete. It must be completed not in malice, not in narrowness; nor artificial progress, nor in efforts at mere temporary political gain, nor in abuse of another section or race. Standing as I do today in the home of Garrison and Phillips and Sumner, my heart goes out to those who wore gray as well as to those clothed in blue; to those who returned defeated, to destitute homes, to face blasted hopes and shattered political and industrial system. To them there can be no prouder reward for defeat than by a supreme effort to place the Negro on that footing where he will add material, intellectual and civil strength to every department of State.

This work must be completed in public school, industrial school and college. The most of it must be completed in the effort of the Negro himself, in his effort to withstand temptation, to economize, to exercise thrift, to disregard the superficial for the real—the shadow for the substance, to be great and yet small, in his effort to be patient in the laying of a firm foundation, to so grow in skill and knowledge that he shall place his services in demand by reason of his intrinsic and superior worth. This, is the key that unlocks every door of opportunity, and all others fail. In this battle of peace the rich and poor, the black and white may have a part.

What lesson has this occasion for the future? What of hope, what of encouragement, what of caution? "Watchman tell us of the night; what the signs of promise are." If through me, an humble representative, nearly ten millions of my people might be permitted to send a message to Massachusetts, to the survivors of the 54th regiment, to the committee whose untiring energy has made this memorial possible, to the family who gave their only boy that we might have life more abundantly, that message would be, "Tell them that the sacrifice was not in vain, that up from the depth of ignorance and poverty, we are coming, and if we come through oppression out of the struggle, we are gaining strength. By the way of the school, the well cultivated field, the skilled hand, the Christian home, we are coming up; that we propose to invite all who will to step up and occupy this position with us. Tell them that we are learning that standing ground for the race, as for the individual, must be laid in intelligence, industry, thrift and property, not as an end, but as a means to the highest privileges; that we are learning that neither the conqueror's bullet nor that of law, could make an ignorant voter an intelligent voter, could make a dependent man an independent man, could give one citizen respect for another, a bank account, nor a foot of land, nor an enlightened fireside. Tell them that, as grateful as we are to artist and patriotism for placing the figures of Shaw and his comrades in physical form of beauty and magnificence, that after all, the real monument, the greater monument, is being slowly but safely builded among the lowly in the South, in the struggles and sacrifices of a race to justify all that has been done and suffered for it."

One of the wishes that lay nearest Col. Shaw's heart was, that his black troops might be permitted to fight by the side of white soldiers. Have we not lived to see that wish realized, and will it not be more so in the future? Not at Wagner, not with rifle and bayonet, but on the field of peace, in the battle of industry, in the struggle for good government, in the lifting up of the lowest to the fullest opportunities. In this we shall fight by the side of white men, North and South. And if this be true, as under God's guidance it will, that old flag, that emblem of progress and security, which brave Sergeant Carney never permitted to fall on the ground, will still be borne aloft by Southern soldier and Northern soldier, and in a more potent and higher sense, we shall all realize that

"The slave's chain and the master's alike are broken;
The one curse of the race held both in tether;
They are rising, all are rising—
The black and the white together."

# 4

## Open Letter to the Louisiana Constitutional Convention, February 19, 1898

*Washington took an active role in the struggle against the erosion of black political rights in the late nineteenth century. This letter to the Louisiana Constitutional Convention argued that any restrictions placed on suffrage should apply equally to whites and blacks, and warned of the economic and social consequences of limiting access to and funding of educational facilities for blacks. While the tone of Washington's correspondence is nonconfrontational, he clearly indicates his position on the issues at hand and also describes rather bluntly the dangers inherent in closing the doors to progress to African Americans. This letter was published in the February 21, 1898, issues of both the New Orleans* Picayune *and the New Orleans* Times-Democrat; *it was reprinted in* BTW Papers *4: 381–84.*

Tuskegee, Alabama, Feb. 19, 1898

To the Louisiana State Constitutional Convention: In addressing you this letter, I know that I am running the risk of appearing to meddle with something that does not concern me. But since I know that nothing but sincere love for our beautiful Southland, which I hold as near to my heart as any of you can, and a sincerer love for every black and white man within her borders, is the only thing actuating me to write, I am willing to be misjudged, if need be, if I can accomplish a little good.

But I do not believe that you, gentlemen of the Convention, will misinterpret my motives. What I say will, I believe, be considered in the same earnest spirit in which I write.

I am no politician; on the other hand, I have always advised my race to give attention to acquiring property, intelligence and character, as the necessary bases of good citizenship, rather than to mere political agitation. But the question upon which I write is out of the region of ordinary politics; it affects the civilization of two races, not for a day alone, but for a very long time to come; it is up in the region of duty of man to man, of Christian to Christian.

Since the war, no State has had such an opportunity to settle for all time the race question, so far as it concerns politics, as is now given in Louisiana. Will your Convention set an example to the world in this respect? Will Louisiana take such high and just grounds in respect to the Negro that no one can doubt that the South is as good a friend to the Negro as he possesses elsewhere? In all this, gentlemen of the Convention, I am not pleading for the Negro alone, but for the morals, the higher life of the white man, as well. For the more I study this question, the more I am convinced that it is not so much a question as to what the white man will do with the Negro, as to what the Negro will do with the white man's civilization.

The Negro agrees with you that it is necessary to the salvation of the South that restriction be put upon the ballot. I know that you have two serious problems before you; ignorant and corrupt government on the one hand, and on the other, a way to restrict the ballot so that control will be in the hands of the intelligent, without regard to race. With the sincerest sympathy with you in your efforts to find a way out of the difficulty, I want to suggest that no State in the South can make a law that will provide an opportunity or temptation for an ignorant white man to vote and withhold the same opportunity from an ignorant colored man, without injuring both men. No State can make a law that can thus be executed, without dwarfing for all time the morals of the white man in the South. Any law controlling the ballot, that is not absolutely just and fair to both races, will work more permanent injury to the whites than to the blacks.

The Negro does not object to an educational or property test, but let the law be so clear that no one clothed with State authority will be tempted to perjure and degrade himself, by putting one interpretation upon it for the white man and another for the black man. Study the history of the South, and you will find that where there has been the most dishonesty in the matter of voting, there you will find to-day the lowest moral condition of both races. First, there was the temptation to act wrongly with the Negro's ballot. From this it was an easy step to dishonesty with the white man's ballot, to the carrying of concealed weapons, to the murder of a Negro, and then to the murder of a white man, and then to lynching. I entreat you not to pass such a law as will prove an eternal millstone about the neck of your children.

No man can have respect for government and officers of the law, when he knows, deep down in his heart, that the exercise of the franchise is tainted with fraud.

The road that the South has been compelled to travel during the last thirty years has been strewn with thorns and thistles. It has been as one groping through the long darkness into the light. The time is not distant when the world will begin to appreciate the real character of the burden that was imposed upon the South when 4,500,000 ex-slaves, ignorant and impoverished, were given the franchise. No people had ever been given such a problem to solve. History had blazed no path through the wilderness that could be followed. For thirty years, we wandered in the wilderness. We are beginning to get out. But there is but one road out, and all makeshifts, expedients, "profit and loss calculations," but lead into the swamps, quicksands, quagmires and jungles. There is a highway that will lead both races out into the pure, beautiful sunshine, where there will be nothing to hide and nothing to explain, where both races can grow strong and true and useful in every fibre of their being. I believe that your Convention will find this highway; that it will enact a fundamental law which will be absolutely just and fair to white and black alike.

I beg of you, further, that in the degree that you close the ballot-box against the ignorant, that you open the school house. More than one half of the people of your State are Negroes. No State can long prosper when a large percentage of its citizenship is in ignorance and poverty, and has no interest in government. I beg of you that you do not treat us as alien people. We are not aliens. You know us; you know that we have cleared your forests, tilled your fields, nursed your children and protected your families. There is an attachment between us that few understand. While I do not presume to be able to advise you, yet it is in my heart to say that if your Convention would do something that would prevent, for all time, strained relations between the two races, and would permanently settle the matter of political relations in our Southern States, at least, let the very best educational opportunities be provided for both races; and add to this the enactment of an election law that shall be incapable of unjust discrimination, at the same time providing that in proportion as the ignorant secure education, property and character, they will be given the right of citizenship. Any other course will take from one-half your citizens interest in the State, and hope and ambition to become intelligent producers and taxpayers—to become useful and virtuous citizens. Any other course will tie the white citizens of Louisiana to a body of death.

The Negroes are not unmindful of the fact that the white people of your State pay the greater proportion of the school taxes, and that the poverty of the State prevents it from doing all that it desires for public education; yet I believe you will agree with me, that ignorance is more costly to the State than education; that it will cost Louisiana more not to educate her Negroes than it will cost to educate them. In connection with a generous provision for public schools, I believe that nothing will so help my own people in your State as provision at some institution for the highest academic and normal training, in connection with thorough training in agriculture, mechanics and domestic economy. The fact is that 90 per cent. of our people depend upon the common occupations for their living, and outside of the cities 85 per cent. depend upon agriculture for support. Notwithstanding this, our people have been educated since the war in everything else but the very thing that most of them live by. First-class training in agriculture, horticulture, dairying, stock-raising, the mechanical arts and domestic economy, will make us intelligent producers, and not only help us to contribute our proportion as taxpayers, but will result in retaining much money in the State that now goes outside for that which can be produced in the State. An institution that will give this training of the hand, along with the highest mental culture, will soon convince our people that their salvation is in the ownership of property, industrial and business development, rather than in mere political agitation.

The highest test of the civilization of any race is in its willingness to extend a helping hand to the less fortunate. A race, like an individual, lifts itself up by lifting others up. Surely no people ever had a greater chance to exhibit the highest Christian fortitude and magnanimity than is now presented to the people of Louisiana. It requires little wisdom or statesmanship to repress, to crush out, to retard the hopes and aspirations of a people, but the highest and most profound statesmanship is shown in guiding and stimulating a people so that every fibre in the body, mind and soul shall be made to contribute in the highest degree to the usefulness and nobility of the State. It is along this line that I pray God the thoughts and activities of your Convention be guided. Respectfully submitted,

---

# 5
## Letter to W.E.B. Du Bois, October 26, 1899

*For several years around the turn of the century, Washington actively recruited Du Bois for the faculty at Tuskegee. These efforts ceased as the two men became increasingly estranged. See also the letter from Du Bois to Washington, document 3 in section II of this collection. This letter can be found in the Booker T. Washington Papers, Library of Congress, container 282A; it also has been reprinted in* BTW Papers *5: 245.*

[Tuskegee, Ala.], Oct. 26, 1899

Dear Sir: I have delayed writing you a little longer than I intended to do, but this has been an exceedingly busy fall with me.

I write to renew the proposition that you connect yourself permanently with this institution. What I wish you to do is to make your home here and to conduct sociological studies that will prove helpful to our people, especially in the gulf states, including both the country districts, smaller towns and cities. I am especially anxious that some systematic and painstaking work be done with the country districts in the Black Belt. Our printing office will be wholly at your service and you could use it in a way that would scatter your writings all through the country.

I should like, if possible, for you to teach at least one class in our institution, this would result in keeping the students in close touch with the line of work which you would be pursuing.

All the work of course would be done in your own name and over your own signature. I should like, of course, for the name of the institution to be in some way attached to whatever publications you should make. I repeat that it would be the policy of the school to leave you free to use your time as you decide would be most desirable.

I would have made you this offer several years ago but I did not feel it would be doing you justice to ask you to come here and tie your hands with routine work. For this work we can pay you a salary of fourteen hundred dollars ($1400.) per year and furnish you a comfortable and convenient house. If any portion of this proposition is not satisfactory to you I shall be glad to make any reasonable changes in it.

I had a letter a few days ago from Prof. Hart asking whether or not we had come to any definite decision. Yours truly,

---

# 6

## Interview, Atlanta *Constitution*, November 10, 1899

*Washington expanded on the arguments that he made in his letter to the Louisiana Constitutional Convention almost two years earlier in an interview published in the Atlanta* Constitution, *November 10, 1899. Again he calls for suffrage laws that treat blacks and whites equally. This interview was reprinted at Tuskegee as a pamphlet in 1902; and in* BTW Papers *5: 261–65.*

### WASHINGTON URGES EQUAL TREATMENT

#### Danger to the South in Unjust Race Discrimination

### GIVES DETAILED OPINION

#### Thinks Law Would Injure White People in the End

### AN ELOQUENT PLEA FOR FAIRNESS

#### The Great Negro Leader Discusses Election Law Tendencies, Wherein Danger, as He Sees It, Lies

Professor Booker T. Washington, the head of the famous industrial school for colored youths at Tuskegee, and probably the foremost man of his race today, gave his views on the question of franchise restriction to a representative of The Constitution yesterday. Professor Washington spent the day in the city, having come here on business.

When asked for an expression on the Hardwick bill, he said that he did not care to discuss that or any other specific measure, but on the subject of an educational qualification restricting the ballot to the intelligence of the country, he had very decided views.

"I dread the idea of seeming to intrude my views too often upon the public," said Professor Washington, "but I feel that I can speak very frankly upon this subject, because I am speaking to the south and the southern people. It has been my experience that when our southern people are convinced that one speaks from the heart and tries to speak that which he feels is for the permanent good of both races, he is always accorded a respectful hearing. No possible influence could tempt me to say that which I thought would tend merely to stir up strife or to induce my own people to return to the old-time method of political agitation rather than give their time, as most of them are now doing, to the more fundamental principles of citizenship, education, industry and prosperity.

## Decision Left to the South

"The question of the rights and elevation of the negro is now left almost wholly to the south, as it has been long pleaded should be done," added Professor Washington. "The south has over and over said to the north and her representatives have repeated it in congress, that if the north and the federal government would 'hands off,' the south would deal justly and fairly with the negro. The prayer of the south has been almost wholly answered. The world is watching the south as it has never done before.

"Not only have the north and the federal congress practically agreed to leave the matter of the negro's citizenship in the hands of the south, but many conservative and intelligent negroes in recent years have advised the negro to cast his lot more closely with the southern white man and to cease a continued senseless opposition to his interests. This policy has gained ground to such an extent that the white man controls practically every state and every county and township in the south.

## Various Election Laws

"There is a feeling of friendship and mutual confidence growing between the two races that is most encouraging. But in the midst of this condition of things one is surprised and almost astounded at the measures being introduced and passed by the various lawmaking bodies of the southern states. What is the object of these election laws? Since there is white domination throughout the south, there can be but one object in the passing of these laws—to disfranchise the negro. At the present time the south has a great opportunity as well as responsibility. Will she shirk this opportunity, or will she look matters in the face and grapple with it bravely, taking the negro by the hand and seeking to lift him up to the point where he will be prepared for citizenship?

"None of the laws passed by any southern state, or that are now pending, will do this. These new laws will simply change the form of the present bad election system and widen the breach between the two races, when we might, by doing right, cement the friendship between them.

## Dangerous All Around

"To pass an election law with an 'understanding' clause simply means that some individual will be tempted to perjure his soul and degrade his whole life by deciding in too many cases that the negro does not 'understand' the constitution and that a white man, even though he be an ignorant white foreigner with but recently acquired citizenship, does 'understand' it.

"In a recent article President Hadley, of Yale University, covers the whole truth when he says: 'We cannot make a law which shall allow the right exercise of a discretionary power and prohibit its wrong use.' The 'understanding' clause may serve to keep negroes from voting, but the time will come when it will also be used to keep white men from voting if any number of them disagree with the election officer who holds the discretionary power.

"While discussing this matter, it would be unfair to the white people of the south and to my race if I were not perfectly frank. What interpretation does the outside world and the negro put upon these 'understanding' clauses? Either that they are meant to leave a loophole so that the ignorant white man can vote or to prevent the educated negro from voting. If this interpretation is correct in either case the law is unjust. It is unjust to the white man because it takes away from him incentive to prepare himself to become an intelligent voter. It is unjust to the negro because it makes him feel that no matter how well he prepares himself in education for voting he will be refused a vote through the operation of the 'understanding' clause.

## In a False Position

"And what is worse this treatment will keep alive in the negro's breast the feeling that he is being wrongfully treated by the southern white man and therefore he ought to vote against him, whereas with just treatment the years will not be many before a large portion of the colored people will be willing to vote with the southern white people.

"Then again I believe that such laws put our southern white people in a false position.

"I cannot think that there is any large number of white people in the south who are so ignorant or so poor that they cannot get education and property enough that will enable them to stand the test by the side of the negro in these respects. I do not believe that these white people want it continually advertised to the world that some special law must be passed by which they will seem to be given an unfair advantage over the negro by reason of their ignorance or poverty.

"It is unfair to blame the negro for not preparing himself for citizenship by acquiring intelligence and then when he does get education and property, to pass a law that can be so operated as to prevent him from being a citizen even though he may be a large taxpayer. The southern white people have reached the point where they can afford to be just and generous; where there will be nothing to hide and nothing to explain. It is an easy matter, requiring little thought, generosity or statesmanship, to push a weak man down when he is struggling to get up. Any one can do that. Greatness, generosity, statesmanship are shown in stimulating, encouraging every individual in the body politic to make of himself the most useful, intelligent and patriotic citizen possible. Take from the negro all incentive to make himself and [his] children useful property-holding citizens and can any one blame him for becoming a beast capable of committing any crime?

**Repression Will Fail**

"I have the greatest sympathy with the south in its efforts to find a way out of present difficulties, but I do not want to see the south tie itself to a body of death. No form of repression will help matters. Spain tried that for 400 years and was the loser. There is one, and but one, way out of our present difficulties and that is the right way. All else but right will fail. We must face the fact that the tendency of the world is forward, and not backward. That all civilized countries are growing in the direction of giving liberty to their citizens, not withholding it. Slavery ceased because it was opposed to the progress of both races and so all forms of repression will fail—must fail—in the long run. Whenever a change is thought necessary to be made in the fundamental law of the states, as Governor Candler says in his recent message:

" 'The man who is virtuous and intelligent, however poor or humble; or of whatever race or color, may be safely intrusted with the ballot.'

"And as the recent industrial convention at Huntsville, Ala., composed of the best brains of the white south puts it:

" 'To move the race problem from the domain of politics, where it has so long and seriously vexed the industrial progress of the south, we recommend to the several states of the south the adoption of an intelligent standard of citizenship THAT WILL EQUALLY APPLY TO BLACK AND WHITE ALIKE.'

"We must depend upon the mental, industrial and moral elevation of all the people to bring relief. The history of the world proves that there is no other safe cure. We may find a way to stop the negro from selling his vote, but what about the conscience of the man who buys his vote? We must go to the bottom of the evil.

**Should Be Equality of Treatment**

"Our southern states cannot afford to have suspicion of evil intention resting upon them. It not only will hurt them morally, but financially.

"In conclusion let me add that the southern states owe it to themselves not to pass unfair election laws because it is against the constitution of the United States and each state is under a solemn obligation that every citizen, regardless of color, shall be given the full protection of the laws. No state can make a law that can be so interpreted to mean one thing when applied to a black man and another thing when applied to a white man, without disregarding the constitution of the United States. In the second place, unfair election laws in the long run, I repeat, will injure the white man more than the negro, such laws will not only disfranchise the negro, but the white man as well.

"The history of the country shows that in those states where the election laws are most just, there you will find the most wealth, the most intelligence and the smallest percentage of crime. The best element of white people in the south are not in favor of oppressing the negro, they want to help him up, but they are sometimes mistaken as to the best method of doing this.

"While I have spoken very plainly, I do not believe that any one will misinterpret my motives. I am not in politics, per se, nor do I intend to be, neither would I encourage my people to become mere politicians, but the question I have been discussing strikes at the very fundamental principles of citizenship."

---

# 7
## Letter to W.E.B. Du Bois, March 11, 1900

*In this letter Washington agreed to recommend Du Bois for the position of assistant superintendent for colored schools in Washington, D.C. (see letter from Du Bois to Washington, February 17, 1900, in section II below). The cryptic nature of the advice in this letter convinced Du Bois that Washington was not honestly supporting him for the position. This suspicion, together with the fact that Du Bois did not get the position, were among the factors that soured relations between the two men. This letter is available in the W.E.B. Du Bois Papers, University of Massachusetts, Amherst; it was reprinted in* BTW Papers *5: 458–59.*

Grand Union Hotel, New York. Mar. 11, 1900

Dear Dr. Du Bois: Please consider the contents of this letter strictly private. If you have not done so, I think it not best for you to use the letter of recommendation which I have sent you. I have just received a letter direct from one of the Commissioners in the District asking me to recommend some one for the vacancy there and I have recommended you as strongly as I could. Under the circumstances it would make your case stronger for you not to present the letter which I have given you for the reason that it would tend to put you in the position of seeking the position. It is pretty well settled, judging by the Commissioner's letter, that some one outside of the District is going to be appointed.

This will be my address for the next week. Yours truly,

---

# 8

## Letter to the Editor of the Montgomery *Advertiser,* September 23, 1901

*This very interesting letter supposes a connection between the assassination of William McKinley by the anarchist Leon Czolgosz and the anarchism of lynching. The letter was printed in the Montgomery* Advertiser, *September 24, 1901; a revised version appeared in the* Tuskegee Student, *September 28, 1901, and it was reprinted in* BTW Papers *6: 217–18.*

Tuskegee, Ala., Sept. 23, 1901

Editor The Advertiser: "Mob rule is destructive of all government." These are the words just spoken by the Hon. Adlai E. Stevenson.

In the midst of the season of deepest grief, when the heart of a nation is shedding tears of sorrow as perhaps it has never before done for an individual, is it not a fitting time to stop to take our bearings that we may know whither we are drifting? With united voice we condemn the individual who was the direct cause of removing the, perhaps, most tenderly and universally loved President the nation has ever had. But in all sincerity, I want to ask, is Czolgosz alone guilty? Has not the entire nation had a part in this greatest crime of the century? What is anarchy but a defiance of law and has not the nation reaped what it has been sowing? According to a careful record kept by The Chicago Tribune, 2,516 persons have been lynched in the United States during the past sixteen years and every State in the Union except five, has had its lynching. A conservative estimate would place the number of persons engaged in these lynchings at about fifty per individual lynched, so that there are or have been engaged in this anarchy of lynching nearly 125,000 persons to say nothing of the many organized bands of technically organized anarchists. Those composing these mobs have defied Governors, Judges, Sheriffs and helped create a disregard for law and authority that, in my mind, has helped to lay the foundation for the great disgrace and disaster that has overtaken the country.

We cannot sow disorder and reap order. We cannot sow death and reap life.

To check the present tendency, it seems to me there are two duties that face us: first, for all classes to unite in an earnest effort to create such a public sentiment as will make crime disappear, and especially is it needful that we see that there is no idle, dissolute, purposeless class permitted in our midst with which and among whom crime usually originates.

Second, for all to unite in a brave effort to bring criminals to justice, and where a supposed criminal is found, no matter what the charge against him is, to see that he has a fair, patient, legal trial. One criminal put to death through the majesty of the law does more, to my mind, to prevent crime than ten put to death by the hand of lynching anarchists.

At the present time, when governors, judges, the pulpit and the press in all parts of the country are condemning lynching and anarchy as never before, is the time to begin the reform.

When the practice of lynching was begun, it was said that lynching would be inflicted, but for one crime, but the actual facts show that so true is it that lawlessness breeds lawlessness, that more people are now lynched each year for other supposed crimes than for the crime for which it was begun.

Let us heed the words of our departed and beloved Chief, as he lay upon his dying bed, referring to his murderer: "I hope he will be treated with fairness." If William McKinley, as he was offering up his life in behalf of the nation, could be brave enough, thoughtful and patriotic enough to request that his assailant should be fairly and honestly tried and punished, surely we can afford to heed the lesson. The best way, it seems to me, to show our love and reverence for William McKinley is to reach the conclusion in every community, in every part of the country, that the majesty of the law must be upheld at any cost.

---

# 9
## Letter to Theodore Roosevelt, October 16, 1901

*In this letter Washington accepted Roosevelt's invitation to dine at the White House. The invitation came only a few weeks after Roosevelt assumed the presidency, and it was the first time that an African American had dined at the White House. Washington was sharply criticized throughout the South for accepting this invitation; he defended his action by noting that the invitation was just reciprocating for Washington's having hosted former President William McKinley at dinner at Tuskegee. This letter is available in the Theodore Roosevelt Papers, Library of Congress; it was reprinted in* BTW Papers *6: 243.*

Washington, D.C., October 16, 1901

My dear Mr. President—I shall be very glad to accept your invitation for dinner this evening at seven-thirty. Yours very truly,

---

# 10
## The Negro and the Signs of Civilization

*In "The Negro and the Signs of Civilization," printed as an article in the* Tuskegee Student, *November 9, 1901, Washington outlines his standard argument that economic advancement is the key to black progress in the South; but this message also includes a warning to the South of the consequences it will face if black progress is thwarted. The article was reprinted in* BTW Papers *6: 299–302.*

There are certain visible signs of civilization and strength which the world demands that each individual or race exhibit before it is taken seriously into consideration in the affairs of the world. Unless these visible evidences of ability and strength are forthcoming, mere abstract talking and mere claiming of "rights" amount to little. This is a principle that is as broad and old as the world and is not confined to the conditions that exist between the white man and the black man in the South. We may be inclined to exalt intellectual acquirements over the material, but all will acknowledge that the possession of the material has an influence that is lasting and unmistakable. As one goes through our Western States and sees the Norwegians in Minnesota, for example, owning and operating nearly one-third of the farms in the State; and then as he goes through one of the cities of Minnesota and sees block after block of brick stores owned by these Norwegians; as he sees factories and street railways owned and operated by these same people, and as he notes that as a rule these people live in neat, well-kept cottages where there are refinement and culture, on nice streets, that have been paid for, he can't help but have confidence in and respect for such people, no matter how he has been educated to feel regarding them. The material, visible and tangible elements in this case teach a lesson that almost nothing else can. It may be said in opposition to this view that this is exalting too high the material side of life. I do not take this view. Let us see what is back of this material possession. In the first place the possession of property is an evidence of mental discipline, mental grasp and control. It is an evidence of self-sacrifice. It is an evidence of economy. It is an evidence of thrift and industry. It is an evidence of fixedness of character and purpose. It is an evidence of interest in pure and intelligent government, for no man can possess property without having the deepest interest in all that pertains to local and national government. The black man who owns $50,000 worth of property in a town is going to think a good many times before he votes for the officer who will have the liberty of taxing his property. If he thinks that a colored law-maker will use his taxing power wrongfully, he is not likely to vote for him merely for the sentimental reason that he is a black man. The black man who owns $50,000 worth of property in a town is not likely to continue to vote for a Republican law-maker if he knows that a Democratic one will bring lower taxes and better protection to his property. Say or think what we will there is but one way for the Negro to get up and that is for him to pay the cost, and when he has paid the cost—paid the price of his freedom—it will appear in the beautiful, well-kept home, in the increasing bank account, in the farm, and crops that are free from debt, in the ownership of railroad and municipal stocks and bonds (and he who owns the majority of stock in a railroad will not have to ride in a "Jim Crow car"), in the well-kept store, in the well-fitted laundry, in the absence of mere superficial display. These are a few of the universal and indisputable signs of the highest civilization, and the Negro must possess them or be debarred. All mere abstract talk about the possibility of possessing them, or his intention to possess them, counts for little. He must actually possess them, and the only way to possess them is to possess them. From every standpoint of interest it is the duty of the Negro himself, and the duty of the Southern white man as well as the white man in the North, to see that the Negro be helped forward as fast as possible towards the possession of these evidences of civilization. How can it best be done? Where is the beginning to be made? It can be done by the Negro beginning right now and where he finds himself. What I am anxious for is for the Negro to be in actual possession of all the elements of the highest civilization, and when he is so possessed, the burden of his future treatment by the white man must rest upon the white man.

I repeat, let the Negro begin right where he is, by putting the greatest amount of intelligence, of skill and dignity into the occupations by which he is surrounded. Let him learn to do common things in an uncommon manner. Whenever in the South, for example, the Negro is the carpenter, let him realize that he cannot remain the carpenter unless people are sure that no one can excel him as a carpenter. This black carpenter should strive in every way possible to keep himself abreast of the best wood work done in the world. He should be constantly studying the best journals and books bearing on carpentry. He should watch for every improvement in his line. When this carpenter's son is educated in college or elsewhere, he should see that his son studies mechanical and architectural drawing. He should not only have his son taught practical carpentry, but should see that in addition to his literary education that he is a first class architect as well—that, if possible, he has an idea of landscape gardening and house furnishing. In a word, he should see that his son knows so much about wood work, house construction, and everything that pertains to making a house all that it should be, that his services are in constant demand. One such Negro in each community will give character to a hundred other Negroes. It is the kind of effort that will put the Negro on his feet. What I have said of carpentry, is equally true of dozens of occupations now within the Negro's hands. The second or third generation of this black man's family need not be carpenters, but can aspire successfully to something higher because the foundation has been laid.

It is not only the duty of the Negro to thus put himself in possession of the signs of civilization, but it is also the plainest duty of the white man, North and South, to help the Negro to do so in a more generous manner than ever before. One-third of the population of the South is black. Ignorance in any country or among any people is the sign of poverty, crime and incompetency. No State can have the highest civilization and prosperity with one-third of its population down. This one-third will prove a constant millstone about the neck of the other two-thirds. Every one-room Negro cabin in the South, where there is ignorance, poverty and stupidity, is an adverse advertisement of the State, the bad effects of which no white man in the next generation can escape.

# 11
## Statement on Suffrage, Philadelphia *North American*

*This statement on black political rights and suffrage was printed in the Philadelphia* North American, *June 7, 1903, and reprinted in* BTW Papers 7: 171–73. *Washington again outlined his views on suffrage in a firm but nonconfrontational manner.*

### Negro and the White

I believe it is the duty of the negro—as the greater part of the race is already doing—to deport himself modestly in regard to political claims, depending on the slow but sure influences that proceed from the possession of property, intelligence and high character for the full recognition of his political rights.

I think that the according of the full exercise of political rights is going to be a matter of natural, slow growth, not an over-night, gourd-vine affair. I do not believe that the negro should cease voting, for a man cannot learn the exercise of self-government by ceasing to vote, any more than a boy can learn to swim by keeping out of the water; but I do believe that in his voting he should more and more be influenced by those of intelligence and character who are his next-door neighbors.

I know colored men who, through the encouragement, help and advice of Southern white people, have accumulated thousands of dollars worth of property, but who, at the same time, would never think of going to those same persons for advice concerning the casting of their ballots. This, it seems to me, is unwise and unreasonable, and should cease. In saying this, I do not mean that the negro should truckle, or not vote from principle, for the instant he ceases to vote from principle he loses the confidence and respect of the Southern white man even.

## Suffrage Laws Unjust

I do not believe that any State should make a law that permits an ignorant and poverty-stricken white man to vote and prevents a black man in the same condition from voting.

Such a law is not only unjust, but it will react, as all unjust laws do, in time; for the effect of such a law is to encourage the negro to secure education and property, and at the same time it encourages the white man to remain in ignorance and poverty. I believe that in time, through the operation of intelligence and friendly race relations, all cheating at the ballot-box in the South will cease.

It will become apparent that the white man who begins by cheating a negro out of his ballot soon learns to cheat a white man out of his, and that man who does this ends his career of dishonesty by the theft of property or by some equally serious crime.

In my opinion, the time will come when the South will encourage all of its citizens to vote. It will see that it pays better, from every standpoint, to have healthy, vigorous life than to have that political stagnation which always results when one-half the population has no share and no interest in the government.

As a rule, I believe in universal, free suffrage, but I believe that in the South we are confronted with peculiar conditions that justify the protection of the ballot in many of the States, for a while at least, either by an educational test, a property test, or by both combined; but whatever tests are required they should be made to apply with equal and exact justice to both races.

# 12

## Statement Before the Washington Conference on the Race Problem in the United States

*Booker T. Washington made these remarks at the Washington Conference on the Race Problem in the United States held in Washington, D.C., November 9–12, 1903, by the National Sociological Society. At this conference Washington, while not rejecting agitation as an appropriate tool in the struggle for civil rights, reminded his listeners that blacks living in the South faced different realities and different constraints than did those living in the North. These remarks were printed in the* Proceedings of the Washington Conference on the Race Problem in the United States under the Auspices of the National Sociological Society, Washington, D.C., November 9, 10, 11, 12, 1903 *(Washington, 1904), 141–44; they were reprinted in* BTW Papers *7: 340–42.*

[Booker T. Washington entered the church where the conference was held while a session was under way. He was greeted with prolonged applause that brought the proceedings to a halt. Kelly Miller, who had been speaking, acknowledged Washington's arrival and offered the floor to him.]

PROF. KELLY MILLER:

Mr. Chairman: I notice that the great Tuskegeeian, Prof. Booker T. Washington, has entered the house, and I move you that unanimous consent be granted him to speak on any subject agreeable to him.

Consent was granted, and Prof. Washington spoke as follows:

PROF. BOOKER T. WASHINGTON:

My remarks will be very few and very short.

For once I want to have the privilege of listening and not talking. In fact, as I grow older I sometimes have the feeling that if I had listened more and talked less I would have accomplished more work than I have accomplished. I came here at the cost of much precious time, away from many pressing and important duties, and if I do not stay to the finish of your Conference I hope that you will not consider that I am not deeply interested in what you are doing; it will be because I am forced to go away for interests especially pressing us in certain sections of the South. I am very glad that this Conference has been called, and I hope that we will learn more and more, as the years pass by, that no one organization, no one institution, no one individual, can represent all the interests of the race.

We need organizations, both national and local in character, in order that all the issues of the race may be reached and may be emphasized, and I hope that through such an organization as this that the lesson of organization will be more and more emphasized. We are all trying to reach the same end. We may travel, for a time at least, on different lines, but the goal is the same. You can do a certain work in this organization if you follow the suggestions which have been outlined and emphasized in the printed matter concerning it, a work that perhaps no other organization can do. There are three or four others that can do a work that this organization cannot do, and it is only through the various organizations, as I have said, that all sides of race issues can be emphasized and properly represented. That Mr. Lawson, or another, may not belong to all of these organizations should not be taken to indicate that he is not as deeply interested in the problems of those organizations as those in them. I repeat that you have a work to do in this organization that is not being done by any other, and a work that will redound to the great good of the entire race. I am glad that we are getting to the point where we can talk without regard to denomination, without regard to political parties, and discuss our race interests in a large and broad sense, as I see we are doing here this evening.

Now, there are two things that I want to say before I finish. One is that I hope you will always bear in mind that the great body of our people live in the South. There are eight millions and more of us down there, and the problem is there. If you can help us to bear our conditions, I hope you will keep in close touch and sympathy with those who are striving for better conditions right there in the South. There are some who, at all hazards, mean to remain there. If they suffer, they mean to remain there—right there in the heart of the South—as long as the bulk of our people are there. It is comparatively easy for you in these atmospheres to discuss the problem, but do so always with a view of looking not to your own interests, but to those of the larger masses of our people in the South.

In the discussion of these questions it seems that we should bear in mind that agitation, as one gentleman said a minute ago, should have a very large and important part. That is proper. The condemnation of wrong should always have a very large and important place; the demands for rights withheld should have a large and important place; but a very large place in all of our discussion and in all of our efforts should be given to something that is constructive. Now, some of us live in the section of the country where we hear of these wrongs. We eat them for our breakfast, for our dinner, for our supper. We live on them day in and day out. Some of them we know pretty well. Along with the condemnation I hope that such a thoughtful body as this will turn its attention more and more in the constructive direction. What we can construct, what we can project, is what will bring us relief. I have great hope when I see such an intelligent and conscientious body doing something in this high-reaching and constructive period.

Question—By REV. HARVEY JOHNSON: I believe what you say, that we must construct; we must do, if we can convince the people who are opposed to us that we can do. Have we not constructed something? Something that is operative. Has that construction effected or accomplished the end in view? Do you note any tendency on the part of the Southern white people to accord you justice on the score of the great, great work that you have accomplished in Alabama, or to accept you and yours and me and mine in this section more than before, because of that construction?

PROFESSOR WASHINGTON: We have got to do our duty. In a great many cases you have got to wait patiently for results. If we keep on doing our duty, whether we see immediate results or not, the results will take care of themselves.

---

# 13
## Speech to the National Afro-American Council

*Booker T. Washington presented this address at the meeting of the National Afro-American Council in Louisville, Kentucky, on July 2, 1903. At this meeting Washington confronted growing criticism of his leadership, spearheaded by William Monroe Trotter, but Washington and his allies maintained control of the meeting. In his address, he urged blacks to remain patient and not give in to the urgings of extremists even in the face of increasing racial violence. This speech was printed in Ernest Davidson Washington,* Selected Speeches of Booker T. Washington *(Garden City, N.Y.: Doubleday, Doran and Co., 1932), 92–100, and reprinted in* BTW Papers 7: 187–92.

### Rights and Duties of the Negro

In the midst of the present deep interest growing out of matters connected with our race, it can be stated that recent events, as regretable as they are, have tended to simplify the problem in one direction at least. The events to which I refer show that the questions pertaining to our race are each day more and more becoming national ones, rather than local and sectional ones. When we carry the question up into the atmosphere where men of all races, North and South, will discuss it with calmness, with absence of passion and sectional feelings, I believe we shall have made a distinct advance.

While my remarks tonight will relate to the race in its national aspect, I speak also as one who was born in the South, who loves it, and expects to abide there permanently. I am glad this great meeting is held south of the Mason and Dixon line. It is in the South that the great masses of our people dwell, and will abide in the future as now. It is fitting that this body should have its hearing and perform its work in the section of our country where the Negro race lives; it is equally important that this organization speak its words and perfect its plans in the midst of the white people who are most directly concerned about the future of the race.

Whatever progress is made in the years that are to come will result largely from open, frank discussion and a sympathetic cooperation between the highest types of whites and the same class of blacks. One thing of which I feel absolutely sure is that without mutual confidence and cooperation there is little hope for the progress which we all desire. In the present season of anxiety, and almost of despair, which possesses an element of the race, there are two things which I will say as strongly as I may.

First, let no man of the race become discouraged or hopeless. Though their voices may not be often or loudly lifted, there are in this country, North and South, men who mean to help see that justice is meted out to the race in all avenues of life. Such a man is Judge Thomas G. Jones, of Alabama, to whom more credit should be given for blotting out the infamous system of peonage than to any other. Judge Jones represents the very highest type of Southern manhood, and there are hosts of others like him. There is a class of brave, earnest men in the South, as well as in the North, who are more determined than ever before to see that the race is given an opportunity to elevate itself; and we owe it to these friends as well as to ourselves to see that no act of ours causes them embarrassment.

Second, let us keep before us the fact that, almost without exception, every race or nation that has ever got upon its feet has done so through struggle and trial and persecution; and that out of this very resistance to wrong, out of the struggle against odds, it has gained strength, self-confidence, and experience which it could not have gained in any other way.

And not the least of the blessings of such struggle is that it keeps one humble and nearer to the heart of the Giver of all gifts. Show me the individual who is permitted to go through life without anxious thought, without ever having experienced a sense of poverty and wrong, want and struggle, and I will show you a man who is likely to fail in life. "Whom the Lord loveth, He chasteneth."

No one should seek to close his eyes to the truth that the race is passing through a very serious and trying period of its development, a period that calls for the use of our ripest thought, our most sober judgment, and frequent appeals to Him who has promised strength to the weak.

During the season through which we are now passing, I wish to ask, with all the emphasis I am able to command, that each individual of the race keep a calm mind and exercise the greatest self-control; and that we all keep a brave heart. Let nothing lead us into extremes of utterance or action. By this method of procedure we shall be able to justify the faith of our friends and confound our enemies. In the affairs of a race, as with great business enterprises, it is the individual of few words and conservative action who commands respect and confidence. Vastly more courage is often shown in one's ability to suffer in silence, or to keep the body under control when sorely tempted, than acting through the medium of a mob. In the long run it is the race or individual that exercises the most patience, forbearance, and self-control in the midst of trying conditions that wins its course and the respect of the world. Such a course will, in the end, draw to our side all men, North and South, whose good will and support are worth having. Let nothing induce us to descend to the level of the mob, but rather direct our course in a dignified atmosphere.

In advocating this policy I am not asking that the Negro act the coward; we are not cowards. The part which we have played in defending the flag of our country in every war in which we have been engaged is sufficient evidence of our courage when the proper time comes to manifest it.

The recent outbreaks of government by the mob emphasize two lessons, one for our race and one for the other citizens of our country, South and North; for it is to be noted, I repeat, that the work of the lyncher is not confined to one section of the country.

The lesson for us is that we should see to it that so far as the influence of parent, of school, of pulpit, and of press is concerned, no effort be spared to impress upon our people, especially the youth, that idleness and crime should cease, and that no excuse be given the world to label any large proportion of the race as idlers and criminals; and that we show ourselves as anxious as any other class of citizens to bring to punishment those who commit crime, when proper legal procedure is sure. We should let the world know on all proper occasions that we consider no legal punishment too severe for the wretch of any race who attempts to outrage a woman.

The lesson for the other portion of the nation to learn is that, both in the making and the execution, the same laws should be made to apply to the Negro as to the white man. There should be meted out equal justice to the black man and the white man whether it relates to citizenship, the protection of property, the right to labor, or the protection of human life. Whenever the nation forgets, or is tempted to forget, this basic principle, the whole fabric of government for both the white and the black man is weakened and threatened with destruction. This is true whether it relates to conditions in Texas, Indiana, or Delaware.

To show how far we have already been led astray by those who disregard the majesty of the law and would insult governors and judges, by those who would uphold the law in one case and trample it under foot in another, we have but to call attention to the lamentable fact that the most careful and systematic investigation into the subject of lynching that has ever been made in this country shows that only thirty-five per cent of those lynched have ever been charged with violence to women. To attempt to say that all these thirty-five per cent were guilty would be to argue that the judgment of the mob is more unerring than that of the court. We cannot, and should not, escape the punishment for our sins of commission or of omission.

It is with a nation as with an individual: whatsoever we sow, that shall we also reap; if we sow crime, we shall reap lawlessness. If we break the law when a helpless Negro is concerned, it will not be very long before the same law is disregarded when a white man is concerned. Out of the present conditions there is one sign more encouraging than all others; and that is that in the South as well as in the North the voice of the press is speaking out as never before in favor of upholding the majesty of the law.

The Negro in this country constitutes the most compact, reliable, and peaceful element of labor; one which is almost the sole dependence for production in certain directions; and I believe that, if for no higher reason than the economic one, the people will see that it is worth while to keep so large an element of labor happy, contented, and prosperous, by surrounding and guarding it with every protection and encouragement of the laws. In the long run, nothing is more costly and unsatisfactory than discontented, unhappy, and restless labor. Few people are wise enough to learn the economic value of justice.

In our efforts to go forward, we should keep in mind the difference between the problem presented previous to the Civil War and the one now confronting us. Before our freedom a giant tree was growing in the garden, which all considered injurious to the progress of the whole nation. The work to be done was direct and simple—destroy the hurtful tree. The work before us now is not the destruction of a tree, but the growing of one. Slavery presented a problem of destruction; freedom presents one of construction. This requires time, patience, preparation of the soil, watering, pruning, and the most careful nursing.

In this connection we should bear in mind that our ability and our progress will be measured largely by evidences of tangible, visible worth. We have a right in a conservative and sensible manner to enter our complaints, but we shall make a fatal error if we yield to the temptation of believing that mere opposition to our wrongs, and the simple utterance of complaint, will take the place of progressive, constructive action, which must constitute the bedrock of all true civilization. The weakest race or individual can condemn a policy; it is the work of a statesman to construct one. A race is not measured by its ability to condemn, but to create. Let us hold up our heads and with firm and steady tread go manfully forward. No one likes to feel that he is continually following a funeral procession.

Let us not forget to lay the greatest stress upon the opportunities open to us, especially here in the South, for constructive growth in labor, in business and education. Back of all complaint, all denunciation, must be evidences of character and economic foundation. An inch of progress is worth more than a yard of complaint.

The whites and the blacks are to reside together in this country permanently, and we should lose no opportunity to cultivate in every straightforward, manly way the greatest harmony between the races. Whoever, North or South, black or white, by word or deed needlessly stirs up strife is an enemy to both races and to his country. While making our appeals for help and sympathy, we should not forget that in the last analysis the most effective appeal will consist in laying our case before the community and state in which we reside; nor that usefulness in our own homes will constitute our most lasting and most potent protection.

I appreciate from the bottom of my heart the tremendous and trying strain that is now upon us, and how difficult it is for us to make progress under such circumstances; but I believe the momentous period through which we are now passing will draw to our assistance in larger numbers the good will, the sympathy, and helpful cooperation of white men in the South, as well as in the North, if we only exercise due patience, self-control, and courage.

---

# 14
## Letter to W.E.B. Du Bois, January 27, 1904

*This letter chronicles one of the last examples of behind-the scenes cooperation between Washington and Du Bois in attacking civil rights issues in the South. The "committee" mentioned here is the Committee of Twelve for the Advancement of the Interests of the Negro Race, envisioned as an executive committee of national black leadership which would attempt to maintain cooperation and harmony between factions in African American leadership. Washington and Du Bois were responsible for organizing the committee. Du Bois's conviction that he was excluded from this process accentuated the split between the two men. This letter is available in the Booker T. Washington Papers, Library of Congress, container 20; it was reprinted in* BTW Papers 7: 414–15.

January 27, 1904

Dear Dr. Du Bois: Even before our committee is formed, I think there are one or two matters that we might attend to effectively. First. I presume you have seen something of the recent decision handed down by the U.S. Supreme Court bearing upon the question of colored men serving upon juries. So far as I can get hold of the facts, this is a clear, clean cut decision in our favor, and I think it will be a good idea for you, Mr. Browne and myself to arrange to have Mr. Wilford H. Smith, the lawyer who had charge of the case, make up a letter of instruction that might serve as a guide to colored people throughout the South and have this circular printed as far as possible in the colored papers and distributed also separately as far as possible. If the facts and proper instruction as to methods of procedure are put before the colored people and they do not secure representation upon the juries they will have no one to blame but themselves. Please let me have your idea as soon as possible upon the advisability of taking this course.

Second. Either before or soon after the committee of twelve has been formed, I think it well to get Mr. Smith, or some competent authority, to make a digest of the various requirements for voting in the various Southern States and put it in pamphlet form for large circulation among the colored people throughout the South. I find that in many cases the people do not vote simply because they are careless or ignorant of the law. For example, as the law now stands in Alabama, a very large number of colored people could vote if they were aware of the fact that they must pay their poll tax between now and February 1st. Unless some individual however, takes it upon himself to keep the poll tax matter constantly before them between now and February, comparatively few of them will pay this tax. It seems to me that our committee might have for one of its objects the keeping of such matters constantly before the people.

I do not mind saying for your private information that I think I could get Mr. Smith to compile the circular bearing on the jury system without charge since I employed him to take the case through the Supreme Court. Yours very truly,

---

# 15
## A Protest against Lynching

*"A Protest against Lynching" was published as a letter to the editor of the Birmingham* Age-Herald, *February 29, 1904. This is one of Washington's strongest statements against lynching. Excerpts from this letter were also printed in the* New York Times, *February 29, 1904; it was reprinted in* BTW *Papers 7: 447–48.*

Tuskegee, Ala., February 22, 1904

Within the last fortnight three members of my race have been burned at the stake; of these one was a woman. Not one of the three was charged with any crime even remotely connected with the abuse of a white woman. In every case murder was the sole accusation. All of these burnings took place in broad daylight and two of them occurred on Sunday afternoon in sight of a Christian church.

In the midst of the nation's busy and prosperous life few, I fear, take time to consider where these brutal and inhuman crimes are leading us. The custom of burning human beings has become so common as scarcely to excite interest or attract unusual attention.

I have always been among those who condemned in the strongest terms crimes of whatever character committed by members of my race, and I condemn them now with equal severity; but I maintain that the only protection of our civilization is a fair and calm trial of all people charged with crime and in their legal punishment if proved guilty.

There is no shadow of excuse for departure from legal methods in the cases of individuals accused of murder. The laws are as a rule made by the white people and their execution is in the hands of the white people; so that there is little probability of any guilty colored man escaping.

These burnings without a trial are in the deepest sense unjust to my race; but it is not this injustice alone which stirs my heart. These barbarous scenes followed, as they are, by publication of the shocking details are more disgraceful and degrading to the people who inflict the punishment than those who receive it.

If the law is disregarded when a Negro is concerned, it will soon be disregarded when a white man is concerned; and, besides, the rule of the mob destroys the friendly relations which should exist between the races and injures and interferes with the material prosperity of the communities concerned.

Worst of all these outrages take place in communities where there are Christian churches; in the midst of people who have their Sunday schools, their Christian Endeavor Societies and Young Men's Christian Associations, where collections are taken up for sending missionaries to Africa and China and the rest of the so-called heathen world.

Is it not possible for pulpit and press to speak out against these burnings in a manner that shall arouse a public sentiment that will compel the mob to cease insulting our courts, our Governors and legal authority; cease bringing shame and ridicule upon our Christian civilization?

---

# 16
## The Negro and the Labor Problem of the South

*"The Negro and the Labor Problem of the South" was published as an article in the Atlanta* Constitution, *November 27, 1904. This article introduces a theme that Washington will repeat for the next ten years: that African American labor will remain in the rural South (where it is most needed) only if blacks are provided with adequate educational facilities and protected from racial violence. Although written expressly for the Atlanta* Constitution, *the article was printed simultaneously in thirty southern newspapers. It was also reprinted in* BTW Papers *8: 139–45.*

Recent industrial changes bring into prominence two facts, first, that the South is likely for all time to be the cotton center of the world, and second, that the continued increase in the use of cotton goods among all nations will give to every acre of land in the South a value that it has not heretofore possessed. With these facts in mind, a natural inquiry is, what can the Negro do to help forward the interests of the South, and what can the white man do to help the Negro and himself?

I shall hope to suggest an answer to both of these questions. A few days ago I spent a day in one of the rural counties of Georgia and heard a great deal of discussion about the scarcity of efficient farm labor. After spending the day in the country, I returned to Atlanta for the night. Between 10 and 11 o'clock I made a tour through Decatur Street and several streets in that vicinity. I think I do not exaggerate when I say that I found in and near Decatur Street enough people who were not regularly employed to operate successfully fifty of the largest plantations in the state of Georgia. This single example would mean little except that it represents a condition more or less prevalent in practically all of our larger cities and all of our Southern States.

As an economic problem, we have on the one hand a surplus of idle labor in the cities, and on the other, much vacant land, unpicked cotton and a scarcity of farm labor; it is a tremendously difficult situation. The problem of changing these conditions not only confronts the South, and it is not by any means confined to my race, but for the present I desire to deal with it mainly as it affects my race and the land owner of the South, be that land owner white or black.

In order that what I may say on this subject be of any value to the white man or to my own race, I shall have to ask the privilege of perfect frankness. The many subjects affecting the interests of both races require perfect frankness on both sides. Your readers will agree with me, I think, when I say that it is possible for a Negro to know more of the feelings and motives of colored people than a white man can possibly know.

In my recent visit to Atlanta I did that which I have often done in large cities of the South wherever I have found a floating class of colored people. I made individual inquiry as to why they preferred uncertain existence in the city to a life of comparative prosperity upon a farm, either as owners, renters, or laborers. While I shall not attempt to use their exact words, I sum up the reasons they gave me in a few sentences. Just now the South is in the midst of the season when land owners are making plans for another year's crop, some of the matters that were brought out, and which I shall try to discuss a little fully and maybe with profit to land owners.

In the South, as elsewhere, there are two classes: those whom labor seeks, and those who have to seek labor. The first group is comparatively small, but such a class exists; it can and ought to be increased. There are, in my opinion, two classes of faults as between white farmers and black labor: one, on the part of the white people, the other on the part of the black people. To find and state faults, however, is easy. To suggest a remedy, one that shall promote the prosperity and happiness of both races is the aim of this article.

To return to the main complaints of the colored people as they have stated them to me time and time again— These people who have talked may be right, they may be wrong, they may state facts or they may state untruths, but this I know, they represent the attitude of a large class of colored people, who give the following as chief reasons for leaving the farms: Poor dwelling houses, loss of earnings each year, because of unscrupulous employers, high priced provisions, poor schoolhouses, short school terms, poor school teachers, bad treatment generally, lynchings and whitecapping, fear of the practice of peonage, a general lack of police protection and want of encouragement. Let us assume that these conditions do exist in some sections, and with certain individual planters. As a mere matter of dollars and cents, if for no higher reason, I believe that it will pay every owner of a plantation throughout the South to see to it that the houses of the tenants are not only made comfortable, but attractive in a degree. The land owner who thinks that he can secure the best class of colored people when he provides only a broken-down, one-room cabin for them to live in, will find himself mistaken. The chances are that the planter who provides comfortable houses for his tenants will keep them much longer, and will have a more reliable service. The matter of being cheated out of his earnings at the end of the year is, of course, a complaint that is very hard to discuss, and I know is likely to involve much exaggeration, and the more ignorant the aggrieved person is, the more given is he to such complaint and exaggeration, but I must not conceal the fact that such feeling is deep and wide-spread, and I ought to make the same statement regarding the high prices charged during the year for provisions, etc., supplied.

Some of the colored people who have migrated into the cities give as their reason for leaving the country the poor school facilities in the rural communities. In practically every large city in the South the colored man is enabled by public, missionary, and private schools, to keep his child in school eight or nine months in the year. Not only is this true, but the schoolhouses are comfortable, and the teachers are efficient. In many of the rural communities, the location of the schoolhouse is far from the home of the child, the building is uncomfortable, the term lasts but four or five months, and the teacher's salary is so small that it generally invites a most inefficient class of teachers. I know one community that has had great trouble this year in getting cotton pickers and other laborers, and inquiry reveals the fact that the Negro children in that community were in school last year only four months, and the teacher received from the public fund but eleven dollars per month for his services. Under such conditions who can blame a large number of colored people for leaving the plantations of the country districts?

Purely as an economic proposition, I believe that it will not only pay the land owners of the South, either as individuals, or by united effort, to see that good schoolhouses are provided on or near their plantations, that the school is kept open six or eight months in a year, and that there is a good teacher regularly employed; where the school fund is not large enough to supply a good school-house, they should extend the school term and provide a first-class, moral teacher. Further, it will pay to lead the way in seeing that reasonable facilities are otherwise provided.

This, I repeat, will lead to a demand for land and increase of efficiency in the labor force. Financially, there will soon be a great difference in the price of land when there are tenants bidding for opportunities instead of going to cities as now. Wherever it is practicable, I would urge that at least a primary course in agriculture be given in every country school. This would lead to a love of farm work and of country life. Again, many are not on the farms, as they say, because they have not been treated fairly. To illustrate: I recall that some years ago a certain white farmer asked me to secure for him a young colored man to work about the house and to work in the field. The young man was secured, a bargain was entered into to the effect that he was to be paid a certain sum monthly and his board and lodging furnished as well. At the end of the colored boy's first day on the farm he returned. I asked the reason, and he said that after working all the afternoon he was handed a buttered biscuit for his supper and no place was provided for him to sleep.

At night he was told he could find a place to sleep in the fodder loft. This white farmer, whom I know well, is not a cruel man and seeks generally to do the right thing, but in this case he simply overlooked the fact that it would have paid him better in dollars and cents to give some thought and attention to the comfort of his helper. This case is more or less typical. Had this boy been well cared for he would have so advertised the place that others would have sought work there.

The readers of your paper know too well that in a few counties of several of our Southern States there has been such a reign of lawlessness led by whitecappers and lynchers that many of the best colored people have been driven from their homes and have sought in large cities safety and police protection. In too many cases the colored people who have been molested have been those, who by their thrift and diligence, have secured homes and other property. These colored people have been oppressed in most instances not by the property-holding, intelligent white people, but by the worst and most shiftless element of whites. Have the higher class of whites escaped responsibility for letting their affairs be controlled by the worst element? The practice of peonage in a few counties of the South has also caused a fear among an element of the colored people that prevents their going into or remaining in the country districts that they may be forced to labor involuntarily and without proper remuneration. I have said that such lawless conditions exist in only a "few" counties in the South, and I used the word advisedly. In the majority of the counties in the South life and property are just as safe as anywhere in the United States, but the harm comes because of the wide-spread notoriety that a few lawless communities and counties have given the South, and this serves to spread the idea pretty generally among the colored people that if they want police protection when they are charged with crime or under suspicion they must hastily seek the confines of a city. I repeat that fear has stripped some counties of its most valuable colored labor and left the dregs of that population. In the matter of law and order, my constant appeal is that there be hearty cooperation between the best whites and the best blacks.

Nothing is clearer than that crime is rarely committed by the colored man who has education and owns property. I have not failed either to say to the colored people on more than one occasion, "We should see to it that crime in all its phases is condemned by the race and a public sentiment kept alive that will make it impossible for a criminal to be shielded or protected by any member of the race, at any time or in any place."

Few white people realize how far a little encouragement goes in helping to make better and more useful citizens of the colored people. Some months ago I recall that I listened for an hour to a white man in the South who was making a political speech. He was in a state where a revised constitution had disfranchised nineteen-twentieths of the colored voters fifteen years ago and there was not the slightest chance of any political uprising, or even opposition on the part of the colored people, yet two-thirds of this man's address was devoted to ridicule and abuse of the colored people. The sad feature of such an address lies in the fact that in many parts of the country such a speech is taken seriously. To most of those who heard it and to those who knew the man in that community it did no especial harm, for the people knew that his talk did not tally with his actions, but he had become so accustomed to making that kind of speech that he repeated it by force of habit. This man had drawn his first life's sustenance from the breast of a colored woman, had been reared by one, and at that moment he had dozens of the best colored people in that section on his plantation, any one of whom would have laid down his life for him, and the man himself would have fought to the death in defense of these colored servants of his.

Every year these same laborers were making him richer and richer by their patient, faithful labor, and he would trust them with all that he possessed. In this community the Negroes have never made an unavailing appeal to this man for aid in building churches or schoolhouses, or in supporting a school. Few white men anywhere in the world in their actual daily practice had done more to help the black man. Yet, such a speech read in the newspaper at a distance would give the impression to thousands of colored laborers that the county in which the speaker lived was for them absolutely unsafe. Such a speech was not calculated to gain a single vote, but it was calculated, in my opinion, to lose to the community a good many bales of cotton. I repeat that few understand how much good could be accomplished in the way of helping the colored people to lead law-abiding and useful lives if more white people would take occasion both in private and in public to praise their good qualities instead of reviling and ridiculing them.

In regard to the duties and obligations of my own people, I would say that unless they realize fully the opportunities that are before them in the South and seize every chance to improve their methods of labor, the time will come when Italians and other foreigners will attempt to displace them in the labor work of the South, just as the Chinese are displacing the Negro in South Africa.

One charge frequently brought against us is that we cannot be depended upon for constant and uninterrupted labor; that an excursion or other excitement will take laborers from the very places where their services are most needed. The complaint is frequently made that if paid on Saturday night the laborers will probably not return to work until all the cash received has been expended, and that on the plantation the colored tenant takes little interest in caring for the property of the landlord. These things our people should change.

I hope I may be pardoned for speaking so plainly and in so much detail and at such length, but I believe that the South is on the eve of a season of prosperity, such as it has never before experienced, and that by mutual understanding and sympathetic co-operation each of these two races of the South can help forward the interests of the other, and thus cement a friendship between them that shall be an object lesson for all the world.

---

# 17
## Letter to President Theodore Roosevelt, December 26, 1904

*Washington advised Roosevelt on the contents of his Lincoln Birthday speech —an important political address that would be looked at closely by Republicans and African Americans. The Platt bill was a proposal to reduce representation in Congress for those states that restricted black suffrage. Washington urged Roosevelt to address a number of issues that were of importance to blacks, but the positions he advocated were quite moderate. This letter can be found in the Booker T. Washington Papers, Tuskegee Institute, Tuskegee, Alabama; it was printed in* BTW Papers *8: 162–64. The ellipses indicate an illegible line.*

*Personal*                                                         December 26, 1904

My dear Mr. President: So anxious am I about your Lincoln Birthday speech that I am writing you again, and may write you several times on the subject before the address is delivered.

I hope you will bear in mind in the preparation of this address

First, that the whole country has endorsed your principles and acts in a way that no other President has ever been endorsed, and that nothing will creep into the address which will give those who have stood by you so loyally the least impression that you are not standing by the principles upon which you were re-elected so overwhelmingly. In stating your position on the Platt bill for reduction of representation, I wonder if it would not be wise in some way to recognize the fact that the national platform adopted at Chicago called for an investigation of conditions. This, of course, does not commit the party to reduction. You stated very clearly in your letter of acceptance that you approved of the whole platform. The average man has the idea that the platform called for reduction, which it did not. This is merely a suggestion. Second, the discussion of the question of "Social Equality" is a very delicate matter and one out of which all kinds of harm may grow unless it is handled very carefully. The Southern white man understands one thing about social equality and the Northern and Western white man quite another thing. The Southern white man is constantly confusing civil privileges with social intercourse. The more I have thought over it since I saw you . . . cussing that subject rather than to hear from Bishop Strange. I happen now to recall that I am quite sure this is the same address which I heard Bishop Strange deliver in St. Thomas's Church, New York, about two months ago, and the effect which it made upon the audience, I mean the part relating to social equality and the separation of the races, was not satisfactory to any element in the congregation and I heard it rather severely criticised by many afterwards. On the question of Negro domination and social equality I send you an extract from an address which I delivered in Montgomery, Alabama, a short while ago.

So far as I can discern, the Negro in no part of the country feels it necessary to have purely social intercourse with the white man, nor does he hanker after it, but the difficulty in discussing the question grows out of the fact that in the South many of the white people regard the matter of riding in the same railroad coach or on the same seat in a street car or in the same waiting room at a depot "social equality." The Negro does not object so much to the separation of the races in these regards in itself, but he knows by experience that in nine cases out of ten where the Negroes are so separated the colored man gets the bad end of the bargain, that is to say in the vast majority of the cases in the South the colored man pays the same fare as the white man on the railroad trains but gets an accommodation that is far from equal. This is the ground of opposition.

It will be very hard for you to use the quotation from Bishop Strange's address without making the Northern white people feel that they must begin drawing the same lines that are drawn in the South.

I wonder if what you have to say against the amalgamation of the races would not go far towards answering the point which you have in mind?

These are mere suggestions. The Address so far as it is completed is strong and is going to produce a great impression as a whole as I said to you when you read it to me. Yours very truly,

Booker T. Washington

P.S. I wonder if you could not properly, in your Lincoln Birthday address, congratulate the country and the South upon the fact that now for two months there has not been a single lynching in any part of the country. This, I think you will find has not been true for any two months since the year 1885. This will be all the more powerful since so many have tried to produce the impression that your administration had resulted in creating more lynchings in the South than had ever occurred before. If you decide to take this matter up, it might be safe for you to get the latest and most direct information from the Chicago Tribune which is an authority on the subject.

If you take up the subject of lynching, I think it well for you to bear in mind that most of the daily newspapers, especially the Atlanta Constitution, Montgomery Advertiser as well as the grand juries and ministers, deserve great credit for taking the lead in this movement in the South to blot out lynching. Not the least part of the effective work has been the fact that the intelligent classes of colored and white people have both cooperated actively and heartily together in forming public sentiment.

---

# 18
## The Negro in the North: Are His Advantages as Great as in the South

*"The Negro in the North: Are His Advantages as Great as in the South" was published as an article in* Congregationalist and Christian World *92 (September 28, 1907): 403–04. Washington outlined his arguments that the interests of African Americans would be best served if they remained in the South. This article was also printed in* The Interior *38 (September 26, 1907): 1259–60; and in* BTW Papers *9: 341–46.*

My attention has been repeatedly called in recent years to the rapid increase of the Negro population in Northern cities, particularly in the larger cities of the North Atlantic States, that is, New England, New York, New Jersey, and Pennsylvania. These states have already considerably more than one-third of all the Northern Negroes and statistics show that from 1880 to 1900 this portion of the population increased one-third more rapidly than the white. The Negroes in Philadelphia increased in the ten years, between 1890 and 1900, from thirty to sixty-two thousand. The colored population in New York was 23,606 in 1890, but in 1900 it had risen to 60,666. Boston's colored population grew more slowly, but it has grown steadily. In 1880 the Negroes of Cambridge and Boston were 7,377, but in 1900 this number had increased to 15,497.

Under normal conditions I doubt whether the existence of 900,000 Negroes scattered over the whole Northern and Western country, and permanently settled on farms and in small towns, as they are to a very large degree in the South, would have attracted particular attention. But the fact is that the Negroes in the Northern States are, to a large extent, part of the floating population. While eighty-two per cent. of the Southern Negroes are on farms and plantations in country districts, more than seventy per cent. of the Northern Negroes are in cities.

This Negro element in the floating population of the Northern cities has grown so rapidly in recent years and has to such an extent complicated the problem of city life, already difficult enough, that some persons have come to regard it as a distinct menace.

**City Life Unfavorable to Health and Morals**

I have more than once said that the masses of the colored people are not yet fitted to survive and prosper in the great cities North and South to which so many of them are crowding. The temptations are too great and the competition with the foreign population with which they come in contact is too severe. Many of these young colored men and women, who leave the country for the city, go almost directly from the farms and plantations of the South, where they have been living on the same soil on which their fathers and mothers worked as slaves and under conditions not far removed from those that existed before emancipation. It is not difficult, under these circumstances, to understand that the colored immigrants from the South are not able at once to adjust themselves to the crowded, strenuous and complicated life of these great modern cities. The vital statistics, which are perhaps the best indicators we have in this matter, show that, of all the races now pouring into the larger American cities from various parts of the world, the Negro is the least prepared to meet the conditions of city life.

It should always be borne in mind that there is this difference between the Negro in the North and the average colored man living on plantations of the country districts in the South, that while he is ignorant he has not been degraded, as a rule, except in rare cases, by vicious habits. In the large cities of the North, it is true of a large element of the Negroes, as it is true of the same class of other races, that they have injured body and soul by degrading habits. There is a vast difference between pure ignorance and degradation.

My own conviction is that this problem, like others which the presence of the Negro race in this land has created, must find its solution ultimately on the farms and plantations of the Southern States. So far as I can understand the disposition of the masses of my own people they have determined to remain for all time upon the soil of the Southern States, where their future, in my opinion, is inextricably bound up with the prosperity of the soil. I do not believe that any large proportion of the Negro people intend to live permanently outside of the South, and I doubt very much if any laborer will be found to supplant permanently the Negro in the Southern cotton field. The problem of the Northern Negro will, to a very large extent, find its solution in the efforts now being made by the United States Department of Agriculture to improve the character and quality of the Negro farmers; in the efforts now being made to increase the number and efficiency of country schools; in the growing disposition among the better class of the white people to secure justice for the Negro and protect him against hectoring and abuse to which he is so often subjected, and finally in the encouragement the Negro is receiving in certain parts of the South to buy land, to build houses and permanently settle on the soil.

The security of the South against danger of race riots and the evils that causes them demands that every man, white and black, should, as far as possible, own a home; a hearth stone around which the interest of the family can find a center; and a permanent place of abode on which the wholesome influences of family life can find a prop.

I believe that those who are seeking a solution of the problem of the Northern Negro will find that they can co-operate in this direction with the more thoughtful class of the Southern people who find that the South is being slowly drained of the labor it needs in the fields and in the trades by emigration Northward.

I have spoken thus far of that part of the population which has but lately arrived in the North. It represents the element of unrest among the Negroes of the South. While a large number of these people have left the South upon a definite promise of higher wages or better treatment, a greater number are mere social drift, drawn into the cities with the tide that sets to the large centers of population from all over the United States.

While I do not deny that there are some advantages for the Negro in the North which he does not have in the South, there are also disadvantages. There are the advantages of better schools and better teachers. The Negro has, for example, the opportunity of using the public library, of entering the colleges and universities. The Northern cities are farther advanced, on the whole, in their methods of dealing with the problem of city life. The Northern people are not haunted by the fear of social equality, and are therefore able to take hold in a more practical way of the problem of uplifting backward races. The Northern cities are richer and more able to provide special education to meet the special needs of special classes of the population.

### Difficulties in Finding Labor

But on the whole I am convinced that the condition of the great mass of Negroes in the Northern cities is not only worse than that of the Negroes on the farms in the South but worse than that of any other portion of the city population. The statistics show that the death rate is much larger among Negroes in the North than it is among the whites, and this greater death rate is, no doubt, the result, not of one, but a number of influences which, in the Northern cities, work to the detriment of the race. The Negro has greater difficulty there in finding satisfactory employment. Large numbers of Negro laborers are induced to leave the South to meet the emergencies of Northern industry. They were brought to Chicago to help dig the Chicago Drainage canal. They were imported to New York to work on the building of the subway. The labor unions, to whose interest it is to limit the supply of labor, have never been favorable to the employment of Negroes. The fact that Negroes are frequently brought North as "strike breakers" helps to intensify the prejudice against them. The tendency of all this is to force the Negro down to the lowest rung of the industrial ladder and to make him, in short, a sort of industrial pariah.

But in spite of these difficulties the facts show that a considerable number of exceptional colored men, spurred on by contact and competition with the swift and thrifty race about them, have made their way and been successful. The number of successful Negro business and professional men is probably larger in proportion to the Negro population in the North than it is in the South. Many of these have become men of influence in the communities in which they live and have worked quietly and steadily in their professions and in other directions for the benefit and building up of the Negro people.

## Greater Opportunities in the South

But the Northern Negro who makes a success in business or in a profession must, in most instances, live beside and work for a people who have no special need of his talents. At best he can but perform for them a service that can be performed as well, if not better, by some one else. In the South, on the contrary, a Negro professional or business man has an opportunity to work for his own people who need his services and will respect and honor him for his work. Land is still cheap in the South. Negroes are better able there than in the North to buy and own their homes, to build their own communities, where they can have their own churches, schools, banks and other places of business, and where the masses of the people are not placed in such direct competition with a race centuries ahead of them in habits, instincts and education. In these communities the masses of the people are enabled to grow slowly and normally, and the educated Negro, the preacher, physician, teacher and business man has an opportunity in directing and controlling the development of his own people, to assist in building up his race and his country, and to gain for himself the honor and gratitude with which the world everywhere rewards real service.

But there is another disadvantage under which the Northern Negro labors which, while it is not so obvious, is none the less real. He is, in relation to the lives and interests of the masses of the Negro race, in a certain sense, an exile, condemned to witness from a distance their struggles to rise, but not able to give them any effectual aid. Very often it happens that the Northern Negro knows little or nothing, except what he can learn from the newspapers, of the actual condition under which the majority of the Negro population live. He hears much of the crime and violence and sees nothing of the deeper constructive forces which are working quietly in the minds and hearts of Southern people, black and white. His protests against what he regards as the wrongs committed against the members of his race in the South are often inspired by impatience and contempt for the Southern Negroes themselves who, as far as he can see, are willing patiently to suffer wrong.

The result has been that while Northern and Southern white people have been steadily coming closer together upon the race question, the Northern and Southern Negro seem to be steadily growing farther apart.

There is a radical group among the Northern Negroes, just as there is a radical section among Southern whites, who insist on making the racial question a political and sectional issue. They are seeking to solve the problem of the races by keeping the North and the South apart and preventing the co-operation of both sections and both races in the task of reconstruction.

My own opinion is that this policy is not only hopeless but mistaken. What the ultimate effect of any systematic effort to intensify the sectional and racial antagonisms that already exist might be I dare not say. Some persons have suggested that it would result in making the Negroes the permanent wards of the several states or of the United States. I do not believe that either the white people or the black people of the South are yet prepared to accept this solution. On the contrary I believe that the races that have lived and worked together for 250 years in slavery will be able, in spite of difficulties, to solve the problem of living together in freedom.

The Negro has too long been a battledore and shuttlecock of political parties. What the South at the present time needs most is racial and sectional peace. What the Negro wants is justice, protection and encouragement to put forth his best efforts in fruitful and productive labor for his own welfare and that of the country as a whole. This is not a sectional, but a national issue.

---

# 19
## Letter to William Howard Taft, June 4, 1908

*Washington wrote this letter to Taft (who at the time was secretary of war and a candidate for the Republican nomination for president) during the 1908 presi-*

*dential campaign. In it he outlined his suggestions for the civil rights plank in the 1908 Republican platform. Here we see Washington using his personal political influence in an attempt to strengthen the Republican Party's commitment to equal rights and to full suffrage for African Americans. This letter is in the Booker T. Washington Papers, Library of Congress, container 7; it was reprinted in* BTW Papers *9: 550–52.*

Personal and Very Confidential                                   June 4, 1908

My dear Mr. Secretary: Enclosed I send you some suggestions for a plank in the Chicago platform. Of course, I presume the wording will be changed, but I have tried to make my meaning clear. I think I know the situation pretty well among the colored people and I do think the substance of what is stated in this suggestion ought to go in the platform in some form. I have put it in plain language as the situation demands plain language, something which cannot be misunderstood or misinterpreted.

My own view is that something like the enclosed would do more good than the meaningless platform about reducing Southern representation. That was in the last platform and made no impression because it did not mean anything, and if another plank goes into the platform about reducing Southern representation I do not believe it will make the least impression, but what I have suggested, in my opinion, if put in some form would help the situation tremendously.

The words "Lily Whitism" may seem inelegant, but the meaning will be clear to all. Yours very truly,

[Enclosures:]

**Suggested Plank for Platform:**

The Republican Party had its origin in an effort to secure equal justice to all men. Above the tariff, above the currency question, is the matter of justice between man and man and as between race and race. The Republican Party, as now constituted, cannot afford to deviate in any degree from the principles of its founders. If the party anywhere has drifted from its original moorings, it should as speedily as possible get back to the original starting point and demand justice for all men regardless of race and regardless of color.

In this connection we applaud and commend the efforts of President Roosevelt to secure equal accommodations on railroads and other public carriers for the white and black races.

The Republican Party demands that wherever any law relating to the civil or political conduct or rights of individuals is framed and promulgated, that that law shall apply with equal and exact justice to all races; especially is this true in regard to the exercise of the franchise. The weak need the protection which the ballot affords. No color line should be recognized in the American ballot. The provision known as the "grandfather clause" in some state constitutions is an insult to American manhood and we condemn and oppose it as unwarranted and un-American.

The National Republican Party unequivocally records itself as opposed to the recognition of any party organization which excludes or discourages men from joining county, state or national organizations because of their race or color; and especially does the party record itself as being opposed to the doctrine known in some parts of the country as "Lily Whiteism." This departure from Republican principles must find no place in the plans or policies of the Republican Party.

**Rights of the Negro:**

The Republican party has been for more than fifty years the consistent friend of the American Negro. It granted to him the freedom & the citizenship which he earned by his valor & service. It wrote into the organic law of the land the declarations that proclaim his civil and political rights, and it believes today that his noteworthy progress in intelligence, industry and good citizenship has earned the respect and encouragement of the Nation. We demand equal justice for all men, without regard to race or color; we approve the efforts of President Roosevelt and the vote of the Republican majority in Congress, over a solid Democratic opposition, to secure equal accommodations on railroads and other public carriers for all citizens, whether white or black; we declare once more, and without reservation, for the enforcement in spirit and letter of all those amendments to the Constitution which were designed for the protection and advancement of the Negro, and we condemn all devices like the so-called "grandfather clause" that have for their real aim his disfranchisement for reasons of color alone, as unfair, un-American and repugnant to the supreme law of the land.

---

# 20
## A Statement on Lynching

*Washington issued this statement a few days after the Springfield, Illinois, race riot. While this is one of Washington's most pointed attacks on lynching, he still apologizes for crime and idleness in the black community. The statement was printed in the New York* World, *August 20, 1908, and reprinted in* BTW Papers *9: 611–13.*

**Booker T. Washington Gives Facts and Condemns Lynchings
in a Statement Telegraphed to the New York World**

Within the past sixty days twenty-five Negroes have been lynched in different parts of the United States. Of this number only four were even charged with criminal assault upon women. Nine were lynched in one day on the charge of being connected with murder. Four were lynched in one day on the charge that they passed resolutions in a lodge approving the murder of an individual. Three were lynched in one day on the charge that they had taken part in the burning of a gin house. The others were lynched for miscellaneous reasons.

One was publicly burned in open daylight in the presence of women and children, after oil had been poured upon his body, at Greenville, Tex., and reports state that a thousand people witnessed the spectacle in the open square of the town. One other victim was eighty years of age. How long can our Christian civilization stand this? I am making no special plea for the Negro, innocent or guilty, but I am calling attention to the danger that threatens our civilization.

*Condemns Negro Loafers*

For the Negro criminal, and especially for the Negro loafer, gambler and drunkard, I have nothing but the severest condemnation, and no legal punishment is too severe for the brute that assaults a woman.

It requires no courage for 500 men to tie the hands of an individual to the stake or to hang or shoot him. But young men and boys who have once witnessed or who have read in the papers of these exciting scenes of burnings and lynchings often get the idea that there is something heroic in attacking some individual in the community who is at least able to defend himself.

No doubt the people who engage in lynchings, and excuse them, believe that they will have the effect of striking terror to the guilty. But who shall say whether the persons lynched are guilty? There is no way of distinguishing the innocent from the guilty except by due process of law. That is what courts are for. Those who have examined into the facts know only too well that in the wild justice of the mob it is frequently the innocent man who is executed.

*Terrify the Innocent*

These lynchings terrify the innocent, but they embolden the criminal. The criminal knows it is much easier to escape the mad fury of the mob than the deliberate vengeance of the law. But no man is so innocent that he can be safe at all times from the frenzy of the mob.

Statistics show that during the past ten years an average of thirty-two Negroes a year have been lynched on the charge of assaulting women. Granting that thirty-two per year are guilty, is that a just reason for condemning over

3,000,000 adult Negro men who have no part in such crimes? Are we as a nation to allow thirty-two criminals a year out of a race of 10,000,000 of people to throw us into a frenzy and change the complexion of our civilization so that we are held up to foreign nations as an uncivilized people not governed by law or order? Again I would say I am not making any special plea for the Negro, but because I feel that lynching is not only wrong, but a mistake—an awful mistake.

### Effect of Mob Justice

Mob justice undermines the very foundation upon which our civilization rests, viz., respect for the law and confidence of its security. There are, in my opinion, two remedies—First of all, let us unite in a determined effort everywhere to see that the law is enforced, that all people at all times and all places see that the man charged with crime is given a fair trial.

Secondly, let all good citizens unite in an effort to rid the communities, especially the large cities, of the idle, vicious and gambling element. And in this connection I would not be just and would not be frank unless I stated that the betters of the black race could use their influence, especially in the cities, to see that the idle element that lives by its wits without permanent or reliable occupation or place of abode is either reformed or gotten rid of in some manner. In most cases it is this element that furnishes the powder for these explosions.

---

# 21
## Letter to the Editor, Montgomery *Advertiser,* December 30, 1910

*Washington again states his argument that blacks have deserted rural areas for southern and northern cities because rural areas generally provide few educational opportunities for blacks, and fail to protect blacks from racial violence. This letter was reprinted in* BTW Papers *10: 513–16.*

Tuskegee, Ala., Dec. 29, 1910

I have seen considerable discussion in the Alabama papers bearing on the question as to why the majority of the "Black Belt" counties have, during the past ten years, lost population. An examination shows that it is the "Black Belt" counties that have no large cities that have decreased in population. Macon County, however, is an exception for instead of losing population it has during the past ten years increased in population. In my opinion there are reasons for this. I may not be able to state all the reasons, but I think I know, at least, one or two reasons why Macon County has gone forward in population instead of going backward.

So far as the negro race is concerned, I am quite sure that Macon County has gained in population because the County Board of Education has been wise enough to encourage and help the colored people to have good public schools in the country districts of the county. The average white man does not realize that no matter what else the average negro will do without, he wants education for his children. I am not taking time now to discuss the wisdom of all the wants of the negro, but to state why there are few negro families in Alabama who would be content to live from year to year in a country community that provides no public school or a school taught in a log cabin for three or four months only during the year and that with a very poor teacher at its head. This condition means that the negro family becomes restless, dissatisfied and seeks as soon as possible to better its condition, and to do this it moves to a community where school facilities are better.

## Little School Money

I do not believe that the leading white people, and especially land owners of the "Black Belt" counties know how little money some negro schools receive. I actually know of communities where negro teachers are being paid only from $15 to $17 per month for services for a period of three or four months in the year. This, of course, means practically no schools. In making this statement, I am not overlooking the fact that even where the disposition exists to help the negro public schools the money is often lacking to a large extent, but I am stating facts so far as I know them. More money is paid for negro convicts than for negro teachers. About $46 per month is now being paid for first-class able bodied negro convicts, $36 for second-class and $26 for third-class, for twelve months in the year.

One other element in the situation that drives negroes from the farms of the "Black Belt" counties is this: In many of the "Black Belt" counties when a negro is charged with a crime, a mob of wild, excited and often intoxicated people go scouring through the country in search of the negro. In many cases it happens, as former Governor Jelks frankly stated, that the wrong negro is caught and often lynched. There have been happenings of this kind in the country districts which have made many of the best colored people feel that the safest thing for them is to move to a large city where they will receive police protection in case they are charged with crime. The experience of the civilized world shows that even where the utmost care and deliberation is exercised on the part of lawyers, judges and jury innocent persons are sometimes punished. In the face of this experience, it is impossible for a wild, frenzied and excited mob of people to pass judgment upon the guilt or innocence of an individual.

In my opinion if the negroes understand that their public schools in the country districts are gradually going to be improved as fast as the state can do so and that they will receive police protection in case they are charged with crime in the country districts as they do in the cities, then the best colored farmers will cease moving from the country districts into the cities.

## Macon County Schools

In Macon County there are good school houses and reasonably good teachers. This is true, I think I am safe in saying, for both races. Ask any white man in Macon County, and he will tell you, I think, that since Macon County has had good public schools it has a more orderly and law-abiding negro population; that labor is much easier to secure and that the colored people work better than they did before.

In addition to this, negro public schools in Macon County have teachers who teach about the things by which they are to earn their living. In addition to teaching the children with books and about the Bible, they teach them how to farm, how to grow vegetables, how to raise poultry, pigs, fruits, etc., they also teach the girls something of cooking, table service and sewing. The result is, the whole community, through the school, is taught to love country life and to respect labor.

Since the state of Alabama is going to spend money on the education of the negro child, I believe it will be better to see that this money is looked after closely and is wisely spent so as to produce good results.

Certainly, so far as "Black Belt" counties are concerned, if they would pursue the policy Macon County is pursuing, they would have a negro population that would be a continual source of usefulness and strength to the whole state.

Another reason why I think Macon County is in such good condition, is because the negroes have good sense enough to realize that they have certain duties to perform themselves—that all the responsibility does not rest with the white people. There are few negroes in Macon County who do not co-operate with the officers of the law in order to get rid of lawbreakers. There are few negroes in Macon County who would refuse to assist the sheriff in ferreting out crime and bringing criminals into a court of justice. And the negroes of Macon County also co-operate heartily with the school officials in building up and sustaining good public schools.

## No Race Problem

We have no race problem in Macon County. We have no race friction. In talking with the sheriff of Macon County, a few days ago, he told me that there is so little crime in Macon County that he can scarcely find enough to keep him busy.

As I have gone into Montgomery, Birmingham, Atlanta and other large cities, I have found colored people who formerly lived in rural communities, and have asked them why they moved to the cities and in nine cases out of ten they have told me that there were no public schools in the communities where they formerly lived.

I believe that the "Black Belt" counties of Alabama will continue to lose in population unless some attention is given to building up good public schools in rural districts. It is just as easy to have a negro population that is happy, contented and prosperous as to have one that is restless and dissatisfied because of poor schools and all such matters. I believe in this respect the two races can co-operate and in this way add to the happiness and prosperity of both.

---

# 22
## Letter to C. Elias Winston, October 2, 1914

*In this unusual letter Washington responded to criticism that he had urged blacks to stop fighting against segregation. Instead, he asserts, he has always opposed segregation, but attempted to do so in a manner that emphasized constructive programs as well as the condemnation of evil. This letter can be found in the Booker T. Washington Papers, Library of Congress, container 523; it was reprinted in* BTW Papers *13: 139–42.*

Tuskegee Institute, Alabama. October 2, 1914

My dear Mr. Winston: I regret the delay in answering your letter owing to the fact that I have been off on a fishing trip for a week.

In your case, I am doing something which I very rarely do, and that is to attempt to correct a misrepresentation of my words. I have found by some experience in public life that if one spends his time in attempting to correct false reports, he will rarely do anything in the way of constructive work, and that the time spent in trying to make such corrections could be better spent, in most cases, in some direct effort in the way of progress.

I am making exception in your case, because you have been kind and thoughtful enough to do that which very few people think of doing, and that is to try to find out directly from the individual, himself, the facts concerning his utterances. In most cases, persons simply hear a rumor, or read a garbled report of one's address and then this report or rumor is passed from one hand to another without anyone taking the precaution to get first-hand, direct information from the person most concerned.

You say that I am quoted in both the white and colored press as making the following remarks: "The Negro should stop fighting segregation and lend his forces towards beautifying the neighborhood in which he lives." Let me say that I have made no such remarks at any time or at any place. On the other hand, I have always opposed the passing of any law to segregate the Negro, either in city, town or country district. I have always said, especially when speaking to Southern white people, that such segregation is unnecessary, unjust, unwise, and from my point of view, illegal, and I have been often surprised at the number of white people in the South who have agreed with my position.

A few weeks ago, when an attempt was made to pass a law segregating colored people in Birmingham, I, in connection with a number of other colored people in Alabama, took the matter up directly with the city commissioners and the law was not passed.

When speaking on the subject of railroad accommodations in Muskogee, I made the following direct remarks to the white people who composed a large part of the audience, "Let us urge upon the railroads throughout this country to provide more equal, more just, more clean and up-to-date railroad facilities for the black people of this country, wherever the law requires such separation. And there is no white man in the United States, no matter where he lives, North or South, who will not agree with us in the statement that, whenever and wherever a Negro pays a railroad fare that is equal to that paid by a white man, he should have accommodations that are just as just and equal, and that are just as clean and decent, as those furnished the white man for the same amount of money. You would not permit the white merchants in Muskogee to sell so many pounds of flour to a Negro customer at a certain price and then sell better flour and more flour to a white customer for the same money; no more should a railroad be permitted to furnish one kind of accommodation to the Negro passenger and another kind of accommodation to the white passenger for the same money."

What I did attempt to say in Muskogee, and what I have attempted on numerous occasions to say when speaking in public, was to urge our people not to become discouraged or disheartened in communities where they were segregated, but notwithstanding such segregation, go forward and make progress. In a word, to overcome evil with good; to make so much progress in the beauty, comfort and convenience of their surroundings that those who have treated them unjustly will be made to blush with shame because of the progress that the colored people are making. In a word, I try to impress upon our people the idea that they should keep a cheerful heart and a strong will and not permit themselves to be continually on the defensive side of life, but to make such progress that the world will admire the rapid strides with which they are going forward.

I realize fully the importance of condemning wrong—such wrongs as segregation —but I realize, too, the danger of our spending too much time and strength in mere condemnation without attempting to aid our cause by progressive, constructive work as well as condemnation. Condemnation is easy; construction is difficult. The constructive action should employ the major portion of our time. The two lines of thought and work must go hand in hand; condemnation of wrong and constructive effort; overcoming injustice through evidences of progress. On this platform we can make an appeal to every white man in the South and in the North whose goodwill and influence is worth having. More and more, throughout the South, the number of white people who feel and see that it never helps to yield to the temptation of mistreating a black man is increasing; throughout this country, the number of black people who feel and see that it never helps a black man to yield to the temptation of mistreating a white man is increasing.

In proportion as we go forward in all parts of the country, making real progress and asking for fair and just treatment by the hands of all people, North and South, our race is going to command the respect and confidence of all the people of all classes.

You are at liberty to make any use of this letter that your judgment dictates. Yours very truly,

---

# 23
## Speech to the National Negro Business League, August 18, 1915

*This address, presented to the annual meeting of the National Negro Business League in Boston, was one of the last public presentations that Washington made before his death on November 14, 1915. It contains Washington's assessment of the racial situation in the United States in mid-1915. This speech was printed in the* Tuskegee Student *27 (September 4, 1915): 1–3, and reprinted in* BTW Papers *13: 345–51.*

Symphony Hall    Boston, Massachusetts
Wednesday Night August 18, 1915

At the beginning of my annual address as President, to this the sixteenth meeting of the National Negro Business League, let me emphasize, in so far as mere human words can, the deep depth of gratitude, which all of us owe to our Secretary, Mr. Emmett J. Scott, for the continued success of this organization. In a large measure, it is the hard work, the loyalty, unselfishness, and resourcefulness of Mr. Scott which make and keep this League the power for good that it is. Nor should I overlook the steadfastness and helpful interest and generosity of all the members of the Executive Committee, as well as the several officers.

In this catalogue there should not be omitted the name of our active and devoted National Organizer, Mr. Charles H. Moore, the loyalty and activity of many of the Local Leagues is a matter of constant surprise and gratification.

The difficult and practical work which has been done by the Boston Local League, together with the Cambridge League, and the citizens of Boston as a whole, to make this meeting a success, is also cause for congratulations and deep gratitude.

I wish now again, as in other years to thank the Colored Press throughout the country for its more than liberal and constant support of the work of this League. We of the Negro Race and of the White Race know little of the self-sacrificing and patriotic work that is constantly being done by the Negro Press.

This National Negro Business League was organized in the city of Boston fifteen years ago with a mere handful of men. The League during the fifteen years of its life has grown in power, in influence, and in usefulness, until, either, through its local leagues or individual members, it reaches practically every part of the country in which there are any considerable number of colored people. After fifteen years of testing useful service and growth, it is fitting that we should return to Boston, the place which gave us birth.

From the first, this National Negro Business League has clung strictly to the object for which it was founded. It was not founded to take the place of other organizations; nor was this league as a league, ever intended to go into business as an organization or to become a close, hide-bound concern, with grips and signs and pass words. We have such organizations and they are doing their work well, but the central purpose of this National Negro Business League has been, from the first to foster, to spread, and to create industrial, business and commercial enterprises among our people in every part of the country. How well we have succeeded, I shall let the facts tell the story later on.

The founders and promoters of the League fully recognize the fact that it cannot meet all the needs of the race, nor satisfy all its ambition. We fully and frankly recognize the fact that there is need for the particular and distinct work to be done by the religious, the educational, the political, the literary, the secret, and the fraternal bodies, as well as those that deal with the civil rights of our people.

All of these have their place and with none of them would we seek to interfere; but the history of civilization, throughout the world, shows that without economic and commercial success there can be no lasting or commanding success in other fields of endeavor. This League then has for one of its objects not the tearing down or weakening of other organizations, but rather to give them strength and stability.

Since our last annual meeting, there have been happenings that are of peculiar interest to our race. Among these has been the observance of a National Health

Week which was promoted very largely by this Business League, acting in co-operation with the Virginia Organization Society. Health Week was perhaps more generally observed by all classes of our people in the South and in the North than has ever been true of any similar movement in the history of the race. Until ten years ago, the death-rate among our people was alarming, but the importance of good health and long life has been called to the attention of the race in so many ways during the last ten years that the death-rate has already been reduced by four per cent in certain parts of the country. It is the wish of many that the Health Week be observed again this year.

Since our last meeting the United States Supreme Court has rendered a decision in the Oklahoma case which is of far-reaching value and importance to our race. The main value of this decision, rendered by a Southern Supreme Court Justice and an ex-confederate soldier and ex-slave-holder, consists in the fact that it makes plain the idea, once and for all by the Supreme Court of the land, that neither color nor race can debar a man in this country from full citizenship.

I regret to note that the number of lynchings, during the first six months of the calendar year, has increased as compared with the same period a year ago. While the number of black people lynched is smaller; the number of white people lynched is larger. The increase in the total number lynched should not discourage but should make us renew our energies and double our determination to blot out the crime of lynching from our civilization, whether the man be a white man or a black man. And I here repeat that which I said in Louisiana a few weeks ago. We must have in this country, law administered by the court and not by the mob. Along with the blotting out of lynchings should go that other relic of barbarism. I refer to public hangings.

In all these matters I am pleading not in the interest of the Negro or the White man, but in the interest of a more strong and perfect civilization.

It is seldom that it is ever so true that, in the space of one generation, that so many evidences of real progress in the fundamental things of life can be seen. Perhaps the changes in Japan are the nearest akin to it.

Since the League met in Boston fifteen years ago, great changes have taken place among our people in property getting and in the promotion of industrial and business enterprises. These changes have taken place not solely because of the work of the League, but this and similar organizations have had much to do with bringing about this progress. Let me be more specific.

We have not the figures covering all the Negro's wealth, but the Federal Census Bureau has just released a document which gives the value of the Negro's farm property alone as $1,142,000,000. From 1900 to 1910, the Negro's farm property increased 128 per cent. In 1863 we had as a race 2000 small business enterprises of one kind and another. At the present time, the Negro owns and operates about 43,000 concerns, with an annual turn-over of about one billion dollars. Within fifty years we have made enough progress in business to warrant the operation of over 50 banks. With all that I have said, we are still a poor race as compared with many others; but I have given these figures to indicate the direction in which we are traveling. During the last 6 years we have experienced as a race not a few business failures, including the closing of several banks. We must not let these failures discourage us. We must remember that it is with a race, as it is with an individual, that it is only through seeming failure, as well as success, that we finally gain that experience and confidence which are necessary to permanent success. With all that I have said, we should remember that we have but scratched the surface of industrial and business success.

Our future is before us, not behind us. We are a new race in a comparatively new country. Let any who may be inclined toward pessimism or discord consider with me for a few moments the opportunities that are before us. It is always of more value to consider our advantages rather than disadvantages. In considering one's opportunities it is worth while not to overlook the size of our race.

There are only 14 nations in the world whose population exceeds the number of Negroes in the United States. Norway has a population of only 2,400,000; Denmark, 2,700,000; Bulgaria, 4,000,000; Chile, 4,000,000; Canada, 7,000,000; Argentina, 9,000,000. When we contemplate these figures, and then remember that we, in the United States alone are 10,000,000 Negroes, we can get some idea of the opportunities that are right about us. Let me be more specific in pointing the way to these opportunities. If you would ask where you are to begin, I would answer, begin where you are. As a rule the gold mine which we seek in a far-off country is right at our door.

Over a million of our people live in the Northern and Western States. In these States at the present time, our people operate about 4000 business enterprises. There are opportunities in the North and West for eight thousand business enterprises, or double the present number. In the Southern States, where the great bulk of our people live, we have about 40,000 business concerns. There should be within the next few years twenty thousand more business concerns. In all this, we should never forget that the ownership and cultivation of the soil constitute the foundation for great wealth and usefulness among our people. I have already indicated that we now operate about 800,000 farms. Within the next decade let us try to double the number. To realize a little more in directions of our opportunities: There are now 4000 truck farms operated by us, we ought to increase this number to 8000. We ought never to forget that in the ownership and cultivation of the soil in a very large measure we must lay the foundation for one's success.

A landless race is like a ship without a rudder. Emphasizing again our opportunities, especially as connected with the soil, we now have, for example, 122 poultry raisers. The number should be increased to 1500. We now have 200 dairymen. The number should be increased to 2000.

At present there are far too many of our people living in the cities in a hand-to-mouth way, dependent on someone else for an uncertain job. Aside from what the soil offers, there are other opportunities in business. For example, we now own and operate 75 bakeries. The number can be increased to 500. From 32 brickmakers the number can be increased to 3000. From 200 sawmills we can increase the number to 1000. From 50 furniture factories, the number can be increased to 300. Where we now have 9000 drygood stores and grocery merchants, we should have in the near future 15,000.

Where we now have 700 drug stores, we should have 3000. Where we now have 700 real estate dealers, we should have 3000. Where we now have 1000 millinery stores, we should have 5000. Where we now have 150 plumbers, we should have 600. Where we have 400 tailors we should have 2000. Where we now have 59 architects we should have 400. We now have 3000 contractors and builders, we should have 5000. Where we now have 51 banks, we should have 500.

Few people are aware of the fact that we now have in our race after only fifty years of freedom, 55 book stores, 18 department stores, 14 five-and-ten cent stores, 20 jewelry stores, 790 junk dealers, 13 warehouses and cold storage plants, 152 wholesale merchants, 200 laundries, 350 livery stables, 953 undertakers, 400 photographers, 10 opticians, 75 hair goods manufacturers, 111 old-rag dealers, 12 buyers and shippers of live stock.

With our race as it has been and always will be with all races without economic and business foundation, it is hardly possible to have educational and religious growth or political freedom.

We can learn some mighty serious lessons just now from conditions in Liberia and Hayti. For years both in Liberia and Hayti, literary education and politics have been emphasized, but while doing this the people have failed to apply themselves to the development of the soil, mines and forests. The result is that, from an economic point of view, those two republics have become dependent upon other nations and races. In both republics the control of finances is in the hands of other nations, this being true not withstanding the fact that the two countries have natural resources greater than other countries similar in size. In the United States there is no hope for us, except in an increasing degree we teach our young people to apply their education to develop the natural resources and to promote human activities in the communities where we live. Mere abstract, unused education means little for a race or individual. An ounce of application is worth a ton of abstraction. We must not be afraid to pay the price for success in business—the price of sleepless nights, the price of toil when others rest, the price of planning today for tomorrow, this year for next year. If someone else endures the hardships, does the thinking, and pays the salaries, someone else will reap the harvest and enjoy the reward.

To accomplish what I have indicated, we must have a united race, men who are big enough and broad enough to forget and overlook personal and local differences and each willing to place upon the altar all that he holds for the benefit of the race and our country.

Sometimes it is suggested that some of us are over optimistic concerning the present conditions and future of our race. In part answer, it might be stated that one on the inside of a house looking out can often see more than the one on the outside looking in. No one enjoys riding in a pullman car so much as the one who has ridden in a freight car.

No matter how poor you are, how black you are, or how obscure your present work and position, I want each one to remember that there is a chance for him and the more difficulties he has to overcome, the greater will be his success.

Everywhere we should be proud of the Negro race and loyal to the great human family of whatever color. Whenever we consider what is now going on in Europe, where all the people are of one color, and then compare these conditions with present conditions and our task for our race, we ought to thank our Creator that conditions are so well with us and that we live beneath the Stars and Stripes.

---

# 24
## My View of Segregation Laws

*"My View of Segregation Laws" was written in September 1915, but published as an article in the* New Republic *5 (December 4, 1915): 113–14, a month following Washington's death.*

In all of my experience I have never yet found a case where the masses of the people of any given city were interested in the matter of the segregation of white and colored people; that is, there has been no spontaneous demand for segregation ordinances. In certain cities politicians have taken the leadership in introducing such segregation ordinances into city councils, and after making an appeal to racial prejudices have succeeded in securing a backing for ordinances which would segregate the negro people from their white fellow citizens. After such ordinances have been introduced it is always difficult, in the present state of public opinion in the South, to have any considerable body of white people oppose them, because their attitude is likely to be misrepresented as favoring negroes against white people. They are, in the main, afraid of the stigma, "negro lover."

It is probably useless to discuss the legality of segregation; that is a matter which the courts will finally pass upon. It is reasonably certain, however, that the courts in no section of the country would uphold a case where negroes sought to segregate white citizens. This is the most convincing argument that segregation is regarded as illegal, when viewed on its merits by the whole body of our white citizens.

Personally I have little faith in the doctrine that it is necessary to segregate the whites from the blacks to prevent race mixture. The whites are the dominant race in the South, they control the courts, the industries and the government in all of the cities, counties and states except in those few communities where the negroes, seeking some form of self-government, have established a number of experimental towns or communities.

I have never viewed except with amusement the sentiment that white people who live next to negro populations suffer physically, mentally and morally because of their proximity to colored people. Southern white people who have been brought up in this proximity are not inferior to other white people. The President of the United States was born and reared in the South in close contact with black people. Five members of the present Cabinet were born in the South; and many of them, I am sure, had black "mammies." The Speaker of the House of Representatives is a Southern man, the chairmen of leading committees in both the United States Senate and the Lower House of Congress are Southern men. Throughout the country to-day, people occupying the highest positions not only in the government but in education, industry and science, are persons born in the South in close contact with the negro.

Attempts at legal segregation are unnecessary for the reason that the matter of residence is one which naturally settles itself. Both colored and whites are likely to select a section of the city where they will be surrounded by congenial neighbors. It is unusual to hear of a colored man attempting to live where he is surrounded by white people or where he is not welcome. Where attempts are being made to segregate the races legally, it should be noted that in the matter of business no attempt is made to keep the white man from placing his grocery store, his dry goods store, or other enterprise right in the heart of a negro district. This is another searching test which challenges the good faith of segregationists.

It is true that the negro opposes these attempts to restrain him from residing in certain sections of a city or community. He does this not because he wants to mix with the white man socially, but because he feels that such laws are unnecessary. The negro objects to being segregated because it usually means that he will receive inferior accommodations in return for the taxes he pays. If the negro is segregated, it will probably mean that the sewerage in his part of the city will be inferior; that the streets and sidewalks will be neglected, that the street lighting will be poor; that his section of the city will not be kept in order by the police and other authorities, and that the "undesirables" of other races will be placed near him, thereby making it difficult for him to rear his family in decency. It should always be kept in mind that while the negro may not be directly a large taxpayer, he does pay large taxes indirectly. In the last analysis, all will agree that the man who pays house rent pays large taxes, for the price paid for the rent includes payment of the taxes on the property.

Right here in Alabama nobody is thinking or talking about land and home segregation. It is rather remarkable that in the very heart of the Black Belt where the black man is most ignorant the white people should not find him so repulsive as to set him away off to himself. If living side by side is such a menace as some people think, it does seem as if the people who have had the bulk of the race question to handle during the past fifty years would have discovered the danger and adjusted it long ago.

A segregated negro community is a terrible temptation to many white people. Such a community invariably provides certain types of white men with hiding places—hiding places from the law, from decent people of their own race, from their churches and their wives and daughters. In a negro district in a certain city in the South a house of ill-repute for white men was next door to a negro denominational school. In another town a similar kind of house is just across the street from the negro grammar school. In New Orleans the legalized vice section is set in the midst of the negro section, and near the spot where stood a negro school and a negro church, and near the place where the negro orphanage now operates. Now when a negro seeks to buy a house in a reputable street he does it not only to get police protection, lights and accommodations, but to remove his children to a locality in which vice is not paraded.

In New Orleans, Atlanta, Birmingham, Memphis—indeed in nearly every large city in the South—I have been in the homes of negroes who live in white neighborhoods, and I have yet to find any race friction; the negro goes about his business, the white man about his. Neither the wives nor the children have the slightest trouble.

White people who argue for the segregation of the masses of black people forget the tremendous power of objective teaching. To hedge any set of people off in a corner and sally among them now and then with a lecture or a sermon is merely to add misery to degradation. But put the black man where day by day he sees how the white man keeps his lawns, his windows; how he treats his wife and children, and you will do more real helpful teaching than a whole library of lectures and sermons. Moreover, this will help the white man. If he knows that his life is to be taken as a model, that his hours, dress, manners, are all to be patterns for someone less fortunate, he will deport himself better than he would otherwise. Practically all the real moral uplift the black people have got from the whites—and this has been great indeed—has come from this observation of the white man's conduct. The South to-day is still full of the type of negro with gentle manners. Where did he get them? From some master or mistress of the same type.

Summarizing the matter in the large, segregation is ill-advised because

1. It is unjust.
2. It invites other unjust measures.
3. It will not be productive of good, because practically every thoughtful negro resents its injustice and doubts its sincerity. Any race adjustment based on

injustice finally defeats itself. The Civil War is the best illustration of what results where it is attempted to make wrong right or seem to be right.

4. It is unnecessary.

5. It is inconsistent. The negro is segregated from his white neighbor, but white business men are not prevented from doing business in negro neighborhoods.

6. There has been no case of segregation of negroes in the United States that has not widened the breach between the two races. Wherever a form of segregation exists it will be found that it has been administered in such a way as to embitter the negro and harm more or less the moral fibre of the white man. That the negro does not express this constant sense of wrong is no proof that he does not feel it.

It seems to me that the reasons given above, if carefully considered, should serve to prevent further passage of such segregation ordinances as have been adopted in Norfolk, Richmond, Louisville, Baltimore, and one or two cities in South Carolina.

Finally, as I have said in another place, as white and black learn daily to adjust, in a spirit of justice and fair play, those interests which are individual and racial, and to see and feel the importance of those fundamental interests which are common, so will both races grow and prosper. In the long run no individual and no race can succeed which sets itself at war against the common good; for "in the gain or loss of one race, all the rest have equal claim."

Tuskegee Institute, Alabama.
September 13, 1915.

# II.  W.E.B. Du Bois

# 1
## Letter to Booker T. Washington, September 24, 1895

*Du Bois sent this letter to Washington while he was a young professor at Wilberforce. At the time he generally endorsed the leadership of Washington and applauded the Atlanta speech, as did most black leaders. This letter can be found in the Booker T. Washington Papers, Library of Congress, container 113; it also has been reprinted in* BTW Papers *4: 26.*

Wilberforce, 24 Sept., '95

My Dear Mr Washington: Let me heartily congratulate you upon your phenomenal success at Atlanta—it was a word fitly spoken.

Sincerely Yours,

---

# 2
## Strivings of the Negro People

*In this article, "Strivings of the Negro People" (*Atlantic Monthly: A Magazine of Literature, Science, Art, and Politics *80 [August 1897]: 194–98), Du Bois further developed the themes that he had introduced in an address at the American Negro Academy in March 1897. Du Bois argued that it was imperative that each race maintain its separate identity to fulfill its destiny, and that the African American consequently had two identities to maintain, his civic identity as an American and his racial identity as an African. With this publication, Du Bois emerged as one of the leading young black intellectuals.*

Between me and the other world there is ever an unasked question: unasked by some through feelings of delicacy; by others through the difficulty of rightly framing it. All, nevertheless, flutter round it. They approach me in a half-hesitant sort of way, eye me curiously or compassionately, and then, instead of saying directly, How does it feel to be a problem? they say, I know an excellent colored man in my town; or, I fought at Mechanicsville; or, Do not these Southern outrages make your blood boil? At these I smile, or am interested, or reduce the boiling to a simmer, as the occasion may require. To the real question, How does it feel to be a problem? I answer seldom a word.

And yet, being a problem is a strange experience,—peculiar even for one who has never been anything else, save perhaps in babyhood and in Europe. It is in the early days of rollicking boyhood that the revelation first bursts upon one, all in a day, as it were. I remember well when the shadow swept across me. I was a little thing, away up in the hills of New England, where the dark Housatonic winds between Hoosac and Taghanic to the sea. In a wee wooden schoolhouse, something put it into the boys' and girls' heads to buy gorgeous visiting-cards— ten cents a package—and exchange. The exchange was merry, till one girl, a tall newcomer, refused my card,— refused it peremptorily, with a glance. Then it dawned upon me with a certain suddenness that I was different from the others; or like, mayhap, in heart and life and longing, but shut out from their world by a vast veil. I had thereafter no desire to tear down that veil, to creep through; I held all beyond it in common contempt, and lived above it in a region of blue sky and great wandering shadows. That sky was bluest when I could beat my mates at examination-time, or beat them at a foot-race, or even beat their stringy heads. Alas, with the years all this fine contempt began to fade; for the world I longed for, and all its dazzling opportunities, were theirs, not mine. But they should not keep these prizes, I said; some, all, I would wrest from them. Just how I would do it I could never decide: by reading law, by healing the sick, by telling the wonderful tales that swam in my head,—some way. With other black boys the strife was not so fiercely sunny: their youth shrunk into tasteless sycophancy, or into silent hatred of the pale world about them and mocking distrust of every- thing white; or wasted itself in a bitter cry, Why did God make me an outcast and a stranger in mine own house? The "shades of the prison-house" closed round about us all: walls strait and stubborn to the whitest, but relentlessly narrow, tall, and unscalable to sons of night who must plod darkly on in resignation, or beat unavailing palms against the stone, or steadily, half hopelessly watch the streak of blue above.

After the Egyptian and Indian, the Greek and Roman, the Teuton and Mongo- lian, the Negro is a sort of seventh son, born with a veil, and gifted with second- sight in this American world,—a world which yields him no self-consciousness, but only lets him see himself through the revelation of the other world. It is a peculiar sensation, this double-consciousness, this sense of always looking at one's self through the eyes of others, of measuring one's soul by the tape of a world that looks on in amused contempt and pity. One ever feels his two-ness,— an American, a Negro; two souls, two thoughts, two unreconciled strivings; two warring ideals in one dark body, whose dogged strength alone keeps it from being torn asunder. The history of the American Negro is the history of this strife,—this longing to attain self-conscious manhood, to merge his double self into a better and truer self. In this merging he wishes neither of the older selves to be lost. He does not wish to Africanize America, for America has too much to teach the world and Africa; he does not wish to bleach his Negro blood in a flood of white Americanism, for he believes— foolishly, perhaps, but fervently —that Negro blood has yet a message for the world. He simply wishes to make it possible for a man to be both a Negro and an American without being cursed and spit upon by his fellows, without losing the opportunity of self-development.

This is the end of his striving: to be a co-worker in the kingdom of culture, to escape both death and isolation, and to husband and use his best powers. These powers, of body and of mind, have in the past been so wasted and dispersed as to lose all effectiveness, and to seem like absence of all power, like weakness. The double-aimed struggle of the black artisan, on the one hand to escape white contempt for a nation of mere hewers of wood and drawers of water, and on the other hand to plough and nail and dig for a poverty-stricken horde, could only result in making him a poor craftsman, for he had but half a heart in either cause. By the poverty and ignorance of his people the Negro lawyer or doctor was pushed toward quackery and demagogism, and by the criticism of the other world toward an elaborate preparation that overfitted him for his lowly tasks. The would-be black savant was confronted by the paradox that the knowledge his people needed was a twice-told tale to his white neighbors, while the knowledge which would teach the white world was Greek to his own flesh and blood. The innate love of harmony and beauty that set the ruder souls of his people a-dancing, a-singing, and a-laughing raised but confusion and doubt in the soul of the black artist; for the beauty revealed to him was the soul-beauty of a race which his larger audience despised, and he could not articulate the message of another people.

This waste of double aims, this seeking to satisfy two unreconciled ideals, has wrought sad havoc with the courage and faith and deeds of eight thousand thousand people, has sent them often wooing false gods and invoking false means of salvation, and has even at times seemed destined to make them ashamed of themselves. In the days of bondage they thought to see in one divine event the end of all doubt and disappointment; eighteenth-century Rousseauism never worshiped freedom with half the unquestioning faith that the American Negro did for two centuries. To him slavery was, indeed, the sum of all villainies, the cause of all sorrow, the root of all prejudice; emancipation was the key to a promised land of sweeter beauty than ever stretched before the eyes of wearied Israelites. In his songs and exhortations swelled one refrain, liberty; in his tears and curses the god he implored had freedom in his right hand. At last it came,—suddenly, fearfully, like a dream. With one wild carnival of blood and passion came the message in his own plaintive cadences:—

"Shout, O children!
Shout, you're free!
The Lord has bought your liberty!"

Years have passed away, ten, twenty, thirty. Thirty years of national life, thirty years of renewal and development, and yet the swarthy ghost of Banquo sits in its old place at the national feast. In vain does the nation cry to its vastest problem,—

"Take any shape but that, and my firm nerves
Shall never tremble!"

The freedman has not yet found in freedom his promised land. Whatever of lesser good may have come in these years of change, the shadow of a deep disappointment rests upon the Negro people,—a disappointment all the more bitter because the unattained ideal was unbounded save by the simple ignorance of a lowly folk.

The first decade was merely a prolongation of the vain search for freedom, the boon that seemed ever barely to elude their grasp,—like a tantalizing will-o'-the-wisp, maddening and misleading the headless host. The holocaust of war, the terrors of the Kuklux Klan, the lies of carpet-baggers, the disorganization of industry, and the contradictory advice of friends and foes left the bewildered serf with no new watchword beyond the old cry for freedom. As the decade closed, however, he began to grasp a new idea. The ideal of liberty demanded for its attainment powerful means, and these the Fifteenth Amendment gave him. The ballot, which before he had looked upon as a visible sign of freedom, he now regarded as the chief means of gaining and perfecting the liberty with which war had partially endowed him. And why not? Had not votes made war and emancipated millions? Had not votes enfranchised the freedmen? Was anything impossible to a power that had done all this? A million black men started with renewed zeal to vote themselves into the kingdom. The decade fled away,—a decade containing, to the freedman's mind, nothing but suppressed votes, stuffed ballot-boxes, and election outrages that nullified his vaunted right of suffrage. And yet that decade from 1875 to 1885 held another powerful movement, the rise of another ideal to guide the unguided, another pillar of fire by night after a clouded day. It was the ideal of "book-learning;" the curiosity, born of compulsory ignorance, to know and test the power of the cabalistic letters of the white man, the longing to know. Mission and night schools began in the smoke of battle, ran the gauntlet of reconstruction, and at last developed into permanent foundations. Here at last seemed to have been discovered the mountain path to Canaan; longer than the highway of emancipation and law, steep and rugged, but straight, leading to heights high enough to overlook life.

Up the new path the advance guard toiled, slowly, heavily, doggedly; only those who have watched and guided the faltering feet, the misty minds, the dull understandings, of the dark pupils of these schools know how faithfully, how piteously, this people strove to learn. It was weary work. The cold statistician wrote down the inches of progress here and there, noted also where here and there a foot had slipped or some one had fallen. To the tired climbers, the horizon was ever dark, the mists were often cold, the Canaan was always dim and far away. If, however, the vistas disclosed as yet no goal, no resting-place, little but flattery and criticism, the journey at least gave leisure for reflection and self-examination; it changed the child of emancipation to the youth with dawning self-consciousness, self-realization, self-respect. In those sombre forests of his striving his own soul rose before him, and he saw himself,—darkly as through a veil; and yet he saw in himself some faint revelation of his power, of his mission. He began to have a dim feeling that, to attain his place in the world, he must be himself, and not another. For the first time he sought to analyze the burden he bore upon his back, that dead-weight of social degradation partially masked behind a half-named Negro problem. He felt his poverty; without a cent, without a home, without land, tools, or savings, he had entered into competition with rich, landed, skilled neighbors. To be a poor man is hard, but to be a poor race in a land of dollars is the very bottom of hardships. He felt the weight of his ignorance,—not simply of letters, but of life, of business, of the humanities; the accumulated sloth and shirking and awkwardness of decades and centuries shackled his hands and feet. Nor was his burden all poverty and ignorance. The red stain of bastardy, which two centuries of systematic legal defilement of Negro women had stamped upon his race, meant not only the loss of ancient African chastity, but also the hereditary weight of a mass of filth from white whoremongers and adulterers, threatening almost the obliteration of the Negro home.

A people thus handicapped ought not to be asked to race with the world, but rather allowed to give all its time and thought to its own social problems. But alas! while sociologists gleefully count his bastards and his prostitutes, the very soul of the toiling, sweating black man is darkened by the shadow of a vast despair. Men call the shadow prejudice, and learnedly explain it as the natural defense of culture against barbarism, learning against ignorance, purity against crime, the "higher" against the "lower" races. To which the Negro cries Amen! and swears that to so much of this strange prejudice as is founded on just homage to civilization, culture, righteousness, and progress he humbly bows and meekly does obeisance. But before that nameless prejudice that leaps beyond all this he stands helpless, dismayed, and well-nigh speechless; before that personal disrespect and mockery, the ridicule and systematic humiliation, the distortion of fact and wanton license of fancy, the cynical ignoring of the better and boisterous welcoming of the worse, the all-pervading desire to inculcate disdain for everything black, from Toussaint to the devil,—before this there rises a sickening despair that would disarm and discourage any nation save that black host to whom "discouragement" is an unwritten word.

They still press on, they still nurse the dogged hope,—not a hope of nauseating patronage, not a hope of reception into charmed social circles of stock-jobbers, pork-packers, and earl-hunters, but the hope of a higher synthesis of civilization and humanity, a true progress, with which the chorus "Peace, good will to men,"

"May make one music as before,
But vaster."

Thus the second decade of the American Negro's freedom was a period of conflict, of inspiration and doubt, of faith and vain questionings, of *Sturm und Drang*. The ideals of physical freedom, of political power, of school training, as separate all-sufficient panaceas for social ills, became in the third decade dim and overcast. They were the vain dreams of credulous race childhood; not wrong, but incomplete and over-simple. The training of the schools we need to-day more than ever,—the training of deft hands, quick eyes and ears, and the broader, deeper, higher culture of gifted minds. The power of the ballot we need in sheer self-defense, and as a guarantee of good faith. We may misuse it, but we can scarce do worse in this respect than our whilom masters. Freedom, too, the long-sought, we still seek,—the freedom of life and limb, the freedom to work and think. Work, culture, and liberty,—all these we need, not singly, but together; for to-day these ideals among the Negro people are gradually coalescing, and finding a higher meaning in the unifying ideal of race,—the ideal of fostering the traits and talents of the Negro, not in opposition to, but in conformity with, the greater ideals of the American republic, in order that some day, on American soil, two world races may give each to each those characteristics which both so sadly lack. Already we come not altogether empty-handed: there is to-day no true American music but the sweet wild melodies of the Negro slave; the American fairy tales are Indian and African; we are the sole oasis of simple faith and reverence in a dusty desert of dollars and smartness. Will America be poorer if she replace her brutal, dyspeptic blundering with the light-hearted but determined Negro humility; or her coarse, cruel wit with loving, jovial good humor; or her Annie Rooney with Steal Away?

Merely a stern concrete test of the underlying principles of the great republic is the Negro problem, and the spiritual striving of the freedmen's sons is the travail of soul whose burden is almost beyond the measure of their strength, but who bear it in the name of an historic race, in the name of this the land of their fathers' fathers, and in the name of human opportunity.

# 3
## Letter to Booker T. Washington, February 17, 1900

*This letter was written at a crucial point in the relationship between the young Du Bois and Booker T. Washington. Du Bois was professor at Atlanta University and an increasingly prominent scholar. Washington had been recruiting Du Bois for the faculty at Tuskegee for several years. In this letter Du Bois asks instead for Washington to help him get the job of assistant superintendent of colored schools in Washington, D.C. When Du Bois failed to get this job, he blamed it on Washington's political machinations; it was one element that soured relations between the two men. This letter can be found in the Booker T. Washington Papers, Library of Congress, container 170; it also has been reprinted in* BTW Papers 3: 443–44.

*Confidential.*                                                    Atlanta, Ga., Feb. 17, 1900

My Dear Mr. Washington: I have taken a rather unreasonable amount of time to consider your kind offer to come to Tuskeegee, and I have not yet fully decided. I want however to lay some considerations before you & then when I come to the Conference as I now think I shall, we can talk further. Since your offer was made I have had two other chances—tho' not formal offers: one to stand for a professorship in Howard University and the other to enter the race for the position of Superintendant of the Washington colored schools. Then of course there are the claims of the work here.

Now the question that really puzzles me in these cases is the one as to where I would really be most useful. Howard I cut from the list without hesitation—I'm sure I shouldn't get on well there for it's a poorly conducted establishment. On the other hand I really question as to how much I am really needed at Tuskeegee. I think to be sure I could be of use there but after all would it not be a rather ornamental use than a fundamental necessity? Would not my department be regarded by the public as a sort of superfluous addition not quite in consonance with the fundamental Tuskeegee idea? On the other hand there is no doubt that I am needed at Atlanta and that in the future as much closer cooperation between Tuskeegee Atlanta & Hampton is possible in the future than in the past. Well this is the line along which I had been thinking some months, when there came letters urging me to seek the position of superintendent of the Washington D.C. schools. It seems that Mr. Cook who has held the position over 20 years has some thoughts of resigning. Now the question comes Is not this the most useful place of the three & could I not serve both your cause & the general cause of the Negro at the National capital better than elsewhere? I wish you'd think this matter over seriously & give me your best advice. Boiled down the questions are: 1st Am I really needed at Tuskeegee. 2nd Considering the assured success of the Tuskeegee institute already are there not weaker places where pioneer work is necessary. 3rd Is not the Washington position—provided always I could get it—such a place?

Of course if I should apply for the W. place your indorsement would go further probably than anyone's else. Could you conscientiously give it?

I write you thus frankly & hope you will consider the matter from my point of view & give me the results of your wisdom. Very Sincerely

---

# 4

## The Evolution of Negro Leadership

*"The Evolution of Negro Leadership" (The Dial 31 [July 16, 1901]: 53–55) was W.E.B. Du Bois's review of Booker T. Washington's autobiography,* Up from Slavery. *Du Bois placed Washington within the context of earlier black leadership as well as within the context of late-nineteenth-century economic, social, and political realities. While the review is not overtly critical, it did raise questions about Washington's racial philosophy and political tactics.*

In every generation of our national life, from Phillis Wheatley to Booker Washington, the Negro race in America has succeeded in bringing forth men whom the country, at times spontaneously, at times in spite of itself, has been impelled to honor and respect. Mr. Washington is one of the most striking of these cases, and his autobiography is a partial history of the steps which made him a group leader, and the one man who in the eyes of the nation typifies at present more nearly than all others the work and worth of his nine million fellows.

The way in which groups of human beings are led to choose certain of their number as their spokesmen and leaders is at once the most elementary and the nicest problem of social growth. History is but the record of this group leadership; and yet how infinitely changeful is its type and history! And of all types and kinds, what can be more instructive than the leadership of a group within a group—that curious double movement where real progress may be negative and actual advance be relative retrogression? All this is the social student's inspiration and despair.

When sticks and stones and beasts form the sole environment of a people, their attitude is ever one of determined opposition to, and conquest of, natural forces. But when to earth and brute is added an environment of men and ideas, then the attitude of the imprisoned group may take three main forms: a feeling of revolt and revenge; an attempt to adjust all thought and action to the will of the greater group; or, finally, a determined attempt at self-development, self-realization, in spite of environing discouragements and prejudice. The influence of all three of these attitudes is plainly to be traced in the evolution of race leaders among American negroes. Before 1750 there was but the one motive of revolt and revenge which animated the terrible Maroons and veiled all the Americas in fear of insurrection. But the liberalizing tendencies of the latter half of the eighteenth century brought the first thought of adjustment and assimilation in the crude and earnest songs of Phillis and the martyrdom of Attucks and Salem.

The cotton-gin changed all this, and men then, as the Lyman Abbotts of to-day, found a new meaning in human blackness. A season of hesitation and stress settled on the black world as the hope of emancipation receded. Forten and the free Negroes of the North still hoped for eventual assimilation with the nation; Allen, the founder of the great African Methodist Church, strove for unbending self-development, and the Southern freedmen followed him; while among the black slaves at the South arose the avenging Nat Turner, fired by the memory of Toussaint the Savior. So far, Negro leadership had been local and spasmodic; but now, about 1840, arose a national leadership—a dynasty not to be broken. Frederick Douglass and the moral revolt against slavery dominated Negro thought and effort until after the war. Then, with the sole weapon of self-defense in perilous times, the ballot, which the nation gave the freedmen, men like Langston and Bruce sought to guide the political fortunes of the blacks, while Payne and Price still clung to the old ideal of self-development.

Then came the reaction. War memories and ideals rapidly passed, and a period of astonishing commercial development and expansion ensued. A time of doubt and hesitation, of storm and stress, overtook the freedmen's sons; and then it was that Booker Washington's leadership began. Mr. Washington came with a clear simple programme, at the psychological moment; at a time when the nation was a little ashamed of having bestowed so much sentiment on Negroes and was concentrating its energies on Dollars. The industrial training of Negro youth was not an idea originating with Mr. Washington, nor was the policy of conciliating the white South wholly his. But he first put life, unlimited energy, and perfect faith into this programme; he changed it from an article of belief into a whole creed; he broadened it from a by-path into a veritable Way of Life. And the method by which he accomplished this is an interesting study of human life.

Mr. Washington's narrative gives but glimpses of the real struggle which he has had for leadership. First of all, he strove to gain the sympathy and cooperation of the white South, and gained it after that epoch-making sentence spoken at Atlanta: "In all things that are purely social we can be as separate as the fingers, yet one as the hand in all things essential to mutual progress. . . ." This conquest of the South is by all odds the most notable thing in Mr. Washington's career. Next to this comes his achievement in gaining place and consideration in the North. Many others less shrewd and tactful would have fallen between these two stools; but as Mr. Washington knew the heart of the South from birth and training, so by singular insight he intuitively grasped the spirit of the age that was dominating the North. He learned so thoroughly the speech and thought of triumphant commercialism and the ideals of material prosperity that he pictures as the height of absurdity a black boy studying a French grammar in the midst of weeds and dirt. One wonders how Socrates or St. Francis of Assissi would receive this!

And yet this very singleness of vision and thorough oneness with his age is a mark of the successful man. It is as though Nature must needs make men a little narrow to give them force. At the same time, Mr. Washington's success North and South, with his gospel of Work and Money, raised opposition to him from widely divergent sources. The spiritual sons of the Abolitionists were not prepared to acknowledge that the schools founded before Tuskegee, by men of broad ideals and self-sacrificing souls, were wholly failures, or worthy of ridicule. On the other hand, among his own people Mr. Washington found deep suspicion and dislike for a man on such good terms with Southern whites.

Such opposition has only been silenced by Mr. Washington's very evident sincerity of purpose. We forgive much to honest purpose which is accomplishing something. We may not agree with the man at all points, but we admire him and cooperate with him so far as we conscientiously can. It is no ordinary tribute to this man's tact and power, that, steering as he must amid so many diverse interests and opinions, he to-day commands not simply the applause of those who believe in his theories, but also the respect of those who do not.

Among the Negroes, Mr. Washington is still far from a popular leader. Educated and thoughtful Negroes everywhere are glad to honor him and aid him, but all cannot agree with him. He represents in Negro thought the old attitude of adjustment to environment, emphasizing the economic phase; but the two other strong currents of feeling, descended from the past, still oppose him. One is the thought of a small but not unimportant group, unfortunate in their choice of spokesman, but nevertheless of much weight, who represent the old ideas of revolt and revenge, and see in migration alone an outlet for the Negro people. The second attitude is that of the large and important group represented by Dunbar, Tanner, Chesnut, Miller, and the Grimkes, who, without any single definite programme, and with complex aims, seek nevertheless that self-development and self-realization in all lines of human endeavor which they believe will eventually place the Negro beside the other races. While these men respect the Hampton-Tuskegee idea to a degree, they believe it falls far short of a complete programme. They believe, therefore, also in the higher education of Fisk and Atlanta Universities; they believe in self-assertion and ambition; and they believe in the right of suffrage for blacks on the same terms with whites.

Such is the complicated world of thought and action in which Mr. Booker Washington has been called of God and man to lead, and in which he has gained so rare a meed of success.

Atlanta University, Atlanta, Ga.

---

# 5
## The Parting of the Ways

*In 1903 W.E.B. Du Bois published* The Souls of Black Folk, *a collection of essays that addressed the issue of race in American life, and the impact of race on African Americans. One essay in the collection, "Of Booker T. Washington and Others," examined very critically Washington's philosophy and leadership and laid out Du Bois's strategy for civil rights. While not attacking Washington's motives or ethics, Du Bois argued that the policies championed by the Tuskegeean failed to resolve the problems that African Americans confronted. In this essay, "The Parting of the Ways" (*World Today 6 [April 1904]: 521–32), Du Bois intensified his criticism of Washington, and outlined his specific differences with the conservative faction of African American leadership. In doing so he defined many of the racial views that later would be embodied in the Niagara Movement and the NAACP.*

The points upon which American Negroes differ as to their course of action are the following: First, the scope of education; second, the necessity of the right of suffrage; third, the importance of civil rights; fourth, the conciliation of the South; fifth, the future of the race in this country.

The older opinion as built up under the leadership of our great dead, Payne, Crummell, Forten and Douglass, was that the broadest field of education should be opened to black children; that no free citizen of a republic could exist in peace and prosperity without the ballot; that self-respect and proper development of character can only take place under a system of equal civil rights; that every effort should be made to live in peace and harmony with all men, but that even for this great boon no people must willingly or passively surrender their essential rights of manhood; that in future the Negro is destined to become an American citizen with full political and civil rights, and that he must never rest contented until he has achieved this.

Since the death of the leaders of the past there have come mighty changes in the nation. The gospel of money has risen triumphant in church and state and university. The great question which Americans ask to-day is, "What is he worth?" or "What is it worth?" The ideals of human rights are obscured, and the nation has begun to swagger about the world in its useless battleships looking for helpless peoples whom it can force to buy its goods at high prices. This wave of materialism is temporary; it will pass and leave us all ashamed and surprised; but while it is here it strangely maddens and blinds us. Religious periodicals are found in the van yelling for war; peaceful ministers of Christ are leading lynchers; great universities are stuffing their pockets with greenbacks and kicking the little souls of students to make them "move faster" through the courses of study, the end of which is ever *"Etwas schaffen"* and seldom *"Etwas sein."* Yet there are signs of change. Souls long cramped and starved are stretching toward the light. Men are beginning to murmur against the lower tendencies and the sound of the Zeitgeist strikes sensitive ears with that harrowing discord which prefigures richer harmony to come.

Meantime an awakening race, seeing American civilization as it is, is strongly moved and naturally misled. They whisper: What is the greatness of the country? is it not money? Well then, the one end of our education and striving should be moneymaking. The trimmings of life, smatterings of Latin and music and such stuff—let that wait till we are rich. Then as to voting, what is the good of it after all? Politics does not pay as well as the grocery business, and breeds trouble. Therefore get out of politics and let the ballot go. When we are rich we can dabble in politics along with the president of Yale. Then, again the thought arises: What is personal humiliation and the denial of ordinary civil rights compared with a chance to earn a living? Why quarrel with your bread and butter simply because of filthy Jim Crow cars? Earn a living; get rich, and all these things shall be added unto you. Moreover, conciliate your neighbors, because they are more powerful and wealthier, and the price you must pay to earn a living in America is that of humiliation and inferiority.

No one, of course, has voiced this argument quite so flatly and bluntly as I have indicated. It has been expressed rather by the emphasis given industrial and trade teaching, the decrying of suffrage as a manhood right or even necessity, the insistence on great advance among Negroes before there is any recognition of their aspirations, and a tendency to minimize the shortcomings of the South and to emphasize the mistakes and failures of black men. Now, in this there has been just that degree of truth and right which serves to make men forget its untruths. That the shiftless and poor need thrift and skill, that ignorance can not vote intelligently, that duties and rights go hand in hand, and that sympathy and understanding among neighbors is prerequisite to peace and concord, all this is true. Who has ever denied it, or ever will? But from all this does it follow that Negro colleges are not needed, that the right of suffrage is not essential for black men, that equality of civil rights is not the first of rights and that no self-respecting man can agree with the person who insists that he is a dog? Certainly not, all answer.

Yet the plain result of the attitude of mind of those who, in their advocacy of industrial schools, the unimportance of suffrage and civil rights and conciliation, have been significantly silent or evasive as to higher training and the great principle of free self-respecting manhood for black folk—the plain result of this propaganda has been to help the cutting down of educational opportunity for Negro children, the legal disfranchisement of nearly 5,000,000 of Negroes and a state of public opinion which apologizes for lynching, listens complacently to any insult or detraction directed against an eighth of the population of the land, and silently allows a new slavery to rise and clutch the South and paralyze the moral sense of a great nation.

What do Negroes say to this? I speak advisedly when I say that the over-whelming majority of them declare that the tendencies to-day are wrong and that the propaganda that encouraged them was wrong. They say that industrial and trade teaching is needed among Negroes, sadly needed; but they unhesitatingly affirm that it is not needed as much as thorough common school training and the careful education of the gifted in higher institutions; that only in this way can a people rise by intelligence and social leadership to a plane of permanent effi-ciency and morality. To be sure, there are shorter and quicker methods of making paying workingmen out of a people. Slavery under another name may increase the output of the Transvaal mines, and a caste system coupled with manual training may relieve the South from the domination of labor unions. But has the nation counted the cost of this? Has the Negro agreed to the price, and ought he to agree? Economic efficiency is a means and not an end; this every nation that cares for its salvation must remember.

Moreover, notwithstanding speeches and the editorials of a subsidized Negro press, black men in this land know that when they lose the ballot they lose all. They are no fools. They know it is impossible for free workingmen without a ballot to compete with free workingmen who have the ballot; they know there is no set of people so good and true as to be worth trusting with the political destiny of their fellows, and they know that it is just as true to-day as it was a century and a quarter ago that "Taxation without representation is tyranny."

Finally, the Negro knows perfectly what freedom and equality mean—oppor-tunity to make the best of oneself, unhandicapped by wanton restraint and unrea-soning prejudice. For this the most of us propose to strive. We will not, by word or deed, for a moment admit the right of any man to discriminate against us simply on account of race or color. Whenever we submit to humiliation and oppression it is because of superior brute force; and even when bending to the inevitable we bend with unabated protest and declare flatly and unswervingly that any man or section or nation who wantonly shuts the doors of opportunity and self-defense in the faces of the weak is a coward and knave. We refuse to kiss the hands that smite us, but rather insist on striving by all civilized methods to keep wide educational opportunity, to keep the right to vote, to insist on equal civil rights and to gain every right and privilege open to a free American citizen.

But, answer some, you can not accomplish this. America will never spell opportunity for black men; it spelled slavery for them in 1619 and it will spell the same thing in other letters in 1919. To this I answer simply: I do not believe it. I believe that black men will become free American citizens if they have the courage and persistence to demand the rights and treatment of men, and cease to toady and apologize and belittle themselves. The rights of humanity are worth fighting for. Those that deserve them in the long run get them. The way for black men to-day to make these rights the heritage of their children is to struggle for them unceasingly, and if they fail, die trying.

---

# 6

## Letter to Oswald Garrison Villard, March 24, 1905

*By 1904 the philosophical differences between Du Bois and Washington were clearly defined. This letter, written to white civil rights supporter Oswald Garrison Villard, provided evidence to support the charge that Du Bois had made in print two months earlier that Washington used "hush money" to buy the support of African American newspaper editors and thereby take control of the black press, using it to undermine or silence his critics. The dozen "exhibits" included in the original letter were supposed to document the charges. While Villard was not convinced by these charges, the incident deepened the rift between Du Bois and Washington. This letter can be found in the Oswald Garrison Villard Papers, Harvard University; it also has been reprinted in* BTW Papers *8: 224–29.*

(confidential.)                                        Atlanta, Ga., March 24, 1905

My dear Mr. Villard: In reply to your letter of the 13th inst, I am going to burden you with considerable matter. I do this reluctantly because it seems like imposing on a busy man. At the same time I want to say frankly that I have been sorry to feel in your two letters a note of impatience and disbelief which seems to me unfortunate and calling for a clear, even, if long, statement.

In the *Voice of the Negro* for January, I made the charge that $3000 of hush money had been used to subsidize the Negro press in five leading cities. The bases upon which that charge was made were in part as follows:

The offer of $3000 to the editor of the Chicago *Conservator* on 2 separate occasions to change its editorial policy, and the final ousting of the editor by the board of management, and the installing of an editor with the required policy; with the understanding that financial benefit would result. (Exhibit A.) The statement of the former editor of the Washington *Record* that he was given to understand that the *Record* received $40 a month from the outside to maintain its policy. (Exhibit B.)

The statement of one of the assistant editors of the Washington *Colored American* that it was worth to them $500 a year to maintain its policy. (Exhibit C.) There is similar testimony in regard to papers in other cities particularly the *Freeman* of Indianapolis, the *Age* of New York and the *Citizen* of Boston. All these papers follow the same editorial policy, print the same syndicated news, praise the same persons and attack the same persons. Besides the more definite testimony there is a mass (Exhibit D) of corroborative circumstantial evidence, and all this leads me to estimate that $3000 is certainly the lowest possible estimate of the sums given these 6 papers in the year 1904; I firmly believe that the real sum expended was nearer $5000 and perhaps more than that.

The object of this distribution of money and other favors was, I believe, to stop the attacks being made on the policy of Mr. B.T. Washington. The reason for this belief is as follows:

1. The fact that these papers praise all that Mr. Washington does with suspicious unanimity.

2. The existence of a literary bureau at Tuskegee under Mr. Washington's private secretary, Emmett Scott. (cf. Exhibit B and F. No. 2.)

3. The sending out of syndicated matter from the bureau to appear simultaneously in the above mentioned papers and several others. This appears often in the form of editorials. (Exhibit E.)

4. The change of policy toward Mr. Washington of such papers as the *Age*, which formerly bitterly opposed his policy.

4. [*sic*] The creation of new papers and buying up of old papers by Mr. Washington's friends or former employes. (Exhibit F.)

5. The rewarding of favorable newspapers by Mr. Washington. (Exhibit G.)

6. The abuse and warning of enemies through the syndicated papers, sending out of cartoons, etc. (Exhibit H.)

7. The use of political patronage to reward and punish.

Finally I was not the first to make this charge. It was common property among colored people, spoken and laughed about and repeatedly charged in the newspapers. (Exhibit J.)

What now ought to be the attitude of thinking Negroes toward this situation, assuming the facts alleged to be substantially true? Two things seem certain:

1. There was some time ago a strong opposition to Mr. Washington's policy developed among Negroes. In many cases this opposition became violent and abusive and in one case even riotous.

2. Since that time by the methods above described and also as the result of conference and statements by Mr. Washington, this opposition has been partially stopped.

Now personally I strongly oppose Mr. Washington's positions: those positions have been considerably modified for the better since the time of my first public dissent from them; but they are still in my mind dangerous and unsatisfactory in many particulars.

At the same time I have been very sorry to see the extremes to which criticism has gone. I anticipated this mud-slinging in my book and deprecated it, although I knew it would come. My rule of criticism has been, (a) to impute no bad motives (b) to make no purely personal attack. This has I think been adhered to in every single public utterance of mine on the subject hitherto. And when others have not adhered to it I have not hesitated to criticise them.

Moreover most of the criticism of Mr. Washington by Negro papers has not been violent. The *Conservator* was insistent but courteous; the *Record* under Cromwell was always moderate and saw things both to praise and condemn; The *Freeman* and *American* were open to the highest bidder on either side; the *Guardian* was at times violent although more moderate now than formerly, and has gained in standing as it has become less bitter. All this was a good sign. The air was clearing itself, the demand of the people known, and a healthy democratic out-come of the controversy seemed possible. It seemed at one time indeed possible that even the *Guardian* would see the situation in a better light. Then gradually a change came in. Criticism suddenly stopped in many quarters and fulsome adulation succeeded. Violent attacks on all opposers were printed in a certain set of papers. National organizations of Negroes were "captured" by indefensible methods. (Exhibit K.)

It thus became clearer and clearer to me and to others that the methods of Mr. Washington and his friends to stop violent attack had become a policy for wholesale hushing of all criticism and the crushing out of men who dared to criticise in any way. I felt it time to speak at least a word of warning.

I could not however make this warning as definite as I would have liked for three reasons.

1st. I did not want to drag Atlanta University into the controversy since the proceeding was altogether of my own initiative.

2nd. I did not want to ask those who privately gave me information to do so publicly. They are poor men and if, for instance, Mr. Cromwell, a teacher in the Washington Colored schools, were to testify as to the facts in public he might lose his position.

3rd. I uttered the warning to a Negro audience and it was addressed particularly to them; so far as possible I want to keep the internal struggles of the race in its own ranks. Our dirty linen ought not be exhibited too much in public.

For this latter reason many of my friends do not agree with me in the policy of speaking out. Kelly Miller, A. H. Grimke and others have repeatedly expressed to me that they are perfectly satisfied that Mr. Washington is furnishing money to Negro newspapers in return for their [the newspapers'] support. But they say: What are you going to do about it? He has the support of the nation, he has the political patronage of the administration, he has apparently unlimited cash, he has the ear of the white press and he is following exactly the methods of that press; and moreover his attitude on the race question is changing for the better. These are powerful arguments, but they do not satisfy me. I am however constrained by such representations to take up the matter cautiously and to see what warnings and aroused conscience in the race will do toward stopping this shameful condition of affairs.

On the other hand when I am convinced that the time has come, that bribery is still going on and gag law manifest, and political bossism saddled on a people advised to let politics alone, I will speak again in no uncertain words and I will prove every statement I make.

I regret to say that honest endeavors on my part in the past to understand and cooperate with Mr. Washington have not been successful. 'I recognize as clearly as anyone the necessity of race unity against a common enemy—but it must be unity against the enemy and not veiled surrender to them.' My attitude is not actuated by my sympathy with Mr. Trotter, editor of the Guardian. There was once a rumor that I was acting jointly with him. My reply to that was made in a letter to George F. Peabody, which I venture to enclose as Exhibit L. I went into conference last winter with Mr. Washington and his friends. Mr. Washington selected the personnel of the conference and it did not altogether please me but I attended and urged such of my friends as were invited to come also. In that conference I did not beat around the bush but told Mr. Washington plainly and frankly the causes of our differences of opinion with him.

Mr. Washington replied in a very satisfactory speech and his friends asked me to draw up a plan of a central committee of 12. This I did. The resulting committee which I helped select was good save in two cases where I was overruled by Mr. Washington and his friend. I was taken ill during the summer and the meeting of the committee was postponed; finally the committee was organized at a meeting to which I was not invited, and of which I knew nothing till 2 weeks afterward. Whether this was by accident or design I do not know. At any rate the committee was so organized as to put the whole power virtually in the hands of an executive committee and the appointment of that committee was left to Mr. Washington. Upon hearing this some two weeks after, I resigned my membership. I could not conscientiously deliver my freedom of thought and action into the hands of Mr. Washington and his special abettors like Fortune.

I am still uncertain as to how Mr. Washington himself ought to be judged in the bribery matter. I especially condemn the bribetakers and despise men like Fortune, Cooper, Alexander, Manly and Knox who are selling their papers. If they agree with Mr. Washington and he wishes to help them, the contributions ought to be open and above board; and if the contrary is the case and it is, to my unwavering belief, in 3 or 4 of the above instances, these men are scamps. Mr. Washington probably would defend himself by saying that he is unifying the Negro press, that his contributions are investments not bribes, and that the Tuskegee press bureau is a sort of Associated Negro Press. The reply to this is that the transactions do not appear to be thus honorable, that the character of the matter sent out is fulsome in praise of every deed of Mr. Washington's and abusive toward every critic, and that the men who are conducting the enterprises are not the better type of Negroes but in many cases the worst, as in the case of Fortune, Cooper, Knox and Thompson. (Exhibit M.)

In the trying situation in which we Negroes find ourselves today we especially need the aid and countenance of men like you. This may look to outsiders as a petty squabble of thoughtless self-seekers. It is in fact the life and death struggle of nine million men. It is easy of course to dismiss my contentions as the result of petty jealousy or short-sighted criticism—but the ease of the charge does not prove its truth. I know something of the Negro race and its condition and dangers, and while I am sure, and am glad to say, that Mr. Washington has done and is doing much to help the Negro, I just as firmly believe that he represents today in much of his work and policy the greatest of the hindering forces in the line of our true development and uplift. I beg to remain Very respectfully yours,

# 7
# Declaration of Principles

*"Declaration of Principles" was authored by Du Bois and adopted by the Niagara Movement. It was then printed as a pamphlet in 1905. It outlined the political beliefs and policies of the Niagara Movement, a civil rights organization founded in 1905 by Du Bois and twenty-eight other black leaders who had become frustrated and impatient by what they believed to be the conservatism and accommodation of Booker T. Washington. This pamphlet is reprinted as "The Niagara Movement, Declaration of Principles, 1905" in* The Complete Published Works of W.E.B. Du Bois, Pamphlets and Leaflets, *ed. by Herbert Aptheker (White Plains, N.Y.: Kraus-Thompson Organization Ltd., 1986), 55–58.*

## Progress

The members of the conference, known as the Niagara Movement, assembled in annual meeting at Buffalo, July 11th, 12th and 13th, 1905, congratulate the

Negro-Americans on certain undoubted evidences of progress in the last decade, particularly the increase of intelligence, the buying of property, the checking of crime, the uplift in home life, the advance in literature and art, and the demonstration of constructive and executive ability in the conduct of great religious, economic and educational institutions.

## Suffrage

At the same time, we believe that this class of American citizens should protest emphatically and continually against the curtailment of their political rights. We believe in manhood suffrage; we believe that no man is so good, intelligent or wealthy as to be entrusted wholly with the welfare of his neighbor.

## Civil Liberty

We believe also in protest against the curtailment of our civil rights. All American citizens have the right to equal treatment in places of public entertainment according to their behavior and deserts.

## Economic Opportunity

We especially complain against the denial of equal opportunities to us in economic life; in the rural districts of the South this amounts to peonage and virtual slavery; all over the South it tends to crush labor and small business enterprises; and everywhere American prejudice, helped often by iniquitous laws, is making it more difficult for Negro-Americans to earn a decent living.

## Education

Common school education should be free to all American children and compulsory. High school training should be adequately provided for all, and college training should be the monopoly of no class or race in any section of our common country. We believe that, in defense of our own institutions, the United States should aid common school education, particularly in the South, and we especially recommend concerted agitation to this end. We urge an increase in public high school facilities in the South, where the Negro-Americans are almost wholly without such provisions. We favor well-equipped trade and technical schools for the training of artisans, and the need of adequate and liberal endowment for a few institutions of higher education must be patent to sincere well-wishers of the race.

## Courts

We demand upright judges in courts, juries selected without discrimination on account of color and the same measure of punishment and the same efforts at reformation for black as for white offenders. We need orphanages and farm schools for dependent children, juvenile reformatories for delinquents, and the abolition of the dehumanizing convict-lease system.

## Public Opinion

We note with alarm the evident retrogression in this land of sound public opinion on the subject of manhood rights, republican government and human brotherhood, and we pray God that this nation will not degenerate into a mob of boasters and oppressors, but rather will return to the faith of the fathers, that all men were created free and equal, with certain unalienable rights.

## Health

We plead for health—for an opportunity to live in decent houses and localities, for a chance to rear our children in physical and moral cleanliness.

## Employers and Labor Unions

We hold up for public execration the conduct of two opposite classes of men: The practice among employers of importing ignorant Negro-American laborers in emergencies, then affording them neither protection nor permanent employment; and the practice of labor unions in proscribing and boycotting and oppressing thousands of their fellow-toilers, simply because they are black. These methods have accentuated and will accentuate the war of labor and capital, and they are disgraceful to both sides.

## Protest

We refuse to allow the impression to remain that the Negro-American assents to inferiority, is submissive under oppression and apologetic before insults. Through helplessness we may submit, but the voice of protest of ten million Americans must never cease to assail the ears of their fellows, so long as America is unjust.

## Color-Line

Any discrimination based simply on race or color is barbarous, we care not how hallowed it be by custom, expediency, or prejudice. Differences made on account of ignorance, immorality, or disease are legitimate methods of fighting evil, and against them we have no word of protest; but discriminations based simply and solely on physical peculiarities, place of birth, color or skin, are relics of that unreasoning human savagery of which the world is and ought to be thoroughly ashamed.

## "Jim Crow" Cars

We protest against the "Jim Crow" car, since its effect is and must be to make us pay first-class fare for third-class accommodations, render us open to insults and discomfort and to crucify wantonly our manhood, womanhood and self-respect.

## Soldiers

We regret that this nation has never seen fit adequately to reward the black soldiers who, in its five wars, have defended their country with their blood, and yet have been systematically denied the promotions which their abilities deserve. And we regard as unjust, the exclusion of black boys from the military and navy training schools.

## War Amendments

We urge upon Congress the enactment of appropriate legislation for securing the proper enforcement of those articles of freedom, the thirteenth, fourteenth and fifteenth amendments of the Constitution of the United States.

## Oppression

We repudiate the monstrous doctrine that the oppressor should be the sole authority as to the rights of the oppressed.

The Negro race in America stolen, ravished and degraded, struggling up through difficulties and oppression, needs sympathy and receives criticism; needs help and is given hindrance, needs protection and is given mob-violence, needs justice and is given charity, needs leadership and is given cowardice and apology, needs bread and is given a stone. This nation will never stand justified before God until these things are changed.

## The Church

Especially we are surprised and astonished at the recent attitude of the church of Christ—on the increase of a desire to bow to racial prejudice, to narrow the bounds of human brotherhood, and to segregate black men in some outer sanctuary. This is wrong, unchristian and disgraceful to the twentieth century civilization.

## Agitation

Of the above grievances we do not hesitate to complain, and to complain loudly and insistently. To ignore, overlook, or apologize for these wrongs is to prove ourselves unworthy of freedom. Persistent manly agitation is the way to liberty, and toward this goal the Niagara Movement has started and asks the co-operation of all men of all races.

**Help**

At the same time we want to acknowledge with deep thankfulness the help of our fellowmen from the abolitionist down to those who to-day still stand for equal opportunity and who have given and still give of their wealth and of their poverty for our advancement.

**Duties**

And while we are demanding, and ought to demand, and will continue to demand the rights enumerated above, God forbid that we should ever forget to urge corresponding duties upon our people:

> The duty to vote.
> The duty to respect the rights of others.
> The duty to work.
> The duty to obey the laws.
> The duty to be clean and orderly.
> The duty to send our children to school.
> The duty to respect ourselves, even as we respect others.

This statement, complaint and prayer we submit to the American people, and Almighty God.

---

# 8
## Two Editorials: "The Crisis" and "Agitation"

*In 1909, following the collapse of the Niagara Movement, Du Bois participated in the organization of the NAACP. Du Bois, the only African American officer of the new organization, moved to New York in August 1910 to assume the position of director of publicity and research. His first goal was to establish and edit a journal,* The Crisis. *In "The Crisis" (The Crisis 1 [November 1910]: 10) and "Agitation" (Ibid., 11), Du Bois outlined his perception of the goals and philosophy of the new civil rights organization and its journal.*

## The Crisis

The object of this publication is to set forth those facts and arguments which show the danger of race prejudice, particularly as manifested to-day toward colored people. It takes its name from the fact that the editors believe that this is a critical time in the history of the advancement of men. Catholicity and tolerance, reason and forbearance can to-day make the world-old dream of human brotherhood approach realization; while bigotry and prejudice, emphasized race conscious-ness and force can repeat the awful history of the contact of nations and groups in the past. We strive for this higher and broader vision of Peace and Good Will.

The policy of THE CRISIS will be simple and well defined:

It will first and foremost be a newspaper: it will record important happenings and movements in the world which bear on the great problem of inter-racial relations, and especially those which affect the Negro-American.

Secondly, it will be a review of opinion and literature, recording briefly books, articles, and important expressions of opinion in the white and colored press on the race problem.

Thirdly, it will publish a few short articles.

Finally, its editorial page will stand for the rights of men, irrespective of color or race, for the highest ideals of American democracy, and for reasonable but earnest and persistent attempt to gain these rights and realize these ideals. The magazine will be the organ of no clique or party and will avoid personal rancor of all sorts. In the absence of proof to the contrary it will assume honesty of purpose on the part of all men, North and South, white and black.

## Agitation

Some good friends of the cause we represent fear agitation. They say: "Do not agitate—do not make a noise; work." They add, "Agitation is destructive or at best negative—what is wanted is positive constructive work."

Such honest critics mistake the function of agitation. A toothache is agitation. Is a toothache a good thing? No. Is it therefore useless? No. It is supremely useful, for it tells the body of decay, dyspepsia and death. Without it the body would suffer unknowingly. It would think: All is well, when lo! danger lurks.

The same is true of the Social Body. Agitation is a necessary evil to tell of the ills of the Suffering. Without it many a nation has been lulled to false security and preened itself with virtues it did not possess.

The function of this Association is to tell this nation the crying evil of race prejudice. It is a hard duty but a necessary one—a divine one. It is Pain; Pain is not good but Pain is necessary. Pain does not aggravate disease—Disease causes Pain. Agitation does not mean Aggravation—Aggravation calls for Agitation in order that Remedy may be found.

## 9

## A Philosophy for 1913

*In the editorial "A Philosophy for 1913" (The Crisis 5 [January 1913]: 127), Du Bois presented his New Year's resolution in the form of a creed which rededicated* The Crisis *to its commitment to confront bigotry and discrimination.*

I am by birth and law a free black American citizen.

As such I have both rights and duties.

If I neglect my duties my rights are always in danger. If I do not maintain my rights I cannot perform my duties.

I will listen, therefore, neither to the fool who would make me neglect the things I ought to do, nor to the rascal who advises me to forget the opportunities which I and my children ought to have, and must have, and will have.

Boldly and without flinching, I will face the hard fact that in this, my fatherland, I must expect insult and discrimination from persons who call themselves philanthropists and Christians and gentlemen. I do not wish to meet this despicable attitude by blows; sometimes I cannot even protest by words; but may God forget me and mine if in time or eternity I ever weakly admit to myself or the world that wrong is not wrong, that insult is not insult, or that color discrimination is anything but an inhuman and damnable shame.

Believing this with my utmost soul, I shall fight race prejudice continually. If possible, I shall fight it openly and decidedly by word and deed. When that is not possible I will give of my money to help others to do the deed and say the word which I cannot. This contribution to the greatest of causes shall be my most sacred obligation.

Whenever I meet personal discrimination on account of my race and color I shall protest. If the discrimination is old and deep seated, and sanctioned by law, I shall deem it my duty to make my grievance known, to bring it before the organs of public opinion and to the attention of men of influence, and to urge relief in courts and legislatures.

I will not, because of inertia or timidity or even sensitiveness, allow new discriminations to become usual and habitual. To this end I will make it my duty without ostentation, but with firmness, to assert my right to vote, to frequent places of public entertainment and to appear as a man among men. I will religiously do this from time to time, even when personally I prefer the refuge of friends and family.

While thus fighting for Right and Justice, I will keep my soul clean and serene. I will not permit cruel and persistent persecution to deprive me of the luxury of friends, the enjoyment of laughter, the beauty of sunsets, or the inspiration of a well-written word. Without bitterness (but also without lies), without useless recrimination (but also without cowardly acquiescence), without unnecessary heartache (but with no self-deception), I will walk my way, with uplifted head and level eyes, respecting myself too much to endure without protest studied disrespect from others, and steadily refusing to assent to the silly exaltation of a mere tint of skin or curl of hair.

In fine, I will be a man and know myself to be one, even among those who secretly and openly deny my manhood, and I shall persistently and unwaveringly seek by every possible method to compel all men to treat me as I treat them.

---

# 10
## The Immediate Program of the American Negro

*By 1915* The Crisis, *with a circulation in excess of 30,000, clearly was a powerful voice in the African American community. In April 1915 Du Bois defined in detail the political program he envisioned for African Americans in the article "The Immediate Program of the American Negro" (*The Crisis 9 *[April 1915]: 310–12). Du Bois's vision was of an assertive program for equal rights in all areas of American life combined with education, economic development, and advances in art and literature.*

The immediate program of the American Negro means nothing unless it is mediate to his great ideal and the ultimate ends of his development. We need not waste time by seeking to deceive our enemies into thinking that we are going to be content with a half loaf, or by being willing to lull our friends into a false sense of our indifference and present satisfaction.

The American Negro demands equality—political equality, industrial equality and social equality; and he is never going to rest satisfied with anything less. He demands this in no spirit of braggadocio and with no obsequious envy of others, but as an absolute measure of self-defense and the only one that will assure to the darker races their ultimate survival on earth.

Only in a demand and a persistent demand for essential equality in the modern realm of human culture can any people show a real pride of race and a decent self-respect. For any group, nation or race to admit for a moment the present monstrous demand of the white race to be the inheritors of the earth, the arbiters of mankind and the sole owners of a heritage of culture which they did not create, nor even improve to any greater extent than the other great division of men—to admit such pretense for a moment is for the race to write itself down immediately as indisputably inferior in judgment, knowledge and common sense.

The equality in political, industrial and social life which modern men must have in order to live, is not to be confounded with sameness. On the contrary, in our case, it is rather insistence upon the right of diversity;—upon the right of a human being to be a man even if he does not wear the same cut of vest, the same curl of hair or the same color of skin. Human equality does not even entail, as is sometimes said, absolute equality of opportunity; for certainly the natural ine- qualities of inherent genius and varying gift make this a dubious phase. But there is a more and more clearly recognized minimum of opportunity and maximum of freedom to be, to move and to think, which the modern world denies to no being which it recognizes as a real man.

These involve both negative and positive sides. They call for freedom on the one hand and power on the other. The Negro must have political freedom; taxation without representation is tyranny. American Negroes of to-day are ruled by tyrants who take what they please in taxes and give what they please in law and administration, in justice and in injustice; and the great mass of black people must stand helpless and voiceless before a condition which has time and time again caused other peoples to fight and die.

The Negro must have industrial freedom. Between the peonage of the rural South, the oppression of shrewd capitalists and the jealousy of certain trade unions, the Negro laborer is the most exploited class in the country, giving more hard toil for less money than any other American, and have less voice in the conditions of his labor.

In social intercourse every effort is being made to-day from the President of the United States and the so-called Church of Christ down to saloons and boot- blacks to segregate, strangle and spiritually starve Negroes so as to give them the least possible chance to know and share civilization.

These shackles must go. But that is but the beginning. The Negro must have power; the power of men, the right to do, to know, to feel and to express that knowledge, action and spiritual gift. He must not simply be free from the politi- cal tyranny of white folk, he must have the right to vote and to rule over the citizens, white and black, to the extent of his proven foresight and ability. He must have a voice in the new industrial democracy which is building and the power to see to it that his children are not in the next generation trained to be the mudsills of society. He must have the right to social intercourse with his fellows. There was a time in the atomic individualistic group when "social intercourse" meant merely calls and tea-parties; to-day social intercourse means theatres, lectures, organizations, churches, clubs, excursions, travel, hotels,—it means in short Life; to bar a group from such methods of thinking, living and doing is to bar them from the world and bid them create a new world;—a task to which no single group is today equal; it is to crucify them and taunt them with not being able to live.

What now are the practical steps which must be taken to accomplish these ends?

First of all before taking steps the wise man knows the object and end of his journey. There are those who would advise the black man to pay little or no attention to where he is going so long as he keeps moving. They assume that God or his vice-gerent the White Man will attend to the steering. This is arrant nonsense. The feet of those that aimlessly wander land as often in hell as in heaven. Conscious self-realization and self-direction is the watchword of modern man, and the first article in the program of any group that will survive must be the great aim, equality and power among men.

The practical steps to this are clear. First we must fight obstructions; by continual and increasing effort we must first make American courts either build up a body of decisions which will protect the plain legal rights of American citizens or else make them tear down the civil and political rights of all citizens in order to oppress a few. Either result will bring justice in the end. It is lots of fun and most ingenious just now for courts to twist law so as to say I shall not live here or vote there, or marry the woman who wishes to marry me. But when to-morrow these decisions throttle all freedom and overthrow the foundation of democracy and decency, there is going to be some judicial house cleaning.

We must *secondly* seek in legislature and congress remedial legislation; national aid to public school education, the removal of all legal discriminations based simply on race and color, and those marriage laws passed to make the seduction of black girls easy and without legal penalty.

*Third* the human contact of human beings must be increased; the policy which brings into sympathetic touch and understanding, men and women, rich and poor, capitalist and laborer, Asiatic and European, must bring into closer contact and mutual knowledge the white and black people of this land. It is the most frightful indictment of a country which dares to call itself civilized that it has allowed itself to drift into a state of ignorance where ten million people are coming to believe that all white people are liars and thieves, and the whites in turn to believe that the chief industry of Negroes is raping white women.

*Fourth* only the publication of the truth repeatedly and incisively and uncompromisingly can secure that change in public opinion which will correct these awful lies. THE CRISIS, our record of the darker races, must have a circulation not of 35,000 chiefly among colored folk but of at least 250,000 among all men who believe in men. It must not be a namby-pamby box of salve, but a voice that thunders fact and is more anxious to be true than pleasing. There should be a campaign of tract distribution—short well written facts and arguments—rained over this land by millions of copies, particularly in the South, where the white people know less about the Negro than in any other part of the civilized world. The press should be utilized—the 400 Negro weeklies, the great dailies and eventually the magazines, when we get magazine editors who will lead public opinion instead of following afar with resonant brays. Lectures, lantern-slides and moving pictures, co-operating with a bureau of information and eventually becoming a Negro encyclopedia, all these are efforts along the line of making human beings realize that Negroes are human.

Such is the program of work against obstructions. Let us now turn to constructive effort. This may be summed up under (1) economic co-operation (2) a revival of art and literature (3) political action (4) education and (5) organization.

Under economic co-operation we must strive to spread the idea among colored people that the accumulation of wealth is for social rather than individual ends. We must avoid, in the advancement of the Negro race, the mistakes of ruthless exploitation which have marked modern economic history. To this end we must seek not simply home ownership, small landholding and saving accounts, but also all forms of co-operation, both in production and distribution, profit sharing, building and loan associations, systematic charity for definite, practical ends, systematic migration from mob rule and robbery, to freedom and enfranchisement, the emancipation of women and the abolition of child labor.

In art and literature we should try to loose the tremendous emotional wealth of the Negro and the dramatic strength of his problems through writing, the stage, pageantry and other forms of art. We should resurrect forgotten ancient Negro art and history, and we should set the black man before the world as both a creative artist and a strong subject for artistic treatment.

In political action we should organize the votes of Negroes in such congressional districts as have any number of Negro voters. We should systematically interrogate candidates on matters vital to Negro freedom and uplift. We should train colored voters to reject the bribe of office and to accept only decent legal enactments both for their own uplift and for the uplift of laboring classes of all races and both sexes.

In education we must seek to give colored children free public school training. We must watch with grave suspicion the attempt of those who, under the guise of vocational training, would fasten ignorance and menial service on the Negro for another generation. Our children must not in large numbers, be forced into the servant class; for menial service is still, in the main, little more than an antiquated survival of impossible conditions. It has always been as statistics show, a main cause of bastardy and prostitution and despite its many marvelous exceptions it will never come to the light of decency and honor until the house servant becomes the Servant in the House. It is our duty then, not drastically but persistently, to seek out colored children of ability and genius to open up to them broader, industrial opportunity and above all, to find that Talented Tenth and encourage it by the best and most exhaustive training in order to supply the Negro race and the world with leaders, thinkers and artists.

For the accomplishment of all these ends we must organize. Organization among us already has gone far but it must go much further and higher. Organization is sacrifice. It is sacrifice of opinions, of time, of work and of money, but it is, after all, the cheapest way of buying the most priceless of gifts—freedom and efficiency. I thank God that most of the money that supports the National Association for the Advancement of Colored People comes from black hands; a still larger proportion must so come, and we must not only support but control this and similar organizations and hold them unwaveringly to our objects, our aims and our ideals.

---

# 11
## "Booker T. Washington" and "An Open Letter to Robert Russa Moton"

*In November 1915, following a brief illness, Booker T. Washington died. The death of his principal adversary gave Du Bois the opportunity to unite the African American community under his leadership. The eulogy "Booker T. Washington" (*The Crisis *11 [December 1915]: 82) and the appeal to Robert Russa Moton, Washington's successor at Tuskegee in "An Open Letter to Robert Russa Moton" (*The Crisis *12 [July 1916]: 136–37) represent Du Bois's efforts to heal the divisions in black leadership.*

### Booker T. Washington

The death of Mr. Washington marks an epoch in the history of America. He was the greatest Negro leader since Frederick Douglass, and the most distinguished man, white or black, who has come out of the South since the Civil War. His fame was international and his influence far-reaching. Of the good that he accomplished there can be no doubt: he directed the attention of the Negro race in America to the pressing necessity of economic development; he emphasized technical education and he did much to pave the way for an understanding between the white and darker races.

On the other hand there can be no doubt of Mr. Washington's mistakes and short comings: he never adequately grasped the growing bond of politics and industry; he did not understand the deeper foundations of human training and his basis of better understanding between white and black was founded on caste.

We may then generously and with deep earnestness lay on the grave of Booker T. Washington testimony of our thankfulness for his undoubted help in the accumulation of Negro land and property, his establishment of Tuskegee and spreading of industrial education and his compelling of the white south to at least think of the Negro as a possible man.

On the other hand, in stern justice, we must lay on the soul of this man, a heavy responsibility for the consummation of Negro disfranchisement, the decline of the Negro college and public school and the firmer establishment of color caste in this land.

What is done is done. This is no fit time for recrimination or complaint. Gravely and with bowed head let us receive what this great figure gave of good, silently rejecting all else. Firmly and unfalteringly let the Negro race in America, in bleeding Hayti and throughout the world close ranks and march steadily on, determined as never before to work and save and endure, but never to swerve from their great goal: the right to vote, the right to know, and the right to stand as men among men throughout the world.

It is rumored that Mr. Washington's successor at Tuskegee will be Robert Russa Moton, Commandant of Cadets at Hampton. If this proves true Major Moton will enter on his new duties with the sympathy and good will of his many friends both black and white.

### An Open Letter to Robert Russa Moton

The CRISIS hastens to extend to you on your accession to the headship of Tuskegee the assurances of its good will and personal respect. The CRISIS does this all the more willingly because it has to some extent been the mouth-piece of many who have had occasion repeatedly to criticize the words and deeds of your predecessor.

It would be a matter of hope and rejoicing if your assumption of new duties could be the beginning of a new era of union and understanding among the various groups of American Negroes.

But understanding and cooperation must be based on frank conference and clear knowledge. As a preliminary step to such understanding the CRISIS ventures in this open letter to express to you publicly its hopes and fears.

It hopes that the aims of the colored American have become sufficiently clear to admit of no misunderstanding or misstatement. We desire to become American citizens with every right that pertains to citizenship:

1. The right to vote and hold office.
2. Equality before the law.
3. Equal civil rights in all public places, and in all public services.
4. A proportional share in the benefits of all public expenditures.
5. Education according to ability and aptitude.

With these rights we correlate our duties as men and citizens—the abolition of poverty, the emancipation of women, the suppression of crime and the overcoming of ignorance.

The CRISIS assumes—indeed, it knows—that in these matters you believe substantially, as we do, and that the real differences between us, if there be such, lie in matters of present emphasis and present procedure.

We assume, without demur, that following the late Booker T. Washington you will place especial emphasis on vocational training, property getting and conciliation of the white South. These are necessary policies, but they have their pitfalls, and against these the CRISIS speaks this warning word:

1. Only the higher and broader training will give any race its ultimate leadership. This Mr. Washington came to realize, and this you must not forget.

2. Individual accumulation of wealth must gradually and inevitably give way to methods of social accumulation and equitable distribution.

3. Finally: Conciliation is wise and proper. But how far shall it go? It is here that the CRISIS confesses to its deepest solicitude in your case. It cannot but remember its unanswered query of you in the case of the St. Louis luncheon. It has before it the heading of a Rochester paper which gives as your opinion that "from North one gets distorted view of South." And finally, there is the recent case of the Pullman car and your family.

The CRISIS will assume in all of these cases that you have not been correctly reported; that you did not voluntarily give up lunching at the St. Louis City Club; that you did not assert that the South was maligned usually at the North, and above all, that you did not say that you had no sympathy with the attempt of members of your family to ride on Pullman cars in the South.

The CRISIS knows only too well the way in which Southern newspapers put such sentiments into the mouths of colored leaders; but the point upon which we insist is this: that such atrocious statements cannot be always passed in silence.

We do not wish the principal of Tuskegee to spend his valuable time in answering calumnies and mis-statements, but we do believe that when so monstrous a statement is made, as in the case of the Pullman car, something besides silence and acquiescence is called for.

We hope to see, therefore, at Tuskegee in the future a carrying out and development of the best of its past work and a continued attempt to come to terms of understanding with the best of the white South; but to these policies we hope to see added a policy of making it clearly understood to the people of this country that Tuskegee does believe in the right to vote; that it does not believe in Jim-Crow cars; that it recognizes the work of the Negro colleges, and that it agrees with Charles Sumner that "Equality of rights is the first of rights."

This, then, is the forward step at Tuskegee which the CRISIS and its friends look for under your administration, and it desires to express its earnest hope, and indeed its faith, that you will not disappoint your fellow workers.

# 12
## Close Ranks

*During Du Bois's first decade with the NAACP he pursued a course of modera-tion, firmly demanding civil rights but avoiding the radical fringe of American politics. His gestures of conciliation following the death of Washington reflected this, as did his unequivocal support of the war effort during World War I. Du Bois's editorial "Close Ranks" (The Crisis 16 [July 1918]: 111), which radicals criticized sharply, illustrated clearly the moderate position that he took at this time in his career.*

This is the crisis of the world. For all the long years to come men will point to the year 1918 as the great Day of Decision, the day when the world decided whether it would submit to military despotism and an endless armed peace—if peace it could be called—or whether they would put down the menace of Ger-man militarism and inaugurate the United States of the World.

We of the colored race have no ordinary interest in the outcome. That which the German power represents today spells death to the aspirations of Negroes and all darker races for equality, freedom and democracy. Let us not hesitate. Let us, while this war lasts, forget our special grievances and close our ranks shoul-der to shoulder with our own white fellow citizens and the allied nations that are fighting for democracy. We make no ordinary sacrifice, but we make it gladly and willingly with our eyes lifted to the hills.

---

# 13
## Returning Soldiers

*As the war came to a close, Du Bois became more radical. The deteriorating racial situation in the United States during the war, the revival of his interest in pan-Africanism, and, later, his renewed commitment to socialism pushed him steadily to the left. "Returning Soldiers" (The Crisis 18 [May 1919]: 13–14) announced a more radical Du Bois.*

We are returning from war! THE CRISIS and tens of thousands of black men were drafted into a great struggle. For bleeding France and what she means and has meant and will mean to us and humanity and against the threat of German race arrogance, we fought gladly and to the last drop of blood; for America and her highest ideals, we fought in far-off hope; for the dominant southern oligarchy entrenched in Washington, we fought in bitter resignation. For the America that represents and gloats in lynching, disfranchisement, caste, brutality and devilish insult—for this, in the hateful upturning and mixing of things, we were forced by vindictive fate to fight, also.

But today we return! We return from the slavery of uniform which the world's madness demanded us to don to the freedom of civil garb. We stand again to look America squarely in the face and call a spade a spade. We sing: This country of ours, despite all its better souls have done and dreamed, is yet a shameful land.

It *lynches*.

And lynching is barbarism of a degree of contemptible nastiness unparalleled in human history. Yet for fifty years we have lynched two Negroes a week, and we have kept this up right through the war.

It *disfranchises* its own citizens.

Disfranchisement is the deliberate theft and robbery of the only protection of poor against rich and black against white. The land that disfranchises its citizens and calls itself a democracy lies and knows it lies.

It encourages *ignorance*.

It has never really tried to educate the Negro. A dominant minority does not want Negroes educated. It wants servants, dogs, whores and monkeys. And when this land allows a reactionary group by its stolen political power to force as many black folk into these categories as it possibly can, it cries in contemptible hypocrisy: "They threaten us with degeneracy; they cannot be educated."

It *steals* from us.

It organized industry to cheat us. It cheats us out of our land; it cheats us out of our labor. It confiscates our savings. It reduces our wages. It raises our rent. It steals our profit. It taxes us without representation. It keeps us consistently and universally poor, and then feeds us on charity and derides our poverty.

It *insults* us.

It has organized a nation-wide and latterly a world-wide propaganda of deliberate and continuous insult and defamation of black blood wherever found. It decrees that it shall not be possible in travel nor residence, work nor play, education nor instruction for a black man to exist without tacit or open acknowledgment of his inferiority to the dirtiest white dog. And it looks upon any attempt to question or even discuss this dogma as arrogance, unwarranted assumption and treason.

This is the country to which we soldiers of Democracy return. This is the fatherland for which we fought! But it is our fatherland. It was right for us to fight. The faults of our country are our faults. Under similar circumstances, we would fight again. But by the God of Heaven, we are cowards and jackasses if now that that war is over, we do not marshal every ounce of our brain and brawn to fight a sterner, longer, more unbending battle against the forces of hell in our own land.

We *return.*

We *return from fighting.*

We *return fighting.*

Make way for Democracy! We saved it in France, and by the Great Jehovah, we will save it in the United States of America, or know the reason why.

---

# 14
# White Co-workers

*In the postwar period Du Bois and the NAACP came under attack from the African American left. In "White Co-workers" (*The Crisis *20 [May 1920]: 6–8), Du Bois responded to charges that the NAACP was irrelevant because it was a white-dominated organization. In doing so he reasserted his commitment to desegregation as the ultimate solution to the race problem.*

There is one charge against the N.A.A.C.P. which is made, now openly and now by veiled innuendo, which it is necessary to answer plainly. It is said that this Association is not a Negro association, but is conducted by white people and that, therefore, it cannot effectively serve the cause of Negro freedom. The veiled assumption is that the efforts of the Negroes in the Association are controlled and largely nullified by whites.

The Association is not an exclusively Negro Association. We do not believe in the color line against either white or black. The N.A.A.C.P. is a union of American citizens of all colors and races who believe that Democracy in America is a failure if it proscribes Negroes, as such, politically, economically, or socially.

That all our officers and members are working wholeheartedly to this end is proven by the fact that this Association has done more for the emancipation of the Negro in the last ten years than any other organization of men, white, black or mixed, in the last half century. The record speaks for itself:

1. The overthrow of segregation
2. Defeat of intermarriage laws in twelve states
3. Cooperation in the "Grandfather" decision case

4. Model Civil Rights bills in New York and Michigan
5. The anti-lynching campaign
6. Movement for Negro Army officers
7. Preventing extradition where lynching was possible
8. Pan-African Congress
9. Spingarn Medal
10. The CRISIS Magazine
11. Over a million pieces of literature, millions of letters, thousands of meetings, appeals, protests, etc.

We have not worked alone; what we have done has been in cooperation with numerous agencies and individuals outside our membership; but ours has been the impulse and initiative and most of the work.

Despite all this we admit frankly and freely that we have not yet settled the Negro problem. The Negro is still disfranchised, lynched, "Jim Crowed," robbed and insulted. But we did not expect to unravel the tangle of 300 years in 10; we *did* expect to start the unravelling and this the most churlish must credit us with doing.

If now anyone can suggest any improvement in our organization or method, we are eager to hear them; but we do not believe that the time has come, or ever will come, when we will not need the help of white Americans. To bar them from our organization would be a monstrous discrimination; it would advertise the fact that we can not or will not work with white people. If this is true, what are we doing in America or indeed in the modern world? What are we fighting for, if it is not the chance to stand with our white fellows, side by side and hand in hand, and fight for right?

We certainly *can* do this for we have. The N.A.A.C.P. consists of about 80,000 Negroes and 10,000 whites. Colored persons predominate on the Board of Directors, on the Committee of Executives and among the executive officers. Most of the white members of the board are there by the earnest invitation and insistence of the colored members, because of their influence and help. On the other hand, at no time has there been the slightest disposition to control the opinion of the colored members or officers. The policy of the N.A.A.C.P. has from the beginning been the policy proposed and advocated by the colored members of the Board and the white members have always been not only willing, but eager to promote the just demands of the Negroes as interpreted by their fellow members. In an experience of twenty-five years in organizations, boards and committees I have never been a member of a board which had more interesting or informing sessions and which, considering the volume and intricacy of its problems, had less friction and lack of good will.

What we have thus accomplished in the N.A.A.C.P. is a sample of what we aim to accomplish in the nation and the world. We propose, as black folk, to work with white folk and red and yellow in this land, as equal partners in promoting the common good; in the world we will to unite with all races and nations in a world Democracy of Humanity. But what shall be said if at the beginning of our world quest we refuse to work with any but Negroes for any object?

What is the meaning of such an attitude? Whither does it tend? Do we want to become American citizens or not? Do we want to share in a world state, or not? If we will neither of these things, then our whole aim and argument since 1863 has been wrong. What we really want is not to *fight* segregation, it *is* segregation. We want separate cities, colonies and states and eventually a separate nation. This is a possible aim. It is an aim which we may be driven by race prejudice sometime to adopt. But it is not our present aim and we cannot consistently or effectively at the same time pursue *both* these aims. We cannot refuse to cooperate with white Americans and simultaneously demand the right to cooperate!

Today we can get the wholehearted cooperation of a few forward looking white Americans and of many Englishmen, Frenchmen and other Europeans; but we can have this only as we are willing to work for a world democracy of *all* men. If we wish in hatred or in selfishness to work simply for ourselves—if we envisage a future policy of *up black, down white*—we not only cannot retain the sympathy of these whites, but we invite the bitter opposition of the world; we invite race conflict of the oldest, cruellest sort; we deny and seek to crucify humanity even as our oppressors have done in time gone.

The N.A.A.C.P. assumes that the Negroes of the United States of America wish to be Americans, but refuse to belong to a subject caste. They demand American citizenship with every right that inheres, but what they ask for themselves they grant just as freely to others. They believe in Negro blood and Negro genius; they seek, in voluntary unions, to develop a new Negro ethos—a music, a literature, a school of art and thought; but they will do this as freemen in a free democracy, joining wholeheartedly with their fellows of all colors whenever that freedom is menaced. Not narrow, excluding, other-hating particularism, but broad, sympathetic, all-embracing nationalism is our aim and spirit.

We are realizing this in our organization. What we realize here we would extend to the nation and the world; and in the midst of this endeavor our own people *accuse* us of having white members and white fellow-officers. It is astounding and it is not altogether sincere. The real animus back of this veiled and half articulate criticism is the fact that a large organization must make enemies— must create dissatisfaction in many quarters, no matter what it does.

Organization is sacrifice. You cannot have absolutely your own way—you cannot be a free lance; you cannot be strongly and fiercely individual if you belong to an organization. For this reason some folk hunt and work alone. It is their nature. But the world's greatest work must be done by team work. This demands organization, and that is the sacrifice of some individual will and wish to the good of all.

# 15
## Marcus Garvey

*One of the sources of the criticism of Du Bois came from Marcus Garvey and the Universal Negro Improvement Association (UNIA). Du Bois responded with a two-part essay analyzing Garvey, his movement, and his accomplishments (The Crisis 21 [December 1920]: 58, 60, and The Crisis 21 [January 1921]: 112–16). The essay was written shortly after Garvey published his UNIA Declaration of Rights, and was selected provisional president of Africa. Du Bois personally investigated the operations of the Black Star Line, and while he may have been overzealous in some of his criticism, on the whole he was balanced, focusing his criticism on Garvey's failures, not on his agenda. (Footnotes are incorporated into the text in parentheses.)*

### Marcus Garvey

Marcus Garvey was born at St. Ann's Bay, Jamaica, about 1885. He was educated at the public school and then for a short time attended the Church of England Grammar School, although he was a Roman Catholic by religion. On leaving school he learned the printing trade and followed it for many years. In Costa Rica he was associated with Marclam Taylor in publishing the *Bluefield's Messenger*. Later he was on the staff of *La Nacion*. He then returned to Jamaica and worked as a printer, being foreman of the printing department of P. Benjamin's Manufacturing Company of Kingston. Later he visited Europe and spent some time in England and France and while abroad conceived his scheme of organizing the Negro Improvement Society. This society was launched August 1, 1914, in Jamaica, with these general objects among others:

"To establish a Universal Confraternity among the race"; "to promote the spirit of race pride and love"; "to administer to and assist the needy"; "to strengthen the imperialism of independent African States"; "to conduct a worldwide commercial and industrial intercourse."

His first practical object was to be the establishment of a farm school. Meetings were held and the Roman Catholic Bishop, the Mayor of Kingston, and many others addressed them. Nevertheless the project did not succeed and Mr. Garvey was soon in financial difficulties. He therefore practically abandoned the Jamaica field and came to the United States. In the United States his movement for many years languished until at last with the increased migration from the West Indies during the war he succeeded in establishing a strong nucleus in the Harlem district of New York City.

His program now enlarged and changed somewhat in emphasis. He began especially to emphasize the commercial development of the Negroes and as an islander familiar with the necessities of ship traffic he planned the "Black Star Line." The public for a long time regarded this as simply a scheme of exploitation, when they were startled by hearing that Garvey had bought a ship. This boat was a former coasting vessel, 32 years old, but it was put into commission with a black crew and a black captain and was announced as the first of a fleet of vessels which would trade between the colored peoples of America, the West Indies and Africa. With this beginning, the popularity and reputation of Mr. Garvey and his association increased quickly.

In addition to the *Yarmouth* he is said to have purchased two small boats, the *Shadyside*, a small excursion steamer which made daily excursions up the Hudson, and a yacht which was designed to cruise among the West Indies and collect cargo in some central spot for the *Yarmouth*. He had first announced the Black Star Line as a Five Million Dollar corporation, but in February, 1920, he announced that it was going to be a Ten Million Dollar corporation with shares selling at Five Dollars. To this he added in a few months the Negro Factories Corporation capitalized at One Million Dollars with two hundred thousand one dollar shares, and finally he announced the subscription of Five Million Dollars to free Liberia and Haiti from debt.

Early in 1920 he called a convention of Negroes to meet in New York City from the 1st to the 31st of August, "to outline a constructive plan and program for the uplifting of the Negroes and the redemption of Africa." He also took title to three apartment houses to be used as offices and purchased the foundation of an unfinished Baptist church which he covered over and used for meetings, calling it "Liberty Hall." In August, 1920, his convention met with representatives from various parts of the United States, several of the West India Islands and the Canal Zone and a few from Africa. The convention carried out its plan of a month's meetings and culminated with a mass meeting which filled Madison Square Garden. Finally the convention adopted a "Declaration of Independence" with 66 articles, a universal anthem and colors,—red, black and green—and elected Mr. Garvey as "His Excellency, the Provisional President of Africa," together with a number of various other leaders from the various parts of the Negro world. This in brief is the history of the Garvey movement.

The question comes (1) Is it an honest, sincere movement? (2) Are its industrial and commercial projects business like and effective? (3) Are its general objects plausible and capable of being carried out?

The central and dynamic force of the movement is Garvey. He has with singular success capitalized and made vocal the great and long suffering grievances and spirit of protest among the West Indian peasantry. Hitherto the black peasantry of the West Indies has been almost leaderless. Its natural leaders, both mulatto and black, have crossed the color line and practically obliterated social distinction, and to some extent economic distinction, between them and the white English world on the Islands. This has left a peasantry with only the rudiments of education and with almost no economic chances, grovelling at the bottom. Their distress and needs gave Garvey his vision.

It is a little difficult to characterize the man Garvey. He has been charged with dishonesty and graft, but he seems to me essentially an honest and sincere man with a tremendous vision, great dynamic force, stubborn determination and unselfish desire to serve, but also he has very serious defects of temperament and training: he is dictatorial, domineering, inordinately vain and very suspicious. He cannot get on with his fellow-workers. His entourage has continually changed. (Of the 16 names of his fellow officers in 1914 not a single one appears in 1918; of the 18 names of officers published in 1918 only 6 survive in 1919; among the small list of principal officers published in 1920 I do not find a single name mentioned in 1919.) He has had endless law suits and some cases of fisticuffs with his subordinates and has even divorced the young wife whom he married with great fanfare of trumpets about a year ago. All these things militate against him and his reputation. Nevertheless I have not found the slightest proof that his objects were not sincere or that he was consciously diverting money to his own uses. The great difficulty with him is that he has absolutely no business sense, no flair for real organization and his general objects are so shot through with bombast and exaggeration that it is difficult to pin them down for careful examination.

On the other hand, Garvey is an extraordinary leader of men. Thousands of people believe in him. He is able to stir them with singular eloquence and the general run of his thought is of a high plane. He has become to thousands of people a sort of religion. He allows and encourages all sorts of personal adulation, even printing in his paper the addresses of some of the delegates who hailed him as "His Majesty." He dons on state occasion, a costume consisting of an academic cap and gown flounced in red and green!

Of Garvey's curious credulity and suspicions one example will suffice: In March, 1919, he held a large mass meeting at Palace Casino which was presided over by Chandler Owen and addressed by himself and Phillip Randolph. Here he collected $204 in contributions on the plea that while in France, W.E.B. DuBois had interfered with the work of his "High Commissioner" by "defeating" his articles in the French press and "repudiating" his statements as to lynching and injustice in America! The truth was that Mr. DuBois never saw or heard of his "High Commissioner," never denied his nor anyone's statements of the wretched American conditions, did everything possible to arouse rather than quiet the French press and would have been delighted to welcome and co-operate with any colored fellow-worker.

(To be concluded in January)

**Marcus Garvey**

(An article in the December CRISIS gave Mr. Garvey's personal history. This article considers his industrial enterprises and the feasibility of his general plans.)

When it comes to Mr. Garvey's industrial and commercial enterprises there is more ground for doubt and misgiving than in the matter of his character. First of all, his enterprises are incorporated in Delaware, where the corporation laws are loose and where no financial statements are required. (Mr. Garvey boasts Feb. 14, 1920: "This week I present you with the Black Star Line Steamship Corporation recapitalized at ten million dollars. They told us when we incorporated this corporation that we could not make it, but we are now gone from a $5,000,000 corporation to one of $10,000,000." This sounds impressive, but means almost nothing. The fee for incorporating a $5,000,000 concern in Delaware is $850. *By paying $250 more the corporation may incorporate with $10,000,000 authorized capital without having a cent of capital actually paid in!* Cf. "General Corporation Laws of the State of Delaware," edition of 1917.) So far as I can find, and I have searched with care, Mr. Garvey has never published a complete statement of the income and expenditures of the Negro Improvement Association or of the Black Star Line or of any of his enterprises, which really revealed his financial situation. A courteous letter of inquiry sent to him July 22, 1920, asking for such financial data as he was willing for the public to know, remains to this day unacknowledged and unanswered.

Now a refusal to publish a financial statement is no proof of dishonesty, but it is proof that either Garvey is ill-advised and unnecessarily courting suspicion, or that his industrial enterprises are not on a sound business basis; otherwise he is too good an advertiser not to use a promising balance-sheet for all it is worth.

There has been one balance sheet, published July 26, 1920, purporting to give the financial condition of the Black Star Line after one year of operation; neither profit or loss is shown, there is no way to tell the actual cash receipts or the true condition of the business. Nevertheless it does make some interesting revelations.

The total amount of stock subscribed for is $590,860. Of this $118,153.28 is not yet paid for, leaving the actual amount of paid-in capital charged against the corporation, $472,706.72. Against this stands only $355,214.59 of assets (viz.: $21,985.21 in cash deposits and loans receivable; $12,975.01 in furniture and equipment, $288,515.37 which is the alleged value of his boats, $26,000 in real estate and $5,739 of insurance paid in advance). To offset the assets he has $152,264.14 of other liabilities (accrued salaries, $1,539.30; notes and accounts payable, $129,224.84; mortgages due $21,500). In other words, his capital stock of $472,706.72 is after a year's business impaired to such extent that he has only $202,960.46 to show for it.

Even this does not reveal the precariousness of his actual business condition. Banks before the war in lending their credit refused to recognize any business as safe unless for every dollar of current liabilities there were *two* dollars of current assets. Today, since the war, they require *three* dollars of current assets to every *one* of current liabilities. The Black Star Line had July 26, $16,485.21 in current assets and $130,764.14 in current liabilities, when recognition by any reputable bank called for $390,000 in current assets.

Moreover, another sinister admission appears in this statement: the cost of floating the Black Star Line to date has been $289,066.27. In other words, it has cost nearly $300,000 to collect a capital of less than half a million. Garvey has, in other words, spent more for advertisement than he has for his boats!

This is a serious situation, and even this does not tell the whole story: the real estate, furniture, etc., listed above, are probably valued correctly. But how about the boats? The *Yarmouth* is a wooden steamer of 1,452 gross tons, built in 1887. It is old and unseaworthy; it came near sinking a year ago and it has cost a great deal for repairs. It is said that it is now laid up for repairs with a large bill due. Without doubt the inexperienced purchasers of this vessel paid far more than it is worth and it will soon be utterly worthless unless rebuilt at a very high cost. (Technically the *Yarmouth* does not belong to the Black Star Line of Delaware, but to the "Black Star Line of Canada, Limited," incorporated in Canada, March 23, 1920, with one million dollars capital. This capital consists of $500 cash and $999,500 "assets." Probably the Black Star Line of Delaware controls this corporation, but this is not known.)

The cases of the *Kanawha* (or *Antonio Maceo*) and the *Shadyside* are puzzling. Neither of these boats is registered as belonging to the Black Star Line at all. The former is recorded as belonging to C.L. Dimon, and the latter to the North and East River Steamboat Company. Does the Black Star Line really own these boats, or is it buying them by installments, or only leasing them? We do not know the facts and have been unable to find out. Under the circumstances they look like dubious "assets."

The majority of the Black Star stock is apparently owned by the Universal Negro Improvement Association. There is no reason why this association, if it will and can, should not continue to pour money into its corporation. Let us therefore consider then Mr. Garvey's other resources.

Mr. Garvey's income consists of (a) dues from members of the U. N. I. Association; (b) shares in the Black Star Line and other enterprises, and (c) gifts and "loans" for specific objects. If the U. N. I. Association has "3,000,000 members" then the income from that source alone would be certainly over a million dollars a year. If, as is more likely, it has under 300,000 paying members, he may collect $150,000 annually from this source. Stock in the Black Star Line is still being sold. Garvey himself tells of one woman who had saved about four hundred dollars in gold: "She brought out all the gold and bought shares in the Black Star Line." Another man writes this touching letter from the Canal Zone: "I have sent twice to buy shares amounting to $125, (numbers of certificates 3752 and 9617). Now I am sending $35 for seven more shares. You might think I have money, but the truth, as I stated before, is that I have no money now. But if I'm to die of hunger it will be all right because I'm determined to do all that's in my power to better the conditions of my race" (P.N. Gordon).

In addition to this he has asked for special contributions. In the spring of 1920 he demanded for his coming convention in August, "a fund of two million dollars ($2,000,000) to capitalize this, the greatest of all conventions." In October he acknowledged a total of something over $16,000 in small contributions. Immediately he announced "a constructive loan" of $2,000,000, which he is presumably still seeking to raise. ("The Universal Negro Improvement Association is raising a constructive loan of two million dollars from its members. Three hundred thousand dollars out of this two million has been allotted to the New York Local as its quota, and already the members in New York have started to subscribe to the loan, and in the *next seven days* the three hundred thousand dollars will be oversubscribed. The great divisions of Pittsburgh, Philadelphia, Boston, Chicago, Cleveland, Wilmington, Baltimore and Washington will also oversubscribe their quota to make up the two million dollars. Constructive work will be started in *January* 1921, when the first ship of the Black Star Line on the African trade will sail from New York with materials and workmen for this constructive work." Eleven days later, November 6th, the *Negro World* is still "raising the loan" but there is no report of the amount raised.)

From these sources of income Mr. Garvey has financed his enterprises and carried on a wide and determined propaganda, maintained a large staff of salaried officials, clerks and agents, and published a weekly newspaper. Notwithstanding this considerable income, there is no doubt that Garvey's expenditures are pressing hard on his income, and that his financial methods are so essentially unsound that unless he speedily revises them the investors will certainly get no dividends and worse may happen. (It might be argued that it is not absolutely necessary that the Black Star Line, etc., should pay financially. It is quite conceivable that Garvey should launch a business philanthropy, and that without expectation of return, colored people should contribute for a series of years to support Negro enterprise. But this is not Garvey's idea. He says plainly in a circular: "The Black Star Line Corporation presents to every Black Man, Woman and Child the opportunity to climb the great ladder of industrial and commercial progress. If you have ten dollars, one hundred dollars, or one or five thousand dollars to invest for profit, then take out shares in the Black Star Line, Inc. This corporation is chartered to trade on every sea and all waters. The Black Star Line will turn over large profits and dividends to stockholders, and operate to their interest even whilst they will be asleep.") He is apparently using the familiar method of "Kiting"—i.e., the money which comes in as investment in stock is being used in current expenses, especially in heavy overhead costs, for clerk hire, interest and display. Even his boats are being used for advertisement more than for business—lying in harbors as exhibits, taking excursion parties, etc. These methods have necessitated mortgages on property and continually new and more grandiose schemes to collect larger and larger amounts of ready cash. Meantime, lacking business men of experience, his actual business ventures have brought in few returns, involved heavy expense and threatened him continually with disaster or legal complication.

On the other hand, full credit must be given Garvey for a bold effort and some success. He has at least put vessels manned and owned by black men on the seas and they have carried passengers and cargoes. The difficulty is that he does not know the shipping business, he does not understand the investment of capital, and he has few trained and staunch assistants.

The present financial plight of an inexperienced and headstrong promoter may therefore decide the fate of the whole movement. This would be a calamity. Garvey is the beloved leader of tens of thousands of poor and bewildered people who have been cheated all their lives. His failure would mean a blow to their faith, and a loss of their little savings, which it would take generations to undo.

Moreover, shorn of its bombast and exaggeration, the main lines of the Garvey plan are perfectly feasible. What he is trying to say and do is this: American Negroes can, by accumulating and ministering their own capital, organize industry, join the black centers of the south Atlantic by commercial enterprise and in this way ultimately redeem Africa as a fit and free home for black men. This is true. It is *feasible*. It is, in a sense, practical; but it will take for its accomplishment long years of painstaking, self-sacrificing effort. It will call for every ounce of ability, knowledge, experience and devotion in the whole Negro race. It is not a task for one man or one organization, but for co-ordinate effort on the part of millions. The plan is not original with Garvey but he has popularized it, made it a living, vocal ideal and swept thousands with him with intense belief in the possible accomplishment of the ideal.

This is a great, human service; but when Garvey forges ahead and almost single-handed attempts to realize his dream in a few years, with large words and wild gestures, he grievously minimizes his task and endangers his cause.

To instance one illustrative fact: there is no doubt but what Garvey has sought to import to America and capitalize the antagonism between blacks and mulattoes in the West Indies. This has been the cause of the West Indian failures to gain headway against the whites. Yet Garvey imports it into a land where it has never had any substantial footing and where today, of all days, it is absolutely repudiated by every thinking Negro; Garvey capitalizes it, has sought to get the cooperation of men like R.R. Moton on this basis, and has aroused more bitter color enmity inside the race than has ever before existed. The whites are delighted at the prospect of a division of our solidifying phalanx, but their hopes are vain. American Negroes recognize no color line in or out of the race, and they will in the end punish the man who attempts to establish it.

Then too Garvey increases his difficulties in other directions. He is a British subject. He wants to trade in British territory. Why then does he needlessly antagonize and even insult Britain? He wants to unite all Negroes. Why then does he sneer at the work of the powerful group of his race in the United States where he finds asylum and sympathy? Particularly, why does he decry the excellent and rising business enterprises of Harlem—intimating that his schemes alone are honest and sound when the facts flatly contradict him? He proposes to settle his headquarters in Liberia—but has he asked permission of the Liberian government? Does he presume to usurp authority in a land which has successfully withstood England, France and the United States,—but is expected tamely to submit to Marcus Garvey? How long does Mr. Garvey think that President King would permit his anti-English propaganda on Liberian soil, when the government is straining every nerve to escape the Lion's Paw?

And, finally, without arms, money, effective organization or base of operations, Mr. Garvey openly and wildly talks of "Conquest" and of telling white Europeans in Africa to "get out!" and of becoming himself a black Napoleon! (He said in his "inaugural" address: "The signal honor of being Provisional President of Africa is mine. It is a political job; it is a political calling for me to redeem Africa. It is like asking Napoleon to take the world. He took a certain portion of the world in his time. He failed and died at St. Helena. But may I not say that the lessons of Napoleon are but stepping stones by which we shall guide ourselves to African liberation?")

Suppose Mr. Garvey should drop from the clouds and concentrate on his industrial schemes as a practical first step toward his dreams: the first duty of a great commercial enterprise is to carry on effective commerce. A man who sees in industry the key to a situation, must establish sufficient business-like industries. Here Mr. Garvey has failed lamentably.

The *Yarmouth*, for instance, has not been a commercial success. Stories have been published alleging its dirty condition and the inexcusable conduct of its captain and crew. To this Mr. Garvey may reply that it was no easy matter to get efficient persons to run his boats and to keep a schedule. This is certainly true, but if it is difficult to secure one black boat crew, how much more difficult is it going to be to "build and operate factories in the big industrial centers of the United States, Central America, the West Indies and Africa to manufacture every marketable commodity"? and also "to purchase and build ships of larger tonnage for the African and South American trade"? and also to raise "Five Million Dollars to free Liberia" where "new buildings are to be erected, administrative buildings are to be built, colleges and universities are to be constructed"? and finally to accomplish what Mr. Garvey calls the "Conquest of Africa"!

To sum up: Garvey is a sincere, hard-working idealist; he is also a stubborn, domineering leader of the mass; he has worthy industrial and commercial schemes but he is an inexperienced businessman. His dreams of Negro industry, commerce and the ultimate freedom of Africa are feasible; but his methods are bombastic, wasteful, illogical and ineffective and almost illegal. If he learns by experience, attracts strong and capable friends and helpers instead of making needless enemies; if he gives up secrecy and suspicion and substitutes open and frank reports as to his income and expenses, and above all if he is willing to be a co-worker and not a czar, he may yet in time succeed in at least starting some of his schemes toward accomplishment. But unless he does these things and does them quickly he cannot escape failure.

Let the followers of Mr. Garvey insist that he get down to bed-rock business and make income and expense balance; let them gag Garvey's wilder words, and still preserve his wide power and influence. American Negro leaders are not jealous of Garvey—they are not envious of his success; they are simply afraid of his failure, for his failure would be theirs. He can have all the power and money that he can efficiently and honestly use, and if in addition he wants to prance down Broadway in a green shirt, let him—but do not let him foolishly overwhelm with bankruptcy and disaster one of the most interesting spiritual movements of the modern Negro world.

# 16
## A Lunatic or a Traitor

*Three years later Du Bois presented a less balanced and far more critical assessment of Garvey. By this time Garvey had denigrated Du Bois and the NAACP for their color prejudice, and had been convicted of mail fraud. For Du Bois the solution was simple: Garvey must go ("A Lunatic or a Traitor," The Crisis 28 [May 1924]: 8–9).*

In its endeavor to avoid any injustice toward Marcus Garvey and his followers, THE CRISIS has almost leaned backward. Notwithstanding his wanton squandering of hundreds of thousands of dollars we have refused to assume that he was a common thief. In spite of his monumental and persistent lying we have discussed only the larger and truer aspects of his propaganda. We have refrained from all comment on his trial and conviction for fraud. We have done this too in spite of his personal vituperation of the editor of THE CRISIS and persistent and unremitting repetition of falsehood after falsehood as to the editor's beliefs and acts and as to the program of the N. A. A. C. P.

In the face, however, of the unbelievable depths of debasement and humiliation to which this demagog has descended in order to keep himself out of jail, it is our duty to say openly and clearly:

Marcus Garvey is, without doubt, the most dangerous enemy of the Negro race in America and in the world. He is either a lunatic or a traitor. He is sending all over this country tons of letters and pamphlets appealing to Congressmen, business men, philanthropists and educators to join him on a platform whose half concealed planks may be interpreted as follows:

That no person of Negro descent can ever hope to become an American citizen.

That forcible separation of the races and the banishment of Negroes to Africa is the only solution of the Negro problem.

That race war is sure to follow any attempt to realize the program of the N. A. A. C. P.

We would have refused to believe that any man of Negro descent could have fathered such a propaganda if the evidence did not lie before us in black and white signed by this man. Here is a letter and part of a symposium sent to one of the most prominent business men of America and turned over to us; we select but a few phrases; the italics are ours:

Do you believe the Negro to be a *human being?*

Do you believe the Negro *entitled to all the rights of humanity?*

Do you believe that the Negro should be taught *not to aspire to the highest political positions in Governments of the white race,* but to such positions among his own race in a Government of his own?

Would you help morally *or otherwise* to bring about such a possibility? Do you believe that the Negro should be *encouraged to aspire* to the highest industrial and commercial positions in the countries of the white man in competition with him and to his exclusion?

Do you believe that the Negro should be encouraged to regard and *respect the rights of all other races* in the same manner as other races would respect the rights of the Negro.

The pamphlets include one of the worst articles recently written *by a Southern white man* advocating the deportation of American Negroes to Liberia and several articles by Garvey and his friends. From one of Garvey's articles we abstract one phrase:

"THE WHITE RACE CAN BEST HELP THE NEGRO BY TELLING HIM THE TRUTH, AND NOT BY FLATTERING HIM INTO BELIEVING THAT HE IS AS GOOD AS ANY WHITE MAN."

Not even Tom Dixon or Ben Tillman or the hatefulest enemies of the Negro have ever stooped to a more vicious campaign than Marcus Garvey, sane or insane, is carrying on. He is not attacking white prejudice, he is grovelling before it and applauding it; his only attack is on men of his own race who are striving for freedom; his only contempt is for Negroes; his only threats are for black blood. And this leads us to a few plain words:

1. No Negro in America ever had a fairer and more patient trial than Marcus Garvey. He convicted himself by his own admissions, his swaggering monkey-shines in the court room with monocle and long tailed coat and his insults to the judge and prosecuting attorney.

2. Marcus Garvey was long refused bail, not because of his color, but because of the repeated threats and cold blooded assaults charged against his orga-

nization. He himself openly threatened to "get" the District Attorney. His followers had repeatedly to be warned from intimidating witnesses and one was sent to jail therefor. One of his former trusted officials after being put out of the Garvey organization brought the long concealed cash account of the organization to this office and we published it. Within two weeks the man was shot in the back in New Orleans and killed. We know nothing of Garvey's personal connection with these cases but we do know that today his former representative lies in jail in Liberia sentenced to death for murder. The District Attorney believed that Garvey's "army" had arms and ammunition and was prepared to "shoot up" colored Harlem if he was released. For these and no other reasons Garvey was held in the Tombs so long without bail and until he had made abject promises, apologizing to the judge and withdrawing his threats against the District Attorney. Since his release he has not dared to print a single word against white folk. All his vituperation has been heaped on his own race.

Everybody, including the writer, who has dared to make the slightest criticism of Garvey has been intimidated by threats and threatened with libel suits. Over fifty court cases have been brought by Garvey in ten years. After my first and favorable article on Garvey, I was not only threatened with death by men declaring themselves his followers, but received letters of such unbelievable filth that they were absolutely unprintable. When I landed in this country from my trip to Africa I learned with disgust that my friends stirred by Garvey's threats had actually felt compelled to have secret police protection for me on the dock!

Friends have even begged me not to publish this editorial lest I be assassinated. To such depths have we dropped in free black America! I have been exposing white traitors for a quarter century. If the day has come when I cannot tell the truth about black traitors it is high time that I died.

The American Negroes have endured this wretch all too long with fine restraint and every effort at cooperation and understanding. But the end has come. Every man who apologizes for or defends Marcus Garvey from this day forth writes himself down as unworthy of the countenance of decent Americans. As for Garvey himself, this open ally of the Ku Klux Klan should be locked up or sent home.

---

# 17
## The Tragedy of "Jim Crow"

*In this essay, "The Tragedy of 'Jim Crow'" The Crisis 26 [August 1923]: 169–72), Du Bois confronted the complexity of the issue of desegregation and came to conclusions that anticipated the controversial position he took on this issue in the 1930s. What troubled Du Bois was the reality that attacking all forms of segregation could result in the undermining of effective black institutions.*

There is developing within the Negro race a situation bordering on tragedy in regard to the "Jim Crow" movement now growing and spreading in the North. The tragedy has been with us before but it has been more or less dormant and unspoken. To-day it is flaring to red flame and we must sit down and reason together.

I stood yesterday before three thousand folk in Philadelphia and said at length what I am saying now more concisely and definitely. It was an earnest crowd quivering with excitement and feeling, and the thing that it had in mind was this:

For 90 years, Pennsylvania has had a private colored school founded by Richard Humphreys, a West Indian ex-slave-holder. The institute was located first on Lombard Street, Philadelphia, then on Bainbridge Street and finally in 1911 was removed to Cheyney, twenty miles from Philadelphia in a beautiful section where new buildings were erected and a normal school equipped.

Many distinguished persons have been at the head of the school including Charles L. Reason of New York, Ebenezer D. Bassett, afterward Minister to Haiti, the late Fannie Jackson Coppin, Hugh Brown and at present Leslie P. Hill, Harvard '03, Phi Beta Kappa. In 1914, the school began to receive State aid at the rate of $6,000 every two years. In 1920, the school was made a State Normal School with an appropriation of $125,000 per year for two years.

Meantime the Northern states slowly struggled out from the shadow of "Jim Crow" school legislation. The schools of New York City became mixed and Negro teachers were appointed who taught without segregation. The same thing happened in Massachusetts, in Northern Illinois and Northern Ohio; in Pennsylvania it became in 1881, "unlawful" to make "any distinction whatever" on account of race among public school children.

Notwithstanding this, separate Negro schools with Negro teachers in Northern states continued to exist. For some time they declined in number; then came the growing concentration of Negroes in cities and finally the new Negro migration from the South. This meant quiet but persistent and renewed attempts at school segregation. The number of separate schools increased in the North, and in Kansas segregation was legalized by permissive legislature.

In Philadelphia particularly separation was carried far by administrative action despite the law, so that to-day while the high school and 200 common schools have colored and white pupils, there are eleven schools with Negro pupils alone, and colored teachers are appointed only in those schools. Thus segregated schools are on the increase in the North and there is no doubt but what we shall see a larger and larger number of them as the flood tide of Southern Negro migration increases.

What shall be our attitude toward this segregation? The National Association for the Advancement of Colored People together with its organ, THE CRISIS, and all thinking men, white and black, have long since taken strong ground against compulsory racial segregation of any sort. This has been true from the foundation of the Association; and we have especially insisted that of all the sorts of segregation and discrimination that meet the Negroes in the United States, that in the common public schools is most dangerous, most insidious, the most far reaching.

Education in the public schools by races or by classes means the perpetuation of race and class feeling throughout the land. It means the establishment of group hostility in those tender years of development when prejudices tend to become "natural" and "instinctive." It is the plain duty of all true Americans who believe in democracy and broad human development to oppose this spread of segregation in the public schools.

On the other hand we are to-day, as practical thinkers and workers, faced by the grim fact of a school segregation already in being: of public common schools, private common schools, high schools and colleges attended exclusively by Negroes and manned wholly and largely by Negroes. Our educational plight is still precarious but without the self-sacrificing efficient colored teacher of colored youth to-day, we would face positive disaster. These teachers have in their ranks some of the finest trained men and women in the world and the black race can never repay them for the work they have done under difficulty and deprivation, obloquy and insult, and sometimes even with the hatred and abuse of colored folk themselves.

Here then we face the amazing paradox: we must oppose segregation in schools; we must honor and appreciate the colored teacher in the colored school.

How can we follow this almost self-contradictory program? Small wonder that Negro communities have been torn in sunder by deep and passionate differences of opinion arising from this pitiable dilemma.

Despite all theory and almost unconsciously we are groping on. We recognize one thing worse than segregation and that is ignorance. There is, for instance, among the Negroes of the United States no effort to disestablish the separate public schools of the South. Why? They are wrong; they are undemocratic; they are ridiculously and fatally costly; they mean inferior schools for colored people, discrimination in equipment and curriculum; and yet so long as the race feeling is what it is in the South, mixed schools are utterly impossible. Even if by law we could force colored children into the white schools, they would not be educated. They would be abused, brow-beaten, murdered, kept in something worse than ignorance. What is true in the South is true in most parts of the border states and in some parts of the North. In some of these regions where there are mixed schools innocent colored children of tender years are mercilessly mistreated and discriminated against and practically forced out of school before they have finished the primary grades. Even in many of the best Northern states colored

pupils while admitted and treated fairly, receive no inspiration or encouragement.

How else can we explain the astonishing fact that with practically the same
kinds of colored population in cities like Washington, Baltimore, Philadelphia
and New York, the 200,000 Negroes in Washington and Baltimore send out 400
colored High School graduates every year, while 250,000 Negroes in Philadelphia and New York send out only 50? Moreover the academic standards of these
colored High Schools have been proven to be fairly high by the success of their
graduates in Northern colleges. What are we going to do about this? First and
foremost and more important than anything else, Negro children must not be
allowed to grow up in ignorance. This is worse than segregation, worse than
anything we could contemplate.

There is only one method to avoid both this and segregation and that is by
efforts such as are being made in New York City. The movement is still young
and wavering, but it is a beginning. We are trying there to superintend the course
of colored children in the mixed public school. We are seeking to guide them
there and to help them at home; we try to discover and oppose prejudiced
teachers; we encourage their enrollment in High Schools. There is no reason why
a movement like this, pushed with unwavering determination, should not succeed in bringing the High School enrollment of black New York up to the level
of Washington, Baltimore and St. Louis.

In Philadelphia no such movement is manifest. On the contrary with the
colored citizens largely asleep for a long time, the solution of separate colored
schools has been accepted with only half-hearted protest. To-day, however,
strangely enough protest has risen to fever heat, and why? Because two years
ago, Cheyney was made a colored State Normal School. We say colored advisedly because there is no use of stickling at facts or dodging behind legal
quibbles.

Cheyney is to-day a State Normal School for Negroes. Is this a fault, and if so
whose fault is it? A large number of honest and earnest colored people in Philadelphia—persons who have cooperated with this Association and who believe in
its work and possibilities, have taken this stand:

1. There is a conspiracy in Philadelphia to segregate all colored teacher training of the state in Cheyney, where with inferior equipment, colored teachers will
be educated and sent out for use in a growing system of segregated colored
public schools.

2. That Leslie Hill and his teachers are at least in part responsible for the
programme and have aided and abetted it.

Without a shadow of a doubt many white people of Pennsylvania have the
programme above in mind; without doubt principals of many of the other thirteen Normal Schools and some public school officials would welcome and push

to the limit of the law and past it, the segregation of colored teachers and pupils; but there is no proof that all white folk in authority want this; there is no proof that the state does not intend to make Cheyney the equal of any other State Normal School; moreover according to present law no Negro is compelled to attend Cheyney. All of the other 13 normal schools of the State remain absolutely open to those who wish to attend them. And above all, proof is absolutely lacking that Hill and his teachers are dishonest betrayers of the interests of their race.

Leslie Hill and his wife Jane Hill have had honorable and self-sacrificing records. He has surrounded himself by the best faculty his limited funds would allow: Harvard, Radcliffe, the University of London and similar schools have trained them. I have seen schools in two continents and ten countries and I have yet to see a finer group in character and service than the teachers of Cheyney. And yet for three months these people were actually deprived of bread and butter by legal injunctions and pursued by denunciation, ostracism and innuendo, while the real culprits, the white "Jim Crow" officials, publicists and philanthropists stood aside unscathed and smiling to see the "darkies" quarrel.

I am not for a moment calling in question the motives and sincerity of those in Philadelphia who are fighting segregation. In such a fight I am with them heart and soul. But when this fight becomes a fight against Negro school teachers I quit. I believe in Negro school teachers. I would to God white children as well as colored could have more of them. With proper training they are the finest teachers in the world because they have suffered and endured and nothing human is beneath their sympathy.

I know perfectly well that there have been colored educators and leaders who in order to get funds for their schools and enterprises and positions for their friends and children have betrayed and sold out the interests of their race and humanity. I have denounced and will denounce such men unsparingly. But it does not follow that when a black man makes a black enterprise the best and most efficient for its purpose that he is necessarily a traitor or that he believes in segregation by race. A condition, not a theory confronts him. It was the duty of Hill to make Cheyney a school. He did not found Cheyney. It was founded half a century before he was born. He did try and is trying to raise it from the status of a second class High School without funds, equipment or recognition, to one of the best normal schools of one of the greatest states of the Union. Those folk, white or black, who seek to saddle this programme with a permanent "Jim Crow" school policy in the commonwealth of William Penn deserve the damning of every decent American citizen; and those folk are not black folk—they are white and wealthy and powerful, and many of them are distinguished Quakers.

The real fight in Philadelphia and Pennsylvania should be made on the following lines:

1. To stop by agitation, political power and legal method, all further increase of public common schools segregated by race. The appointment and election of openly sympathetic school officials is the first step in this campaign

2. To continue to insist on the appointment of colored teachers in white schools

3. To support the efforts to make the present segregated schools the very best possible and to open them to white children

4. To make Cheyney the best Normal School in the state and to encourage the entry of white students

5. To see to it by scholarships and local efforts that colored pupils are kept in every other normal school of the state

6. To make the colored teacher feel that no calling is so fine and valuable as his and that the Negro race and the world knows it.

---

# 18
## The New Crisis

*In celebration of the fifteenth year of* The Crisis *(and the beginning of its thirtieth semi-annual volume), Du Bois wrote this editorial, "The New Crisis" (*The Crisis *30 [May 1925]: 7–9), which outlined the composition of the new Crisis. To its commitment to equal rights, Du Bois added a commitment to economic justice through the support of organized labor, a commitment to pan-Africanism, and a commitment to art and literature.*

We have assumed, with the Spring, with the beginning of our 30th semi-annual volume, with our 175th number and with the closing of a fateful quarter century, something of a new dress and a certain renewal of spirit.

How long may a CRISIS last? one might ask, sensing between our name and age some contradiction. To which we answer: What is long? 15 or 5000 years? But even in 15 years we see curious and suggestive change. In November, 1910, we wrote:

> "The object of this publication is to set forth those facts and arguments which show the danger of race prejudice, particularly as manifested today toward colored people. It takes its name from the fact that the editors believe that this is a critical time in the history of the advancement of men. Catholicity and tolerance, reason and forbearance can today make the world-old dream of human brotherhood approach realization; while bigotry and prejudice, emphasized race consciousness and force can repeat the awful history of the contact of nations and groups in the past. We strive for this higher and broader vision of Peace and Good Will."

Then we set forth the plan to make THE CRISIS (1) a newspaper, (2) a review of opinion, (3) a magazine with "a few short articles."

This initial program has unfolded itself, changed and developed. There is no longer need of a monthly newspaper for colored folk. Colored weeklies have arisen with an efficiency and scope in news-gathering that was not dreamed of in 1910. Our news therefore has transformed itself into a sort of permanent record of a few matters of widespread and historic importance. Our review of opinion continues in both "Opinion" and "Looking Glass," but rather as interpretation than as mere quotation. Particularly has our policy changed as to articles. They have increased in number, length and authority. And above all, out of the broad vagueness of our general policy have emerged certain definite matters which we shall pursue with increased earnestness. We name them in something like the order in which they appeal to us now:

1. Economic Development

At Philadelphia, the N. A. A. C. P. made a suggestion of alliance among the laboring people of the United States across the color line. The American Federation of Labor has as yet made no active response to our overtures. Meantime, however, we are not waiting and we propose to make a crusade in THE CRISIS covering the next three years and taking up in succession the history and significance of the Labor Movement in the modern world, the present actual relation of Negroes to labor unions and a practical plan of future cooperation.

2. Political Independence

We shall stress as never before political independence. No longer must Negroes be born into the Republican Party. If they vote the Republican ticket or any other ticket it must be because the candidates of that party in any given election make the best promises for the future and show the best record in the past. Above all we shall urge all Negroes, male and female, to register and vote and to study political ethics and machinery.

3. Education and Talent

We shall stress the education of Negro youth and the discovery of Negro talent. Our schools must be emancipated from the secret domination of the Bourbon white South. Teachers, white or black, in Negro schools who cannot receive and treat their pupils as social equals must go. We must develop brains, ambition, efficiency and ideals without limit or circumscription. If our own Southern colleges will not do this, and whether they do it or not, we must continue to force our way into Northern colleges in larger and larger numbers and to club their doors open with our votes. We must provide larger scholarship funds to support Negroes of talent here and abroad.

4. Art

We shall stress Beauty—all Beauty, but especially the beauty of Negro life and character; its music, its dancing, its drawing and painting and the new birth of its literature. This growth which THE CRISIS long since predicted is sprouting and coming to flower. We shall encourage it in every way—by reproduction, by publication, by personal mention—keeping the while a high standard of merit and stooping never to cheap flattery and misspent kindliness.

5. Peace and International Understanding

Through the Pan-African movement we shall press for better knowledge of each other by groups of the peoples of African descent; we shall seek wider understanding with the brown and yellow peoples of the world and thus, by the combined impact of an appeal to decency and humanity from the oppressed and insulted to those fairer races who today accidentally rule the world, we shall seek universal peace by abolishing the rivalries and hatreds and economic competition that lead to organized murder.

6. The Church

We shall recognize and stress the fact that the American Negro church is doing the greatest work in social uplift of any present agency. We criticize our churches bitterly and in these plaints THE CRISIS has often joined. At the same time we know that without the help of the Negro church neither the N. A. A. C. P. Nor THE CRISIS could have come into being nor could they for a single day continue to exist. Despite an outworn creed and ancient methods of worship the black church is leading the religious world in real human brotherhood, in personal charity, in social uplift and in economic teaching. No such tremendous force can be neglected or ignored by a journal which seeks to portray and expound the truth. We shall essay, then, the contradictory task of showing month by month the accomplishment of black religious organization in America and at the same time seeking to free the minds of our people from the futile dogma that makes for unreason and intolerance.

7. Self-criticism

THE CRISIS is going to be more frankly critical of the Negro group. In our fight for the sheer crumbs of decent treatment we have become habituated to regarding ourselves as always right and resenting criticism from whites and furiously opposing self-criticism from within. We are seriously crippling Negro art and literature by refusing to contemplate any but handsome heroes, unblemished heroines and flawless defenders; we insist on being always and everywhere all right and often we ruin our cause by claiming too much and admitting no fault. Here THE CRISIS has sinned with its group and it purposes hereafter to examine from time to time judicially the extraordinary number of very human faults among us—both those common to mankind and those born of our extraordinary history and experiences.

8. Criticism

This does not mean that we propose for a single issue to cease playing the gadfly to the Bourbon South and the Copperhead North, to hypocritical Philanthropy and fraudulent Science, to race hate and human degradation.

All this, we admit, is an enormous task for a magazine of 52 pages, selling for 15 cents and paying all of its own expenses out of that 15 cents and not out of the bribes of Big Business. We shall probably fall far short of its well doing but we shall make the attempt in all seriousness and good will. And, Good Reader, what will you do? Write and tell us.

---

# 19
## Race Relations in the United States

*This article, "Race Relations in the United States" (*Annals of the American Academy of Political and Social Science *140 [November 1928]: 6–10), represented one of the rare occasions that an African American gained access to the pages of a mainstream scholarly journal in the 1920s. Du Bois used this opportunity to summarize his views on race in the United States at the end of the 1920s.*

In our present discussion of the relations between the white and black races in the United States, we are facing an astonishing paradox. In the first place, the increasingly certain dictum of science is that there are no "races," in any exact scientific sense; that no measurements of human beings, of bodily development, of head form, of color and hair, of psychological reactions, have succeeded in dividing mankind into different, recognizable groups: that so-called "pure" races seldom, if ever, exist and that all present mankind, the world over, are "mixed" so far as the so-called racial characteristics are concerned.

Notwithstanding these facts, and indeed, in the very face of them, we have serious discussions of race in the United States and of race relations; scientific investigations, based on race measurements; and widespread assumption among intelligent people that there are between certain large groups of men ineradicable, and, for all practicable purposes, unchangeable racial differences; and that the limitations of race can, to some extent, be measured; and that the question of the relations between these groups is the greatest of social problems.

When, now, a nation of reasonable human beings faces such a contradiction and paradox, the danger to their development and culture is great. The greatest danger lies not in the so-called "problems" of race, but rather in the integrity of national thinking and in the ethics of national conduct. Such a nation, if it persists in its logical contradictions, is bound to develop fools and hypocrites: fools, who in the presence of plain facts, cannot think straight; and hypocrites, who in the face of clear duty, refuse to do the right thing and yet pretend to do it.

## Problems of Logic and Ethics

It is, of course, clear as to what most people mean by races and race problems in the United States; they refer to national groups who are not of English descent; religious groups like Jews; "colored" people like the Japanese and Chinese; or, more especially, they have in mind the group of twelve million Americans who are descended from former Negro slaves. This group has a certain historical unity, a large percentage of common blood and the average level of their intelligence, efficiency and income, is below that of the average of the nation. But with this broad general unity, goes great diversity: these "Negroes" represent a wide intermixture of blood; they have produced individuals of unusual intelligence and efficiency, and they have accumulated large amounts of property. Neither their blood nor their condition constitute them a closed racial group, and yet we treat them as such, in flat contradiction of well-known facts and scientific proof.

This paradox in the United States has given rise to a series of subtle reactions which we loosely denominate "race problems," but which are in truth problems of logic and ethics. Take the matter of lynching: we have in the last forty-three years allowed mobs to murder over 4,000 persons accused of crime. Public opinion has largely condoned this because most of these victims were of Negro descent. Men have refused to take into account the fact that slavery, ignorance and poverty are a sufficient explanation of crime among American freedmen, without any additional subtle and immeasurable racial characteristics; and that "racial" crime is no different and calls for no other remedies than any other kind of crime.

On account of the "Negro problem" we are making democratic government increasingly impossible in the United States. When the two old parties become corrupt and inefficient, no Third Party can hope to win because the minority party is too strong to disappear. This arises because we have let the Democratic party establish itself in perpetuity by permitting it to use the political power of the black men and white men which it has illegally disfranchised. And we excuse this because of arguments of race inferiority. Yet it is clear that the political corruption of the Negro is a result of inexperience, ignorance and poverty and not of the color of his skin. This has been proven by numberless Negro officials of ability and honor from Reconstruction times down to our own day.

We have submitted in the United States to widespread customs, sometimes written into law, and sometimes enforced by mob violence, which insult the manhood and sense of decency of self-respecting human beings. In various parts of the United States a traveler may be compelled to pay first-class fare for third-class accommodations, may be publicly stigmatized and affronted despite his dress, character and attainment, and simply because he has or is suspected of having a Negro ancestor; families may be ousted from their homes and made to lose their property without due process of law; children may be deprived of their proper education; youth kept from an opportunity to work and age from the public enjoyment of wealth which it has helped create, not for any individual fault or failing, but because the majority of the group, thus singled out for public insult, are descendants of slaves, and, therefore, as a class, less well-clothed, less well-educated, with smaller incomes and with more difficulties to encounter than other people.

We have submitted to corrupt political conditions in great cities, like Philadelphia, Chicago and Memphis, because we would rather have corruption than recognize the manhood of the best class of Negro citizens. Classifying all persons of Negro descent in one conglomerate heap, we make it impossible for them to achieve even a semblance of municipal freedom except by submission to political bosses of the lowest type. Negroes get colored school teachers and policemen in New York by serving Tammany; they get representation in the Civil Service and in the city council in Philadelphia by following [William S.] Vare; they get to the legislature and to Congress by supporting [William "Big Bill"] Thompson in Chicago. Much as Southerners, Quakers and Illinoisians may want decent government, numbers of them prefer government by bootleggers and scoundrels rather than by the highest type of colored voters and officials.

We treat crime in the United States, not as a curable social phenomenon, but as a chance for the exhibition of class and racial hatred. And in large areas of the country we deliberately buy and sell colored criminals like slaves; bad as our jails are for whites, the chain-gangs and prisons for Negroes are inhuman breeding grounds for crime and disease.

Education was once the foundation stone of our democracy. But because we long hesitated and still hesitate to admit the descendants of slaves into the body politic, we have not only made the education of Negro children a half-hearted, incomplete enterprise, but have begun to hesitate over giving the white poor a chance for high school and college. After a half century of Negro public schools in the South there are states where the expenditures for Negro schools are less than a fifth of those for whites and yet the white schools are not good. A large group of public school officials and intelligent white folk, in the South, still believe that so far as black folk are concerned, ignorance is a more profitable investment than intelligence.

Hand in hand with all this, this country professes loudly and blatantly a religion of mercy, humanity and sacrifice; we profess to regard all men as brothers, and teach that we should turn the other cheek to evil; and that all human distinctions, not based on individual character and desert, are false and wrong. Yet, at the mere presence of a colored face, again and again our whole moral fabric falls, fails and collapses, in simple matters of human intercourse, in larger matters of social service and in the very pews of the church itself.

What is going to become of a country which allows itself to fall into such an astonishing intellectual and ethical paradox? Nothing but disaster. Intellectual and ethical disaster in some form must result unless immediately we compel the thought and conscience of America to face the facts in this so-called racial problem.

## Slavery and Emancipation

Nor are the facts hidden or difficult to find: black slaves were imported into the United States in the seventeenth, eighteenth and nineteenth centuries, because their labor was profitable for the white inhabitants. On slave labor the economic foundations of the United States were laid. As industry developed, slave labor remained profitable, only in agriculture, and chiefly in the raising of cotton, sugar, rice and such semi-tropical crops. Here for a long time it was immensely profitable and the whole country, north and south and west, shared in this prosperity built on slavery. The nineteenth century, however, brought changes—the factory system, a labor movement and democratic humanitarianism. The impoverishment of Southern land, on the other hand, meant that slavery could only survive by means of a new slave trade and imperial aggression in the tropics which should annex new rich land to the United States. But imperialism and slave labor meant severe competition with white labor and the new industries of the North. The result was a Civil War which emancipated the slaves.

These emancipated slaves were victims who had been bred deliberately in sloth, ignorance, poverty and crime. Their emancipation meant that they must either be killed off, gotten rid of by compulsory migration, or that they must be educated and trained.

The United States was forced to adopt the last course to insure its victory over the rebellious states and to justify the war in the eyes of the civilized world. The country was encouraged in its course by the Abolitionists, the Christian churches and the humanitarians; but particulary by the sincere and almost desperate cooperation of the freedmen. The result has been astonishing. It has repeatedly been said that never before in a similar period of history has so large a group of people made the social, intellectual and economic advance that American Negroes have made. It is not a question as to whom credit for this belongs. That a part of it belongs to the white South is true. That a larger part of it belongs to the Abolition North is also true. But by far the largest part of the credit surely belongs to the struggling Negroes themselves.

## Future Race Problems

But the question is not one of credit and praise. It is a question as to what place these emancipated and advancing people are going eventually to occupy in the United States of America. Some people have long hoped that the country would not have to face this question, and that according to time-honored tradition, the emancipated black man would be unable to withstand civilization and would die out. The American Negro has firmly refused this invitation. Others have acted as though they hoped to goad the Negro into open revolt and then kill him, by police, mobs and machine guns. Much as these methods have been tried in the last half century, they have not been wholly successful. They have doubtless cowed black men; they have made hereditary cowards of large numbers of them; they have given Negroes a widespread inferiority complex; but, notwithstanding all this, Negroes as a mass are still surging forward, and pushing upward, determined, ambitious and rising masses of humanity.

Now the real problem of race relations in the United States which the majority of Americans are seldom willing to face frankly, is this: Must such people be recognized as full-fledged Americans or must they be compelled to occupy a caste position of inferiority until such time as they die out, migrate or commit suicide by voluntary revolt?

There is no doubt that Negroes are today and in the mass, poorer, less intelligent and less efficient than whites. It takes no elaborate "intelligence" tests to prove what would be a miracle if it were not true. But there is also not the slightest doubt but that there are Negroes and increasing numbers of them, who are equal to, and above the average of the white nation by any standard of measurement. There is no reason to believe that the possibility of improvement among blacks is not just as great as among whites. How then, is the black group to be treated, especially those of them who are by any measurement the equal of the whites?

This is the real problem which we do not like to face, and we do not like to face it because we believe that its solution involves miscegenation.

**Miscegenation**

If groups of people live together there is going to be more or less intermingling of blood. This was true in the slave South. It is true today in caste-ridden United States. It will be true tomorrow whether the American Negro becomes really free or sinks to greater serfdom. Will this intermingling of races be hastened if the American Negro reaches the economic and intellectual average of the American white man? Or if numbers of Negroes become superior in training and ability to the average of white Americans? This question no man can answer off-hand. If the greatest ambition of the Negro is to become white, then certainly his advance would bring him greater opportunities for intermarriage with the whites. But why should he want to be white if there is no reason because of treatment or opportunity? Because of political freedom or social contact? It is quite conceivable that the advance of the American Negro might mean not more but less intermingling of blood.

This again brings us face to face with facts, perfectly well known, but continually ignored. A foreigner might go over the literature of the Negro problem and come to believe that there are in the United States facing each other today, two absolutely unmixed groups of whites and blacks. Yet nothing is further from the truth. The so-called American Negro is probably less than 25 per cent of pure

African descent. There is reason to believe that over 70 per cent of these so-called Negroes are descendants of American whites and that 40 per cent of them have as much white blood as Negro. Such intermingling of blood took place, moreover, mainly during slavery and mainly at the demand of white folk. Assuming that there is today no such demand from whites, it is difficult to see how in the future there could come from self-respecting, educated persons of Negro descent, any demand for this mingling of blood which would bring as much miscegenation in the near future as in the past.

In the far future miscegenation is going to be widely practised in the world and that despite the likes and dislikes of present living beings. We today can at least determine whether such race mixture shall be between intelligent, self-respecting and self-determining people, or between masters and slaves. Any attempt to stop miscegenation today by forcing millions of men into pauperism and ignorance and by making their women prostitutes and concubines is too nasty and barbaric to be faced even by hypocritical America.

## Segregation

Moreover, those persons who are determined at any cost: at the cost of religious hypocrisy, political disarrangement, and intellectual clarity, to keep American Negroes from becoming men, must remember this will prevent an intermingling of blood only in case it is followed up by actual physical segregation. This means the forceable removal of millions of human beings from this country to some other and the setting aside of lands and territories claimed and in part occupied by whites. Such forceable migration since the slave trade is a chimera which no civilized people has contemplated; neither Kenya nor the Union of South Africa with all their color hatred and Negro degradation have been able to assign separate lands.

And why is this? Because the industrial organization of the modern world and the incomes of white folk demand today as never before a world with the "Open Door" and unsegregated and free contact of all races and peoples. Here the paradox of race appears in its world guise as demanding, on the one hand, no race equality, and, on the other, complete racial contact and the paradox persists because it rests based on the pious hope that by low wage and little education "lower" races will remain lower and satisfied.

What has the United States to contribute to this world problem? Darkness rather than light—paradox rather than logic. "Lower" races can be educated. We have proven this. What shall the world do—prevent their education and exploit them as ignorant slaves, or let them struggle up and then beat them back? How fine an alternative and how brilliant a program of World Peace for the land which the World War placed at the head of the nations!

# 20
## Economic Disfranchisement

*As the Great Depression worsened, Du Bois turned more and more to socialism as the ultimate solution to the problems confronting African Americans in the United States. In the article "Economic Disfranchisement" (The Crisis 37 [August 1930]: 281–82), he argued that public ownership of public service companies is the only way that blacks will achieve a voice in the operation in these companies, and the only way that they can guarantee that they will not be excluded from decent jobs.*

There is no universal suffrage in modern industry. So far as the government conducts industry, as in the case of the post office and, in some instances, the transportation system, universal political suffrage indirectly controls the industry. But there are great public services, like the railroad, the telephone, gas and electric lighting, the telegraph and others, where the industry, although public in nature, is private in ownership, and conducted by an autocracy, except insofar as public opinion and the granting of privileges and franchises gives remote control to the voters.

The disfranchisement, therefore, of the mass of workers in this case is the most extraordinary and vital disfranchisement in the modern world. When we talk of industrial democracy, we mean the increased right of the working people to determine the policies of great public services, either through direct public ownership or by private negotiation in the shape of shop committees, working agreements and the like.

What is the attitude of the Negro here? Most Negroes would have no attitude at all, so far as public ownership was concerned. They would not be interested; and yet, they are, or should be, tremendously interested. Take, for instance, the telephone service. It is wellnigh universal. The number of telephones in use by colored people runs into the millions. It is not possible that Negroes in the United States spend less than $10,000,000 a year for telephone service, and they may spend three times as much as this. In the organization of work and trade a balance is always assumed between a service rendered or goods delivered on one side and a reciprocal service rendered and goods delivered, on the other. If the exchange is not direct it must be indirect, or the whole industrial combination fails. Yet in the case of the colored people and the telephone there is no reciprocity. The Telephone Company in the North, almost without exception, employs no colored help whatsoever; no laborers, no telephone girls, no clerks, no officials. The whole service is absolutely closed to Negroes. In the South, a few colored men are employed as laborers and linemen, but not many.

Here then is a situation where a quasi-public institution absolutely refuses to let millions of citizens earn a decent living, while taxing them along with other citizens for this public service. This compulsory exclusion is, of course, not confined to colored people. It is exercised against Jews; it is exercised against various groups of foreign-born; it is exercised even against certain social classes among American-born citizens. But in the case of the Negroes, we can see it openly, just as in those chemical experiments where an artificially colored liquid reveals diffusion and reaction.

What now must Negroes do? If this sort of thing goes on, then disfranchisement in industry is going to be a vital factor in their elimination from modern civilization. By consolidations and mergers, by holding companies and interlocking directorates, the great industries of the world are becoming integrated into vast private organizations, which means that the work of the world,—the skilled work, the best paid work,—in the vast majority of the cases, is subject to this social and racial exclusion; to this refusal to allow certain classes of men to earn a decent living.

It is an intolerable situation. Attempts have been made to correct it by appeal. In Chicago and in High Harlem, New York, these appeals have been effective in the case of small store chains, and even to a slight extent with a corporation like the Western Union Telegraph Company. But the Telephone Company remains adamant. The Gas Company is absolutely deaf and unsympathetic.

In this case there is only one thing to do, and that is for the Negro voters with intelligence and far-reaching memory to see that by their votes no further privileges and franchises are granted to these public service companies; and to see that the work of these companies, just as far as possible and as soon as possible, is transferred to the government. Government ownership is the only solution for this present industrial disfranchisement of the Negro.

There are, of course, many other reasons and arguments for public ownership beside this personal and racial reason. But all these arguments simply bring home to the mass of people the fact that public service cannot be carried on endlessly for private advantage and private profit.

---

# 21
## Marxism and the Negro Problem

*In the 1930s Du Bois turned sharply to the left, embracing Marxism, pan-Africanism, and a more class-conscious, nationalist view of race in the United*

*States. Du Bois's Marxism was more analytical and less doctrinaire than that of many of his contemporaries. In this essay, "Marxism and the Negro Problem"* *(*The Crisis *40 [May 1933]: 103–04, 118), he argued that Marxism was relevant, but acknowledged that it needed to be modified before it could be the basis for a solution to the problems that blacks faced in America.*

Karl Marx was a Jew born at Treves, Germany, in March, 1818. He came of an educated family and studied at the Universities of Bonn and Berlin, planning first to become a lawyer, and then to teach philosophy. But his ideas were too radical for the government. He turned to journalism, and finally gave his life to economic reform, dying in London in 1883, after having lived in Germany, Belgium, France, and, for the last thirty-five years of his life, in England. He published in 1867, the first volume of his monumental work, "Capital."

There are certain books in the world which every searcher for truth must know: the Bible, the Critique of Pure Reason, the Origin of Species, and Karl Marx' "Capital."

Yet until the Russian Revolution, Karl Marx was little known in America. He was treated condescendingly in the universities, and regarded even by the intelligent public as a radical agitator whose curious and inconvenient theories it was easy to refute. Today, at last, we all know better, and we see in Karl Marx a colossal genius of infinite sacrifice and monumental industry, and with a mind of extraordinary logical keenness and grasp. We may disagree with many of the great books of truth that I have named, and with "Capital," but they can never be ignored.

At a recent dinner to Einstein, another great Jew, the story was told of a professor who was criticized as having "no sense of humor" because he tried to explain the Theory of Relativity in a few simple words. Something of the same criticism must be attached to anyone who attempts similarly to indicate the relation of Marxian philosophy and the American Negro problem. And yet, with all modesty, I am essaying the task knowing that it will be but tentative and subject to much criticism, both on my own part and that of other abler students.

The task which Karl Marx set himself was to study and interpret the organization of industry in the modern world. One of Marx's earlier works, "The Communist Manifesto," issued in 1848, on the eve of the series of democratic revolutions in Europe, laid down this fundamental proposition.

"That in every historical epoch the prevailing mode of economic production and exchange, and the social organization necessarily following from it, form the basis upon which is built up, and from which alone can be explained, the political and intellectual history of that epoch; that consequently the whole history of mankind . . . has been a history of class struggles, contest between exploiting and exploited, ruling and oppressed classes; that the history of these class struggles forms a series of evolution in which, now-a-days, a stage has been reached where the exploited and oppressed class (the proletariat) cannot attain its emancipation from the sway of the exploiting and ruling class (the bourgeoisie) without, at the same time, and once and for all, emancipating society at large from all exploitation, oppression, class-distinction and class-struggles."

All will notice in this manifesto phrases which have been used so much lately and so carelessly that they have almost lost their meaning. But behind them still is living and insistent truth. The *class struggle* of exploiter and exploited is a reality. The capitalist still today owns machines, materials, and wages with which to buy labor. The laborer even in America owns little more than his ability to work. A wage contract takes place between these two and the resultant manufactured commodity or service is the property of the capitalist.

Here Marx begins his scientific analysis based on a mastery of practically all economic theory before his time and on an extraordinary, thoroughgoing personal knowledge of industrial conditions over all Europe and many other parts of the world.

His final conclusions were never all properly published. He lived only to finish the first volume of his "Capital," and the other two volumes were completed from his papers and notes by his friend Engels. The result is an unfinished work, extraordinarily difficult to read and understand and one which the master himself would have been first to criticize as not properly representing his mature and finished thought.

Nevertheless, that first volume together with the fairly evident meaning of the others, lay down a logical line of thought. The gist of that philosophy is that the value of products regularly exchanged in the open market depends upon the labor necessary to produce them; that capital consists of machines, materials and wages paid for labor; that out of the finished product, when materials have been paid for and the wear and tear and machinery replaced, and wages paid, there remains a surplus value. This surplus value arises from labor and is the difference between what is actually paid laborers for their wages and the market value of the commodities which the laborers produce. It represents, therefore, exploitation of the laborer, and this exploitation, inherent in the capitalistic system of production, is the cause of poverty, of industrial crises, and eventually of social revolution.

This social revolution, whether we regard it as voluntary revolt or the inevitable working of a vast cosmic law of social evolution, will be the last manifestation of the class struggle, and will come by inevitable change induced by the very nature of the conditions under which present production is carried on. It will come by the action of the great majority of men who compose the wage-earning proletariat, and it will result in common ownership of all capital, the disappearance of capitalistic exploitation, and the division of the products and services of industry according to human needs, and not according to the will of the owners of capital.

It goes without saying that every step of this reasoning and every presentation of supporting facts have been bitterly assailed. The labor theory of value has been denied; the theory of surplus value refuted, and inevitability of revolution scoffed at; while industrial crises—at least until this present one—have been defended as unusual exceptions proving the rule of modern industrial efficiency.

But with the Russian experiment and the World Depression most thoughtful men today are beginning to admit:

That the continued recurrence of industrial crises and wars based largely on economic rivalry, with persistent poverty, unemployment, disease and crime, are forcing the world to contemplate the possibilities of fundamental change in our economic methods; and that means thorough-going change whether it be violent, as in France or Russia, or peaceful, as seems just as possible, and just as true to the Marxian formula, if it is fundamental change; in any case, Revolution seems bound to come.

Perhaps nothing illustrates this better than recent actions in the United States: our re-examination of the whole concept of Property; our banking moratorium; the extraordinary new agriculture bill; the plans to attack unemployment, and similar measures. Labor rather than gambling is the sure foundation of value and whatever we call it—exploitation, theft or business acumen—there is something radically wrong with an industrial system that turns out simultaneously paupers and millionaires and sets a world starving because it has too much food.

What now has all this to do with the Negro problem? First of all, it is manifest that the mass of Negroes in the United States belong distinctly to the working proletariat. Of every thousand working Negroes less than a hundred and fifty belong to any class that could possibly be considered bourgeois. And even this more educated and prosperous class has but small connection with the exploiters of wage and labor. Nevertheless, this black proletariat is not a part of the white proletariat. Black and white work together in many cases, and influence each other's rates of wages. They have similar complaints against capitalists, save that the grievances of the Negro worker are more fundamental and indefensible, ranging as they do, since the day of Karl Marx, from chattel slavery, to the worst paid, sweated, mobbed and cheated labor in any civilized land.

And while Negro labor in America suffers because of the fundamental inequities of the whole capitalistic system, the lowest and most fatal degree of its suffering comes not from the capitalists but from fellow white laborers. It is white labor that deprives the Negro of his right to vote, denies him education, denies him affiliation with trade unions, expels him from decent houses and neighborhoods, and heaps upon him the public insults of open color discrimination.

It is no sufficient answer to say that capital encourages this oppression and uses it for its own ends. This may have excused the ignorant and superstitious Russian peasants in the past and some of the poor whites of the South today. But the bulk of American white labor is neither ignorant nor fanatical. It knows exactly what it is doing and it means to do it. William Green and Mathew Woll of the A.F. of L. have no excuse of illiteracy or religion to veil their deliberate intention to keep Negroes and Mexicans and other elements of common labor, in a lower proletariat as subservient to their interests as theirs are to the interests of capital.

This large development of a petty bourgeoisie within the American laboring class is a post-Marxian phenomenon and the result of the tremendous and world wide development of capitalism in the 20th Century. The market of capitalistic production has gained an effective world-wide organization. Industrial technique and mass production have brought possibilities in the production of goods and services which out-run even this wide market. A new class of technical engineers and managers has arisen forming a working class aristocracy between the older proletariat and the absentee owners of capital. The real owners of capital are small as well as large investors—workers who have deposits in savings banks and small holdings in stocks and bonds; families buying homes and purchasing commodities on installment; as well as the large and rich investors.

Of course, the individual laborer gets but an infinitesimal part of his income from such investments. On the other hand, such investments, in the aggregate, largely increase available capital for the exploiters, and they give investing laborers the capitalistic ideology. Between workers and owners of capital stand today the bankers and financiers who distribute capital and direct the engineers.

Thus the engineers and the saving better-paid workers, form a new petty bourgeois class, whose interests are bound up with those of the capitalists and antagonistic to those of common labor. On the other hand, common labor in America and white Europe far from being motivated by any vision of revolt against capitalism, has been blinded by the American vision of the possibility of layer after layer of the workers escaping into the wealthy class and becoming managers and employers of labor.

Thus in America we have seen a wild and ruthless scramble of labor groups over each other in order to climb to wealth on the backs of black labor and foreign immigrants. The Irish climbed on the Negroes. The Germans scrambled over the Negroes and emulated the Irish. The Scandinavians fought forward next to the Germans and the Italians and "Bohunks" are crowding up, leaving Negroes still at the bottom chained to helplessness, first by slavery, then by disfranchisement and always by the Color Bar.

The second influence on white labor both in America and Europe has been the fact that the extension of the world market by imperial expanding industry has established a world-wide new proletariat of colored workers, toiling under the worst conditions of 19th century capitalism, herded as slaves and serfs and furnishing by the lowest paid wage in modern history a mass of raw material for industry. With this largess the capitalists have consolidated their economic power, nullified universal suffrage and bribed the white workers by high wages, visions of wealth and the opportunity to drive "niggers." Soldiers and sailors from the white workers are used to keep "darkies" in their "places" and white foremen and engineers have been established as irresponsible satraps in China and India, Africa and the West Indies, backed by the organized and centralized ownership of machines, raw materials, finished commodities and land monopoly over the whole world.

How now does the philosophy of Karl Marx apply today to colored labor? First of all colored labor has no common ground with white labor. No soviet of technocrats would do more than exploit colored labor in order to raise the status of whites. No revolt of a white proletariat could be started if its object was to make black workers their economic, political and social equals. It is for this reason that American socialism for fifty years has been dumb on the Negro problem, and the communists cannot even get a respectful hearing in America unless they begin by expelling Negroes.

On the other hand, within the Negro groups, in the United States, in West Africa, in South America and in the West Indies, petty bourgeois groups are being evolved. In South America and the West Indies such groups drain off skill and intelligence into the white group, and leave the black labor poor, ignorant and leaderless save for an occasional demagog.

In West Africa, a Negro bourgeoisie is developing with invested capital and employment of natives and is only kept from the conventional capitalistic development by the opposition and enmity of white capital, and the white managers and engineers who represent it locally and who display bitter prejudice and tyranny; and by white European labor which furnishes armies and navies and Empire "preference." African black labor and black capital are therefore driven to seek alliance and common ground.

In the United States also a petty bourgeoisie is being developed, consisting of clergymen, teachers, farm owners, professional men and retail businessmen. The position of this class, however, is peculiar: they are not the chief or even large investors in Negro labor and therefore exploit it only here and there; and they bear the brunt of color prejudice because they express in word and work the aspirations of all black folk for emancipation. The revolt of any black proletariat could not, therefore, be logically directed against this class, nor could this class join either white capital, white engineers or white workers to strengthen the color bar.

Under these circumstances, what shall we say of the Marxian philosophy and of its relation to the American Negro? We can only say, as it seems to me, that the Marxian philosophy is a true diagnosis of the situation in Europe in the middle of the 19th Century despite some of its logical difficulties. But it must be modified in the United States of America and especially so far as the Negro group is concerned. The Negro is exploited to a degree that means poverty, crime, delinquency and indigence. And that exploitation comes not from a black capitalistic class but from the white capitalists and equally from the white proletariat. His only defense is such internal organization as will protect him from both parties, and such practical economic insight as will prevent inside the race group any large development of capitalistic exploitation.

Meantime, comes the Great Depression. It levels all in mighty catastrophe. The fantastic industrial structure of America is threatened with ruin. The trade unions of skilled labor are double-tongued and helpless. Unskilled and common white labor is too frightened at Negro competition to attempt united action. It only begs a dole. The reformist program of Socialism meets no response from the white proletariat because it offers no escape to wealth and no effective bar to black labor, and a mud-sill of black labor is essential to white labor's standard of living. The shrill cry of a few communists is not even listened to, because and solely because it seeks to break down barriers between black and white. There is not at present the slightest indication that a Marxian revolution based on a united class-conscious proletariat is anywhere on the American far horizon. Rather race antagonism and labor group rivalry is still undisturbed by world catastrophe. In the hearts of black laborers alone, therefore, lie those ideals of democracy in politics and industry which may in time make the workers of the world effective dictators of civilization.

---

# 22
## Pan-Africa and New Racial Philosophy

*The second leg of Du Bois's new radicalism was his renewed commitment to pan-Africanism. In the article "Pan-Africa and New Racial Philosophy" (*The Crisis *40 [November 1933]: 247, 262), in words somewhat reminiscent of those of Marcus Garvey, Du Bois called upon his readers to remember that they were not white, and that their economic survival depended on cooperation with other peoples of Africa or of African descent.*

During the last ten months, we have tried in the CRISIS magazine to make a re-statement of the Negro problem in certain of its aspects. We began with the question of health and disease among us. Then we took up in succession our physical rate of increase, "Karl Marx and the Negro," "The Problem of Earning a Living," "Marxism and the Negro Problem," "The Negro Vote," "The Class Struggle Within the Race," "Negro Education," and "Our Problems of Religion."

We have considered all these matters in relation to the American Negro but our underlying thought has been continually that they can and must be seen not against any narrow, provincial or even national background, but in relation to the great problem of the colored races of the world and particularly those of African descent.

There are still large numbers of American Negroes who in all essential particulars conceive themselves as belonging to the white race. And this, not on
account of their color, which may be yellow, brown or black, but on account of
their history and their social surroundings. They react as white Americans. They
have all the racial prejudices of white America, not only against Asiatics and
Jews, but even against Mexicans and West Indians. In all questions of human
interest, they would flock to white America before they would flock to the brown
West Indies or to black Africa or to yellow Asia.

This, of course, is quite natural, and in a sense proves how idiotic most of our
racial distinctions are. Here is a boy, born in America, of parents who were born
in America, of grandparents and great grandparents born in America. He speaks
the American twang, he reads American history, he gets his news from American
papers, and he understands American baseball. It is impossible for that boy to
think of himself as African, simply because he happens to be black. He *is* an
American. But on the other hand, as he grows up and comprehends his surroundings, he is going to be made to think of himself as at least a peculiar sort of
American. Against this, he is going to protest, logically and emotionally, and
dwell upon the anomaly of a person being outcast and discriminated against in
his own home. Gradually, however, he is going to find that this protest has only
limited effect; that to most white Americans of today, Negro prejudice is something that is beyond question and will. It is a stark, true fact and little or nothing
can be done about it at present. In the future, the long future, things may change.
But they are not going to change in the lifetime of those now living.

So long now as this is an academic question, a matter of attitudes and
thoughts and spiritual likes and dislikes, we can leave it there. But when it
becomes an economic problem, a stark matter of bread and butter, then if this
young, black American is going to survive and live a life, he must calmly face
the fact that however much he is an American there are interests which draw him
nearer to the dark people outside of America than to his white fellow citizens.

And those interests are the same matters of color caste, of discrimination, of
exploitation for the sake of profit, of public insult and oppression, against which
the colored peoples of Mexico, South America, the West Indies and all Africa,
and every country in Asia, complain and have long been complaining. It is,
therefore, simply a matter of ordinary common sense that these people should
draw together in spiritual sympathy and intellectual co-operation, to see what can
be done for the freedom of the human spirit which happens to be incased in dark
skin.

This was the idea that was back of the Pan-African Congresses, started in
Paris directly after the war, and carried on for several years. These Congresses
brought upon themselves the active enmity and disparagement of all the colony-
owning powers. Englishmen, Frenchmen, Belgians and others looked upon the
movement as a political movement designed to foment disaffection and strife
and to correct abuse by force.

It may be that in the end nothing but force will break down the injustice of the color line. But to us who have seen and known the futility of war, the ghastly paradox of talking about Victor and Vanquished in the last world holocaust, there is a feeling that we must desperately try methods of thought and co-operation and economic re-adjustment before we yield to councils of dispair. And in this program, all that has been said about economic readjustment in America for American Negroes can be said with even more emphasis concerning the Negroes of the world and concerning the darker peoples. These people raise everything necessary to satisfy human wants. They are capable of carrying on every process by which material, transported and re-made, may satisfy the needs and appetites of men. They are all of them willing and eager to work, and yet because their work is misdirected in order to make a profit for white people, these dark people must starve and be unemployed.

Here in the United States the net result of the National Recovery Act so far has been to raise wages for a small number of favored white workers and to decrease wages or push out of employment entirely the Negro. It is possible that this present result may in time be changed, and we note with interest what Secretary Ickes has said to the State Engineers and Public Works Administration:

"It is important to bear in mind that the Public Works Administration is for the benefit of all the people of the country. The established policy in the construction of public-buildings and public works under its control is that in the employment of mechanics and labor, preference be given to local labor to the extent that it is available and competent, and that there be no discrimination exercised against any person because of color or religious affiliation."

Nevertheless, this we feel is going to make little difference so long as the American people believe that any white man of whatever character or education is better than any possible colored man.

It is, therefore, imperative that the colored peoples of the world, and first of all those of Negro descent, should begin to concentrate upon this problem of their economic survival, the best of their brains and education. Pan-Africa means intellectual understanding and co-operation among all groups of Negro descent in order to bring about at the earliest possible time the industrial and spiritual emancipation of the Negro peoples.

Such a movement must begin with a certain spiritual housecleaning. American Negroes, West Indians, West Africans and South Africans must proceed immediately to wipe from their minds the preconcepts of each other which they have gained through white newspapers. They must cease to think of Liberia and Haiti as failures in government; of American Negroes as being engaged principally in frequenting Harlem cabarets and Southern lynching parties; of West Indians as ineffective talkers; and of West Africans as parading around in breech-clouts.

These are the pictures of each other which white people have painted for us and which with engaging naiveté we accept, and then proceed to laugh at each other and criticize each other before we make any attempt to learn the truth. There are, for instance, in the United States today several commendable groups of young people who are proposing to take hold of Liberia and emancipate her from her difficulties, quite forgetting the fact that Liberia belongs to Liberia. They made it. They suffered and died for it. And they are not handing over their country to any group of young strangers who happen to be interested. If we want to help Liberia, our business is to see in what respect the Liberians need help, and the persons best able to give this information are the Liberians themselves.

It is a large and intricate problem but the sooner we put ourselves in position to study it with a vast and increasing area of fact and with carefully guided and momentarily tested effort, the sooner we shall find ourselves citizens of the world and not its slaves and pensioners.

---

# 23
## Segregation

*Du Bois's increasing political radicalism in the early 1930s became a concern for Walter White and other board members of the NAACP. Then, in early 1934 with the editorial "Segregation" (*The Crisis *41 [January 1934]: 20), Du Bois challenged a fundamental tenet of the NAACP. Even though the concepts that Du Bois proposed were not entirely new, the debate that followed quickly undermined his position in the NAACP.*

The thinking colored people of the United States must stop being stampeded by the word segregation. The opposition to racial segregation is not or should not be any distaste or unwillingness of colored people to work with each other, to cooperate with each other, to live with each other. The opposition to segregation is an opposition to discrimination. The experience in the United States has been that usually when there is racial segregation, there is also racial discrimination.

But the two things do not necessarily go together, and there should never be an opposition to segregation pure and simple unless that segregation does involve discrimination. Not only is there no objection to colored people living beside colored people if the surroundings and treatment involve no discrimination, if streets are well lighted, if there is water, sewerage and police protection, and if anybody of any color who wishes can live in that neighborhood. The same way in schools, there is no objection to schools attended by colored pupils and taught by colored teachers. On the contrary, colored pupils can by our own contention be as fine human beings as any other sort of children, and we certainly know that there are no teachers better than trained colored teachers. But if the existence of such a school is made reason and cause for giving it worse housing, poorer facilities, poorer equipment and poorer teachers, then we do object, and the objection is not against the color of the pupils' or teachers' skins but against the discrimination.

In the recent endeavor of the United States government to redistribute capital so that some of the disadvantaged groups may get a chance for development, the American Negro should voluntarily and insistently demand his share. Groups of communities and farms inhabited by colored folk should be voluntarily formed. In no case should there be any discrimination against white and blacks. But at the same time, colored people should come forward, should organize and conduct enterprises, and their only insistence should be that the same provisions be made for the success of their enterprise that is being made for the success of any other enterprise. It must be remembered that in the last quarter of a century, the advance of the colored people has been mainly in the lines where they themselves working by and for themselves, have accomplished the greatest advance.

There is no doubt that numbers of white people, perhaps the majority of Americans, stand ready to take the most distinct advantage of voluntary segregation and cooperation among colored people. Just as soon as they get a group of black folk segregated, they use it as a point of attack and discrimination. Our counter attack should be, therefore, against this discrimination; against the refusal of the South to spend the same amount of money on the black child as on the white child for its education; against the inability of black groups to use public capital; against the monopoly of credit by white groups. But never in the world should our fight be against association with ourselves because by that very token we give up the whole argument that we are worth associating with.

Doubtless, and in the long run, the greatest human development is going to take place under experiences of widest individual contact. Nevertheless, today such individual contact is made difficult and almost impossible by petty prejudice, deliberate and almost criminal propaganda and various survivals from prehistoric heathenism. It is impossible, therefore, to wait for the millennium of free and normal intercourse before we unite to cooperate among themselves in groups of like-minded people and in groups of people suffering from the same disadvantages and the same hatreds.

It is the class-conscious working man uniting together who will eventually emancipate labor throughout the world. It is the race-conscious black man cooperating together in his own institutions and movements who will eventually emancipate the colored race, and the great step ahead today is for the American Negro to accomplish his economic emancipation through voluntary determined cooperative effort.

# 24
## The Board of Directors on Segregation

*The debate over segregation culminated in May 1934. In the editorial "The Board of Directors on Segregation" (*The Crisis *41 [May 1934]: 149), Du Bois listed his proposal on segregation, a compromise position, and the statement approved by the NAACP board. In May the board also passed a resolution stating that no salaried officer could criticize the policy, work, or officers of the NAACP in* The Crisis. *Du Bois resigned. Ironically, Du Bois's enemies accused him of embracing the discredited policies of Booker T. Washington.*

This is the vote which was proposed to the Board of Directors by W.E.B. Du Bois:

"The segregation of human beings purely on a basis of race and color, is not only stupid and unjust, but positively dangerous, since it is a path that leads straight to national jealousies, racial antagonisms, and war.

"The N.A.A.C.P., therefore, has always opposed the underlying principle of racial segregation, and will oppose it.

"On the other hand, it has, with equal clearness, recognized that when a group like the American Negroes suffers continuous and systematic segregation, against which argument and appeal are either useless or very slow in effecting changes, such a group must make up its mind to associate and co-operate for its own uplift and in defense of its self-respect.

"The N.A.A.C.P., therefore, has always recognized and encouraged the Negro church, the Negro college, the Negro public school, Negro business and industrial enterprises, and believes they should be made the very best and most efficient institutions of their kind judged by any standard; not with the idea of perpetuating artificial separations of mankind, but rather with the distinct object of proving Negro efficiency, showing Negro ability and discipline, and demonstrating how useless and wasteful race segregation is."

This is the modification of the Du Bois proposal, as rewritten by the Committee of Administration, and placed before the Board at its April meeting:

"The National Association for the Advancement of Colored People has always opposed the segregation of human beings on the basis of race and color. We have always as a basic principle of our organization opposed such segregation and we will always continue to oppose it.

"It is true that we have always recognized and encouraged the Negro church, the Negro college, the Negro school, and Negro business and industrial enterprises, and we shall continue to encourage them, so that they may serve as proofs of Negro efficiency, ability and discipline. Not merely external necessity but our faith in the genius of the Negro race has made us do this. But this does not alter our conviction that the necessity which has brought them into being is an evil, and that this evil should be combated to the greatest extent possible.

"We reserve to ourselves complete liberty of action in any specific case that may arise, since such liberty is essential to the statesmanship necessary to carry out any ideal; but we give assurance to the white and colored peoples of the world that this organization stands where it has always stood, as the chief champion of equal rights for black and white, and as unalterably opposed to the basic principle of racial segregation."

This is the resolution passed by the Board:

"The National Association for the advancement of Colored People is opposed both to the principle and the practice of enforced segregation of human beings on the basis of race and color.

"Enforced segregation by its very existence carries with it the implication of a superior and inferior group and invariably results in the imposition of a lower status on the group deemed inferior. Thus both principle and practice necessitate unyielding opposition to any and every form of enforced segregation."

These proposals and this vote will be discussed in the June issue of THE CRISIS.

It would be interesting to know what the Board means by the resolution.

Does it mean that it does not approve of the Negro Church or believe in its segregated activities in its 26,000 edifices where most branches of the N.A.A.C.P. meet and raise money to support it?

Does it mean that it lends no aid or countenance to Fisk, Atlanta, Talladega, Hampton, Howard, Wiley and a dozen other Negro Colleges?

Does it disapprove of the segregated public school system where two million Negro children are taught by 50,000 Negro teachers?

Does it believe in 200 Negro newspapers which spread N.A.A.C.P. news and propaganda?

Does it disapprove of slum clearance like the Dunbar Apartments in New York, the Rosenwald Apartments in Chicago and the $2,000,000 projects in Atlanta?

Does it believe in Negro business enterprise of any sort?

Does it believe in Negro history, Negro literature and Negro art?

Does it believe in the Negro spirituals?

*And if it does believe in these things is the Board of Directors of the N.A.A.C.P., afraid to say so?*

# 25
## A Negro Nation within the Nation

*Following his departure from the NAACP, Du Bois returned to the faculty of Atlanta University, where he continued to write about the economic and social crisis confronting the African American. In this article, "A Negro Nation within the Nation"* (Current History *42 [June 1935]: 265–270), he developed in greater detail the arguments that he had introduced in the 1934 debate on segregation in* The Crisis. *Like A. Philip Randolph (and even echoing some aspects of Booker T. Washington), Du Bois saw consumer cooperatives and building viable economic and political institutions within the black community as the keys to survival.*

No more critical situation ever faced the Negroes of America than that of today —not in 1830, nor in 1861, nor in 1867. More than ever the appeal of the Negro for elementary justice falls on deaf ears.

Three-fourths of us are disfranchised; yet no writer on democratic reform, no third party movement says a word about Negroes. The Bull Moose crusade in 1912 refused to notice them; the La Follette uprising in 1924 was hardly aware of them; the Socialists still keep them in the background. Negro children are systematically denied education; when the National Education Association asks for Federal aid to education it permits discrimination to be perpetuated by the present local authorities. Once or twice a month Negroes convicted of no crime are openly and publicly lynched, and even burned; yet a National Crime Convention is brought to perfunctory and unwilling notice of this only by mass picketing and all but illegal agitation. When a man with every qualification is refused a position simply because his great-grandfather was black there is not a ripple of comment or protest.

Long before the depression Negroes in the South were losing "Negro" jobs, those assigned them by common custom—poorly paid and largely undesirable toil, but nevertheless life-supporting. New techniques, new enterprises, mass production, impersonal ownership and control have been largely displacing the skilled white and Negro worker in tobacco manufacturing, in iron and steel, in lumbering and mining, and in transportation. Negroes are now restricted more and more to common labor and domestic service of the lowest paid and worst kind. In textile, chemical and other manufactures Negroes were from the first nearly excluded, and just as slavery kept the poor white out of profitable agriculture, so freedom prevents the poor Negro from finding a place in manufacturing. The world-wide decline in agriculture has moreover carried the mass of black farmers, despite heroic endeavor among the few, down to the level of landless tenants and peons.

The World War and its wild aftermath seemed for a moment to open a new door; 2,000,000 black workers rushed North to work in iron and steel, make automobiles and pack meat, build houses and do the heavy toil in factories. They met first the closed trade union which excluded them from the best paid jobs and pushed them into the low-wage gutter, denied them homes and mobbed them. Then they met the depression.

Since 1929 Negro workers, like white workers, have lost their jobs, have had mortgages foreclosed on their farms and homes, have used up their small savings. But, in the case of the Negro worker, everything has been worse in larger or smaller degree; the loss has been greater and more permanent. Technological displacement, which began before the depression, has been accelerated, while unemployment and falling wages struck black men sooner, went to lower levels and will last longer.

Negro public schools in the rural South have often disappeared, while Southern city schools are crowded to suffocation. The Booker Washington High School in Atlanta, built for 1,000 pupils, has 3,000 attending in double daily sessions. Above all, Federal and State relief holds out little promise for the Negro. It is but human that the unemployed white man and the starving white child should be relieved first by local authorities who regard them as fellow-men, but often regard Negroes as subhuman. While the white worker has sometimes been given more than relief and been helped to his feet, the black worker has often been pauperized by being just kept from starvation. There are some plans for national rehabilitation and the rebuilding of the whole industrial system. Such plans should provide for the Negro's future relations to American industry and culture, but those provisions the country is not only unprepared to make but refuses to consider.

In the Tennessee Valley beneath the Norris Dam, where do Negroes come in? And what shall be their industrial place? In the attempt to rebuild agriculture the Southern landholder will in all probability be put on his feet, but the black tenant has been pushed to the edge of despair. In the matter of housing, no comprehensive scheme for Negro homes has been thought out and only two or three local projects planned. Nor can broad plans be made until the nation or the community decides where it wants or will permit Negroes to live. Negroes are largely excluded from subsistence homesteads because Negroes protested against segregation, and whites, anxious for cheap local labor, also protested.

The colored people of America are coming to face the fact quite calmly that most white Americans do not like them, and are planning neither for their survival, nor for their definite future if it involves free, self-assertive modern manhood. This does not mean all Americans. A saving few are worried about the Negro problem; a still larger group are not ill-disposed, but they fear prevailing public opinion. The great mass of Americans are, however, merely representatives of average humanity. They muddle along with their own affairs and scarcely can be expected to take seriously the affairs of strangers or people whom they partly fear and partly despise.

For many years it was the theory of most Negro leaders that this attitude was the insensibility of ignorance and inexperience, that white America did not know of or realize the continuing plight of the Negro. Accordingly, for the last two decades, we have striven by book and periodical, by speech and appeal, by various dramatic methods of agitation, to put the essential facts before the American people. Today there can be no doubt that Americans know the facts; and yet they remain for the most part indifferent and unmoved.

The main weakness of the Negro's position is that since emancipation he has never had an adequate economic foundation. Thaddeus Stevens recognized this and sought to transform the emancipated freedmen into peasant proprietors. If he had succeeded, he would have changed the economic history of the United States and perhaps saved the American farmer from his present plight. But to furnish 50,000,000 acres of good land to the Negroes would have cost more money than the North was willing to pay, and was regarded by the South as highway robbery.

The whole attempt to furnish land and capital for the freedmen fell through, and no comprehensive economic plan was advanced until the advent of Booker T. Washington. He had a vision of building a new economic foundation for Negroes by incorporating them into white industry. He wanted to make them skilled workers by industrial education and expected small capitalists to rise out of their ranks. Unfortunately, he assumed that the economic development of America in the twentieth century would resemble that of the nineteenth century, with free industrial opportunity, cheap land and unlimited resources under the control of small competitive capitalists. He lived to see industry more and more concentrated, land monopoly extended and industrial technique changed by wide introduction of machinery.

As a result, technology advanced more rapidly than Hampton or Tuskegee could adjust their curricula. The chance of an artisan's becoming a capitalist grew slimmer, even for white Americans, while the whole relation of labor to capital became less a matter of technical skill than of basic organization and aim.

Those of us who in that day opposed Booker Washington's plans did not foresee exactly the kind of change that was coming, but we were convinced that the Negro could succeed in industry and in life only if he had intelligent leadership and far-reaching ideals. The object of education, we declared, was not "to make men artisans but to make artisans men." The Negroes in America needed leadership so that, when change and crisis came, they could guide themselves to safety.

The educated group among American Negroes is still small, but it is large enough to begin planning for preservation through economic advancement. The first definite movement of this younger group was toward direct alliance of the

Negro with the labor movement. But white labor today as in the past refuses to respond to these overtures.

For a hundred years, beginning in the Thirties and Forties of the nineteenth century, the white laborers of Ohio, Pennsylvania and New York beat, murdered and drove away fellow-workers because they were black and had to work for what they could get. Seventy years ago in New York, the centre of the new American labor movement, white laborers hanged black ones to lamp posts instead of helping to free them from the worst of modern slavery. In Chicago and St. Louis, New Orleans and San Francisco, black men still carry the scars of the bitter hatred of white laborers for them. Today it is white labor that keeps Negroes out of decent low-cost housing, that confines the protection of the best unions to "white" men, that often will not sit in the same hall with black folk who already have joined the labor movement. White labor has to hate scabs; but it hates black scabs not because they are scabs but because they are black. It mobs white scabs to force them into labor fellowship. It mobs black scabs to starve and kill them. In the present fight of the American Federation of Labor against company unions it is attacking the only unions that Negroes can join.

Thus the Negro's fight to enter organized industry has made little headway. No Negro, no matter what his ability, can be a member of any [of] the railway unions. He cannot be an engineer, fireman, conductor, switchman, brakeman or yardman. If he organizes separately, he may, as in the case of the Negro Firemen's Union, be assaulted and even killed by white firemen. As in the case of the Pullman Porters' Union, he may receive empty recognition without any voice or collective help. The older group of Negro leaders recognize this and simply say it is a matter of continued striving to break down these barriers.

Such facts are, however, slowly forcing Negro thought into new channels. The interests of labor are considered rather than those of capital. No greater welcome is expected from the labor monopolist who mans armies and navies to keep Chinese, Japanese and Negroes in their places than from the captains of industry who spend large sums of money to make laborers think that the most worthless white man is better than any colored man. The Negro must prove his necessity to the labor movement and that it is a disastrous error to leave him out of the foundation of the new industrial State. He must settle beyond cavil the question of his economic efficiency as a worker, a manager and controller of capital.

The dilemma of these younger thinkers gives men like James Weldon Johnson a chance to insist that the older methods are still the best; that we can survive only by being integrated into the nation, and that we must consequently fight segregation now and always and force our way by appeal, agitation and law. This group, however, does not seem to recognize the fundamental economic bases of social growth and the changes that face American industry. Greater democratic control of production and distribution is bound to replace existing autocratic and monopolistic methods.

In this broader and more intelligent democracy we can hope for progressive softening of the asperities and anomalies of race prejudice, but we cannot hope for its early and complete disappearance. Above all, the doubt, deep-planted in the American mind, as to the Negro's ability and efficiency as worker, artisan and administrator will fade but slowly. Thus, with increased democratic control of industry and capital, the place of the Negro will be increasingly a matter of human choice, of willingness to recognize ability across the barriers of race, of putting fit Negroes in places of power and authority by public opinion. At present, on the railroads, in manufacturing, in the telephone, telegraph and radio business, and in the larger divisions of trade, it is only under exceptional circumstances that any Negro, no matter what his ability, gets an opportunity for position and power. Only in those lines where individual enterprise still counts, as in some of the professions, in a few of the trades, in a few branches of retail business and in artistic careers, can the Negro expect a narrow opening.

Negroes and other colored folk, nevertheless, exist in larger and growing numbers. Slavery, prostitution to white men, theft of their labor and goods have not killed them and cannot kill them. They are growing in intelligence and dissatisfaction. They occupy strategic positions, within nations and besides nations, amid valuable raw material and on the highways of future expansion. They will survive, but on what terms and conditions? On this point a new school of Negro thought is arising. It believes in the ultimate uniting of mankind and in a unified American nation, with economic classes and racial barriers leveled, but it believes this is an ideal and is to be realized only by such intensified class and race consciousness as will bring irresistible force rather than mere humanitarian appeals to bear on the motives and actions of men.

The peculiar position of Negroes in America offers an opportunity. Negroes today cast probably 2,000,000 votes in a total of 40,000,000, and their vote will increase. This gives them, particularly in Northern cities, and at critical times, a chance to hold a very considerable balance of power, and the mere threat of this being used intelligently and with determination may often mean much. The consuming power of 2,800,000 Negro families has recently been estimated at $166,000,000 a month—a tremendous power when intelligently directed. Their man power as laborers probably equals that of Mexico or Yugoslavia. Their illiteracy is much lower than that of Spain or Italy. Their estimated per capita wealth about equals that of Japan.

For a nation with this start in culture and efficiency to sit down and await the salvation of a white God is idiotic. With the use of their political power, their power as consumers, and their brain power, added to that chance of personal appeal which proximity and neighborhood always give to human beings, Negroes can develop in the United States an economic nation within a nation, able to work through inner cooperation, to found its own institutions, to educate its genius, and at the same time, without mob violence or extremes of race hatred, to keep in helpful touch and cooperate with the mass of the nation. This has happened more often than most people realize, in the case of groups not so obviously separated from the mass of people as are American Negroes. It must happen in our case, or there is no hope for the Negro in America.

Any movement toward such a program is today hindered by the absurd Negro philosophy of Scatter, Suppress, Wait, Escape. There are even many of our educated young leaders who think that because the Negro problem is not in evidence where there are few or no Negroes, this indicates a way out! They think that the problem of race can be settled by ignoring it and suppressing all reference to it. They think that we have only to wait in silence for the white people to settle the problem for us; and finally and predominantly, they think that the problem of 12,000,000 Negro people, mostly poor, ignorant workers, is going to be settled by having their more educated and wealthy classes gradually and continually escape from their race into the mass of the American people, leaving the rest to sink, suffer and die.

Proponents of this program claim, with much reason, that the plight of the masses is not the fault of the emerging classes. For the slavery and exploitation that reduced Negroes to their present level or at any rate hindered them from rising, the white world is to blame. Since the age-long process of raising a group is through the escape of its upper class into welcome fellowship with risen peoples, the Negro intelligentsia would submerge itself if it bent its back to the task of lifting the mass of people. There is logic in this answer, but futile logic.

If the leading Negro classes cannot assume and bear the uplift of their own proletariat, they are doomed for all time. It is not a case of ethics; it is a plain case of necessity. The method by which this may be done is, first, for the American Negro to achieve a new economic solidarity.

There exists today a chance for the Negroes to organize a cooperative State within their own group. By letting Negro farmers feed Negro artisans, and Negro technicians guide Negro home industries, and Negro thinkers plan this integration of cooperation, while Negro artists dramatize and beautify the struggle, economic independence can be achieved. To doubt that this is possible is to doubt the essential humanity and the quality of brains of the American Negro.

No sooner is this proposed than a great fear sweeps over older Negroes. They cry "No segregation"—no further yielding to prejudice and race separation. Yet any planning for the benefit of American Negroes on the part of a Negro intelligentsia is going to involve organized and deliberate self-segregation. There are plenty of people in the United States who would be only too willing to use such a plan as a way to increase existing legal and customary segregation between the races. This threat which many Negroes see is no mere mirage. What of it? It must be faced.

If the economic and cultural salvation of the American Negro calls for an increase in segregation and prejudice, then that must come. American Negroes must plan for their economic future and the social survival of their fellows in the firm belief that this means in a real sense the survival of colored folk in the world and the building of a full humanity instead of a petty white tyranny. Control of their own education, which is the logical and inevitable end of separate schools, would not be an unmixed ill; it might prove a supreme good. Negro schools once meant poor schools. They need not today; they must not tomorrow. Separate Negro sections will increase race antagonism, but they will also increase economic cooperation, organized self-defense and necessary self-confidence.

The immediate reaction of most white and colored people to this suggestion will be that the thing cannot be done without extreme results. Negro thinkers have from time to time emphasized the fact that no nation within a nation can be built because of the attitude of the dominant majority, and because all legal and police power is out of Negro hands, and because large-scale industries, like steel and utilities, are organized on a national basis. White folk, on the other hand, simply say that, granting certain obvious exceptions, the American Negro has not the ability to engineer so delicate a social operation calling for such self-restraint, careful organization and sagacious leadership.

In reply, it may be said that this matter of a nation within a nation has already been partially accomplished in the organization of the Negro church, the Negro school and the Negro retail business, and, despite all the justly due criticism, the result has been astonishing. The great majority of American Negroes are divided not only for religious but for a large number of social purposes into self-supporting economic units, self-governed, self-directed. The greatest difficulty is that these organizations have no logical and reasonable standards and do not attract the finest, most vigorous and best educated Negroes. When all these things are taken into consideration it becomes clearer to more and more American Negroes that, through voluntary and increased segregation, by careful autonomy and planned economic organization, they may build so strong and efficient a unit that 12,000,000 men can no longer be refused fellowship and equality in the United States.

# III.  Marcus Garvey

# 1
## The Negro's Greatest Enemy

*"The Negro's Greatest Enemy" was printed in* Current History *18 (September 1923): 951–57. The article was published while Garvey was released on bond pending appeal of his June 18, 1923, conviction for mail fraud for activities related to the operation of the Black Star Line. This piece is presented out of chronological order because it provides an autobiographical account of Garvey's early life, immigration to the United States, and activities in this country. It also contains his explanation for events associated with the failure of the Black Star Line. This article was reprinted in Amy Jacques-Garvey, ed.,* Philosophy and Opinions of Marcus Garvey, *vol. 2 (New York: Atheneum, 1969), 124–34, and in several other books.*

This article, which is largely a chapter of autobiography, was
written by the author—the founder of the Universal Negro
Improvement Association

*Starting a movement in opposition to negroes who do not want to be negroes—
A country for the black man—
Attempts to capture the Universal Negro Improvement Association*

I WAS born in the Island of Jamaica, British West Indies, on Aug. 17, 1887. My parents were black negroes. My father was a man of brilliant intellect and dashing courage. He was unafraid of consequences. He took human chances in the course of life, as most bold men do, and he failed at the close of his career. He had a fortune; he died poor. My mother was a sober and conscientious Christian, too soft and good for the time which she lived. She was the direct opposite of my father. He was severe, firm, determined, bold and strong, refusing to yield even to superior forces if he believed he was right. My mother, on the other hand, was always willing to return a smile for a blow, and ever ready to bestow charity upon her enemy. Of this strange combination I was born thirty-six years ago, and ushered into a world of sin, the flesh and the devil.

I grew up with other black and white boys. I was never whipped by any, but made them all respect the strength of my arms. I got my education from many sources—through private tutors, two public schools, two grammar or high schools and two colleges. My teachers were men and women of varied experiences and abilities; four of them were eminent preachers. They studied me and I studied them. With some I became friendly in after years, others and I drifted apart, because as a boy they wanted to whip me, and I simply refused to be whipped. I was not made to be whipped. It annoys me to be defeated; hence to me, to be once defeated is to find cause for an everlasting struggle to reach the top.

I became a printer's apprentice at an early age, while still attending school. My apprentice master was a highly educated and alert man. In the affairs of business and the world he had no peer. He taught me many things before I reached twelve, and at fourteen I had enough intelligence and experience to manage men. I was strong and manly, and I made them respect me. I developed a strong and forceful character, and have maintained it still.

To me, at home in my early days, there was no difference between white and black. One of my father's properties, the place where I lived most of the time, was adjoining that of a white man. He had three girls and two boys; the Wesleyan minister, another white man whose church my parents attended, also had property adjoining ours. He had three girls and one boy. All of us were playmates. We romped and were happy children playmates together. The little white girl whom I liked most knew no better than I did myself. We were two innocent fools who never dreamed of a race feeling and problem. As a child, I went to school with white boys and girls, like all other negroes. We were not called negroes then. I never head the term negro used once until I was about fourteen.

At fourteen my little white playmate and I parted. Her parents thought the time had come to separate us and draw the color line. They sent her and another sister to Edinburgh, Scotland, and told her that she was never to write or try to get in touch with me, for I was a "nigger." It was then that I found for the first time that there was some difference in humanity, and that there were different races, each having its own separate and distinct social life. I did not care about the separation after I was told about it, because I never thought all during our childhood association that the girl and the rest of the children of her race were better than I was; in fact, they used to look up to me. So I simply had no regrets. I only thought them "fresh."

After my first lesson in race distinction, I never thought of playing with white girls any more, even if they might be next door neighbors. At home my sister's company was good enough for me, and at school I made friends with the colored girls next to me. White boys and I used to frolic together. We played cricket and baseball, ran races and rode bicycles together, took each other to the river and to the sea beach to learn to swim, and made boyish efforts while out in deep water to drown each other, making a sprint for shore crying out "shark, shark, shark." In all our experiences, however, only one black boy was drowned. He went under on a Friday afternoon after school hours, and his parents found him afloat half eaten by sharks on the following Sunday afternoon. Since then we boys never went back to sea.

## "You Are Black"

At maturity the black and white boys separated, and took different courses in life. I grew up then to see the difference between the races more and more. My schoolmates as young men did not know or remember me any more. Then I realized that I had to make a fight for a place in the world, that it was not so easy to pass on to office and position. Personally, however, I had not much difficulty in finding and holding a place for myself, for I was aggressive. At eighteen I had an excellent position as manager of a large printing establishment, having under my control several men old enough to be my grandfathers. But I got mixed up with public life. I started to take an interest in the politics of my country, and then I saw the injustice done to my race because it was black, and I became dissatisfied on that account. I went traveling to South and Central America and parts of the West Indies to find out if it was so elsewhere, and I found the same situation. I set sail for Europe to find out if it was different there, and again I found the same stumbling-block—"You are black." I read of the conditions in America. I read "Up From Slavery," by Booker T. Washington, and then my doom—if I may so call it—of being a race leader dawned upon me in London after I had traveled through almost half of Europe.

I asked, "Where is the black man's Government?" "Where is his King and his kingdom?" "Where is his President, his country, and his ambassador, his army, his navy, his men of big affairs?" I could not find them, and then I declared, "I will help to make them."

Becoming naturally restless for the opportunity of doing something for the advancement of my race, I was determined that the black man would not continue to be kicked about by all the other races and nations of the world, as I saw it in the West Indies, South and Central America and Europe, and as I read of it in America. My young and ambitious mind led me into flights of great imagination. I saw before me then, even as I do now, a new world of black men, not peons, serfs, dogs and slaves, but a nation of sturdy men making their impress upon civilization and causing a new light to dawn upon the human race. I could not remain in London any more. My brain was afire. There was a world of thought to conquer. I had to start ere it became too late and the work be not done. Immediately, I boarded a ship at Southampton for Jamaica, where I arrived on July 15, 1914. The Universal Negro Improvement Association and African Communities (Imperial) League was founded and organized five days after my arrival, with the program of uniting all the negro peoples of the world into one great body to establish a country and Government absolutely their own.

Where did the name of the organization come from? It was while speaking to a West Indian negro who was a passenger on the ship with me from Southampton, who was returning home to the West Indies from Basutoland with his Basuto wife, that I further learned of the horrors of native life in Africa. He related to me in conversation such horrible and pitiable tales that my heart bled within me. Retiring from the conversation to my cabin, all day and the following night I pondered over the subject matter of that conversation, and at midnight, lying flat on my back, the vision and thought came to me that I should name the organization the Universal Negro Improvement Association and African Communities (Imperial) League. Such a name I thought would embrace the purpose of all black humanity. Thus to the world a name was born, a movement created, and a man became known.

I really never knew there was so much color prejudice in Jamaica, my own native home, until I started the work of the Universal Negro Improvement Association. We started immediately before the war. I had just returned from a successful trip to Europe, which was an exceptional achievement for a black man. The daily papers wrote me up with big headlines, and told of my movement. But nobody wanted to be a negro. "Garvey is crazy; he has lost his head," "Is that the use he is going to make of his experience and intelligence?"—such were the criticisms passed upon me. Men and women as black as I, and even more so, had believed themselves white under the West Indian order of society. I was simply an impossible man to use openly the term "negro"; yet every one beneath his breath was calling the black man a negro.

I had to decide whether to please my friends and be one of the "black-whites" of Jamaica, and be reasonably prosperous, or come out openly and defend and help improve and protect the integrity of the black millions and suffer. I decided to do the latter, hence my offence against "colored-black-white" society in the colonies and America. I was openly hated and persecuted by some of these colored men of the island who did not want to be classified as negroes, but as white. They hated me worse than poison. They opposed me at every step, but I had a large number of white friends, who encouraged and helped me. Notable among them were the then Governor of the Colony, the Colonial Secretary and several other prominent men. But they were afraid of offending the "colored gentry" that were passing for white. Hence my fight had to be made alone. I spent hundreds of pounds (sterling) helping the organization to gain a footing. I also gave up all my time to the promulgation of its ideals. I became a marked man, but I was determined that the work should be done.

The war helped a great deal in arousing the consciousness of the colored people to the reasonableness of our program, especially after the British at home had rejected a large number of West Indian colored men who wanted to be officers in the British army. When they were told that negroes could not be officers in the British army they started their own propaganda, which supplemented the program of the Universal Negro Improvement Association. With this and other contributing agencies a few of the stiff-necked colored people began to see the reasonableness of my program, but they were firm in refusing to be known as negroes. Furthermore, I was a black man and therefore had absolutely no right to lead; in the opinion of the "colored" element, leadership should have been in the hands of a yellow or a very light man. On such flimsy prejudices our race has been retarded. There is more bitterness among us negroes because of the caste of color than there is between any other peoples, not excluding the people of India.

I succeeded to a great extent in establishing the association in Jamaica with the assistance of a Catholic Bishop, the Governor, Sir John Pringle, the Rev. William Graham, a Scottish clergyman, and several other white friends. I got in touch with Booker Washington and told him what I wanted to do. He invited me to America and promised to speak with me in the Southern and other States to help my work. Although he died in the Fall of 1915, I made my arrangements and arrived in the United States on March 23, 1916.

Here I found a new and different problem. I immediately visited some of the then so-called negro leaders, only to discover, after a close study of them, that they had no program, but were mere opportunists who were living off their so-called leadership while the poor people were groping in the dark. I traveled through thirty-eight States and everywhere found the same condition. I visited Tuskegee and paid my respects to the dead hero, Booker Washington, and then returned to New York, where I organized the New York division of the Universal Negro Improvement Association. After instructing the people in the aims and objects of the association, I intended returning to Jamaica to perfect the Jamaica organization, but when we had enrolled about 800 or 1,000 members in the Harlem district and had elected the officers, a few negro politicians began trying to turn the movement into a political club.

**Political Faction Fight**

Seeing that these politicians were about to destroy my ideals, I had to fight to get them out of the organization. There it was that I made my first political enemies in Harlem. They fought me until they smashed the first organization and reduced its membership to about fifty. I started again, and in two months built up a new organization of about 1,500 members. Again the politicians came and divided us into two factions. They took away all the books of the organization, its treasury and all its belongings. At that time I was only an organizer, for it was not then my intention to remain in America, but to return to Jamaica. The organization had its proper officers elected, and I was not an officer of the New York division, but President of the Jamaica branch.

On the second split in Harlem thirteen of the members conferred with me and requested me to become President for a time of the New York organization so as to save them from the politicians. I consented and was elected President. There then sprung up two factions, one led by the politicians with the books and the money, and the other led by me. My faction had no money. I placed at their disposal what money I had, opened an office for them, rented a meeting place, employed two women secretaries, went on the streets of Harlem at night to speak for the movement. In three weeks more than 2,000 new members joined. By this time I had the association incorporated so as to prevent the other faction using the name, but in two weeks the politicians had stolen all the people's money and had smashed up their faction.

The organization under my Presidency grew by leaps and bounds. I started The Negro World. Being a journalist, I edited this paper free of cost for the association, and worked for them without pay until November, 1920. I traveled all over the country for the association at my own expense, and established branches until in 1919 we had about thirty branches in different cities. By my writings and speeches we were able to build up a large organization of over 2,000,000 by June, 1919, at which time we launched the program of the Black Star Line.

To have built up a new organization, which was not purely political, among negroes in America was a wonderful feat, for the negro politician does not allow any other kind of organization within his race to thrive. We succeeded, however, in making the Universal Negro Improvement Association so formidable in 1919 that we encountered more trouble from our political brethren. They sought the influence of the District Attorney's office of the County of New York to put us out of business. Edwin P. Kilroe, at that time an Assistant District Attorney, on the complaint of the negro politicians, started to investigate us and the association. Mr. Kilroe would constantly and continuously call me to his office for investigation on extraneous matters without coming to the point. The result was that after the eighth or ninth time I wrote an article in our newspaper, The Negro World, against him. This was interpreted as criminal libel, for which I was indicted and arrested, but subsequently dismissed on retracting what I had written.

During my many tilts with Mr. Kilroe, the question of the Black Star Line was discussed. He did not want us to have a line of ships. I told him that even as there was a White Star Line, we would have, irrespective of his wishes, a Black Star Line. On June 27, 1919, we incorporated the Black Star Line of Delaware, and in September we obtained a ship.

The following month (October) a man by the name of Tyler came to my office at 56 West 135th Street, New York City, and told me that Mr. Kilroe had sent him to "get me," and at once fired four shots at me from a .38-calibre revolver. He wounded me in the right leg and the right side of my scalp. I was taken to the Harlem Hospital, and he was arrested. The next day it was reported that he committed suicide in jail just before he was to be taken before a City Magistrate.

## Record-Breaking Convention

The first year of our activities for the Black Star Line added prestige to the Universal Negro Improvement Association. Several hundred thousand dollars worth of shares were sold. Our first ship, the steamship Yarmouth, had made two voyages to the West Indies and Central America. The white press had flashed the news all over the world. I, a young negro, as President of the corporation, had become famous. My name was discussed on five continents. The Universal Negro Improvement Association gained millions of followers all over the world. By August, 1920, over 4,000,000 persons had joined the movement. A convention of all the negro peoples of the world was called to meet in New York that month. Delegates came from all parts of the known world. Over 25,000 persons packed the Madison Square Garden on Aug. 1 to hear me speak to the first International Convention of Negroes. It was a record-breaking meeting, the first and the biggest of its kind. The name of Garvey had become known as a leader of his race.

Such fame among negroes was too much for other race leaders and politicians to tolerate. My downfall was planned by my enemies. They laid all kinds of traps for me. They scattered their spies among the employes of the Black Star Line and the Universal Negro Improvement Association. Our office records were stolen. Employes started to be openly dishonest; we could get no convictions against them; even if on complaint they were held by a Magistrate, they were dismissed by the Grand Jury. The ships' officers started to pile up thousands of dollars of debts against the company without the knowledge of the officers of the corporation. Our ships were damaged at sea, and there was a general riot of wreck and ruin. Officials of the Universal Negro Improvement Association also began to steal and be openly dishonest. I had to dismiss them. They joined my enemies, and thus I had an endless fight on my hands to save the ideals of the association and carry out our program for the race. My negro enemies, finding that they alone could not destroy me, resorted to misrepresenting me to the leaders of the white race, several of whom, without proper investigation, also opposed me.

With robberies from within and from without, the Black Star Line was forced to suspend active business in December, 1921. While I was on a business trip to the West Indies in the Spring of 1921, the Black Star Line received the blow from which it was unable to recover. A sum of $25,000 was paid by one of the officers of the corporation to a man to purchase a ship, but the ship was never obtained and the money was never returned. The company was defrauded of a further sum of $11,000. Through such actions on the part of dishonest men in the shipping business, the Black Star Line received its first setback. This resulted in my being indicted for using the United States mails to defraud investors in the company. I was subsequently convicted and sentenced to five years in a Federal penitentiary. My trial is a matter of history. I know I was not given a square deal, because my indictment was the result of a "frame up" among my political and business enemies. I had to conduct my own case in court because of the peculiar position in which I found myself. I had millions of friends and a large number of enemies. I wanted a colored attorney to handle my case, but there was none I could trust. I feel that I have been denied justice because of prejudice. Yet I have an abundance of faith in the courts of America, and I hope yet to obtain justice on my appeal.

## Association's 6,000,000 Membership

The temporary ruin of the Black Star Line has in no way affected the larger work of the Universal Negro Improvement Association, which now has 900 branches with an approximate membership of 6,000,000. This organization has succeeded in organizing the negroes all over the world and we now look forward to a renaissance that will create a new people and bring about the restoration of Ethiopia's ancient glory.

Being black, I have committed an unpardonable offense against the very light colored negroes in America and the West Indies by making myself famous as a negro leader of millions. In their view, no black man must rise above them, but I still forge ahead determined to give to the world the truth about the new negro who is determined to make and hold for himself a place in the affairs of men. The Universal Negro Improvement Association has been misrepresented by my enemies. They have tried to make it appear that we are hostile to other races. This is absolutely false. We love all humanity. We are working for the peace of the world which we believe can only come about when all races are given their due.

We feel that there is absolutely no reason why there should be any differences between the black and white races, if each stop to adjust and steady itself. We believe in the purity of both races. We do not believe the black man should be encouraged in the idea that his highest purpose in life is to marry a white woman, but we do believe that the white man should be taught to respect the black woman in the same way as he wants the black man to respect the white woman. It is a vicious and dangerous doctrine of social equality to urge, as certain colored leaders do, that black and white should get together, for that would destroy the racial purity of both.

We believe that the black people should have a country of their own where they should be given the fullest opportunity to develop politically, socially and industrially. The black people should not be encouraged to remain in white people's countries and expect to be Presidents, Governors, Mayors, Senators, Congressmen, Judges and social and industrial leaders. We believe that with the rising ambition of the negro, if a country is not provided for him in another 50 or 100 years, there will be a terrible clash that will end disastrously to him and disgrace our civilization. We desire to prevent such a clash by pointing the negro to a home of his own. We feel that all well disposed and broad minded white men will aid in this direction. It is because of this belief no doubt that my negro enemies, so as to prejudice me further in the opinion of the public, wickedly state that I am a member of the Ku Klux Klan, even though I am a black man.

I have been deprived of the opportunity of properly explaining my work to the white people of America through the prejudice worked up against me by jealous and wicked members of my own race. My success as an organizer was much more than rival negro leaders could tolerate. They, regardless of consequences, either to me or to the race, had to destroy me by fair means or foul. The thousands of anonymous and other hostile letters written to the editors and publishers of the white press by negro rivals to prejudice me in the eyes of public opinion are sufficient evidence of the wicked and vicious opposition I have had to meet from among my own people, especially among the very lightly colored. But they went further than the press in their attempts to discredit me. They organized clubs all over the United States and the West Indies, and wrote both open and anonymous letters to city, State and Federal officials of this and other Governments to induce them to use their influence to hamper and destroy me. No wonder, therefore, that several Judges, District Attorneys and other high officials have been against me without knowing me. No wonder, therefore, that the great white population of this country and of the world has a wrong impression of the aims and objects of the Universal Negro Improvement Association and of the work of Marcus Garvey.

## The Struggle of the Future

Having had the wrong education as a start in his racial career, the negro has become his own greatest enemy. Most of the trouble I have had in advancing the cause of the race has come from negroes. Booker Washington aptly described the race in one of his lectures by stating that we were like crabs in a barrel, that none would allow the other to climb over, but on any such attempt all would continue to pull back into the barrel the one crab that would make the effort to climb out. Yet, those of us with vision cannot desert the race, leaving it to suffer and die.

Looking forward a century or two, we can see an economic and political death struggle for the survival of the different race groups. Many of our present-day national centres will have become overcrowded with vast surplus populations. The fight for bread and position will be keen and severe. The weaker and unprepared group is bound to go under. That is why, visionaries as we are in the Universal Negro Improvement Association, we are fighting for the founding of a negro nation in Africa, so that there will be no clash between black and white and that each race will have a separate existence and civilization all its own without courting suspicion and hatred or eyeing each other with jealousy and rivalry within the borders of the same country.

White men who have struggled for and built up their countries and their own civilizations are not disposed to hand them over to the negro or any other race without let or hindrance. It would be unreasonable to expect this. Hence any vain assumption on the part of the negro to imagine that he will one day become President of the Nation, Governor of the State, or Mayor of the city in the countries of white men, is like waiting on the devil and his angels to take up their residence in the Realm on High and direct there the affairs of Paradise.

---

# 2
## Letter to Robert Russa Moton, February 29, 1916

*This letter was sent by Marcus Garvey to Robert Russa Moton, Booker T. Washington's successor at Tuskegee, on February 29, 1916, from Jamaica shortly before Garvey's first trip to the United States. The attachment outlines Garvey's assessment of the racial situation in Jamaica. Interestingly, many of the issues that Garvey would later raise in the United States were anticipated in the difficulties he reported in Jamaica. This letter can be found in the Robert Russa Moton Papers, Hollis Burke Frissell Library, Tuskegee Institute; it was also printed in* The Marcus Garvey and Universal Negro Improvement Associa- *tion Papers, 7 vols., ed. by Robert A. Hill (Berkeley: University of California Press, 1983) 1: 177–83 (hereafter cited as* MG&UNIA *Papers). The original contained a number of hand-written corrections; these have been incorporated into the text.*

Kingston, Jamaica, Febry, 29 1916

My dear Major Moton/

As promised in my letter of yesterday's I now send you the attached com- munication which I must ask you to read and study as the honest views of a true man who believes himself called to service in the interest of his unfortunate people.

I desired an interview with you, and I also desired that my Association be honoured justly by welcoming you and Mrs. Moton to our shores, and we were making arrangements to this end, but we were discouraged by the unkindly attitude of my personal enemies who have been using their unrighteous influence to defeat the purpose of having the Association do honour to an illustrious brother. I respect very much the desire of Mr. Murray to have you spend a pleasant time here, so I calmly withdrew my intention, feeling that you will all the same appreciate the desire of the Association.

My Association was founded in Jamaica eighteen months ago immediately after my return from a long tour and study of Europe. Personally I have spent nearly every cent I possessed to found the Society and keep it alive, and I can only say that the work has been most harassing and hard generally. My Association is well appreciated by the cultured white people of the country, and in a small way they have come to my assistance to help me along. From His Excellency the Governor down, among the whites, I have been helped by kindly encouragement, and I can say that some of the most influential of them have paid us the honour of coming amongst us. His Excellency the Governor, the Colonial Secretary, Hon. H. Bryan, C.M.G., Sir John Pringle, Hon. Brig-General L.S. Blackden, all members of the Privy Council, have been our patrons on several occasions and they are still friends of the Association. The Brig-General has lectured to us, as also His Lordship Bishop J.J. Collins, S.J., His Worship the Mayor of Kingston, Hon. H.A.L. Simpson, M.L.C., Mr. R.W. Bryant, J.P. Ex-Mayor of Kingston who has visited us more than a dozen times and many other prominent dignitaries of the country. The Hon. Colonial Secretary has himself attended a function along with his wife to which he was especially invited.

Whilst we have been encouraged and helped by the cultured whites to do something to help in lifting the masses[,] the so called representative[s] of our own people have sought to draw us down and ever since they have been waging a secret campaign to that end, hence even on your coming here you will find such men parading themselves as "wolves in sheep's clothing" who are desirous of destroying the existence of a Negro Society.

I am engaged in fighting a battle with foes of my own all around, but I am prepared to fight on with the strength given me by Almighty God.

I have many large schemes on my mind for the advancement of my people that I cannot expose at the present to the public as in such a case my hope of immediate success would be defeated, as my enemies are so many, and they are ever anxious to misrepresent me. I have firstly to fund a press of our own and to get some working start so as to demonstrate my true intention.

I have on my programme the establishing of an Industrial Farm and Institute here on the lines of the Tuskegee Institute where we could teach our people on the objects of race pride, race development, and other useful subjects.

I have been planning a tour of America where I am to lecture for five months and I am hoping to leave on Thursday this week if possible or later on in next month. I intend visiting Tuskegee. Dr. Washington during his life time promised to assist me there under cover of 12th April 1915. I wanted was to have had an interview with you along with my secretaries, before I leave, if I go on Thursday, but up to now I have heard nothing definite from those to whom I have applied. If by accident I am unable to meet you here I hope to in America.

One of your experience, will readily realize what enemies in a cause mean.—They are the carrier of poison, so the "tongue" of the serpent sometimes stings without doing harm. I would really like to be able to interview you on Wednesday and I shall take the chance to call on you then so as to further explain the cause of my Association. Trusting you will enjoy your stay, With very best wishes. Yours faithfully,

Major R. Moton/ Tuskegee
Normal & Industrial Institute
"On Visit to Jamaica"

**Attachment**

30 Charles Street, Kingston,
Febry., 29th. 1916

Dear Sir,

You, being a prominent American Negro Leader, coming into a strange country, and I, being a resident here, and one who also claims the distinction of being a race leader, I think it but right that I should try to enlighten you on the conditions existing amoung our people, hence I now take the opportunity of laying before you my views on the local aspect of Negro life.

Jamaica is unlike the United States where the race question is concerned. We have no open race prejudice here, and we do not openly antagonise one another. The extremes here are not between white and black, hence we have never had a case of lynching or anything so desperate. The black people here form the economic asset of the country, they number 6 to 1 of coloured and white combined and without them in labour or general industry the country would go bankrupt.

The black people have had seventy eight years of Emancipation, but all during that time they have never produced a leader of their own, hence they have never been led to think racially but in common with the destinies of the other people with whom they mix as fellow citizens. After Emancipation, the Negro was unable to cope intellectually with his master, and per-force he had to learn at the knees of his emancipator.

He has, therefore, grown with his master's ideals, and up to today you will find the Jamaica Negro unable to think apart from the customs and ideals of his old time slave masters. Unlike the American Negro, the Jamaican has never thought of race ideals, much to his detriment, as instead of progressing generally, he has become a serf in the bulk, and a gentleman in the few.

Racial ideals do no people harm, therefore, the Jamaica Negro has done himself a harm in not thinking on racial ideals with the scattered Negroes of other climes. The coloured and white population have been thinking and planning on exclusive race ideals—race ideals which are unwritten and unspoken. The deplomacy of one race or class of people is the means by which others are outdone, hence the deplomacy of the other races prevent them leading the race question in Jamaica, a question that could have been understood and regarded without friction.

You will find the Jamaican Negro has been sleeping much to his loss, for others have gained on top of him and are still gaining.

Apparently you will think that the people here mix at the end of a great social question, but in truth it is not so. The mixture is purely circumstancial and not genuine. The people mix in business, but they do not mix in true society. The whites claim superiority, as is done all over the world, and, unlike other parts, the coloured, who ancestrially are the illigitimate off-springs of black and white claim a positive superiority over the blacks. They train themselves to believe that in the slightest shade the coloured man is above the black man and so it runs right up to white. The black man naturally is kept down at the foot of the ladder and is trampled on by all the shades above. In a small minority he pushes himself up among the others, but when he "gets there" he too believes himself other than black and he starts out to think from a white and coloured mind much to the detriment of his own people whom he should have turned back to lead out of surrounding darkness.

The black man lives directly under the white man's institutions and the influence over him is so great that he is only a play-thing in the moulder's hand. The blackman of Jamaica cannot think for himself, and because of this he remains in the bulk the dissatisfied "beast of burden." Look around and see to what proportion [t]he black man appears a gentleman in office. With a small exception the black man is not in office at all. The only sphere that he dominates in is that of the teaching profession and he dominates there because the wage is not encouraging enough for others; and even in this department the Negro has the weapon to liberate himself and make himself a man, for there is no greater weapon than education; but the educated teacher, "baby-like" in his practice, does not think apart from the written code, hence he, himself, is a slave to what is set down for him to do and no more.

If you were to go into all the offices throughout Jamaica you will not find one per cent of black clerks employed. You will find nearly all white and coloured persons including men and women; for proof please go through our Post Office, Government Offices and stores in Kingston, and you see only white and coloured men and women in positions of importance and trust and you will find the black men and women, as store-men, messengers, attendants & common servants. In the country parts you will find the same order of things. On the Estates and Plantations you will find the blackman and woman as the labourer, the coloured man as clerk and sometimes owner and the white man generally as master. White and coloured women are absent from the fields of labor. The professions are generally taken up by the white and coloured men because they have the means to equip themselves.

Whenever a black man enters the professions, he per force, thinks from a white and coloured mind, and for the time being he enjoys the apparent friendship of the classes until he is made a bankrupt or forced into difficulties which naturally causes him to be ostracised.

The entire system here is bad as affecting the Negro and the Negro of education will not do anything honestly and truly to help his brethren in the mass. Black Ministers and Teachers are moral cowards, they are too much afraid to speak to their people on the pride of race. Whenever the blackman gets money and education he thinks himself white and coloured, and he wants a white and coloured wife, and he will spend his all to get this; much to his eternal misery.

Black professionals who have gone abroad have nearly all married white women who on their arrival here leave them and return home. Others marry highly coloured women and others taking in the lessons of others refuse to marry in preference to marrying the black girls. You will find a few educated blackmen naturally having black wives but these are the sober minded ones who have taken the bad lessons home. Our black girls are taught by observation to dispise blackmen as they are naturally poor and of social discount; hence you will find a black girl willing to give herself up to any immoral suggestion of white or coloured men, and positively refusing the good attentions of a blackman at the outset.

Not until when she has been made a fool of by white and coloured before she turns back to the black man and wants him as a companion. Our morality is destroyed this way. Ninety per cent of the coloured people are off-springs of immorality, yet they rule next to the whites over the blacks.

This is shameful, but our men hav'nt the courage to stem the tide. Our ministers are funning at the "teaching of the gospel" and they have been often criticised for their inactivity in correcting vice and immorality. I am sorry I have to say this; nevertheless it is true.

The blackman here is a slave of destiny, and it is only by bold and conscientious leadership that he can emancipate, and I do trust your visit will be one of the means of helping him. I am now talking with you as a man with a mission from the High God. Your education will enable you to understand me clearly. I do not mean literary education alone, for that we have here among a goodly number of Blacks as teachers and ministers. I mean the higher education of man's appreciation for his fellowman; of man's love for his race. Our people here are purely selfish and no man or people can lead if selfishness is the cardinal principle.

One Negro here hates to see the other Negro succeed and for that he will pull him down every time he attempts to climb and defame him. The Negro here will not help one another, and they have no sympathy with one another. Ninety per cent of our people are labourers and serfs, the other ten per cent are mixed up in the professions, trades and small proprietorships. I mean the black people, not coloured or white. You look out for here carefully. We have no social order of our own we have to flatter ourselves into white and coloured society to our own disgrace and discomforture, because we are never truly appreciated. Among us we have an excess of crimes and the prison houses, alm houses, and mad houses are over crowded with our people much to the absense of the other classes.

Our prisoners are generally chained and marched through the streets of the city while on their way to the Penitentiary. You should pay a visit to the Prisons, Alms house, and Asylum to test the correctness of my statements. We have a large prison in Kingston and another one at Spanish Town. You will find Alms Houses all over the Island, but the Union Poor House is near to Kingston in St Andrew.

Our women are prostituted, and if you were to walk the lower sections of Kingston after night fall you will see hundreds of Black prostitutes in the lanes, streets and allies.

Our people in the bulk do not live in good houses, they live in "huts" and "old shanties," and you will see this as you go through the country. If you care to see this in Kingston you can visit places like Smith's Village and Hannah's Town. Our people in the bulk can't afford to wear good clothes and boots. Generally they wear rags and go bare-footed in the bulk during the week, and some change their garbs on Sundays when they go to church, but this is not general.

The people have no system of sanitation. They keep themselves dirty and if you were to mix in a crowd on a hot day you would be stifled with the bad odour. You can only see the ragged and dirty masses on alarming occassions when you will see them running from all directions. If a band of music were to parade the city then you would have a fair illustration of what I mean. Our people are not encouraged to be clean and decent because they are kept down on the lowest wage with great expences hanging over them.

Our labour get anything from nine pence (eighteen cent) 1/- (25 cents) 1/6 (36 cents) to fifty cents a day, on which they have to support a family.

This is the grinding system that keeps the blackman down here, hence I personally, have very little in common with the educated class of my own people for they are the bitterest enemies of their own race. Our people have no respect for one another, and all the respect is shown to the white and coloured people.

The reception that will be given you will not be genuine from more than one reasons which I may explain later on to you.

Black men here are never truly honoured. Don't you believe like coloured Dr. Du Bois that the "race problem is at an end here" except you want to admit the utter insignificance of the black man.

It was never started and has not yet begun. It is a paradox. I personally would like to solve the situation on the broadest humanitarian lines. I would like to solve it on the platform of Dr. Booker T. Washington, and I am working on those lines hence you will find that up to now my one true friend as far as you can rely on his friendship, is the whiteman.

I do not mean to bring any estrangement between black and white. I want to have Jamaica a country of "Black and White" all living in peace and harmony but with equal rights and opportunities.

I would not advise you to give yourself too much away to the desire and wishes of the people who are around you for they are mostly hypocrites. They mean to deceive you on the conditions here because we can never blend under the existing state of affairs—it would not be fair to the blackman.—To blend we must all in equal proportion "show our hands."

Your intellect, I believe, is too deep to be led away by "sham sentiment." Population of Jamaica White 15,605, coloured 163,201; black *630,181*, East Indian 17,380, chinese 2,111, 2,905 colour not stated. If you desire to do Jamaica a turn, you might ask those around you on public platforms to explain to what proportion the different people here enjoy the wealth and resources of the country. Impress this, and *let them answer* it *for publication*, and then you will have the whole farce in a *nut shell*. When you are travelling to the mountains parts, stop a while and observe properly the rural life of your people as against the life of others of the classes.

I have much more to say, but I must close for another time.

Again I wish you a pleasant stay. Yours in the Brotherhood,

P/S. Another condition that I would like you to observe is how our people attend church. The churches are generally crowded with women with an opposite absence of men. The women are of different classes but the majority of them are people of questionable morality who parade themselves in the garbs of vice for which the men have to pay.

---

# 3
# West Indies in the Mirror of Truth

*"West Indies in the Mirror of Truth" was printed in* Champion Magazine *1 (January 1917), 167–68. In this essay, written eight months after his arrival in the United States, Garvey viewed the progress made by African Americans in the half century following emancipation in contrast to the lack of progress among Jamaican blacks. This article was reprinted in* MG&UNIA Papers, *1: 197–201.*

I have been in America eight months. My mission to this country is to lecture and raise funds to help my organization—the Universal Negro Improvement Association of Jamaica—to establish an industrial and educational institute to assist in educating the Negro youth of that island. I am also engaged in the study of Negro life in this country.

I must say, at the outset, that the American Negro ought to compliment himself, as well as the early prejudice of the South, for the racial progress made in fifty years, and for the discriminating attitude that had led the race up to the high mark of consciousness preserving it from extinction.

I feel that the Negro who has come in touch with western civilization is characteristically the same, and but for the environment, there would have been no marked difference between those of the scattered race in the western hemisphere. The honest prejudice of the South was sufficiently evident to give the Negro of America the real start—the start with a race consciousness, which I am convinced is responsible for the state of development already reached by the race.

A Fred Douglass or a Booker Washington never would have been heard of in American national life if it were not for the consciousness of the race in having its own leaders. In contrast, the West Indies has produced no Fred Douglass, or Booker Washington, after seventy-eight years of emancipation, simply because the Negro people of that section started out without a race consciousness.

I have traveled a good deal through many countries, and from my observations and study, I unhesitatingly and unreservably say that the American Negro is the peer of all Negroes, the most progressive and the foremost unit in the expansive chain of scattered Ethiopia. Industrially, financially, educationally and socially, the Negroes of both hemispheres have to defer to the American brother, the fellow who has revolutionized history in race development inasmuch as to be able within fifty years to produce men and women out of the immediate bond of slavery, the latchets of whose shoes many a "favored son and daughter" has been unable to loose.

As I travel through the various cities I have been observing with pleasure the active part played by Negro men and women in the commercial and industrial life of the nation. In the cities I have already visited, which include New York, Boston, Philadelphia, Pittsburgh, Baltimore, Washington and Chicago, I have seen commercial enterprises owned and managed by Negro people. I have seen Negro banks in Washington and Chicago, stores, cafes, restaurants, theaters and real estate agencies that fill my heart with joy to realize, in positive truth, and not by sentiment, that at one center of Negrodom, at least, the people of the race have sufficient pride to do things for themselves.

The acme of American Negro enterprise is not yet reached. You have still a far way to go. You want more stores, more banks, and bigger enterprises. I hope that your powerful Negro press and the conscientious element among your leaders will continue to inspire you to achieve; I have detected, during my short stay, that even among you there are leaders who are false, who are mere self-seekers, but on the other hand, I am pleased to find good men and, too, those whose fight for the uplift of the race is one of life and death. I have met some personalities who are not prominently in the limelight for whom I have a strong regard as towards their sincerity in the cause of race uplift, and I think more of their people as real disciples working for the good of our race than many of the men whose names have become nationally and internationally known. In New York, I met John E. Bruce, a man for whom I have the strongest regard inasmuch as I have seen in him a true Negro, a man who does not talk simply because he is in a position for which he must say or do something, but who feels honored to be a member. I can also place in this category Dr. R.R. Wright, Jr., Dr. Parks, vice-president of the Baptist Union, and Dr. Triley of the M.E. church of Philadelphia, the Rev. J.C. Anderson of Quinn Chapel and Mrs. Ida Wells Barnett of Chicago. With men and women of this type, who are conscientious workers and not mere life service dignitaries, I can quite understand that the time is at hand when the stranger, such as I am, will discover the American Negro firmly and strongly set on the pinnacle of fame.

The West Indian Negro who has had seventy-eight years of emancipation has nothing to compare with your progress. Educationally, he has, in the exception, made a step forward, but generally he is stagnant. I have discovered a lot of "vain bluff" as propagated by the irresponsible type of West Indian Negro who has become resident of this country—bluff to the effect that conditions are better in the West Indies than they are in America. Now let me assure you, honestly and truthfully, that they are nothing of the kind. The West Indies in reality could have been the ideal home of the Negro, but the sleeping West Indian has ignored his chance ever since his emancipation, and today he is at the tail end of all that is worth while in the West Indies. The educated men are immigrating to the United States, Canada and Europe; the laboring element are to be found by the thousands in Central and South America. These people are leaving their homes simply because they haven't pride and courage enough to stay at home and combat the forces that make them exiles. If we had the spirit of self-consciousness and reliance, such as you have in America, we would have been ahead of you, and today the standard of Negro development in the West would have been higher. We haven't the pluck in the West Indies to agitate for or demand a square deal and the blame can be attributed to no other source than idolence and lack of pride among themselves.

Let not the American Negro be misled; he occupies the best position among all Negroes up to the present time, and my advice to him is to keep up his constitutional fight for equity and justice.

The Negroes of the West Indies have been sleeping for seventy-eight years and are still under the spell of Rip Van Winkle. These people want a terrific sensation to awaken them to their racial consciousness. We are throwing away good business opportunities in the beautiful islands of the West. We have no banks of our own, no big stores and commercial undertakings; we depend on others as dealers while we remain consumers. The file is there open and ready for anyone who has the training and ability to become a pioneer. If enterprising Negro Americans would get hold of some of the wealthy Negroes of the West Indies and teach them how to trade and to do things in the interest of their people, a great good would be accomplished for the advancement of the race.

The Negro masses in the West Indies want enterprises that will help them to dress as well as the Negroes in the North of the United States; to help them to live in good homes and to provide them with furniture on the installment plan; to insure them in sickness and health and to prevent a pauper's grave.

---

# 4

## Editorials in *Negro World:* "Advice of the Negro to Peace Conference" and "Race Discrimination Must Go"

*Garvey wrote two editorials, "Advice of the Negro to Peace Conference" and "Race Discrimination Must Go," which he published in* Negro World, *November 30, 1918. In these essays Garvey defined his international perspective on the race issue and introduced his argument that the next world war will be a race war between whites, blacks, and Asians. These editorials were also printed in MG&UNIA Papers 1: 302–305.*

### Advice of the Negro to Peace Conference

Now that the statesmen of the various nations are preparing to meet at the Peace Conference, to discuss the future government of the peoples of the world, we take it as our bounden duty to warn them to be very just to all those people who may happen to come under their legislative control. If they, representing the classes, as they once did, were alive to the real feeling of their respective masses four and one-half years ago, today Germany would have been intact, Austria-Hungary would have been intact, Russia would have been intact, the spirit of revolution never would have swept Europe, and mankind at large would have been satisfied. But through graft, greed and selfishness, the classes they represented then, as some of them represent now, were determined to rob and exploit the masses, thinking that the masses would have remained careless of their own condition for everlasting.

It is a truism that you "fool half of the people for half of the time, but you cannot fool all of the people for all of the time"; and now that the masses of the whole world have risen as one man to demand true equity and justice from the "powers that be," then let the delegates at the Peace Conf[e]rence r[e]alize, just now, that the Negro, who forms an integral part of the masses of the world, is determined to get no less than what other men are to get. The oppressed races of

Europe are to get their freedom, which freedom will be guaranteed them. The Asiatic races are to get their rights and a larger modicum of self-government.

We trust that the delegates to the Peace Conference will not continue to believe that Negroes have no ambition, no aspiration. There are no more timid, cringing Negroes; let us say that those Negroes have now been relegated to the limbo of the past, to the region of forgetfulness, and that the new Negro is on the stage, and he is going to play his part good and well. He, like the other heretofore oppressed peoples of the world, is determined to get restored to him his ancestral rights.

When we look at the map of Africa today we see Great Britain with fully five million square miles of our territory, we see France with fully three million five hundred thousand square miles, we see that Belgium has under her control the Congo, Portugal has her sway over Southeast Africa, Italy has under her control Tripoli, Italian Somaliland on the Gulf of Aden and Erythria on the Red Sea. Germany had clamored for a place in the sun simply because she had only one million square miles, with which she was not satisfied, in that England had five millions and France three millions five hundred thousand. It can be easily seen that the war of 1914 was the outcome of African aggrandizement, that Africa, to which the white man has absolutely no claim, has been raped, has been left bleeding for hundreds of years, but within the last thirty years the European powers have concentrated more than ever on the cleaning up of that great continent so as to make it a white man's country. Among those whom they have killed are millions of our people, but the age of killing for naught is passed and the age of killing for something has come. If black men have to die in Africa or anywhere else, then they might as well die for the best of things, and that is liberty, true freedom and true democracy. If the delegates to the Peace Conference would like to see no more wars we would advise them to satisfy the yellow man's claims, the black man's claims and the white man's claims, and let all three be satisfied so that there can be indeed a brotherhood of men. But if one section of the human race is to arrogate to itself all that God gave for the benefit of mankind at large, then let us say human nature has in no way changed, and even at the Peace Conference where from the highest principles of humanity are supposed to emanate there will come no message of peace.

There will be no peace in the world until the white man confines himself politically to Europe, the yellow man to Asia and the black man to Africa. The original division of the earth among mankind must stand, and any one who dares to interfere with this division creates only trouble for himself. This division was made by the Almighty Power that rules, and therefore there can be no interference with the plans Divine.

Cowardice has disappeared from the world. Men have died in this world war so quickly and so easily that those who desire liberty today do not stop to think of death, for it is regarded as the price which people in all ages will have to pay to be free; that is the price the weaker people of Europe have paid; that is the price the Negro must pay some day.

Let the Peace Conference, we suggest, be just in its deliberations and in its findings, so that there can be a true brotherhood in the future with no more wars.

## Race Discrimination Must Go

At last the darker peoples of the world have started out to make their united demands on Occidental civilization. The world war will not have been waged in vain if the principal peace aim of Japan, representing the interests of the races who are discriminated against in the world, is upheld.

The Universal Negro Improvement Association and African Communities' League of the World, on the night of November 10, held a mass convention of American, West Indian and African Negroes in the Palace Casino, at which the Negro's peace aims were formulated and adopted, and on the Monday following cabled to Europe for circulation all over the world. But a few days after the Japanese press picked up the sentiment of the peace aims of the Negro and embodied one of the principal clauses in their declaration "That racial discrimination throughout the world shall be abolished." The report that comes from Tokio, bearing date of November 10, is as follows: "Japanese newspapers are suggesting that Japan and China raise the race question at the forthcoming Peace Conference with the object of seeking an agreement to the effect that in the future there shall be no further racial discrimination throughout the world." Another report from Japan, bearing date of November 21, says that Japan is coaching China how to enter the Peace Conference.

This report is very suggestive. In it can be seen immediate preparation by the yellow man of Asia for the new war that is to be wagered—the war of the races. This is no time for the Negro to be found wanting in anything. He must prepare himself, he must be well equipped in every department, so that when the great clash comes in the future he can be ready wherever he is to be found. Japan has become the acknowledged leader of the yellow races: the white races are already leading themselves; the Negro must now concentrate on his leadership, casting all his strength there, so that whenever the world again becomes disrupted he can be led into the affray under the leadership which will lead him on to real democracy. It is impossible for the world to change itself in a day through human agencies, and since human nature has not changed, it can be seen plainly that there will be many more wars before mankind will be at peace.

We hope Japan will succeed in impressing upon her white brothers at the Peace Conference the essentiality of abolishing racial discrimination. If she does not succeed, then it will be only the putting off of a thing that must come, only that it could have come about easier in peaceful settlement than by disruption among the races.

# 5
## George Cross Van Dusen to J. Edgar Hoover, March 19, 1921

*As early as 1918 Garvey attracted the attention of the United States government. He was placed under surveillance by the State Department, military intelligence, and the Federal Bureau of Investigation. The following material was sent by George Cross Van Dusen of the U.S. Military Intelligence Division of the War Department to J. Edgar Hoover, of the Federal Bureau of Investigation, on March 19, 1921. This report chronicles Garvey's background and his political activities in the United States. Emphasis is placed on his reported advocacy of racial violence in speeches he gave between 1918 and 1921. The ellipses reproduced here appear in the original document. This letter is located in the National Archives, Records of the Federal Bureau of Investigation, File BS 198940–107; it was also reprinted in* MG&UNIA Papers, *3: 255–60.*

**Marcus Garvey: Information Exclusively from the Files of the Military Intelligence Division and State Department**

*Personal History*

Marcus Garvey was born in St. Ann's Bay, Jamaica, 1887 and lived on the island for twenty years attending the Church of England school although a Roman Catholic. He learned the printing trade and followed it for years until he went abroad, although he had the reputation of never sticking to one job long. He attended [Birkbeck] College in England graduating in 1913. He travelled in England, France and the Central European countries, returning to Jamaica shortly after graduating from [Birkbeck]. While abroad he conceived his idea of organizing the Negro Improvement Society. On his return to Jamaica he organized, together with his sweetheart Amy Ashwood, the Jamaica Improvement Association which appears to have been a sort of Forum for the agitation of Negro questions. Garvey acquired debts he could not pay and moved from place to place finally leaving for Port Limón, Costa Rica, coming to New York in 1916. He arrived penniless and devoted himself at once to matters affecting his race. He announced himself to be Marcus Gar[ve]y Jr. of the Jamaica Improvement Association, Kingston, Jamaica, W.I. and collected some money for schools to be established on the Island for colored girls. He posed as a Roman Catholic, securing the use of their churches to lecture in, acquiring the confidence of colored people and even their financial support and that of the Catholic

Church. The schools were never built. At the same time he started his soap box campaign for the "back to Africa" idea and for the Negro control of the continent. He next raised "a large sum of money" to build a school for colored children in New York to teach them anti-white ideas. The school was never built. He obtained loans to start a negro daily paper and then bought out "The Negro World," a weekly. Until June 1919 he was about bankrupt and had seven "convictions" for non-payment of wages.

He then launched his "Black Star Navigation Co" project and began raising money to build ships to be controlled by a negro company, manned by negroes, run to Africa and to carry negro made goods.

## Form of Early Propaganda, and His Change of Attitude

Before leaving Jamaica he agitated the establishment of a negro industrial school which did not materialize but after his arrival in the United States he changed his form of agitation and took the attitude that industrial education would merely mean the eternal submission of the black to the white race and that complete independence of the black race from the white was the only object to be sought for.

He even went so far as to denounce the Pope to the Catholic colored people as it meant the submission to the white race in religious matters.

His popularity was greatly heightened after the formation of the Universal Negro Improvement Association by the organization of the Black Star Navigation Company and the Negro Factories Company.

## Black Star Navigation Company

This is a Delaware corporation with an authorized capital of [$]10,000,000 divided into 2,000,000 five dollar shares. He and a corps of promoters have been active selling the stock among negroes and have been extravagant in their statements as to [what] the company has accomplished and what it is to do. They [have] three ships; two small [steamers] and one small Hudson River excursion boat. They have been in continuous trouble and litigation, the Yarmouth which is the largest, having been libeled and all the boats requiring extensive repairs.

Trade with the West Indies is to be established and then a line of passenger and freight steamers operated to Africa.

Garvey claims two trips have been made by his ships to the West Indies but the only clear record of a trip is the start made by the Yarmouth for Cuba with a cargo of liquor in 1920(?)[.] The ship sprung a leak and was towed into Norfolk and libeled for extensive repairs and towage charges. The Hudson [R]iver boat was used as an excursion steamer during the convention of negroes in New York in 1920.

Garvey and his Black Star Navigation Company have been in trouble twice for stock selling in violation of state laws, once in Illinois where Garvey was arrested and fined $100.00 [ ... ] and costs for selling stock without a license and once in Virginia where he had applied for a license to sell stock and it was denied because his representative had already sold stock (about $5,000) around Norfolk. The Post Office Department states that there had been no violation of the postal laws.

### Negro Factories Company

This is a corporation with an authorized capital of a million dollars. Its purpose is to stimulate the manufacture of any article of trade by negroes by the production of which the economic status of the negro race can be improved.

### Universal Negro Improvement Association

Little information is contained in the M.I.D. files as to the actual organization of this association. It is essentially a propaganda agency through which Garvey carries on his agitation. Its official publication is the Negro World. I will not go into detail in regard to the Negro Factories Company, the Universal Negro Improvement Association or the Negro World as they are fully covered by Department of Justice files.

### Criminal Record of Garvey

I find no record of Garvey's ever having been convicted of a felony in or out of the United States. Mention has been made above of his having been in trouble because of stock selling on behalf of the Black Star Navigation Company in violation of the laws of Illinois and Virginia. He has been the defendant in numerous civil actions arising out of debts he contracted and it is reported he was found guilty of criminal libel on August 28, 1919 in New York in an action brought by District Attorney Kilroe based on an article published in the Negro World. I have also heard this action was compromised out of court and never went to trial.

### Recent References

The following two recent references to the activities of Garvey are of interest:—

1. Under date of January 21, 1921 the Intelligence Officer at Governor's Island writes as follows:—

Cyril V. Briggs, Editor of the "Crusader," when interviewed by an operative of the M.I.D. states in regard to Garvey that the racial question from a radical point of view was progressing very favorably. The Universal Negro Improvement Association has a membership of 600,000 and while not as radical as he

(Briggs) would wish still is doing good work. Says Garvey has done good by arousing negroes out of their lethargy and making them realize their power. Says Negro World has a circulation of 40,000 and that Garvey gets a good income from it.

[File] 10218–412

2. An article in the New York Call of March [1]9, 1921:—

Garvey is reported in Havana, March 8th as agitating among Cuban negroes despite the disapproval of the Cuban Government to "fight and die for liberty." Government objections merely passive and based on fear of race friction. Garvey said to intend touring the West Indies.

### *Extracts from his Speeches*

He has advocated that for every negro lynched in the south, the negro ought to lynch a white in the north. This statement is reported as made at a mass meeting held by the Universal Negro Improvement Association in Harlem, New York, December 1918. At this meeting, he also preached that the next war would be between the negro and the whites, and with Japan's assistance, the negro will win. He has frequently stated that the balance of power in the wars to come will be the negro.

[File] 10218–261–53

Extracts from Garvey's address at Bethel A.M.E. Church, Baltimore, Maryland, December 18, 1918:

"We, like Josephus Daniels, believe that the next world war will be a war of the races, and I believe that that war will start between the white and the yellow peoples. Negroes should make no compromise with either the white men or the yellow men. We have become the balance of power between the white men of Europe and the yellow men of Asia.

"Can die on the battlefields of France and Flanders to give liberty to an alien race and cannot die somewhere to give liberty to himself.

"Out of this war we have produced the American, or the West Indian, or the African Napoleon who will ultimately lead the 400,000,000 black people of the world to Victory.

"Must organize to know what we are to get out of the next war and see that we get it before one sacrifice is made."

[File] 10218–261–38

"A big reunion of negroes of America, Africa, the West Indies, South and Central America and Canada, the biggest ever staged in the United States of America" was widely advertised to be held in Carnegie Hall Monday night,

August 25th, 1919, attracting the attention of Assistant District Attorney Archibald Stephenson, of counsel for the Lusk Committee, who attended with detectives of the Bomb Squad and stenographers who took notes of the speeches. It is expected that action will be taken against Garvey for he had previously promised the District Attorney to sell no more shares in the Black Star Line, and to "tone down" his public utterances. Garvey's speech in part was as follows:

"Within the next few months our organization will be in such condition that if there is a lynching in the South and a white man cannot be held to account down there, the button will be pushed here and a white man in New York will be lynched. . . . Shall continue the war until we get democracy. Woe betide the man or nation which stands in the way of the negro. The negro shed his blood in the great war and that same blood will continue to be sacrificed until we get the rights we demand. We are striving to make Africa a republic, and the white man here harries us in this plan. In America and England the negroes are asked by the white man 'What are you doing here?' The negro in Africa will soon ask the white man, 'What are you doing here?' We are out to get what belongs to us politically, economically, socially and in every other way. . . . The white man is the barrier to a black republic in Africa, and it is for his interest to clear out of there. . . . [We] are not Bolshevik, I.W.W., Democratic, Republican, or Socialists, we are pro-negro and our fight is for the new negro race, that is to be."

File 10218–344–3

Address Peop[le']s Church, 16th and Chris[tian] Sts., Phila. September 22, 191[9].

"The masses are going to rule. The few little despots and robbers who used to run the world are now being sent to their graves, and before another ten years roll by all of them will be buried by the hands of the masses."

[File] 10218–304–7

The following letter from Marcus Garvey, dated Chicago, Oct. 1st, and addressed to Fellowmen of the Negro Race, was published in the "Negro World" issue of Oct. 11, 1919 under the caption "Black Men All Over the World Should Prepare to Protect Themselves"—"Negroes Should Match Fire with Hell Fire.". . .

[File] 10218–364–13

At a meeting at Liberty Hall, New York on February 1, 1920, Garvey said:

"We are engaged in a great warfare. It is a fight that must be fought to the finish; it is a fight that will take the last drop of blood of some of us, but we are

prepared to give it. . . . So, in conclusion, I adjure you to be courageous, I ask
that you continue the fight. Cease not until victory comes."

[File] 10218–364–22

## Suggestions

John E. Bruce of Bruce and Franklin, publishers of negro literature 2109 Madison Avenue, New York should be interviewed as to Garvey's statements as he
has followed Garvey's activities for some time and is opposed to his plans for
the future of his race.

Bruce should be especially interrogated in regard to Garvey's having left
Jamaica with "several hundred pounds" he had collected for a school there and
which he appropriated for his own use.

This could perhaps be connected up with his other fake school projects for
which he raised money in the United States.

It would seem as though an investigation of the affairs of the Black Star
Navigation Company would develop a violation of the postal laws.

There is, in addition, the possibility of violation of the Mann Act on the part
of Garvey which seems to be more than merely suggested by the Justice files.

## State Department File

J. E. H. please refer to my confidential memorandum to you on this subject dated
March 19, 1921.

GEO. C. VAN DUSEN

---

# 6
# Address to the New York City Division of the UNIA,
# January 26, 1919

*This speech was presented by Marcus Garvey to the New York Division of the
UNIA on January 26, 1919, and printed in* Negro World, *February 1, 1919.
Garvey remarked on his vision of the world that would emerge out of the Versailles peace conference. Ellipses indicate material that was missing or was
indecipherable in the newspaper report of the speech. This material is reprinted
in* MG&UNIA Papers *1: 353–57.*

**Marcus Garvey at the Crescent Hall Big Meeting of New York
Division of Universal Negro Improvement Association—
Many New Members Added to Movement**

Last Sunday the New York Division of the Universal Negro Improvement Association met in their hall at 36–38 West 135th street, at 3 o'clock P.M., in regular session. There was a large attendance of officers and members. Among those present were Mr. Marcus Garvey, president; Miss Janie Jenkins, president of the Ladies' Division; Mr. George Tobias, second vice-president; Mr. W. Wells, third vice-pres[id]ent; Miss Irene Wingfield, first vice-president of the Ladies' Division; Mrs. Hannah Nicholas, second vice-president; Mrs. G. Woodford, third vice-president; Mr. James E. Linton, treasurer; Rev. John T. Wilkins, executive secretary; Mr. Cecil Hope, general secretary; Miss May Clarke, associate lady secretary; Mr. G. Cox, secretary general of the parent body, and Mr. J.E. Johnson, high chancellor.

The meeting was opened by the singing of the hymn, "Fr[o]m Greenland's Icy Mountains," after which the prayer of the association was read. The minutes were also read and confirmed. The next item on the agenda for the day was the address of the president. He took as his theme a passage from the speech made by President Wilson before the Peace Conference on the topic of the League of Nations. The following is the passage:

**"The select c[l]asses of mankind are no longer the governors of mankind. The fortunes of mankind are now in the hands of the plain people of the whole world. Satisfy them and you have justified their confidence not only, but established peace. Fail to satisfy them, and no arrangement that you can make will either set up or steady the peace of the world."**—President Wilson to the Congress.

Mr. Garvey said President Wilson had become the spokesman of the Socialist party of the world. The passage is read by him he interpreted to be a direct compromise with Socialistic ideas. Those ideas which are now laying hold on the minds of the masses of white people all over the world. Indeed, to him, he said, the President was speaking the language of the people. He could not do better because it had been plainly demonstrated by the many upheavals in Europe and the uprisings abroad that the millions of toilers of all countries were not prepared to entrust their fortunes to any select group within their own nations. The aristocracy that once ruled the common people must be destroyed according to the will of the common people. They have started to destroy that privileged aristocracy in Russia, in Germany, in Austro-Hungary, and there is every indication that within the next ten years Great Britain will be swept by this threatening revolution. The equality of man has become indisputable. There can be but one . . . today and that is labor. The aristocracy of privilege. . . . to defeat, and the President . . . this, is endeavoring to save his class the world over. Hence, this significant passage that can be interpreted as rank Socialism. By the declaration of the President before the Peace Conference, it can easily be seen that labor has forced his hands. It has also forced the hands of David Lloyd George and will eventually force the hands of every statesman in Europe.

To his way of thinking, he believes Gompers to be a greater force in American national life than even President Wilson, because Gompers stands out as the exponent of labor, and labor is determined to bring about a change, caring not what the cost may be, and every intelligent observer can see that that change is bound to occur except a compromise is made with labor before hand. It is this compromise that President Wilson is endeavoring to effect why he has so openly declared himself. How is it that labor has become such a force in the world? Can you not remember, ladies and gentlemen, that some years ago trades unionism was regarded as an impracticable thing? Can you not remember in the years gone by when a few men used to strike for higher wages and they were turned down by their employers and forced to accept their conditions? How is it that this change has come about then? It is because people who were imbued with the ideal of trades unionism years ago stuck to it. They were determined to fight their battles until victory came. It took them years, it took them decades, but today the victory is theirs. All has been accomplished through organization. Organization is the force that rules the world. It is that force that has changed the destiny of governments and of races. This, therefore, is a fair example to us as Negroes, that if we are to impose our wills on the powers that be, we must be as solidly organized as labor is today. If the Negro peoples of the world were organized as labor in America is organized among the whites, as it is organized in England and in France, simultaneously the President would have declared on behalf of African emancipation when he, without any reserve, made it known to his compatriots in the Peace Conference that the fortunes of mankind were now in the hands of the plain people of the whole world, who, in other words, are called workers.

I am somewhat persuaded to believe that the Negro has lost his premier chance through unpreparedness in this present war, but there is still another chance for him which, to my mind, will be in the next conflict that is sure to come. It is because I would like to see my people taking advantage of that chance when it again presents itself why I am today preparing your minds not only in America but all over the world, so that at the psychological moment as the opportunity presents itself, we may universally move as if we were one to bring home to us those things we have longed for.

What impression President Wilson is able to make on the toiling masses I am not prepared to say. But this I do know, that the masses of workers all over the world have bec[o]me so educated out of this bloody war that it takes more than a superman to infringe on their right without their detecting it. I do not mean to say by this . . . President has not spoken with the conviction of truth as touching the [workers] of the world, but from past experiences, peoples who have suffered, classes that have suffered must perforce become suspicious of anything coming from the opposite classes. For instance, D[a]vid Lloyd George[,] the Premier of England during the election of 1912, made great promises to the Irish people. Home rule for Ireland was practically written on the statutes of England, and up to now those people have not gained their freedom. Can the Irishman still continue to have confidence in English professions. I hardly believe that there is an Irishman in any part of the world who would lead himself to believe that the English statesman of today, when he speaks, means any good of Ireland. [As] the Irishman is suspicious of the man who has suppressed him for hundreds of years, so are the workers suspicious of the class that has kept him down for centuries. So when any one from within that class speaks in the language of the workers, it suggests that there may be enthusiasm over the declarations, but not a whole-hearted confidence.

As far as Negroes are concerned, there is absolutely no one, no nation, or no race that they can place their confidence in. We have listened to the various statesmen of the world for long enough and they have said nothing and done nothing to encourage us in the belief that they mean to be fair to our race. From the great centres of civilization news ha[s] come and are still coming which enlighten us of the fact that there can be no abiding peace until all oppression has been removed from the people. That is the fiat of the working classes of Europe. It is the fiat of the working classes of America. And all these white people mean to pay the cost of the realization of their object even by their very lives. As Negroes, we have not yet set ourselves a determination. It is because we have never been determined on any one thing or our own good why we are ignored in the world today, but as soon as we fall in line with the radical changes determined to impose our will for the sake of emancipating ourselves, then we will become a great force to be reckoned with. What other men in other ages of the race have failed to do, let us, as the Universal Negro Improvement Association and African Communities' League of the World, do today. Let us rededicate ourselves to the cause of bleeding Africa and scattered Ethiopia. Let us stretch our hands across to the brother wherever he be and say to him, even in the language of the white man of the past, "You are one of us and we must rise or fall together." Europe, when she becomes again settled, will rise and fall as she originated. Asia will rise and fall as she originated. So must Africa rise and fall as she was originated.

Let us not lose sight of the fact that as scattered children of the bleeding Fatherland, we owe a responsibility that is not light and the quicker we get to realize it, the better it will be.

At the close of Mr. Garvey's address several persons joined the association. The association meets at 3 o'clock every Sunday and at 8:15 on Wednesday and Friday nights of every week.

# 7

## Address to UNIA Supporters in Philadelphia, October 21, 1919

*Marcus Garvey presented this speech in Philadelphia on October 21, 1919, during a campaign to recruit new members and establish new chapters of the UNIA. In this address Garvey detailed his maturing political and racial philosophy, including his conviction that African Americans have no future in the United States. This speech was printed in* Negro World, *November 1, 1919. Some of the original headlines have been abbreviated. Ellipses indicate material missing or material that was indecipherable in the newspaper report of the speech. This speech is also printed in* MG&UNIA Papers *2: 89–98.*

**Hon. Marcus Garvey, Foremost Orator of the Race, Delivers Brilliant Speech in Philadelphia—Big Success for Universal Negro Improvement Association**

Last night the People's Church, corner of Fifteenth and Christian street, was the scene of wild enthusiasm, when the Honorable Marcus Garvey, president-general of the Universal Negro Improvement Association and president of the Black Star Line Steamship Corporation, appeared to speak. Mr. Garvey opened a campaign here last Sunday which opening was very successful. Thousands jammed the church, and thousands were turned away unable to get admittance.

*Mr. Garvey's Speech*

Mr. President, Lady President, Ladies and Gentlemen: Once more it is my pleasure to be with you. That you have turned out in such large numbers tonight proves beyond the shadow of a doubt that you good people of the race in Philadelphia are very much alive to the principles, to the aims, to the objects of the greatest movement among Negroes in the world today—the Universal Negro Improvement Association and African Communities League. It is the greatest movement in the world, because it is the only movement today that is causing the white man to tremble in his shoes. (Cheers.) The white man has had the policies of our great men or the great leaders of the past. They have had the policies of Booker Washington, they have had the policies of the other great leaders of this country, of the West Indies and of Africa, but out of these policies nothing ever came to the Negro, and the white man was satisfied. They have buried our great leader in America, Booker Washington, and yet we have achieved nothing by way of our own initiative. They have buried the great leaders of the Negro race of other countries, and yet we have achieved nothing, except in the Republic of Haiti, where one Negro repelled them and established an independent republic. I speak of Haiti. They did not like Toussaint L'O[u]verture because he had initiative. They lied to him, they deceived him, and when he had just a little faith still in them they destroyed that faith. They made a prisoner of him, took him to France, and there he died. Thank God, as Toussaint L'Ouverture in his time was able to inspire the other men of his country to carry on the work until Haiti was made a free country, so today we have inspired not one, not two, but hundreds of thousands to carry out the work even if they imprison one or kill one.

It is for me to say to you faithful members and followers of the Universal Negro Improvement Association in Philadelphia that the movement that you are in is a movement that is causing not merely the individual white man, but governments to be living in fear as touching the outcome of the Negro peoples of the world through their determination in the Universal Negro Improvement Association.

### Thousands Jammed Hall

Last night, after I was through addressing my people in New York, about 5,000 of them jammed themselves into Liberty Hall, overtaxing the capacity of that building, and we had to turn away about 10,000, and there were fully 3,000 around the building, trying to get in last night. The biggest meeting we ever had in Harlem was last night, when we had fully between twenty and thirty thousand Negroes trying to get into Liberty Hall. After I was through addressing the good people there, one of the members brought me a letter he had received from his friend in Panama. They did not know that the Universal Negro Improvement Association has secret service men all over the world now, and the letter said that just two hours before he read a cable which was sent by the Canal Commission in Panama beseeching Washington not to give a passport to Marcus Garvey to visit Panama, because if he landed there, there would be trouble for the white man there. Now, you know who are the people who are controlling the Panama Canal under this administration. They are Southern white men. The chicken is going home to roost. We told those Southern crackers that one day the Negro would get even with them. You see how cowardly they are. Now, I am quite away in New York and they are begging the people here not to let me get out of New York to go there. But to show you how puzzled they are: My District Attorney friend in New York has been trying for many months to get me expelled from the country. Some want me to go and some don't want me to go. What must I do? To my mind, it is a question of being between hell and the powder house. (Laughter.)

### Ancient Foe Puzzled

Now, that is what we can compliment ourselves for today. We have our foe, our ancient foe, puzzled. He does not know what to do with the New Negro; but the

New Negro knows what to do with himself. And the thing that we are going to do is to blast a way to complete independence and to that democracy which they denied us even after we left the battlefields of France and Flanders. We, the New Negroes, say there is no turning back for us now. There is nothing else but a going forward, and if they squeal in America or anywhere else we are going forward. Why, we are not organized as four hundred millions yet, and they are so scared. Now, what will happen in the next five years when the entire four hundred millions will have been organized? All the lynching in the South will be a thing of the past. We are determined in this association to bring the white man to his senses. We are not going to fight and kill anybody because he has more than we have. But if there is anybody taking advantage of the Negro, whether he be white, red or blue, we are going to organize to stop him. We believe that white men have as much right to live as yellow men; we believe that yellow men have as much right to live as red men; we believe red men have as much right to live as black men, and we believe that black men have as much right to live as all men. Therefore, if any race of mankind says that the other race must die, it is time for that race that is dying to organize to prevent themselves from dying. And as for me, the sweetest life in the world to me is the life of my race. I cannot change my race overnight. You cannot change your race overnight. We have not been able to change our race for three hundred years. No one can change our race overnight. God created us what we are and we are going to remain what we are until Gabriel blows his horn.

Therefore we are of the Negro race and we are suffering simply because we are of the Negro race, and, since we are four hundr[e]d million strong, it is for us to organize that strong to protect our race. And I want you young men, you middle aged men and you old men of the race and women also to realize that this is the age of action—action on the part of each and every individual of every race. If there is a white man who does not love the white race, to his race he is an outcast; if there is a yellow man that does not love his race, to the yellow race he is an outcast: if there is a Negro who does not love the black race, to his race such a Negro is an outcast and should be trampled to death.

*Farce of Brotherhood*

We have lived upon the farce of brotherhood for hundreds of years, and if there is anybody who has suffered from that farce it is the Negro. The white man goes forth with the Bible and tells us that we are all brothers, but it is against the world to believe, against all humanity to believe, that really there is but one brotherhood. And if there are six brothers in any family, at least those six brothers from natural tie ought to be honest in their dealings with each other to the extent of not seeing any of the six starve. If one has not a job, naturally the others would see to it that the one that is out of a job gets something to eat and a place to sleep so as to prevent him from starving and dying. This is brotherhood. Now there is one brother with all the wealth; he has more than he wants, and there is the other brother. What is he doing to the other brother? He is murdering the other brother. He is lynching the other brother, and still they are brothers. Now, if I have any brother in my family who has no better love for me than to starve me, to whip me and to burn me, I say, brother, I do not want your relationship at all. To hell with it.

No, sir, I strike against the idea of brotherhood as coming from that man. I believe in the brotherhood of man. I believe in the fatherhood of God, but as man sinned and lost his purpose ever since the fall of Adam and Eve, I also realize that man has lost his closest connection, his closest tie, with his God. And since man is human, since man has lost his instinct divine, I am not going to trust man. From the attitude of man, from the action of man today, I can see that every one is looking out for himself where the question of race comes in. The white race is looking out for the white race; the yellow race is looking out for the yellow race or Asiatic race. The time has come when the Negro should look out for himself and let the others look out for themselves. This is the new doctrine today. It is the doctrine of Europe. Europe is looking out for the white man. It is the doctrine of Asia. Asia is looking out for the yellow man. So should Africa look out for the black man, the Negro. And since they (the whites) have divided up Africa, having a part in America, a part in Canada, a part in the West Indies, a part in Central America, a part in South America and a part remaining in Africa, we are saying that the time has come that there should be a united Africa. And before a united Africa comes, Ethiopia, as scattered as she is, must stretch forth her hands unto God.

*Time to Help Self*

Tonight the Universal Negro Improvement Association is endeavoring to teach Negroes that the time has come for them to help themselves. We have helped the white man in this Western Hemisphere for over three hundred years until he has become so almighty that he respects not even God himself. The white man believes that there is only one God, and that is the white man. We have a different idea about God. We believe that there is but one God, and he is in a place called heaven. There is a heaven, we believe, and a God presides over that heaven, and as far as the Negro is concerned that God is the only being in the world whom we respect. We believe with Theodore Roosevelt, "FEAR GOD AND KNOW NO OTHER FEAR." And if every Negro in Philadelphia could just get that one thought into his or her mind, to fear God and him alone and let the world take care of itself, the better it would be for each and every one.

*White Man's Imperial Majesty*

The white man comes before you in his imperial and majestic pomp and tries to impress upon you the idea that he is your superior. Who made him your superior? You stick his face with a pin and blood runs out. You stick the black man's face with a pin and blood runs out. Starve the white man and he dies. Starve the black man and he dies. What difference is there, therefore, in black and white. If you stick the white man, blood come[s] out. If you starve the white man he dies. The same applies to the black man. They said the white man was the superior being and the black man was the inferior being. That is the old time notion, but today the world knows that all men were created equal. We were created equal and were put into this world to possess equal rights and equal privileges, and the time has come for the black man to get his share. The white man has got his share and more than his share for thousands of years, and we are calling upon him now to give up that which is not his, so that we can have ours. Some of them will be wise enough and sensible enough to give up what is not theirs to save confusion. You know when a man takes what is not his, the one from whom he took that thing is going to take him to court so as to recover his loss. Now, the Negro is going to take somebody to a court of law one day. This court is not going to be presided over by the white man. It is the court to be presided over and decided by the sword. Yes; the sword will decide to whom belongs the right.

### Africa to Call for a Judgment

And I want you men of Africa, you men of the Negro race, to prepare for the day when Africa will call for a judgment. Africa is preparing to call for a judgment, and that judgment we must have, and it will be a judgment in favor of four hundred million oppressed people. And the marshal who will carry out the authority of the court will be the new Toussaint L'Ouverture with the sword and the banner of the new African Republic. You black men of Philadelphia sit here tonight as jurors in the case where judgment is to be given in favor of the Negro, and I am now asking you jurymen: Gentlemen of the jury, what is your verdict? Cries of: "Africa must be free!" Now, if Africa is to be free, it means, therefore, that Philadelphia has given her verdict as we have in New York. It is now for the judge to give his finding. The judge will give his finding after all the jurors of the Negro race, four hundred million, will have given their verdict. And then after the judge gives his finding he will have to find a marshal to serve the writ, who will require the New Negro to help him to serve this writ, because the man to whom this writ is to be served is of a desperate character, because he prefers to shed blood and take lives before he will give up what is not his. You have to spill blood in Africa before you get what is belonging to you.

### A Negro Government

Therefore, you will realize that the Universal Negro Improvement Association is no joke. It is a serious movement. It is as serious a movement as the movement of the Irish today to have a free Ireland; as the determination of the Jew to recover Palestine. The Negro peoples of the world should be so determined to reclaim Africa and found a government there, so that if any black man in any part of the world is abused we can call the mighty power of Africa to come to our aid. Men, a Negro government we had once, and a Negro government we must have again. Tell me that I must live everlastingly under the domination of a white man, that I must bequeath to my children white overlordship, then I say, let me die now, Almighty God. If there is no better future in the world for me than to be the slave of a white man, I say, take the life you gave me. I do not want it. You would not be my God if you created me to be a slave to other men; but you are my God and will continue to be my God if you created me an equal of all men.

*Life Given for a Purpose*

Men, I want you to realize that the life you live was given you for a purpose; not for the purpose of being a slave, not for the purpose of being a serf, but for the purpose of being a man, and for that purpose you must live, or it is better you die.

*The Negro Will Die Economically*

Now I want to come to the practical, common sense side of this question. We have started an agitation all over the world. It is the agitation of self-reliance wherein the Negro must do for himself. I want you to understand that if you do not get behind this agitation and back it up morally and financially you are only flirting with your own downfall, because the world in which we live is today more serious than ever it was. White and yellow men have become more selfish today than they were before causing the terrible war, the terrible conflict, of 1914 to 1918. They destroyed all that they spent years and years to build and all the time and energy they gave us counted for nought because of the destruction. They have, therefore, lost their sympathies for other men. They have lost their sympathies for other races and have settled down to see nothing else but their own interest until they will have succeeded in rebuilding themselves. During this selfish, soulless age it falls to the province of the Negro to take the initiative and do for himself; otherwise he is going to die. He is going to d[ie] as I stand on this platform tonight[,] economically in America; he is going to die economically under the yoke of Britain, of France and of Germany. He is going to die in the next one hundred years if he does not start out now to do for himself.

*Dear America for White Men*

I want you to realize that this dear America, the greatest democracy in the world for white men, the greatest republic in the world for white men, that this America is becoming more prejudiced every day against the Negro. Month by month they are lynching more Negroes than they ever did before; month by month more riots are going on in the industrial sections of this country than ever before. This is an indication of the spirit of the people that are living today. It is the spirit that will be bequeathed to their children and to the unborn posterity of the white race. If you think that the white man is going to be more liberal to Negroes than they are at present, you are making a big mistake. Every succeeding generation of the white race is getting more prejudiced against the Negro. It is time, therefore, for the Negro to look out for the future for himself.

## Four Hundred Million Whites

We have in America ninety million white fellow citizens, and they are lynching us by the dozen every day. In the next one hundred years you are going to have four hundred million people (white) in America. Now, if they are lynching twelve a day with their ninety millions, how many are they going to lynch when they are four hundred millions. I want you to figure this out for yourselves. And it is because our old time leaders failed to see this that we of the Universal Negro Improvement Association say that the old time leadership must go.

## Negroes Flirting with Their Graves

Again I want you to understand that economically we are flirting with our graves if we do not start out to make ourselves economically independent. This war brought about new conditions in America and all over the world. America sent hundreds of thousands of colored soldiers to fight the white man's battles, during which time she opened the doors of industry to millions of white American men and women and created a new problem in the industrial market. And now the war is over and those millions who took the places of the soldiers who have returned home say: "We are not going to give up our jobs. We are going to remain in the industrial life of the world.["] This makes it difficult for returned soldiers to get work now. There will be sufficient jobs now for returned soldiers and for white men, because abnormal conditions are still in existence, but in the next two years these abnormal conditions will pass away and the industries will not be opened up for so long. It means that millions are going to starve. Do you think the white industrial captains are going to allow the white men and the white women to starve and give you bread? To the white man blood is thicker than water.

Therefore, in the next two years there is going to be an industrial boomerang in this country, and if the Negroes do not organize now to open up economic and industrial opportunities for themselves there will be starvation among all Negroes. It is because we want to save the situation when this good time shall have passed by and the white man calls you, "My dear John, I haven't any job for you today," and you can leave the white man's job as a porter and go into the Negro factory as a clerk, you can leave the white man's kitchen and go into your home as the wife of a big Negro banker or a corporation manager.

### The Black Star Line

That is why we want the Black Star Line so as to launch out to the Negro peoples of the world, and today the richest people of the world are the Negro people of Africa. Their minerals, their diamonds, their gold and their silver and their iron have built up the great English, French, German and Belgian Empires. Men, how long are we going to allow those parasites to suck the blood out of our children? How long? I answer for those who are active members of the Universal Negro Improvement Association and African Communities League, "Not one day longer." No parasite shall continue to feed off my body, because I want to have a healthy body. I have not sufficient blood to give to any parasite, because when I get sick I will need every drop of my blood to sustain me until I am well, so while I am well I will have to take off that parasite and throw it away. The time has come for the Negro to exert his energy to the utmost to do. Men and women of Philadelphia, the question is now for you to decide. Are you ready tonight or are you going to wait for two years more to be ready. The answer is, "You must be ready now[.]" Thank God, there are millions of us who are ready already, and when the Black Star Line sails out, by the demonstration of the Black Star Line spontaneously and simultaneously, millions will become . . . .

### Some Bad Negroes

Some bad Negroes, and I understand some are in Philadelphia, say there will be no Black Star Line. I am only sorry that I have not the time to waste or the strength or energy to give away that when I come against those bad Negroes to just get a big stick and give them a good walloping, because such Negroes are not entitled to courteous treatment. I want you active members not to waste time with such Negroes, but to put them down. Mark them well, because those are the same guys who, after you have achieved through your sacrifice, will go around and say: "We did it; we did it." The so-called big Negroes are the ones who have kept back the race. Some of them are doctors and lawyers and other professionals. They feel they are not belonging to the other class of Negroes. Those are the people who have done nothing to help the race because they sell out the race. This Black Star Line we are putting forward is an industrial proposition, and we are putting this proposition forward not by the big Negroes, but by the small Negroes. The first ship of the Black Star Line that we are to float on the 31st of this month will be owned not by the big Negroes, but by the small Negroes, and on that day we are going to say to the big Negroes, "Now, who are the big Negroes?" We who have made the Black Star Line possible are the big Negroes.

In New York we have discarded that kind of big Negroes. If they want to be big, they have to come right in line with other Negroes and show how big they are. We are not going to take it for granted that you are big. You have to show how big you are, not by the amount of money that you have, not by the automobile that you can afford to run, but by your sacrifice for your race. The sacrifice that you are prepared to make, that is how we are going to make men big. The so-called big Negro tells you that he is an aristocratic Negro; he is a gentleman. I want to know where the Negro aristocrat came from. A little more than fifty years ago Abraham Lincoln took up the pen and liberated four million Negroes. He did not say to any particular one, "You are a big Negro," or "You are an artistocrat," or "You are inferior." Victoria, eighty-two or eighty-three years ago, took up the pen and liberated a few million Negroes in the West Indies, but she did not classify them. All of us got our emancipation on equal terms, and it is for those who have the noblest blood, feeling and sentiment towards humanity to come out and do service so as to distinguish ourselves from the rest. Have they done it? Outside of Booker Washington and Frederick Douglass, there is not another aristocratic Negro in America. Douglass and Washington are the only two Negroes in this country who went out and did service so as to make themselves singular among the Negroes of America. It was not a matter of money that made these two men big Negroes. It was nobility of soul, of spirit, to do service to suffering humanity, and that made them different from the rest of the people. That made them aristocrats among their own. But these fat headed, big belly politicians who have robbed the people in their votes at the polls for a few dollars go among the people and say: "We are the aristocrats; we are the big Negroes." Indeed, I refuse to respect any such big Negroes. Show me the Negro of Booker Washington's stamp, show me the Negro of Frederick Douglass' stamp, and I will say, "There go the aristocratic Negroes of the race!"

*Nobility Through Service*

Men become noble through service. Therefore, if any Negro wants to call himself an aristocrat, a nobleman, before he will get that respect from me he will have to do some service to the Negro race. So you lawyers, you doctors and you politicians who think you are big Negroes we want to tell you that you are nothing for us, of the Universal Negro Improvement Association and African Communities League. You have to do service, and the time will come when we will give you a chance, when we will give you the opportunity to do service, because we are going to want hundreds of you professional men to lead the Negro forces on to VICTORY.

So tonight I want you men and women to understand that there is a chance for every one of you tonight to do service to your race, to humanity, before I leave this building for New York, and that is to help to launch on the 31st of this month the first ship of the Black Star Line. I want you all to buy as many shares as you can. If you can buy twenty, buy them; if you can buy fifteen, buy them; if you can buy ten, buy them. Buy as many as you possibly can, so as to render service to yourselves, service to your race, service to humanity.

---

# 8

## Declaration of the Rights of the Negro Peoples of the World

*The "Declaration of the Rights of the Negro Peoples of the World" was a statement of black grievances and rights drawn up and approved on August 13, 1920, by the first convention of the UNIA, which met in New York, August 1–31, 1920. Garvey viewed this Declaration of Rights as the African/African American equivalent of the Declaration of Independence or the French "Rights of Man." The convention also elected Garvey "Provisional President of Africa." Ellipses indicate that material was missing or indecipherable. We have omitted the signatures affixed to the original document. The Declaration of Rights was printed in* Negro World, *September 11, 1920, and reprinted in Jacques-Garvey,* Philosophy and Opinions of Marcus Garvey, *vol. 2: 135–43, and in* MG&UNIA Papers *2: 571–80.*

### Preamble

*Be It Resolved,* That the Negro people of the world, through their chosen representatives in convention assembled in Liberty Hall, in the City of New York and United States of America, from August 1 to August 31, in the year of Our Lord one thousand nine hundred and twenty, protest against the wrongs and injustices they are suffering at the hands of their white brethren, and state what they deem their fair and just rights, as well as the treatment they purpose to demand of all men in the future.

We complain:

1. That nowhere in the world, with few exceptions, are black men accorded equal treatment with white men, although in the same situation and circumstances, but, on the contrary, are discriminated against and denied the common rights due to human beings for no other reason than their race and color.

We are not willingly accepted as guests in the public hotels and inns of the world for no other reason than our race and color.

2. In certain parts of the United States of America our race is denied the right of public trial accorded to other races when accused of crime, but are lynched and burned by mobs, and such brutal and inhuman treatment is even practiced upon our women.

3. That European nations have parcelled out among them and taken possession of nearly all of the continent of Africa, and the natives are compelled to surrender their lands to aliens and are treated in most instances like slaves.

4. In the southern portion of the United States of America, although citizens under the Federal Constitution, and in some States almost equal to the whites in population and are qualified land owners and taxpayers, we are, nevertheless, denied all voice in the making and administration of the laws and are taxed without representation by the State governments, and at the same time compelled to do military service in defense of the country.

5. On the public conveyances and common carriers in the southern portion of the United States we are jim-crowed and compelled to accept separate and inferior accommodations and made to pay the same fare charged for first-class accommodations, and our families are often humiliated and insulted by drunken white men who habitually pass through the jim-crow cars going to the smoking car.

6. The physicians of our race are denied the right to attend their patients while in the public hospitals of the cities and States where they reside in certain parts of the United States.

Our children are forced to attend inferior separate schools for shorter terms than white children, and the public school funds are unequally divided between the white and colored schools.

7. We are discriminated against and denied an equal chance to earn wages for the support of our families, and in many instances are refused admission into labor unions and nearly everywhere are paid smaller wages than white men.

8. In the Civil Service and departmental offices we are everywhere discriminated against and made to feel that to be a black man in Europe, America and the West Indies is equivalent to being an outcast and a leper among the races of men, no matter what the character attainments of the black men may be.

9. In the British and other West Indian islands and colonies Negroes are secretly and cunningly discriminated against and denied those fuller rights of government to which white citizens are appointed, nominated and elected.

10. That our people in those parts are forced to work for lower wages than the average standard of white men and are kept in conditions repugnant to good civilized tastes and customs.

11. That the many acts of injustices against members of our race before the courts of law in the respective islands and colonies are of such nature as to create disgust and disrespect for the white man's sense of justice.

12. Against all such inhuman, unchristian and uncivilized treatment we here and now emphatically protest, and invoke the condemnation of all mankind.

In order to encourage our race all over the world and to stimulate it to overcome the handicaps and difficulties surrounding it, and to push forward to a higher and grander destiny, we demand and insist on the following Declaration of Rights:

1. Be it known to all men that whereas all men are created equal and entitled to the rights of life, liberty and the pursuit of happiness, and because of this we, the duly elected representatives of the Negro peoples of the world, invoking the aid of the just and Almighty God, do declare all men, women and children of our blood throughout the world free denizens, and do claim them as free citizens of Africa, the Motherland of all Negroes.

2. That we believe in the supreme authority of our race in all things racial; that all things are created and given to man as a common possession; that there should be an equitable distribution and apportionment of all such things, and in consideration of the fact that as a race we are now deprived of those things that are morally and legally ours, we believed it right that all such things should be acquired and held by whatsoever means possible.

3. That we believe the Negro, like any other race, should be governed by the ethics of civilization, and therefore should not be deprived of any of those rights or privileges common to other human beings.

4. We declare that Negroes, wheresoever they form a community among themselves should be given the right to elect their own representatives to represent them in Legislatures, courts of law, or such institutions as may exercise control over that particular community.

5. We assert that the Negro is entitled to even-handed justice before all courts of law and equity in whatever country he may be found, and when this is denied him on account of his race or color such denial is an insult to the race as a whole and should be resented by the entire body of Negroes.

6. We declare it unfair and prejudicial to the rights of Negroes in communities where they exist in considerable numbers to be tried by a judge and jury composed entirely of an alien race, but in all such cases members of our race are entitled to representation on the jury.

7. We believe that any law or practice that tends to deprive any African of his land or the privileges of free citizenship within his country is unjust and immoral, and no native should respect any such law or practice.

8. We declare taxation without representation unjust and tyran[n]ous, and there should be no obligation on the part of the Negro to obey the levy of a tax by any law-making body from which he is excluded and denied representation on account of his race and color.

9. We believe that any law especially directed against the Negro to his detriment and singling him out because of his race or color is unfair and immoral, and should not be respected.

10. We believe all men entitled to common human respect and that our race

should in no way tolerate any insults that may be interpreted to mean disrespect to our race or color.

11. We deprecate the use of the term "nigger" as applied to Negroes, and demand that the word "Negro" be written with a capital "N."

12. We believe that the Negro should adopt every means to protect himself against barbarous practices inflicted upon him because of color.

13. We believe in the freedom of Africa for the Negro people of the world, and by the principle of Europe for the Europeans and Asia for the Asiatics, we also demand Africa for the Africans at home and abroad.

14. We believe in the inherent right of the Negro to possess himself of Africa and that his possession of same shall not be regarded as an infringement on any claim or purchase made by any race or nation.

15. We strongly condemn the cupidity of those nations of the world who, by open aggression or secret schemes, have seized the territories and inexhaustible natural wealth of Africa, and we place on record our most solemn determination to reclaim the treasures and possession of the vast continent of our forefathers.

16. We believe all men should live in peace one with the other, but when races and nations provoke the ire of other races and nations by attempting to infringe upon their rights war becomes inevitable, and the attempt in any way to free one's self or protect one's rights or heritage becomes justifiable.

17. Whereas the lynching, by burning, hanging or any other means, of human beings is a barbarous practice and a shame and disgrace to civilization, we therefore declare any country guilty of such atrocities outside the pale of civilization.

18. We protest against the atrocious crime of whipping, flogging and overworking of the native tribes of Africa and Negroes everywhere. These are methods that should be abolished and all means should be taken to prevent a continuance of such brutal practices.

19. We protest against the atrocious practice of shaving the heads of Africans, especially of African women or individuals of Negro blood, when placed in prison as a punishment for crime by an alien race.

20. We protest against segregated districts, separate public conveyances, industrial discrimination, lynchings and limitations of political privileges of any Negro citizen in any part of the world on account of race, color or creed, and will exert our full influence and power against all such.

21. We protest against any punishment inflicted upon a Negro with severity, as against lighter punishment inflicted upon another of an alien race for like offense, as an act of prejudice and injustice, and should be resented by the entire race.

22. We protest against the system of education in any country where Negroes are denied the same privileges and advantages as other races.

23. We declare it inhuman and unfair to boycott Negroes from industries and labor in any part of the world.

24. We believe in the doctrine of the freedom of the press, and we therefore emphatically protest against the suppression of Negro newspapers and periodicals in various parts of the world, and call upon Negroes everywhere to employ all available means to prevent such suppression.

25. We further demand free speech universally for all men.

26. We hereby protest against the publication of scandalous and inflammatory articles by an alien press tending to create racial strife and the exhibition of picture films showing the Negro as a cannibal.

27. We believe in the self-determination of all peoples.

28. We declare for the freedom of religious worship.

29. With the help of Almighty God we declare ourselves the sworn protectors of the honor and virtue of our women and children, and pledge our lives for their protection and defense everywhere and under all circumstances from wrongs and outrages.

30. We demand the right of an unlimited and unprejudiced education for ourselves and our posterity forever[.]

31. We declare that the teaching in any school by alien teachers to our boys and girls, that the alien race is superior to the Negro race, is an insult to the Negro people of the world.

32. Where Negroes form a part of the citizenry of any country, and pass the civil service examination of such country, we declare them entitled to the same consideration as other citizens as to appointments in such civil service.

33. We vigorously protest against the increasingly unfair and unjust treatment accorded Negro travelers on land and sea by the agents and employes of railroad and steamship companies, and insist that for equal fare we receive equal privileges with travelers of other races.

34. We declare it unjust for any country, State or nation to enact laws tending to hinder and obstruct the free immigration of Negroes on account of their race and color.

35. That the right of the Negro to travel unmolested throughout the world be not abridged by any person or persons, and all Negroes are called upon to give aid to a fellow Negro when thus molested.

36. We declare that all Negroes are entitled to the same right to travel over the world as other men.

37. We hereby demand that the governments of the world recognize our leader and his representatives chosen by the race to look after the welfare of our people under such governments.

38. We demand complete control of our social institutions without interference by any alien race or races.

39. That the colors, Red, Black and Green, be the colors of the Negro race.

40. Resolved, That the anthem "Ethiopia, Thou Land of Our Fathers etc.," shall be the anthem of the Negro race. (Copy anthem appended.)

**The Universal Ethiopian Anthem**
*Poem by Burrell and Ford*

### I.

Ethiopia, thou land of our fathers,
Thou land where the gods loved to be,
As storm cloud at night sudden gathers
Our armies come rushing to thee.
We must in the fight be victorious
When swords are thrust outward to glean;
For us will the victory be glorious
When led by the red, black and green

CHORUS

Advance, advance to victory,
Let Africa be free;
Advance to meet the foe
With the might
Of the red, the black and the green.

### II.

Ethiopia, the tyrant's falling,
Who smote thee upon thy knees
And thy children are lustily calling
From over the distant seas.
Jehovah the Great One has heard us,
Has noted our sighs and our tears,
With His spirit of Love he has stirred us
To be One through the coming years.
CHORUS—Advance, advance, etc.

### III.

O, Jehovah, thou God of the ages
Grant unto our sons that lead
The wisdom Thou gave to Thy sages
When Israel was sore in need.
Thy voice thro' the dim past has spoken,
Ethiopia shall stretch forth her hand,
By Thee shall all fetters be broken
And Heav'n bless our dear fatherland.
CHORUS—Advance, advance, etc.

41. We believe that any limited liberty which deprives one of the complete rights and prerogatives of full citizenship is but a modified form of slavery.

42. We declare it an injustice to our people and a serious impediment to the health of the race to deny to competent licensed Negro physicians the right to practice in the public hospitals of the communities in which they reside, for no other reason than their race and color.

43. We call upon the various government[s] of the world to accept and acknowledge Negro representatives who shall be sent to the said governments to represent the general welfare of the Negro peoples of the world.

44. We deplore and protest against the practice of confining juvenile prisoners in prisons with adults, and we recommend that such youthful prisoners be taught gainful trades under human supervision.

45. Be it further resolved, That we as a race of people declare the League of Nations null and void as far as the Negro is concerned, in that it seeks to deprive Negroes of their liberty.

46. We demand of all men to do unto us as we would do unto them, in the name of justice; and we cheerfully accord to all men all the rights we claim herein for ourselves.

47. We declare that no Negro shall engage himself in battle for an alien race without first obtaining the consent of the leader of the Negro people of the world, except in a matter of national self-defense.

48. We protest against the practice of drafting Negroes and sending them to war with alien forces without proper training, and demand in all cases that Negro soldiers be given the same training as the aliens.

49. We demand that instructions given Negro children in schools include the subject of "Negro History," to their benefit.

50. We demand a free and unfettered commercial intercourse with all the Negro people of the world.

51. We declare for the absolute freedom of the seas for all peoples.

52. We demand that our duly accredited representatives be given proper recognition in all leagues, conferences, conventions or courts of international arbitration wherever human rights are discussed.

53. We proclaim the 31st day of August of each year to be an international holiday to be observed by all Negroes.

54. We want all men to know that we shall maintain and contend for the freedom and equality of every man, woman and child of our race, with our lives, our fortunes and our sacred honor.


These rights we believe to be justly ours and proper for the protection of the Negro race at large, and because of this belief we, on behalf of the four hundred million Negroes of the world, do pledge herein the sacred blood of the race in defense, and we hereby subscribe our names as a guarantee of the truthfulness and faithfulness hereof, in the presence of Almighty God, on this 13th day of August, in the year of our Lord one thousand nine hundred and twenty.

---

# 9

## Editorial Letter in *Negro World,* September 11, 1920

*Garvey wrote this editorial letter printed in* Negro World, *September 11, 1920, to report on events at the recently completed UNIA convention. Garvey underscored the significance of the Declaration of Rights and his election as provisional president of Africa, and committed himself to the liberation of Africa as a homeland for all blacks. Garvey by this time was formulating his theory of the need to separate the world's races into independent homelands. He also urged his readers to purchase shares in the Black Star Line Steamship Corporation. This letter was reprinted in the* MG&UNIA Papers *3: 8–11.*

FELLOW MEN OF THE NEGRO RACE, Greeting:

Owing to the pressure of work in the convention I was unable to keep in closer touch with you during the eventful month of August. However, I embrace this opportunity of writing to you to convey the hearty good wishes of the first International Convention of Negroes which assembled in Liberty Hall, New York, United States of America, from the 1st to the 31st of August. This convention will go down in history as an epoch-making event. It is for me to tell you that for the thirty-one days the honorable Deputies who made up the convention and who were sent to us by the scattered electorate of Negroes in the four hundred millions of the race did their work so nobly and well that they have won for themselves the cognomen of "ABLE COUNSELLORS." It would have made any race or nation's heart feel glad to listen to these honorable Deputies. They came from the four corners of the world with a message for the convention. It was a message of good-will from their section of the world. Indeed, the assemblage was but a pooling of the heartaches and the fraternal greetings of the Negro people of the world. Retrospectively, methinks I hear the unhappy reports of the delegates from Zululand, from Nigeria, from Nyasaland, and from the Congo in Africa. In the same echo methinks I hear also the sad tales of the sufferings in Trinidad, in Jamaica, in Antigua and the other British West Indian Islands. And what did we do? We had to make laws; we had to formulate and adopt a Constitution, a Declaration of Rights, and, thank God, we have given that Declaration of Rights to the world. We wrote fifty-four articles into the Declaration of Rights, and those articles we have given to the world with the warning, with the understanding, that four hundred million Negroes will sacrifice the last drop of their blood to see that every article comes true. No more fear, no more cringing, no more sycophantic begging and pleading; but the Negro must strike straight from the shoulder for manhood rights and for full liberty. Africa calls now more than ever. She calls because the attempt is now being made by the combined Caucasian forces of Europe to subjugate her, to overrun her and to reduce her to that state of alien control that will mean in another one hundred years the complete extermination of the native African. Can we not remember the extermination of the North American Indian which was practiced in a similar manner to the practices now holding sway on the Continent of Africa[?] This convention of August left us full-fledged men; men charged to do our duty, and by the God Divine, and by the Heavens that shelter all humanity, we have pledged ourselves to bring the manhood of our race to the highest plane of human achievement. We cannot, and we must not, falter. There is absolutely no turning back. There must be a going forward to the point of destiny. Destiny leads us to liberty, to freedom; that freedom that Victoria of England never gave; that liberty that Lincoln never meant; that freedom, that liberty, that will see us men among men; that will see us a nation among nations; that will make of us a great and powerful people. Do you tell me you cannot make it? And I say, "Shame on you!" Have you not, you British Negro soldiers, made it for British colonization of the west coast of Africa, when, by your prowess, you conquered the innocent and unsuspecting native tribes? Did you not make it, you American Negro soldiers, for the white Americans in the Revolutionary War, in the Civil War, and when you climbed the heights of San Juan? Did you not make it at the battle of Chateau-Thierry and the Argonne? You French Negro soldiers, did you not make it at the battles of the Marne and Verdun? Then why can you not make it for yourselves, climbing the battle heights of Africa, to plant there the standard of the Red, Black and Green[?] I repeat, you men of the world, there can be no turning back. It means that the Negro must plant the banner of freedom in this twentieth century on the battle plains of Africa or he is lost forever. The world is still in turmoil, the world is still in agony, the world is still in labor. And there will never be a settled world, there will never be a world wherein men will be in peace, one with the other, until the reign of justice is heralded in. But there can be no justice, there will be no ordinary human respect, so long as one race remains at the foot of the great human ladder and the other race sits at the top. It is time that the Negro rise from the foot of the ladder and climb the dizzy heights of fame and meet his brother at the top. What argument, what persuasion, can ever turn us from our course, the course of liberty? Men, be not cowards; men, be not fearful of what the other fellow says. Remember, you are men. God Almighty created us in his image. He gave us all the attributes of men and as men, bearing a semblance to the Divine. Let us rise to the heights that will enable us to say to the race of our brothers, "Indeed, we are of you, and shall remain with you."

The signal honor of being Provisional President of Africa is mine. It is a political job; it is a political calling for me to redeem Africa. It is like asking Napoleon to take the world. He took a certain portion of the world in his time. He failed and died at St. Helena. But may I not say that the lessons of Napoleon are but stepping stones by which we shall guide ourselves to African liberation? We do not desire the conquest of a world; we desire the conquest of Africa; that land that is ours, the land that no one can dispute as being the heritage of the Negro, and for that land I live; for that land I will bleed; for that land I will die, that you have made me its Provisional President. You have also made me President General of the Universal Negro Improvement Association and African Communities League, a social, industrial and commercial organization. This organization seeks no warfare; it seeks not to deprive others of what is theirs; it seeks to build an economic base for the Negro wheresoever he lives. Please give to this organization all the help you possibly can. Help it to become a power of commercial strength so that, as we and our children grow into older manhood, we may be able to find a way by which to live so as to preserve our own existence.

Steamships must be bought and built. In countries like Liberia railroads must be built. Industrial plants must go up if the race is to rise in greatness. Are you prepared to do your part? Men, can you be a commercial power by bowing at the footstools of other races? Can you become an industrial power by giving all energy and wealth to other races? The answer is No. But you can become a great commercial and industrial power by amassing and pooling your own industries and forming your own commercial enterprises. The Declaration of Rights, published in another part of this paper, shall be the Holy Writ of this Negro race of ours. It shall be the very Scriptures by which we shall know ourselves. Alongside the Holy Words of God shall go this Declaration of Rights of this Negro race of ours, and as we pray to Almighty God to save us through his Holy Words so shall we with confidence in ourselves follow the sentiment of the Declaration of Rights and carve our way to liberty. This Declaration of Rights shall take its place alongside of the Declaration of Independence of the United States of America and the Magna Charta of England. Who shall say nay to the Negro in intepreting the sentiment of this Declaration of Rights? He who says nay to the American white man on the principles of his Declaration of Independence; he who says nay to the Englishman on the interpretation of the sentiment of the Magna Charta, then let him say nay to the Negro in his interpretation of this Declaration of Rights, because, as an American white citizen vows that he will give his last drop of blood in defense of his independence and his constitution, and as an Anglo-Saxon will drain the last drop of his blood in defen[s]e of his Constitution and his rights, so I repeat the Negro must drain the last drop of his blood in defense of the sentiments of this Declaration of Rights. Let there be no misunderstanding. The Negro has risen to the fullness of his power. That power he shall preserve down the ages "until the wreck of matter and the crash of worlds."

And now let me say, while we are preparing universally for this new start, let us also remember the Black Star Line Steamship Corporation. The command has gone forth, "Ships and more ships." Africa must be linked to the United States of America. Africa must be linked to South and Central America. Africa must be linked to the West Indies, so that there can be an unbroken intercourse between the four hundred million Negroes of the world. We can only do it by and with more ships, and now is the chance, now is the opportunity for every Negro to do his bit by the Black Star Line Steamship Corporation by buying more shares. Every share you buy is a plate in the great ships of the Negroes' merchant marine. The shares are still going at five dollars each. You may buy two, five, ten, twenty, one hundred or two hundred. The time will come when these shares will bring to you hundreds of dollars. Therefore, while the opportunity presents itself, buy your shares now. Do g[ood] by yourselves in this generation and insure the success of your posterity. You can buy your shares by writing t[o the] Black Star Line Steamship Corporation, 54–56 West 135th Street, New York City, United States of America.

For further information about the Universal Negro Improvement Association, under whose auspices [the first] International Convention of Negroes of the world w[as held] you may write to the Right Honorable Secretary G[eneral,] the Universal Negro Improvement Association, 56 [West] 135th Street, New York. With very best wishes for your success.

Yours fraternally,

---

# 10
## Address to the Second UNIA Convention, New York, August 31, 1921

*Garvey presented this speech at the closing session of the second annual UNIA Convention that met in New York City, August 1–31, 1921. The speech was printed in* Negro World, *September 10, 1921, and reprinted in* MG&UNIA Papers *3: 734–40. Only the section of the* Negro World *article that reported on Garvey's address is reproduced here. Garvey reiterated his argument that an independent African homeland is the only hope for the black people, and protested the continued colonial exploitation of Africa.*

## Marcus Garvey Speaks

Immediately the President-General arose, smiling and bowing to the right and then to the left like a black Napoleon, whereupon the audience again broke into great cheering and hurrahing, followed by the association yell of the Junior Motor Corps girls. When the audience, after a period of about five minutes, had spent itself, and quiet was restored, the President-General spoke as follows:—

May it please your Highness the Potentate, Right Honorable Members of the Executive Council, Deputies and Delegates to the Second International Convention of Negroes of the World, Ladies and Gentlemen:—We are assembled here tonight to bring to a close our great convention of thirty-one days and thirty-one nights. Before we separate ourselves and take our departure to the different parts of the world from which we came, I desire to give you a message; one that you will, I hope, take home and propagate among the scattered millions of Africa's sons and daughters.

We have been here, sent here by the good will of the 400,000,000 Negroes of the world to legislate in their interests, and in the time allotted to us we did our best to enact laws and to frame laws that in our judgment, we hope, will help solve the great problem that confronts us universally. The Universal Negro Improvement Association seeks to emancipate the Negro everywhere, industrially, educationally, politically and religiously. It also seeks a free and redeemed Africa. It has a great struggle ahead; it has a gigantic task to face. Nevertheless, as representatives of the Negro people of the world we have undertaken the task of freeing the 400,000,000 of our race, and of freeing our bleeding Motherland, Africa. We counselled with each other during the thirty-one days; we debated with each other during the thirty-one days, and out of all we did, and out of all we said, we have come to the one conclusion—that speedily Africa must be redeemed! (Applause.) We have come to the conclusion that speedily there must be an emancipated Negro race everywhere (applause); and on going back to our respective homes we go with our determination to lay down, if needs be, the last drop of our blood for the defense of Africa and for the emancipation of our race.

The handwriting is on the wall. You see it as plain as daylight; you see it coming out of India, the tribes of India rising in rebellion against their overlords. You see it coming out of Africa, our dear motherland, Africa; the Moors rising in rebellion against their overlords, and defeating them at every turn. (Applause.) According to the last report flashed to this country from Morocco by the Associated Press, the Moors have again conquered and subdued the Spanish hordes. The same Associated Press flashes to us the news that there is a serious uprising in India, and the English people are marshaling their troops to subdue the spirit of liberty, of freedom, which is now permeating India. The news has come to us, and I have a cable in my pocket that comes from Ireland that the Irish are determined to have liberty and nothing less than liberty. (Applause.)

### *The League of Nations*

The handwriting is on the wall, and as we go back to our respective homes we shall serve notice upon the world that we also are coming; coming with a united effort; coming with a united determination, a determination that Africa shall be free from coast to coast. (Applause.) I have before me the decision of the League of Nations. Immediately after the war a Council of the League of Nations was called, and at that Council they decided that the territories wrested from Germany in West Africa, taken from her during the conflict, should be divided between France and England—608,000 square miles—without even asking the civilized Negroes of the world what disposition shall be made of their own homeland, of their own country. An insult was hurled at the civilized Negroes of the world when they thus took upon themselves the right to parcel out and apportion as they pleased 608,000 square miles of our own land; for we never gave it up; we never sold it. It is still our[s]. (Cries of "Yes!") They parceled it out between these two nations—England and France—gave away our property without consulting us, and we are aggrieved, and we desire to serve notice on civilization and on the world that 400,000,000 Negroes are aggrieved. (Cries of "Yes!" and applause.)

And we are the more aggrieved because of the lynch rope, because of segregation, because of the Jim Crowism that is used, practised and exercised here in this country and in other parts of the world by the white nations of the earth, wherever Negroes happen accidentally or otherwise to find themselves. If there is no safety for Negroes in the white world, I cannot see what right they have to parcel out the homeland, the country of Negroes, without consulting Negroes and asking their permission so to do. Therefore, we are aggrieved. This question of prejudice will be the downfall of civilization (applause), and I warn the white race of this, and of their doom. I hope they will take heed, because the handwriting is on the wall. (Applause.) No portion of humanity, no group of humanity, has an abiding right, an everlasting right, an eternal right to oppress other sections or portions of humanity. God never gave them the right, and if there is such a right, man arrogated it to himself, and God in all ages has been displeased with the arrogance of man. I warn those nations which believe themselves above the law of God, above the commandments of God. I warn those nations that believe themselves above human justice. You cannot long ignore the laws of God; you cannot long ignore the commandments of God; you cannot long ignore human justice, and exist. Your arrogance will destroy you, and I warn the races and the nations that have arrogated to themselves the right to oppress, the right to circumscribe, the right to keep down other races. I warn them that the hour is coming when the oppressed will rise in their might, in their majesty, and throw off the yoke of ages.

The world ought to understand that the Negro has come to life, possessed with a new conscience and a new soul. The old Negro is buried, and it is well the world knew it. It is not my purpose to deceive the world. I believe in righteousness; I believe in truth; I belie[ve] in honesty. That is why I warn a selfish world of the outcome of their actions towards the oppressed. There will come a day, Josephus Daniels wrote about it, a white statesman, and the world has talked about it, and I warn the world of it, that the day will come when the races of the world will marshal themselves in great conflict for the survival of the fittest. Men of the Universal Negro Improvement Association, I am asking you to prepare yourselves, and prepare your race the world over, because the conflict is coming, not because you will it, not because you desire it, but because you will be forced into it. The conflict between the races is drawing nearer and nearer. You see it; I see it; I see it in the handwriting on the wall, as expressed in the uprising in India. You see the handwriting on the wall of Africa; you see it, the handwriting on the wall of Europe. It is coming; it is drawing nearer and nearer. Four hundred million Negroes of the world, I am asking you to prepare yourselves, so that you will not be found wanting when that day comes. Ah! what a sorry day it will be. I hope it will never come. But my hope, my wish, will not prevent its coming. All that I can do is to warn humanity everywhere, so that humanity may change its tactics, and warn them of the danger. I repeat: I warn the white world against the prejudice they are practising against Negroes; I warn them against the segregation and injustice they mete out to us, for the perpetuation of these things will mean the ultimate destruction of the present civilization, and the building up of a new civilization founded upon mercy, justice and equality.

I know that we have good men in all races living at the present time. We have good men of the black race, we have good men of the white race, good men of the yellow race, who are endeavoring to do the best they can to ward off this coming conflict. White men who have the vision, go ye back and warn your people of this coming conflict! Black men of vision, go ye to the four corners of the earth, and warn your people of this coming conflict. Yellow men, go ye out and warn your people of this coming conflict, because it is drawing nearer and nearer; nearer and nearer. Oh! if the world will only listen to the heart-throbs, to the soul-beats of those who have the vision, those who have God's love in their hearts.

I see before me white men, black men and yellow men working assiduously for the peace of the world; for the bringing together of this thing called human brotherhood; I see them working through their organizations. They have been working during the last fifty years. Some worked to bring about the emancipation, because they saw the danger of perpetual slavery. They brought about the liberation of 4,000,000 black people. They passed away, and others started to work, but the opposition against them is too strong; the opposition against them is weighing them down. The world has gone mad; the world has become too material; the world has lost its spirit of kinship with God, and man can see nothing else but prejudice, avarice and greed. Avarice and greed will destroy the world, and I am appealing to white, black and yellow whose hearts, whose souls are touched with the true spirit of humanity, with the true feeling of human brotherhood, to preach the doctrine of human love, more, to preach it louder, to preach it longer, because there is great need for it in the world at this time. Ah! if they could but see the danger—the conflict between the races—races fighting against each other. What a destruction, what a holocaust it will be! Can you imagine it?

Just take your idea from the last bloody war, wherein a race was pitted against itself (for the whole white races united as one from a common origin), the members of which, on both sides, fought so tenaciously that they killed off each other in frightful, staggering numbers. If a race pitted against itself could fight so tenaciously to kill itself without mercy, can you imagine the fury, can you imagine the mercilessness, the terribleness of the war that will come when all the races of the world will be on the battlefield, engaged in deadly combat for the destruction or overthrow of the one or the other, when beneath it and as a cause of it lies prejudice and hatred? Truly, it will be an ocean of blood; that is all it will be. So that if I can sound a note of warning now that will echo and reverberate around the world and thus prevent such a conflict, God help me to do it; for Africa, like Europe, like Asia, is preparing for that day. (Great applause.)

### Africa's Possibilities

You may ask yourselves if you believe Africa is still asleep. Africa has been slumbering; but she was slumbering for a purpose. Africa still possesses her hidden mysteries; Africa has unused talents, and we are unearthening them now for the coming conflict. (Applause.) Oh, I hope it will never come; therefore, I hope the white world will change its attitude towards the weaker races of the world, for we shall not be weak everlastingly. Ah, history teaches us of the rise and fall of nations, races and empires. Rome fell in her majesty; Greece fell in her triumph; Babylon, Assyria, Carthage, Prussia, the German Empire—all fell in their pomp and power; the French Empire fell from the sway of the great Napoleon, from the dominion of the indomitable Corsican soldier. As they fell in the past, so will nations fall in the present age, and so will they fall in the future ages to come, the result of their unrighteousness.

I repeat, I warn the world, and I trust you will receive this warning as you go into the four corners of the earth. The white race should teach humanity. Out there is selfishness in the world. Let the white race teach humanity first, because we have been following the cause of humanity for three hundred years, and we have suffered much. If a change must come, it must not come from Negroes; it must come from the white race, for they are the ones who have brought about this estrangement between the races. The Negro never hated; at no time within the last five hundred years can they point to one single instance of Negro hatred. The Negro has loved eve[n] under the severest punishment. In slavery the Negro loved his master; he protected his master; he saf[e]guarded his master's home. "Greater love hath no man than that he should lay down his life for another." We gave not only our services, our unrequited labor; we gave also our souls, we gave our hearts, we gave our all, to our oppressors.

But, after all, we are living in a material world, even though it is partly spiritual, and since we have been very spiritual in the past, we are going to take a part of the material now, and will give others the opportunity to practice the spiritual side of life. Therefore, I am not telling you to lead in humanity; I am not telling you to lead in the bringing about of the turning of humanity, because you have been doing that for three hundred years, and you have lost. But the compromise must come from the domina[n]t races. We are warning them. We are not preaching a doctrine of hatred, and I trust you will not go back to your respective homes and preach such a doctrine. We are preaching, rather, a doctrine of humanity, a doctrine of human love. But we say love begins at home; "charity begins at home."

We are aggrieved because of this partitioning of Africa, because it seeks to deprive Negroes of the chance of higher national development; no chance, no opportunity, is given us to prove our fitness to govern, to dominate in our own behalf. They impute so many bad things against Haiti and against Liberia, that they themselves circumvented Liberia so as to make it impossible for us to demonstrate our ability for self-government. Why not be honest? Why not be straightforward[?] Having desired the highest development, as they avowed and professed, of the Negro, why not give him a fair chance, an opportunity to prove his capacity for governing? What better opportunity ever presented itself than the present, when the territories of Germany in Africa were wrested from her control by the Allies in the last war—what better chance ever offered itself for trying out the higher ability of Negroes to govern themselves than to have given those territories to the civilized Negroes, and thus give them a trial to exercise themselves in a proper system of government? Because of their desire to keep us down, because of their desire to keep us apart, they refuse us a chance. The chance that they did give us is the chance that we are going to take. (Great applause.) Hence tonight, before I take my seat, I will move a resolution, and I think it is befitting at this time to pass such a resolution as I will move, so that the League of Nations and the Supreme Council of the Nations will understand that Negroes are not asleep; that Negroes are not false to themselves; that Negroes are wide awake, and that Negroes intend to take a serious part in the future government of this world; that God Almighty created him and placed him in it. This world owes us a place, and we are going to occupy that place.

We have a right to a large part in the political horizon, and I say to you that we are preparing to occupy that spot.

Go back to your respective corners of the earth and preach the real doctrine of the Universal Negro Improvement Association—the doctrine of universal emancipation for Negroes, the doctrine of a free and a redeemed Africa!

### *Resolution*

Be It Resolved, That we, the duly elected representatives of the Negro peoples of the world, assembled in this Second Annual Convention, do protest against the distribution of the land of Africa by the Supreme Council and the League of Nations among the white nations of the world. Africa, by right of heritage, is the property of the African races, and those at home and those abroad are now sufficiently civilized to conduct the affairs of their own homeland. This convention believes in the right of Europe for the Europeans; Asia for the Asiatics, and Africa for the Africans, those at home and those abroad. We believe, further, that only a close and unselfish application of this principle will prevent threatening race wars that may cast another gloom over civilization and humanity. At this time humanity everywhere is determined to reach a common standard of nationhood. Hence 400,000,000 Negroes demand a place in the political sun of the world.

> SECOND INTERNATIONAL CONVENTION OF NEGROES.
> Through the Universal Negro Improvement Association,
> Marcus Garvey, President-General.
> Wednesday, August 31, 1921. New York, N.Y.

---

# 11
## Motive of the NAACP Exposed

*Garvey wrote "Motive of the NAACP Exposed," an editorial letter, to* Negro World *on August 31, 1923, while he was serving a sentence for mail fraud in The Tombs prison in New York City; it was published on September 8, 1923. Garvey blamed most of his difficulties on Du Bois, the NAACP, and the color bias of other African American political leaders. This letter was reprinted in* MG&UNIA Papers *5: 437–441, and, with modifications, in Jacques-Garvey,* Philosophy and Opinions of Marcus Garvey, *vol. 2: 55–61.*

FELLOW MEN OF THE NEGRO RACE, Greeting:

The policy of the Universal Negro Improvement Association is so clean-cut, and my personal views are so well known, that no one, for even one moment, could reasonably accuse us of having any other desire than that of working for a united Negro race.

Some of us make the mistake to state in America, the West Indies and Africa that the nearer we approach the white man in color the greater our social standing and privilege, and that we should build up an "aristocracy" based upon caste of color and not achievement in race. It is well known, although no one is honest enough to admit it, that we have been, for the past thirty years at least, but more so now than ever, grading ourselves for social honor and distinction on the basis of color. That the average success in the race has been regulated by color and not by ability and merit; that we have been trying to get away from the pride of race into the atmosphere of color worship, to the damaging extent that the whole world has made us its laughing stock.

There is no doubt that a race that doesn't respect itself forfeits the respect of others, and we are in the moral-social position now of losing the respect of the whole world.

There is a subtle and underhand propaganda fostered by a few men of color in America, the West Indies and Africa to destroy the self-respect and pride of the Negro race by building up what is commonly known to us as a "blue vein" aristocracy and to foster same as the social and moral standard of the race. The success of this effort is very much marked in the West Indies, and coming into immediate recognition in South Africa, and is now gaining much headway in America under the skillful leadership of the National Association for the Advancement of "Colored" People and their silent but scattered agents.

The observant members of our race must have noticed within recent years a great hostility between the National Association for the Advancement of "Colored" People and the Universal "Negro" Improvement Association, and must have wondered why Du Bois writes so bitterly against Garvey and vice versa. Well, the reason is plainly to be seen after the following explanation:

Du Bois represents a group that hates the Negro blood in their veins, and has been working subtly to build up a caste aristocracy that would socially divide the race into two groups: One the superior because of color caste, and the other the inferior, hence the pretentious work of the National Association for the Advancement of "Colored" People. The program of deception was well arranged and under way for success when Marcus Garvey arrived in America, and he, after understudying the artful doctor and the group he represented, fired a "bomb" into the camp by organizing the Universal "Negro" Improvement Association to cut off the wicked attempt of race deception and distinction, and to in truth build up a race united in spirit and ideal with the honest desire of adjusting itself to its own moral-social pride and national self-respect. When Garvey arrived in America and visited the office of the National Association for the Advancement of "Colored" People to interview Du Bois, who was regarded as a leader of the Negro people and who had recently visited the West Indies, he was dum[b]founded when, on approach to the office but for Mr. Dill and Dr. Du Bois himself and the office boy, he could not tell whether he was in a white office or that of the National Association for the Advancement of "Colored" People. The whole staff was either white or very near white, and thus Garvey got his first shock of the advancement hypocrisy. There was no representation of the race there that anyone could recognize. The advancement meant that you had to be as near white as possible, otherwise there was no place for you as stenographer, clerk or attendant in the office of the National Association for the Advancement of "Colored" People. After a short talk with Du Bois, Garvey became so disgusted with the man and his principles that the thought he never contemplated entered his m[i]nd—that of remaining in America to teach Du Bois and his group what real race pride meant.

When Garvey left the office of the National Association for the Advancement of "Colored" People, to travel through and study the social life of Negro America, he found that the policy of the association was well observed in business and professional life as well as in the drawing room, etc., all over the country. In restaurants, drug stores and offices all over the nation where our people were engaged in business it was discoverable that those employed were the very "lightest" members of the race—as waitresses, clerks and stenographers. Garvey asked, "What's the matter? Why were not black, brown-skin and mulatto girls employed?" And he was told it was "for the good of the trade." That to have trade it was necessary and incumbent to have "light" faces, as near white as possible. But the shock did not stop there. In New York, Boston, Washington and Detroit, Garvey further discovered the activities of the "Blue Vein Society" and the "Colonial Club." In New York we had both organizations going. The West Indian "lights" had the "Colonial Club" and the American "lights" had the "Blue Vein Society." The "Colonial Club" would give annual balls outside of its regular weekly or monthly soiree and no one less than a quadroon would be admitted; and gentlemen below that complexion were only admitted if they were lawyers, doctors or very successful business men with plenty of "cash," who were known to uphold the caste aristocracy. At St. Phillip's Church, New York, where the Very Rev. Dr. Daniels held sway and dominion, the "society" had things so arranged that even though this man was a brown-skin clergyman, and his rector a very near white gentleman, he had to draw the line and give the best seats in the church and the places of honor to the "Blue Veins" and the others would have a "look in" when they, by fawning before and "humbling" themselves and by giving lavishly to the church, admitted the superiority of caste. By the way, Dr. Daniels was also an executive officer or director of the National Association for the Advancement of "Colored" People. In Washington one or two of the church[es] did the same thing, but in Detroit the Very Rev. "Bob" Bagnall, now director of branches of the National Association for the Advancement of "Colored" People held sway. In his church no dark person could have a seat in the front, and, to test the truthfulness of it after being told, Garvey, *in cog.*, one Sunday night attempted to occupy one of the empty seats, not so very near the front, and the effort nearly spoiled the whole service, as Brother Bob, who was then ascending the pulpit, nearly lost his "balance" to see such a face so near the "holy of holies." Brother Bob was also an officer of the National Association for the Advancement of "Colored" People. On Garvey's return to New York he made (*in cog.*) a similar test at St. Phillip's Church one Sunday, and the Rev. Daniels was nearly ready to fight.

Now, what does all this mean? It is to relate the hidden program and motive of the National Association for the Advancement of "Colored" People and to warn Negro America of not being deceived by a group of men who have as much love for the Negro blood in their veins as the devil has for holy water.

The National Association for the Advancement of "Colored" People is a scheme to destroy the Negro Race, and the leaders of it hate Marcus Garvey because he has discovered them at their game and because the Universal Negro Improvement Association, without any prejudice to color or caste, is making headway in bringing all the people together for their common good. They hate Garvey because the Universal Negro Improvement Association and the Black Star Line employed every shade of color in the race, according to ability and merit, and put the N.A.A.C.P. to shame for employing only the "lightest" of the race. They hate Garvey because he forced them to fill Shilady's place with a Negro. They hate Garvey because they had to employ "black" Pickens to cover up their scheme after Garvey had discovered it; they hate Garvey because they have had to employ brown-skin "Bob" Bagnall to make a showing to the people that they were doing the "right" thing by them; they hate Garvey because he has broken up the "Pink Tea Set"; they hate Garvey because they have been forced to recognize mulatto, brown and black talent in the association equally with the lighter element; they hate Garvey because he is teaching the unity of race, without color superiority or prejudice. The gang thought that they would have been able to build up in America a buffer class between the white and the Negro, and thus in another fifty years join with the powerful race and crush the blood of their mothers, as is being done in South Africa and the West Indies.

The imprisonment of Garvey is more than appears on the surface, and the National Association for the Advancement of Colored People knows it. Du Bois and those who lead the Association are skillful enough to be using the old method of getting the "other fellow" to destroy himself, hence the activities of "brown-skin" Bagnall and "black" Pickens. Walter White, whom we can hardly tell from a Southern gentleman and who lives with a white family in Brooklyn, is kept in the background, but dark Bagnall, Pickens and Du Bois are pushed to the front to make the attack, so that there would be no suspicion of the motive. They are to drive hard and hot, and then the silent influence would bring up the rear, hence the slogan, "Garvey must go!" and the vicious attacks in the different magazines by Pickens, Du Bois and Bagnall.

Gentlemen, you are very smart, but Garvey has caught your tune. The conspiracy to destroy the Negro race, is so well organized that the moment anything interferes with their program there springs up a simultaneous action on the part of the leaders. It will be observed that in the September issue of the "Crisis" is published on the very last page of its news section what purports to be the opinion of a Jamaica[n] paper about Marcus Garvey and his case. The skillful editor of the "Crisis," Dr. Du Bois, reproduces that part of the article that would tend to show the opinion about Garvey in his own country taken from a paper called the "Gleaner" (edited by one Herbert George De Lesser) and not the property of Negroes.

The article in the original was clipped from the "Gleaner" when it appeared, and was sent by a friend to Garvey, so that he knew all that appeared in it. In it the editor extolled the leadership and virtues of Dr. Du Bois, and said it was the right kind of leadership for the American Negro people, and bitterly denounced Garvey. Du Bois published that part that denounced Garvey, but suppressed the part that gave him the right of leadership; and he failed to enlighten his readers that the editor of the "Gleaner" is a very light man, who hates the Negro blood of his mother and who is part of the international scheme to foster the Blue Vein Society scheme. Dr. Du Bois failed to further enlighten his readers that he visited Jamaica and was part of the "Colonial Society" scheme; he also failed to state that in the plan De Lisser is to "hold down" the West Indian end of the "caste scheme" and he and others to "hold down" the American end, and their agents "hold down" the South African section.

But now we have reached the point where the entire race must get together and stop these schemers at their game. Whether we are light, yellow, black or what not, there is but one thing for us to do, and that is to get together and build up a race. God made us in His own image and He had some purpose when He thus created us. Then why should we seek to destroy ourselves? If a few Du Boises and De Lissers do not want their progeny to remain of our race, why not be satisfied to abide their time and take their peaceful exit? But why try in this subtle manner to humiliate and destroy our race?

We as a people, have a great future before us. Ethiopia shall once more see the day of her glory, then why destroy the chance and opportunity simply to be someone else?

Let us work and wait patiently, for our day of racial triumph will come. Let us not divide ourselves into castes, but let us all work together for the common good. Let us remember the sorrow of our mothers. Let us forget not that it is our duty to remedy any wrong that has already been done, and not of ourselves perpetuate the evil of race destruction. To change our race is no credit. The Anglo-Saxon doesn't want to be a Japanese; the Japanese doesn't want to be a Negro. Then, in the name of God and all that is holy, why should we want to be somebody else?

Let the National Association for the Advancement of Colored People stop its hypocrisy and settle down to real race uplift.

If Du Bois, Johnson, Pickens and Bagnall do not know, let me tell them that they are only being used to weaken the race, so that in another fifty or a hundred years the race can easily be wiped out as a social, economic and political force or "menace." The people who are directing the affairs of the National Association for the Advancement of "Colored" People are keen observers and wise leaders. It takes more than ordinary intelligence to penetrate their motive, hence you are now warned.

All the "gas" about anti-lynching and "social equality" will not amount to a row of pins; in fact, it is only a ruse to raise money to capitalize the scheme and hide the real motive. Negroes, watch your step and save yourselves from deception and subsequent extermination. With best wishes for your success, I have the honor to be, Your obedient servant,

MARCUS GARVEY
President General
Universal Negro Improvement Association

P.S.—This is the first of a series of articles to be written occasionally to expose the motive of the so-called National Association for the Advancement of Certain People. It is also desired to point out that Cyril Briggs, of the so-called African Blood Brotherhood and the Crusader Service, who fought against the Black Star Line, the Universal Negro Improvement Association and Marcus Garvey to destroy them, belongs to the American-West Indian African group, so near white that it is impossible to tell his race. He is from the West Indies and has been most vicious in his attacks upon Marcus Garvey in promoting the Universal Negro Improvement Association. It is alleged that Briggs, like others, believes that the darker element of Negroes should be led and not allowed to lead.

---

# 12
## The Wonders of the White Man in Building America

*Garvey wrote the editorial letter "The Wonders of the White Man in Building America" to* Negro World *on October 23, 1923, while he was traveling in California after being released from The Tombs on bond, pending appeal of his conviction for mail fraud. Garvey had taken the trip partly as a vacation, but partly in an effort to rebuild his organization following his incarceration. In this letter he continued to stress the need for blacks to create a homeland in Africa to avoid racial extinction, and addressed the position of the Ku Klux Klan in the racial debate in the United States. The Dyer that Garvey refers to was Leonidas Carstarphen Dyer, Republican congressman from St. Louis. In April 1918 Dyer introduced a bill in Congress that would make lynching a federal crime. The Dyer Anti Lynching Bill was defeated by a filibuster in the Senate, after being approved in the House in January 1922. The letter was published in* Negro World, *October 27, 1923, and reprinted in* MG&UNIA Papers *5: 484–88.*

Fellow Men of the Negro Race, Greeting:

Away out on the Pacific Coast of America I view with alarm, yet with hope, the future of our race.

I have reached this section of America through a trip of several weeks from New York on the East, and in my travels everywhere I saw before me the wonders wrought by the white man's skill, daring and perseverance. On every hand I came in contact with his rising civilization—that for which he will die, holding it as sacred to his generation and to posterity.

## The Ku Klux Klan

I have traveled through and am now in the stronghold of the Ku Klux Klan, that mighty white organization that faces America with a program that is supported by every second man in the nation, whether he wants to confess it or not.

The Klan has captured the South, the West, the Northwest and the Middle West, and it is only a question of time when that organization will in truth be the most powerful weapon of the white race in prosecuting their ideal of white supremacy in America.

## No Time to Waste

The Universal Negro Improvement Association has never fought the Klan as an organization, and does not intend to do so in America, for it will be useless and non-availing, except to the point when all will unite against us for supremacy—namely, Jew, Catholic and Klan.

The Universal Negro Improvement Association knows America will always be a white man's country, including all elements of that race. Then why waste time in attempting the impossible and in allowing others to make fools of us?

## Responsibility of Saving the Negro

The responsibility of saving the race rests upon our leaders of today, and it is for us to realize that any wholesale antagonism of a group of people who are in a position to enforce their likes and dislikes will but redound to the disadvantage of the unfortunate minority, such as we are, and surrounded as we are by a 90 per cent. Klan spirit, unspoken though it be. Ninety per cent. of white America is sympathetically Klan and would be untrue to itself if it were not. Our relationship, therefore, is like that of the sheep to the lion; the former, then, must be very careful not to be devoured by the latter; and thus we warn the race to be careful in the handling of propaganda against the Knights of the Ku Klux Klan, for the majority of those who seemingly are opposed to the Klan, and who have been inviting Negroes to fight with them against the Klan, are greater and more heartless Klansmen than the Knights themselves. It is purely a question of "NE-GROES, WATCH YOUR STEPS AND YOUR (?) FRIENDS."

## The Solution of the Problem

There is but one solution of this great problem, and that is for the Negro to look toward building for himself, for neither the Klan nor any other group of white men intend to hand over to Negroes the civilization and materialism of America, which they have spent their strength and blood to create. If the Klan and the white race want to make America a white man's country, as they ultimately will, then why not 400,000,000 Negroes unite and make Africa a black man's country, and thus save a conflict of ideals and aspirations that is bound to end disastrously to the weaker race?

America, the country with the program of the greatest good for the greatest number, will always be that of the white man, for he is in the majority. 'Tis hard, 'tis woefully hard, for a Du Bois or a Weldon Johnson to admit this, but how can one wisely "kick against the pricks?"

## Get Busy and Build Nation

Negroes, get busy building a nation of your own, for neither Europe nor America will tolerate us as competitors in another half century. Let's get busy now, and, like the Ku Klux Klan and Knights of Columbus, fight for those ideals that are possible—not to ever see a black President, Governor, Cabinet Officer or Mayor in the country or state where the white man forms the majority population, but of ourselves to build up Africa, where our race will have the opportunity to rise to the highest positions in society, industry and government.

## Don't Be Deceived

I appeal to the black race of America not to allow itself to be deceived by the professions of a Dyer with his antilynching bill, or a Morefield Storey, Spingarn or Mary White Ovington with their oily tongues of hypocrisy and deception. There is no white man in the world who could afford, at this time of the fight for the survival of the fittest, to be more interested in another race than his own. He would either be a traitor or a fool. If the ideals of black and white clash in America, how is it possible for these persons to better serve the black race through the National Association for the Advancement of Colored People than their own? These people tell us to fight the Ku Klux Klan, because they know well that if any one is to suffer for so doing it will not be the advisers, but the doers. They tell us that we must fight against the methods of the President, or the programs of the Republican or Democratic parties; but if any one is to suffer for so doing it is Negroes, and not the "PHILANTHROPISTS."

### Dyer and His Anti-Lynching Bill

Dyer is so sincere in opposing the Klan for Negroes and in carrying an anti-lynching bill in Congress to protect Negroes that in his own State and in his own Congressional District in St. Louis a Negro cannot drink a soda in a white drug store or eat a sandwich in a white restaurant for the want of a civil rights bill! Yet he flies around the nation telling us about the anti-lynching bill, which, if passed, would mean nothing more than other laws already on the statutes, but ineffective in their application to the Negro.

Dyer's bill is not to stop the mob; it is to punish the mob. But the deed is already done. Who will be the judge and jury to punish the mob but the brother and cousins of the violators of the law? And yet Dyer and his gang think they can fool all of the people for all of the time.

### Catching the Negro

Once upon a time the Negro was caught by the brandishing of the red kerchief; then, later, by the beating of the drum, and now in the twentieth century our good friends try to catch us with high-sounding words and promises; but some of us have come from Missouri, Mr. Dyer's own State, and you have to "show us." Dyer gloried in the conviction of Garvey in his speeches for the National Association for the Advancement of Colored People, because he knew that Garvey was one of the Negroes he could not fool for all of the time. If Dyer does not know, let me tell him that I was in his Congressional District in St. Louis two weeks ago and could not get a soda served even by a dirty Greek, who kept his so-called white soda fountain in a Negro section, the section represented by the "famous" anti-lynching advocate. O! the hypocrisy of this world! Here do I leave my untidy home, crusading for the cause of having others clean up that which I failed to do in my own house!

### Congregation of Animals

I was traveling down the street and came upon a great congregation of animals of all kinds. There I saw lions, tigers, elephants, bears, foxes, sheep, goats, dogs, cats, rats and fowls. I observed that every species kept to itself; the tigers were afraid of the company of the lions; the elephants were not uniting with the tigers;

the foxes tried to escape the bears; the rats were running away from the cats, and even the fowls were just nervous about the appearance of the foxes, and therefore I learned a great lesson. The fox hobnobbing with the fowl can have but one object, and that is in some way to steal a chicken. And then do I see that the presence of any opposite animal, human or otherwise, in the midst of others means that some stealing is to be done, either in ideals, character, pride, vision or life.

### Telling the Negro the Truth

Those who tell the Negro what they mean are the Negro's greatest friends. Those who hide their intention under the guise of fellowship, philanthropy and Christianity are our greatest enemy. If I were to decide between the Ku Klux Klan and Dyer as friends of the Negro I would choose the Ku Klux Klan, because they are honest enough to tell me what they mean—"white supremacy"—and thereby give me a chance to save myself, rather than the other fellow, who tries to tell me it is daylight when, indeed, he knows that night is approaching. Does Dyer stand for white supremacy or black ascendancy? He does not dare answer in favor of the latter, and be a man and a Christian, even as his colleagues are unable to answer. Then they are to us as much members of the Invisible Empire as any outspoken Klansman, who is not afraid nor ashamed to tell America and the world what he means.

### How the Negro Is to Rise

If the Negro is to rise he must look to himself and to those of the white race who are honest enough to tell him his faults and help him to be the best of himself and not expect to be the nearest imitation of a white man.

### Room for Everybody

There is room in the world for white and black, both having their eye set upon ideals of their own without deception or hypocrisy. There is room enough in America for the white man and there is room enough in Africa for the black man. Then let us strive after those things that are possible and not be deceived. With best wishes for your success, I have the honor to be Your obedient servant,

MARCUS GARVEY
President-General
Universal Negro Improvement Association

# 13
## What We Believe

*In this editorial letter written on January 1, 1924, and published in* Negro World, *January 12, 1924, Garvey summarizes the racial philosophy of the UNIA. Garvey clearly rejected the integrationist position championed at this time by the NAACP and W.E.B. Du Bois. This letter was reprinted in MG&UNIA Papers 5: 512.*

The Universal Negro Improvement Association advocates the uniting and blending of all Negroes into one strong healthy race. It is against miscegenation and race suicide.

It believes that the Negro race is as good as any other, and therefore should be as proud of itself as others are.

It believes in the purity of the Negro race and the purity of the white race.

It is against rich blacks marrying poor whites.

It is against rich or poor whites taking advantage of Negro women.

It believes in the spiritual Fatherhood of God and the Brotherhood of Man.

It believes in the social and political physical separation of all people to the extent that they promote their own ideals and civilization, with the privilege of trading and doing business with each other. It believes in the promotion of a strong and powerful Negro nation.

It believes in the rights of all men.

> Universal Negro Improvement Assn.
> MARCUS GARVEY
> President-General

---

# 14
## Editorial Letter Written to *NEGRO WORLD*, February 10, 1925

*On February 2, 1925, the Federal Appeals Court rejected Garvey's appeal of his conviction for mail fraud. Garvey was taken into custody in New York City and sent to the federal penitentiary in Atlanta where he would serve his sentence. In this letter, written shortly after he arrived in Atlanta, Garvey accepts his martyrdom, and continues to charge Du Bois and the NAACP with betraying the colored race. This letter was printed in* Negro World, *February 14, 1925, and reprinted in* MG&UNIA Papers 6: 96–98, *and, with revisions, in Jacques-Garvey,* Philosophy and Opinions of Marcus Garvey, *vol. 2: 237–39.*

FELLOW MEN OF THE NEGRO RACE, *Greeting:*

I am delighted to inform you that your humble servant is as happy in suffering for you and our cause as is possible under the circumstances of being viciously outraged by a group of plotters who have connived to do their worst to humiliate you through me in the fight for real emancipation and African Redemption.

## Lying Propaganda

I do trust that you have given no credence to the vicious lies of white and enemy newspapers and those who have spoken in reference to my surrender. The liars plotted in every way to make it appear that I was not willing to surrender to the court. My attorney advised me that no mandate would have been handed down for ten or fourteen days, as is the custom of the courts, and that would have given me time to keep speaking engagements I had in Detroit, Cincinnati and Cleveland. I hadn't left the city for ten hours when the liars flashed the news that I was a fugitive. That was good news to circulate all over the world to demoralize the millions of Negroes in America, Africa, Asia, the West Indies and Central America, but the idiots ought to know by now that they can't fool all the Negroes at the same time.

I do not want at this time to write anything that would make it difficult for you to meet the opposition of the enemy without my assistance. Suffice it to say that the history of the outrage shall form a splendid chapter in the history of Africa redeemed when black men will no longer be under the heels of others, but have a civilization and country of their own.

The whole affair is a disgrace, and the whole black world knows it. We shall not forget. Our day may be fifty, a hundred or two hundred years ahead, but let us watch, work and pray, for the civilization of injustice is bound to crumble and bring destruction down upon the heads of the unjust.

## Seeds of Black Nationalism Well Planted

The idiots thought that they could humiliate me personally, but in that they are mistaken. The minutes of suffering are counted, and when God and Africa come back and measure out retribution these minutes may multiply by thousands for the sinners. Our Arab and Riffian friends will be ever vigilant, as the rest of Africa and ourselves shall be. Be assured that I planted well the seed of Negro or black nationalism which cannot be destroyed even by the foul play that has been meted out to me.

### Dr. W.E.B. Du Bois and the N.A.A.C.P.

Continue to pray for me and I shall ever be true to my trust. I want you, the black peoples of the world, to know that W.E.B. Du Bois and that vicious Negro-hating organization known as the [National] Association for the Advancement of "Colored" People are the greatest enemies the black people have in the world. I have so much to do in the few minutes at my disposal that I cannot write exhaustively on this or any other matter, but be warned against these two enemies. Don't allow them to fool you with fine sounding press releases, speeches and books; they are the vipers who have planned with others the extinction of the "black" race.

My work is just begun, and when the history of my suffering is complete, then future generations of Negroes will have in their hands the guide by which they shall know the "sins" of the twentieth century. I, and I know you, too, believe in time, and we shall wait patiently for two hundred years, if need be, to face our enemies through our generations.

### Support Those at the Helm

You will cheer me much if you will now do even more for the organization than when I was among you. Hold up the hands of those who are carrying on. Help them to make good, so that the work may continue to spread from pole to pole.

I am also making a last minute appeal for support to the Black Cross Navigation and Trading Company. Please send in and make your loans so as to enable the directors to successfully carry on the work.

### "The Bravest Little Woman"

All I have I have given to you. I have sacrificed my home and my loving wife for you. I entrust her to your charge, to protect and defend her in my absence. She is the bravest little woman I know. She has suffered and sacrificed with me for you; therefore, please do not desert her at this dismal hour, when she stands alone. I have left her penniless and helpless to face the world, because I gave you all, but her courage is great and I know she will hold up for you and me.

### In Life or Death

After my enemies are satisfied[,] in life or death I shall come back to you to serve even as I have served before. In life I shall be the same; in death I shall be a terror to the foes of Negro liberty. If death has power, then count on me in death to be the real Marcus Garvey I would like to be. If I may come in an earthquake, or a cyclone, or plague, or pestilence, or as God would have me, then be assured that I will never desert you and make your enemies triumph over you. Would I not go to hell a million times for you? Would I not, like Macbeth's ghost, walk the earth forever for you? Would I not lose the whole world and eternity for you? Would I not cry forever before the footstool of the Lord Omnipotent for you? Would I not die a million deaths for you? Then, why be sad? Cheer up, and be assured that if it takes a million years, the sins of our enemies shall visit the millionth generation of those that hinder and oppress us.

## Will Serve to the End

Remember that I have sworn by you and my God to serve to the end of all time, the wreck of matter and the crash of worlds. The enemies think that I am defeated. Did the Germans defeat the French in 1870? Did Napoleon really conquer Europe? If so, then I am defeated, but I tell you the world shall hear from my principles even two thousand years hence. I am willing to wait on time for my satisfaction and the retribution of my enemies. Observe my enemies and their children and posterity, and one day you shall see retribution settling around them.

## "If I Die in Atlanta"

If I die in Atlanta my work shall then only begin, but I shall live, in the physical or spiritual to see the day of Africa's glory. When I am dead wrap the mantle of the Red, Black and Green around me, for in the new life I shall rise with God's grace and blessings to lead the millions up the heights of triumph with the colors that you well know. Look for me in the whirlwind or the storm, look for me all around you, for, with God's grace, I shall come and bring with me countless millions of black slaves who have died in America and the West Indies and the millions in Africa to aid you in the fight for liberty, freedom and life.

## 20th Century Civilization Drunk with Power

The civilization of today is gone drunk and crazy with its power and by such it seeks through injustice, fraud and lies to crush the unfortunate. But if I am apparently crushed by the system of influence and misdirected power, my cause shall rise again to plague the conscience of the corrupt. For this I am satisfied, and for you, I repeat, I am glad to suffer and even die. Again, I say, cheer up, for better days are ahead. I shall write the history that will inspire the millions that

are coming and leave the posterity of our enemies to reckon with the hosts for
the deeds of their fathers. With God's dearest blessings, I leave you for awhile.
With very best wishes, your humble and obedient servant,

MARCUS GARVEY
President-General
Universal Negro Improvement Association

---

# 15
# Two Editorial Letters from New Orleans,
# December 10, 1927

*Garvey was released from the Atlanta Federal Penitentiary on November 26,
1927; he was immediately taken into custody by the Immigration Bureau, and
transported to New Orleans where he was deported on December 2, 1927. These
two letters are Garvey's farewell to his supporters in the United States. The
letters were printed in* Negro World, *December 10, 1927, and reprinted in*
MG&UNIA Papers *6: 617–21.*

## [Special Message from New Orleans, November 29, 1927]

The first chapter in the history of the Universal Negro Improvement Association
is written, and I am about to open the second chapter in the urge toward African
Nationalism. My simple enemies think they have triumphed in having me rail-
roaded, but their weakness is to be found in their very desperation.

They are counting without the tremendous odds of righteousness which is on
our side, and which will cause us to win under the leadership of GOD.

I am forced to leave you, but I am going to prepare a greater and grander
UNIVERSAL NEGRO IMPROVEMENT ASSOCIATION. Keep up your courage and your
faith. Don't allow the enemy to get the better of you by misrepresenting me. We
are winning, but GOD knows how. The Organization shall continue the same
under my direction until the next INTERNATIONAL CONVENTION in August, 1929.
You must give me time and the help necessary to put into effect my plans and
study for your benefit, that I have developed during my two years and nine
months of quiet imprisonment. It will take me some little time to write the new
creed of the Association and to perfect the sign by which we shall conquer. I am
now appealing to you for the first time in all my efforts for personal financial

help, for I am without funds, having given you everything I had, even to my very name. I cannot fight singlehanded. I have much work to do, but you must now personally help me.

You shall hear from me shortly and constantly. Read THE NEGRO WORLD, and digest carefully my every word, for every word shall have a meaning. I shall publish in a few days the names of the national committee, under the direction of Mr. E.B. Knox, who shall carry on the work of the Association until the next INTERNATIONAL CONVENTION. Keep cheerful and believe that I shall be true to you till death. I send this message to you by my loving and devoted wife, who I ask that you send to me as early as possible. GOD be with you till we meet again. Obediently and Sincerely Yours.

> MARCUS GARVEY
> President General
> Universal Negro Improvement Association

**[Editorial Letter from New Orleans, *ca.* 2  December 1927]**

*Masterly and Trenchant Expose of White Hypocrisy*
*by Marcus Garvey, Mastermind*

To the millions of members of the Universal Negro Improvement Association in America, and my friends, I say good-bye. I leave you thus early because others who are in power today say I must go. What do I care? They ran the Christ out of Jerusalem, but that did not kill the urge of Christianity. They crucified Him in preference to Barabbas, but neither Caiaphas, Herod nor Pontius Pilate could stop the mighty resurrection. These modern fools who play politics against the cause of righteousness shall in the end see their own defeat, of which the floods, storms and earthquakes are but the sign of the doom.

I am not sore with the innocent people of white America because they know no better than what the tricky politicians care to have them know and do; but honest white America will one day wake up and then the cheap politician will have sung his requiem.

*Only One Regret*

There is only one regret I have, and that is, that the Negro is to a certain extent sleeping under the deception of the tricky white politicians and statesmen who have planned his complete elimination and gradual extermination from the body politic with the aid and connivance of the corrupt and heartless Negro politician and leader. Lying white newspapers and magazines are all in the scheme to fool the Negro and suppress his growth.

### The "Liberal" New York World

The New York World still continues to profess friendship for you, but loses sight of no opportunity to stab you in the back by holding up your honest and honorable leadership to ridicule. It is by propaganda and ridicule that they hope to defeat the steady rise of the Negro to nationalism, as they did in defeating the Germans. But for us "they shall not pass." The New York World has just published that I "took in" (whatsover that means) $5,000,000 and that I have half a million put away for some imaginary rainy day. My rainy day is every day. Then why put it away when I could purchase at least four more ships with that much money, to show the white man he shall never completely succeed in driving us off the seas. If I had half a million cents I should not be personally so broke, but what do I care about money, when I possess my character that no evil white man nor newspaper can take away from me?

The white man (unreasonable) in the face of history is simple to think he can dispose of determined characters in world movements for human liberty by mere ridicule.

### Shall Not Be Intimidated

I promise you as God liveth that I shall, with the leadership of Christ and Simon, the Cyrenian, blast a way to African freedom. No fear, no intimidation, no punishment, no death shall ever deter me in the fight for African redemption. Good God! What do these unreasonable white people think? That they are going to buy and fool every Negro who comes upon the scene? It is laughable. They may railroad me out of America, but they also ran Christ out of Jerusalem, but that did not stop the sweeping potency of Christianity.

During the two years and ten months I remained in Atlanta penitentiary they, as planned, robbed you of all your assets in New York and prevented me from properly defending the Morter Estate—a gross loss of over half a million dollars. They imprisoned me for an empty envelope that was not worth a cent, then caused you to lose half a million dollars. But that is only a drop in the bucket in the urge to African freedom. We shall win and recover every cent we have been robbed of with compound interest. Why worry over such small matters when the bigger urge of liberty calls!

### Never Felt in Better Shape

I am feeling fine and never better in my life. They sent me to Atlanta to die, but the God who took care of Daniel in the lions' den and the faithful in the fiery furnace took care of me in Atlanta. They tried their damnedest to hold me down, but truth shall rise even from the dust.

They now, in their press reports, are calling me a "black Ponzi." The thing is laughable. If I am a Ponzi what are the white men who have been robbing even the dead since God Almighty said, "Let there be light"? Has the white man forgotten his history of plunder and universal robbery? Does he want me to tell him about it? If so, I shall surely accom[m]odate him: from the time of Ancient Greece to the time of the politically corrupt 20th century.

### The Business of Fooling Negroes

Negroes, keep your heads high. The day of the unscrupulous of the white race fooling all the Negroes is over. They will have to remake the universe to fool me. In no department of learning can they close my eyes. I am ready for all their tricks, sociologically, anthropologically, economically, industrially, commercially, politically, biologically, ethnically, philosophically and religiously. They use propaganda to throw dust into the eyes of the world, but they shall never blind me in the storm.

They tried to call me crooked because I am honest and did not fall for the methods of corruption. But if I am crooked, than I shall present them their history that even the devil would be ashamed of.

### Work Is Just Begun

Believe that our work is just started. And all those who calculate on my defeat have another thought to experience. Here is one black man who shall not be downed by injustice and unrighteousness. I shall fight on with God on my side, with all the legions of hell let loose. For me there is no fear but the fear of God. Cast fear to the winds, Negroes, and go forward to your own creative destiny.

I feel happy that I have started the good work. Carry on, carry on, and let the standard of the Red, Black and Green fly!

### Cheer Up; Keep Cool

Those of you who have financial interests in the organization as members, don't be discouraged or fooled out of your rights. We shall take care of everything at the next International Convention, and although the enemies have robbed you, and I was imprisoned principally to take all you had so as to discourage and scatter you, believe me that you shall lose nothing. Just wait awhile and help us to rearrange the work of the movement. Hold fast to the principles of the Association, never say die. Cheer up, keep cool, and remember that I am in splendid fighting shape. God bless and be with you.

I have the honor to be, Your obedient servant,

MARCUS GARVEY
First Provisional President of Africa
and President General
Universal Negro Improvement Association
of the World

# IV.  A. Philip Randolph

# 1
## The Negro in Politics

*The essay "The Negro in Politics," published in* The Messenger *2 (July 1918): 15–19, summarized the political history of African Americans from the end of the Civil War to 1918. Reflecting his commitment to leftist politics, Randolph argued that the traditional political parties failed to answer the needs of American blacks, and that their political future was with the Socialist Party.*

The Negro has had a pathetic and unpromising history in American politics.

His eventful and hapless career began under the shadows of the institution of slavery, from which he had just emerged. He was played upon by two forces, viz., the open opposition from his former masters, on the one hand, and the fraud and deception of the white carpet-baggers, who swarmed South, like vultures, to prey upon his ignorance and credulity.

### Reconstruction Period

We have but to take a glimpse into the history of the Reconstruction period, to witness his tragical political flight, wrought by a paradoxial combination of his Northern Republican friends and his Southern Democratic enemies.

During this period the Negro was a political football between his former slave-masters and Northern political adventurers. The economic basis of this contest was the power to tax; to float bonds; to award franchises; in short, to gain control over the financial resources of the newly organized States. These were big stakes for which to contend. Hence, the carpet-baggers used the enfranchised Negro to assist them in securing control over the Southern State governments and the Southern politicians fought the Negro viciously to prevent this Carpet-bagger-Negro political ascendancy.

This period of storm and stress gave birth to two significant social organizations, the Union of Loyal League of Negroes and the Ku Klux Klan, which attempted to protect the political interests of the Negroes and Southern whites, respectively.

They only served, however, to engender bitterness: to breed and to foster suspicion and hate between the races, which resulted in lawlessness, crime and general social anarchy. These, too, were natural political and social consequences of the Reconstruction policy. The inordinate lust for power, overwhelming ambition to rule, the instinct to secure an advantage, impels individuals and social groups to adopt the philosophy of force, the policy of fraud, or the method of education: whichever policy is available, and is recognized as likely to secure the more permanent results.

Such were the political vicissitudes of the Negro in the South. The Ku Klux Klan and the tissue ballot were social and political inventions of intimidation to discourage the Negroes' participation in politics. The Thirteenth, Fourteenth and Fifteenth Amendments to the Federal Constitution, the Federal Army and the Carpet-Baggers were designed to protect the Negroes' suffrage, in order that the Negro might entrench, reenforce and fortify the Republican party's control over Congress. The lessons of this period had been hard, bitter and disappointing to the Negro. The army, the arm of protection of the Federal Government, had been withdrawn. The Negro office holders and their Republican supporters had been hurled from power. The Reconstruction legislation had been emasculated from the statute books. The Southern States had begun a systematic and organized campaign of nullification of the freedom and enfranchisement of the Negro. In fact, the Negro had been reduced to serfdom. And in 1876 the last vestige of Reconstruction governments had disappeared. And it cannot be maintained by the sober and dispassionate historian that the Negro had legislated and administered the State governments wisely and well. As he had ignorantly fought with and tilled the fields for his former masters to maintain slavery, he had also voted to strengthen his Republican political masters, to dominate the government, only to be forsaken, neglected, naked to his enemies. No Negro, with a genius for leadership, had arisen in this period. So much for our Reconstruction history.

**Subsequent Political Course**

What has been the subsequent political course of the Negro?

The complete scheme of the Negroes' disfranchisement was in process of development in the South. The South had resented and ignored the fourteenth amendment which had demanded a reduction in representation in Congress, if the Negroes' suffrage was restricted. Intermittant cries against this political brigandage were heard, but finally subsided. The South continued to weave a fabric of law, the "Grandfather clauses," which gave legal sanction to an already general custom of Negro disfranchisement. The Republican Party, pretended friend and defender, had assented. Yet the Negro remained a Republican. Why? First, the Reconstruction legislation of the Republican party had forged the "Solid South." The Solid South was dominated by the Democratic Party. The Democratic Party had striven to maintain slavery. It had been the father of the "Fugitive Slave Law," the nullification of the Missouri Compromise of 1820, and Chief Justice Taney had handed down the famous Dred Scott's decision, which gave constitutional sanction to the extension of slavery into new territory.

On the other hand, the Republican Party had been the party of the North, the refuge of the fugitive slave, the home of the abolitionists, Wendell Philips, Garrison, Lovejoy and Sumner was in power when freedom came. It had used the Negro as an office holder and continued to distribute political crumbs in the form of collectors of internal revenue, deputy collectors, registrars of the Treasury, Ministers to Hayti, Liberia and such places, that required no administrative ability, no intelligent understanding of the methods, objects and principles of government. In truth, the Negro office-holders were mainly of the "rubber stamp" variety. But it was sufficient that the Republican Party had awarded jobs, to secure the indiscriminating and unquestioning devotion of the Negro. Thus, the Negro became as staunch a Republican as the Irish a Democrat. It was considered race treason for a Negro to profess any other political faith.

Here and there an eccentric Negro had claimed to be a Democrat, but his claim was considered lightly. It is true that in New York City a tiny fraction of Negroes had bolted the Republican ranks and joined Tammany Hall, seeking political jobs.

There had also arisen among the Negroes a political scism, namely a belief in the virtue of dividing the vote. In support of this political heresy, it was maintained that by dividing the vote the Negro would be able to secure the good will of both parties: it was further maintained that it would create fear within the Republican Party which would result in its giving the Negro a fairer consideration, and that the Negro would be sure of political preferment, regardless of which party was in power. And in 1912 and in 1916 a few Negro leaders had professed sympathy for Woodrow Wilson as the Democratic presidential nominee.

The formation of the Progressive Party of 1912 had marked another important rift in the Negro Republican voters. The love for Roosevelt, the expectation of jobs and the general dissatisfaction with President Taft's attitude towards Negro job-holders in the South, had produced this alienation.

In the mayoralty election of New York City, in 1917, occurred another change in the Negroes' political course. This change resulted in 25 per cent. of the Negroes voting the Socialist ticket. This vote, too, it might be observed, was achieved despite the fact that heretofore there had been no Socialist vote among Negroes in New York State.

These movements have had their leaders. Who were they and what did they stand for?

## Types of Negro Political Leaders Evolved

During the Reconstruction period the Negro leaders were unschooled, credulous, gullible. They had been led by the Republican agents from the North, the carpetbaggers.

Ex-Governor Pinchback, Lynch, Moses, etc., had been accomplices to most shameless raids upon the funds of the States destructive legislation and the issuance of spurious, inflated paper.

In Congress White and Bruce had done one thing, they had been loyal to the

Republican Party. During the long years from the passing of Negro representatives in Congress, no Negro of large vision and intelligent grasp of the forces in politics had arisen.

Booker T. Washington had become prominent in the industrial development of the Negro, but had counselled the "let alone policy."

Bishop Walters, W.E.B. Du Bois, James Monroe Trotter, and Rev. James Milton Waldron—Negroes of national standing and prominence—had turned Democratic. Their object was to make the Republican Party repentant. These men had a vision of the rise of a Radical Negro; they had recognized the failure of the Republican Party: they had not caught the message of Socialism and they were still ruled by the belief that the test of the political progress of the Negroes was the number of jobs he held. They had not realized that out of 12,000,000 Negroes but a tiny fraction could become job-holders. The value of workmen's compensation legislation, widow's pensions, social insurance legislation, measures reducing the cost of living, shortening hours of toil and increasing the wages of the masses, had escaped them.

In the Republican Party, Charles W. Anderson, Ralph Tyler, W.T. Vernon and W.H. Lewis are figures of national proportions. These are men of the old school who make much over what they style as "playing the game of politics," which in other words simply means getting next to "campaign slush funds" and landing a rubber stamp job. Their positions rest upon their ability to echo the will of the masters through flamboyant oratory and their unquestioning obedience to the Republican machine.

Even the generous student of politics cannot accord to them any fundamental understanding of the relation between politics and the business of getting a living, the social purpose and economic basis of modern legislation and the scientific methods of administrative government.

They with the ward-heeler-politician identify their personal prosperity with that of the race and insist that their holding of a government job is an unmistakable sign of the Negroes' political progress.

Negro leaders, generally, have been creatures of the Republican or Democratic parties, which hold them in leash and prevent them from initiating anything fundamental in the interest of the Negroes. This brings us to the consideration of the appointment policy.

### Influence of the Appointment Policy

Aptly and truly, too, has it been said that the "power over a man's subsistence is the power over his will" or expressed more popularly "he who pays the fiddler will call the tune."

Since Negro leaders have been the appointees of Republican and Democratic bosses it is but natural that they would obey the voice of their masters. And the Republican and Democratic bosses are servants of the employing or capitalist class which thrives upon low wages and high prices, the ignorance and degradation of the workers of which 12 per cent. are Negroes.

This principle, however, of appointing members of the servant-class to positions in the government or to places of race leadership, has been uniformly adopted by the ruling class in all parts of the world. The social experience is that a member of an oppressed class, invested with power by the master-class becomes the brutal oppressor and exploiter of his class. Note the vicious character of foremen, headwaiters, who are recruited from the working class.

Great Britain employs 250,000 natives of India to hold in subjection 300,000,000. She has also applied this same rule in Ireland and successfully exploited these peoples for 800 years.

Hence, it is apparent that the Negro leaders, the hirelings of the Republican and Democratic bosses who are in turn the agents of anti-labor forces, are the worst enemies of the race.

**The Growth of the Movement for Negro Elective Representation**

The movement is conceived in the idea that those whom the people elect will represent them. But in the light of the history of government, it cannot logically be maintained that all persons elected by the people will represent the people. For instance, during the Reconstruction period the Negro office-holders and legislators, represented the carpet-baggers and not the people. Today, all legislators are elected by the people but the people suffer most from poverty and ignorance, hence it cannot be maintained that the present government represents the people, if by representation we mean the enactment of legislation for the relief of human suffering and the improvement of social conditions. The people elect but the capitalists select.

There are three main conditions to a representative's representing those by whom he is elected. First, his chief interests must be identical with those by whom he is elected; second, he must be the member of a party organization which is controlled by his constituents; and, third, he must be sufficiently intelligent to understand his class interests.

To illustrate: If a real estate owner is elected to the legislature from a district composed largely of working people, his tenants: his chief interests would lie with the members of his class—the real estate owners and in opposition to those who elected him—the tenant-class. If a measure was raised to abolish the "law of dispossess," who would wonder as to how the real estate owners would vote, despite the fact, the measure would be palpably in the interests of those whom he was presumed to represent.

Again, suppose the representative's chief interests are identical with those of his constituents, and is also the member of a political organization which is controlled by forces which are opposed to the chief interests of his district. Is it not plain as to how he would vote? The history of politics is clear on this point.

The lack of regularity would result in his political death. Note the fate of Ex-Governor Sulzer of New York who opposed the Tammany machine which created him. Note Roosevelt's plight who bolted the Republican machine in 1912.

Lastly, given that the two foregoing conditions are satisfied, if the representative was not sufficiently intelligent he might be used as the most effective opponent of his own and his constituent's interests.

Thus, it is apparent that the election of a Negro by Negroes, is not enough and does not guarantee Negroes, of whom 99 per cent. are working people, that their chief interests as working people will be represented.

Just as the election of a woman, by women does not guarantee that their chief interests will be represented.

Witness Jeanette Rankin, woman representative from Montana, lining up with the Republican and Democratic parties in unquestioning support of the capitalists, despite the fact, women and their children are the chief sufferers from long hours of work and low wages in factories and mines.

Witness the election of the Negro assemblyman, E.A. Johnson, from the 21st Assembly District of New York City, introducing a bill to permit children of the tender age of 12 when they are out of school to be exploited at work. Note, too, that he cited as his main reason for this bill, the recent exodus of Negroes from the South and the likelihood of idle Negro children getting into mischief in the streets of New York. This bill was condemned by educators and union leaders, on the ground that children are in need of play and recreation as much as they are in need of book learning. Work stunts the bodies and arrests the mental growth of children.

Here, two facts are evident: first, that the Assemblyman was ignorant of the fundamental recreational and educational needs of children; second, that he is part of the Republican machine, which represents the factory and canneries interests which makes millions out of child labor. Here then is a clear case of a Negro being the father of a measure, from which Negro children will be the chief sufferers, being as they are in more need of education and wholesome recreation.

However, I might observe that I am simply predicting of the Negro representatives what is true of all white representatives of the capitalists parties, Republican and Democratic.

Will the entrance of Negro women into politics change the general tenor of things? My answer is no. The history of women in public affairs, black and white, warrant me in taking this position. Their traditions, education and environment, are similar to those of the men and they may be expected to follow the same course of political thinking. They will also be influenced by their male companions.

However, I might observe here, that Negro women, especially, may profit from the political blunders of Negro men. It is admitted by both white and black that the Negro men have made a mess of politics. It is further admitted that, during his entire political career, he has been nothing else but a Republican, so that the logical deduction is that to follow in the course of the Negro men is to make a similar mess of politics.

## The Rise of Political Radicalism Among Negroes

The political radicalism of the Negro has been marked by three definite movements: First, the entrance of the Negro into the Democratic Party; second, the transition to the elective idea of representation; third, and the most fundamental and significant of all is, the change from the old parties to Socialism.

The last of these changes has been the result of the rise of a new type of leaders. The old Negro leaders have had the intent to serve the interest of the Negroes, but they have lacked the knowledge as to how they could best serve them. And it is recognized today that the possession of an intent to do good without the knowledge is more fatal than the possession of knowledge without the intent. To illustrate: History attests that during the early Christian era, Marcus Aurelius was the most savage persecutor of the Christians, yet he was one of the most upright of men and it is maintained that he persecuted them on the ground that he was saving them from the consequences of their folly. His intent was to do good. Even Protestant historians accord to those who maintained the Spanish Inquisition, honest intentions, while they murdered, massacred and outraged the heretics of their day. The suppression of free speech, the freedom of the press and the lynching of Negroes and I.W.W. are based upon the intent to subserve the country's interests. The system which produces these conditions, determines the social consequences of the policies, adopted by both good and bad men. Thus, it is apparent that an individual's power to do social and personal mischief is, in proportion to the intensity of his belief in the rightness of his act and the absence of knowledge as to its social consequences. An ignorant man may take Bicloride of mercury for quinine; the result is death, though his intent and desire was to live.

## The Future of the Negro in American Politics

Thus it is obvious that the hope of the Negro lies, first, in the development of Negro leaders with a knowledge of the science of government and economics, scientific history and sociology; and second, in the relegation to the political scrap heap, those Negro leaders whose only qualifications are the desire to lead and the intent to do good.

The old Negro leaders have been factors in producing and perpetuating a patent contradiction in American politics: the alliance of a race of poverty, the Negro, with a party of wealth, the Republican Party.

The Republican Party has been an instrumentality in American politics of abolishing agricultural feudalism of the South for the establishment of industrial capitalism of the North. Industrial slavery has been substituted for human slavery.

But how is the Negro to know which party to support? Before answering this question may I observe that a party is a body of individuals who agree upon a political program and who strive to gain control of the government in order to secure its adoption. Its campaigns are made possible by a fund created by those persons who desire the adoption of its program. It is natural and plain then that those who supply the funds will control and direct the party.

Now, it is a fact of common knowledge that the Republican and Democratic parties receive their campaign funds from Rockefeller, Morgan, Schwab, Shonts, Ryan, Armour and other capitalists. It is also a fact of common knowledge, that the chief interests of these capitalists are: to make large profits by employing cheap labor and selling their goods at high prices to the public.

Thus, since the chief interests of the workers are more wages, less work, cheaper food, clothing and shelter, it is apparent that their chief interests are opposed to those of their employers—the capitalists which are represented by the Republican and Democratic parties.

Now, since almost all Negroes are workers, live on wages and suffer from the high cost of food, clothing and shelter, it is obvious that the Republican and Democratic parties are opposed to their interests.

But since neither the Republican nor Democratic parties represent the Negroes' interests, the question logically arises as to which party in American politics does?

I maintain that since the Socialist Party is supported financially by working men and working women and since its platform is a demand for the abolition of this class struggle between the employer and the worker, by taking over and democratically managing the sources and machinery of wealth production and exchange, to be operated for social service and not for private profits; and, further, since the Socialist Party has always, both in the United States and Europe, opposed all forms of race prejudice, that the Negro should no longer look upon voting the Republican ticket, as accepting the lesser of two evils; but that it is politically, economically, historically and socially logical and sound for him to reject both evils, the Republican and Democratic parties and select a positive good—Socialism.

The Negro, like any other class, should support that party which represents his chief interests. Who could imagine a brewer or saloonkeeper supporting the Prohibition party?

It's like an undertaker seeking the adoption of a law, if possible, to abolish death.

Such is not less ludicrous, however, than that of a Negro, living in virtual poverty, children without education, wife driven to the kitchen or the wash-tub: continually dispossessed on account of high rents, eating poor food on account of the high cost of food, working 10, 12 and 14 hours a day, and sometimes compelled to become sycophant and clownish for a favor, a "tip," supporting the party of Rockefeller, the party of his employer, whose chief interests are to overwork and underpay him. Let us abolish these contradictions and support our logical party—the Socialist party.

---

# 2
## Lynching: Capitalism Its Cause; Socialism Its Cure

*"Lynching: Capitalism Its Cause; Socialism Its Cure" was published in* The Messenger *(March 1919): 9–12. Randolph again took a radical perspective, arguing that lynching was caused by the class conflict inherent in capitalism.*

First, What is lynching?

Lynching, historically speaking, is a loose term applied to various forms of executing popular justice, or what is thought to be justice. It is punishment of offenders or supposed offenders by a summary procedure without due process of law. In short, the essence of lynching is that it is extra-legal.

### What Object Does It Achieve?

From the lynchers' point of view it avenges crime—and is calculated to prevent future crime.

During the Reconstruction period the Klu Klux Klan applied the lynch law to intimidate the newly enfranchised Negro voter; to prevent him from voting the Republican carpet-baggers, from the North, into control of the Southern State Governments. The competition was between the former slave-holding class and the carpet-baggers for the power to levy taxes; to issue paper money; to raise revenue; and to grant franchise to private individuals for the operation of public utilities.

Today lynching is a practice which is used to foster and to engender race prejudice to prevent the lynchers and the lynched, the white and black workers from organizing on the industrial and voting on the political fields, to protect their labor-power.

Why do I affirm this and how is it done? This brings me to the consideration of capitalism as the cause of lynching.

Now, just a word as to the reason for inquiring into the cause. All medical scientists are agreed that precedent to prescribing a remedy for a disease, a diagnosis should be made in order to ascertain its cause. Because in order to remove the effects of a disease, physical or social, you must first remove the cause.

To illustrate: Let us assume that a community is situated beside a swampy marsh where poisonous vapors hover over the putrid, pestiferous, standing waters, and where malarial germs and mosquitoes infest. Let us further assume that the people of this community suffer continually from malarial fever. Scientists have determined that mosquitoes are carriers of malarial germs. Now, is it not logical to assume that the swampy marsh is the cause of the malady and that the mosquito but the occasion and that in order to wipe out the effects, malarial fever, it is necessary to remove the cause of the occasion—the marsh? This, then, is no less true of lynching than of any other disease or social evil, such as child labor, white slavery, intemperance, poverty and criminal acts in general.

For clarity of exposition I shall divide the causes into two classes, and I shall treat them in the order of ultimate and immediate or occasion causes.

But, before proceeding to build our structure of the real causes of lynching, we shall do the excavation work by clearing away the debris of alleged but fallacious causes.

First, it is maintained by most superficial sociologists that "race prejudice" is the cause of lynching.

But the fallacy of this contention is immediately apparent in view of the fact that out of 3337 persons lynched between 1882 and 1903, there were 1192 white persons.

Leo Frank, Frank Little and Robert Prager, all white men, are instances of recent date.

Second, it is held by some that "rape of white women" is the real cause. Again this argument is untenable when it is known that out of the entire number of persons lynched, during the above stated period, only 34 per cent. can be ascribed to rape as the cause.

Third, still others contend that the "law's delay" is the controlling cause. This also is without force when the fact is known that men have had their day in court—taken out and lynched, despite the fact that they (the accused) were convicted or acquitted. Leo Frank is an instance in proof. Thus much for what are some of the occasions but not the causes of lynching.

We shall now consider the real and positive causes of this national evil.

## As to the Meaning of Capitalism

Capitalism is a system under which a small class of private individuals make profits out of the labor of the masses by virtue of their ownership of the machinery and sources of production and exchange. For instance, the railroads of this country are owned by less than 600,000 stockholders who employ more than 3,000,000 persons. The ownership of the railroads by the 600,000 stockholders enables them to make billions of profits out of the labor of the 3,000,000 workers. Now there is the crux of the problem. A busines is carried on for profits. Labor is the chief item in the expense of production. It is to the interest of the employer to work the laborer as long hours and to pay as low wages as possible. On the other hand, it is to the interest of the laborer to get as high wages and to work as short hours as possible. Hence, the conflict between the capitalists and the workers. The desire and the power to make profits of the owner of the means of wealth production, which labor must use in order to make wages with which to live, is at the basis of this conflict.

Let us see how it applies to our proposition in question.

We will now review its economic aspects.

During the Civil War one-third of the man-power of the South was killed off. The Civil War resulted in the abolition of property rights in Negroes. Free labor was abolished. For 250 years the slave-owning class had the right, sanctioned by the government, to use a Negro as a horse, a machine. And the invention of the cotton gin had forced the market value of slaves up. Huge fortunes had been made and the slave-owners had lived in luxury, ease, comfort and splendor off the labor of Negroes.

When the end of this came, the industry of the South was paralyzed. There was a shortage of white labor-power. The Negroes had been freed and they distrusted and suspected their former masters. In short, intoxicated with the new wine of freedom, they were disinclined to work.

But cotton must be picked; lumber must be cut; turpentine must be dipped; railroads must be built. In fact, profits must be made. Negroes must work or be made to work, besides they must work cheaply.

How can this be done? This is how it was and is done:

Vagrancy laws are enacted which provide for the imprisonment of all Negroes who have no visible means of support. Of course, it is impossible for a Negro to show that he has any visible means of support. The result is that hordes of unemployed Negroes are hustled off to jail and the convict camps. Their fines are paid by employers of labor for lumber mills, cotton plantations, railroads, etc., they are assigned into their custody, put to work at a wage of 30 and 40 cents a day. They are also compelled to trade at the company's store, which sells its wares at 100 per cent higher than other stores. A debt for railroad fare to the works and for maintainance while at work 'til payday is made. Moreover, when the fines of imprisoned Negroes are paid, they are required to sign labor contracts, the non-performance of which is presumptive proof of fraudulent intent at the time of making it, which the State laws make a crime. And as a white planter himself tells the story: A planter can arrest a man upon the criminal charge of receiving money under false pretenses, which is equivalent to the charge of stealing; you get him convicted; he is fined, and being pennyless, inlieu of the money to pay the fine he goes to jail; then you pay the fine and cost and the judge assigns him to you to work out the fine and you have him back on your plantation, backed up by the authority of the State. This is peonage. It is maintained for profits. This is capitalism. And this does not apply to Negroes only. It is the common fate of the servant class, black and white. But they must not understand that their interests are common. Hence race prejudice is cultivated. Lynching, jim-crowism segregation is used to widen the chasm between the races.

This profit system of capitalism also applies to the farmer through the crop-lien system. This is a system whereby a lien mortgage is taken upon the crops of the poor white and black farmers for a loan. It operates in this way: The poor farmer being in need of provisions for his family until harvesting time, borrows money on his planted, and sometimes unplanted crop, from a big merchant or bank. The rate of interest is so high, sometimes as high as 1000 per cent on the dolar, according to Comptroller of Currency John Skelton Williams, the farmer is unable to pay the interest to say nothing about the principal.

The farmer's inability to meet his note results in the loss of his farm. He then becomes a farm tenant and works upon the metayer system or the plan of giving a part of the crop produced to the owner for the privilege of cultivating the land. This crop-lien system is profitable to the bankers of the South. Both white and black farmers are fleeced by this financial system. But white and black farmers won't combine against a common foe on account of race prejudice. Race antagonism, then, is profitable to those who own the farms, the mills, the railroads and the banks. This economic arrangement in the south is the fundamental cause of race prejudice, which is the fuse which causes the magazine of capitalism to explode into race conflicts—lynchings.

Prejudice is the chief weapon in the South which enables the capitalists to exploit both races. In the East, North and West, State militias, secret detective strike-breaking agencies, religion or nationality is used. The capitalists play Jewish against Irish Catholic workers. As we have our Waco, Memphis and East St. Louis lynching of Negroes, there are also Bayonne, West Virginia and Ludlow massacres of white workers and their families. The capitalists want profits, they don't care who makes them for them. In the South today over a million little white children are taken from school, put into factories and driven 10 and 12 hours a day until their little bodies are broken upon the wheels of industry; all because their labor is cheaper and more profits can be made out of them than out of grown-ups. They are competing with their fathers and brothers and they force the wage scale down by virtue of their increasing the labor supply.

This is how much the Southern white gentlemen capitalists care about white children whom they prate so much. Capitalism knows no color line. It will coin the blood, sweat and suffering of white women and white children or black women and black children into dollars and dividends. So much for the economic aspects.

But this thing must be supported by laws. And this brings us to the political cause of lynching. How does it operate?

Vagrancy laws are enacted by politicians who are selected by political parties which are controlled by those who supply the campaign funds. These funds are contributed by the bankers, railroad directors, lumber mill and cotton plantation-owners whose large profits depend upon the low wages and long hours of work of the servant class. This has been the work of Vardaman, Tillman and the "Lily white" Republicans. The laws making the nonperformance of a labor contract a crime are placed on the statute books by certain anti-labor and incidentally anti-Negro politicians. Sheriffs into whose custody Negroes charged with criminal acts are placed are nominated, elected or appointed by parties, which are responsible to powerful financial agencies which profit by fostering race prejudice and lynching, etc. This is why sheriffs don't protect their prisoners and not because they are afraid of the mob. So that when a mob demands a Negro in the custody of a sheriff nominated and elected by a political machine whose campaign funds are made up by banks and loan agencies, and by big employers of labor, which lend money to poor white and black farmers, at usurious rates of interest and who hold labor in peonage; you can realize and appreciate how the sheriff will act. Self interest will control his action and he can always be expected to act in the interest of those who have the power to remove him.

The ruling class of the South have, through disfranchisement and the poll-tax, deprived the working class of the power to protect their interests. The electorate there is small. It is easier for the capitalists to control or to corrupt a small electorate than a large one.

Politically race feeling is also capitalized by young, ambitious politicians who make their campaigns on the slogan of "Negro domination."

This is how politics fortifies and re-enforces lynch law in the South.

What are the social causes? There are three, the school, church and press.

An uneducated working class won't revolt, won't organize; hence, the meagre sums of $2.22 and $4.92 are approproated for the education of the black and white child, respectively, per year.

The white church is paid to preach the Christianity of lynch law profits.

The press is owned and controlled by the employing class and it is used to influence the minds of the races; to foment race hatred; it gives wide circulation to that insidious doctrine of the Negroes being the hewers of wood and drawers of water for white men. It features in bold headlines such titles as "lynch the black brute," "young white girl raped by black burly fiend," etc.

This produces a psychology which expresses itself through the mob. Anything may occasion a community to burn a Negro. It might be a well-dressed Negro; a Negro who speaks good English or a Negro who talks back to a white man.

To sum up, capitalism is at the basis of the economic, political and social arrangements of the South and it is defended, supported, promoted and upheld by the Republican and Democratic parties of the North, South, East and West. Neither Republican nor the Democratic party has ever condemned peonage or lynching. They can not. They are owned by the capitalists.

What then is the cure. I hold, maintain and aver that Socialism is the only cure. Why?

First, what is it? Briefly, it is the social ownership and democratic management of the means and sources of production and exchange for social use and not for private profit.

## How Does This Effect Lynching?

Socialism would deprive individuals of the power to make fortunes out of the labor of other individuals by virtue of their ownership of the machinery which the worker must use in order to live. When an individual or class may make profits out of the labor of black and white workers, it is to his or to the interest of the class to use any means to keep them (the workers) from combining in order to raise wages; to lower their hours of work or to demand better working conditions. This is the only reason why prejudice is fostered in the South. Of course, it may not be possible to trace every lynching or act of prejudice to a direct economic cause, but the case may be explained by the law of habit. When social practices are once set they act or recur with a dangerous accuracy. So that it is now a social habit to lynch Negroes. But when the motive for promoting race prejudice is removed, viz., profits, by the social ownership, control and operation of the machinery and sources of production through the government, the government being controlled by the workers; the effects of prejudice, race riots, lynching, etc., will also be removed.

For instance, if railroads were owned and democratically managed by the government, its collective and social service function would not be prostituted to jim-crow cars in order to pander and cater to race prejudice. No individuals would be making profits out of them and consequently there would be no interest in promoting race antagonisms. Lynchings, the product of capitalism, would pass as the burning of heretics and the Spanish Inquisition, the product of religious intolerance, passed.

Besides Socialism would arm every man and woman with the ballot. Education would be compulsory and universal. The vagrancy law, child labor and peonage would no longer exist. Tenant-farming and the crop-lien system would be discarded. And every worker would receive the full product of his toil.

This is the goal of Socialism. This is why every Negro should be a Socialist.

In conclusion, workingmen and women of my race don't allow Republican and Democratic leaders to deceive you. They are paid by Rockefeller, Morgan, Armour, Carnegie, owners of Southern railroads, coal mines, lumber mills, turpentine stills, cotton-plantations, etc., who makes millions out of your labor. Don't be deceived by the small increase in wages which you are receiving; the capitalists are taking it back by increasing the cost of food, fuel, clothing and rent. Don't be deceived by any capitalist bill to abolish lynching; if it became a law, it would never be enforced. Have you not the Fourteenth Amendment which is supposed to protect your life, property, liberty and guarantee you the vote? Does it do it? No. Why? Because it is nullified through administration by capitalists, Republican and Democratic representatives, who profit from lynching; who want lynching to continue. Lynching will not stop until Socialism comes. You can strike a death blow to lynching by voting for Socialism.

Black and white workers unite. You have nothing to lose but your chains; you have the world to gain.

---

# 3
## New Leadership for the Negro

*"New Leadership for the Negro" was an editorial published in* The Messenger *(May–June 1919): 9–10, which criticized mainstream black leadership from a radical perspective. Du Bois is especially castigated for his "Close Ranks" editorial.*

The Negro needs new leadership. The old leadership has failed miserably. Du Bois and Kelly Miller, Pickens and Jas. W. Johnson, W.H. Lewis and Chas. W. Anderson, W.T. Vernon and Roscoe Conkling Simmons, W.H. Tyler and the politicians of Chicago, have simply held jobs, produced school boy rhetoric and lulled Negroes into a false sense of security. Another set of leaders like Geo. E. Haynes, Emmet Scott, Dr. R.R. Moton, Fred R. Moore and T. Thomas Fortune, have preached a gospel of satisfaction and content. With one or two exceptions the whole group lacks information and courage. They demanded nothing during the war, and now that it has closed, they can goad nobody for having failed to keep his promises.

In the midst of the war when black men were giving their lives by the minute, Du Bois wrote his infamous "Close Ranks" editorial in the Crisis which will rank in shame and reeking disgrace with the "Atlanta Compromise" speech of Booker Washington. Kelly Miller's contribution to the reconstruction discussion so far has been that "just as we have been 100 per cent. Americans during the war, we want to be 100 per cent. Americans after the war"—whatever that means! William Picken's contribution was a "good nigger" exhortation with this argument: "If your mother doesn't treat you right, she's your mother just the same." This was handed out to persuade Negroes that they should not complain about lynching, disfranchisement, Jimcrowism and segregation because their mother country did it. What trash! Did Pickens ever read Thomas Paine's "Crisis" and "Common Sense?" In speaking of England as the mother country he argued, "Even brutes do not kill their young or starve them by privation." He there showed that even a mother should be respected only for that which was good in her and rejected and rebuked when she failed to act as a mother. Jas. W. Johnson is a man of considerably more ability than his economic relations will permit him to reveal. He would make a much abler editor of the Crisis than Du Bois. He cannot be accused of using school boy rhetoric and he is inclined to prosecute his study of modern problems more than any of the old liners. His giving credence, however, recently to a suggestion that lynching could be dealt with by a day or week of prayer shocked our opinion of his good judgment. Lewis, Anderson, Vernon and Tyler, of course, are simply old line Republican politicians who have been celebrated for their faithful service to the reactionary Republican machine. Like most appointees they are of no service to the people. They owe their places, not to the votes of the people, but to the white bosses who appointed them; and, therefore, they represent, not the people but the white bosses to whom they owe their jobs. "The power over a man's subsistence is the power over his will." Haynes, Scott, Moton, Fortune and Moore belong to that extremely conservative wing of Negroes, who can qualify to the satisfaction of Tillman, Blease and Vardman. As a matter of fact, just a few months ago, Mr. Fred R. Moore in company with some other Negro leaders, held a conference with Cole Blease! What was done we fear was not in the interest of the Negroes or he would have given out the accomplishments of the conference. In the next issue of the MESSENGER, however, we shall give a full account of what took place in the Cole Blease—Fred Moore Conference. Moton has just been to Europe to urge Negro soldiers to "be modest and unassuming when they get back home." Scott is having Du Bois prepare some rhetoric of praise for the black boys' valor. Poor Fortune is racking his deceased mind over the growth of radicalism among Negroes. Fortune once a fearless spokesman of the people is now wallowing in the shame and chagrin of his own apostacy. Haynes is pouring over figures to find out whether Negroes are actually laboring in the United States. Roscoe Conkling Simmons is to deluge us soon again with a discarded and discredited rhetoric which is distinguished for its power to talk much and say little. At best it is little more than an adroit mode of saying nothing.

All of which we regard as valueless. The Negro soldier is not asking for rhetoric and praise. He wants justice and fair play—a chance to work with a decent wage, freedom from discrimination on railroads and street cars, theatres and hotels, protection of his life from lynching and his property from mob violence, the right to vote and education for his children. Leaders who have not the courage to demand these things are worthless. Our present leaders are not demanding them. We need a new leadership—a leadership of intelligence and manly courage.

# 4
## The Crisis of the Crisis

*"The Crisis of the Crisis" was an editorial published in* The Messenger 2 *(July 1919): 10–12, which sharply attacked the NAACP,* The Crisis, *and especially the leadership of W.E.B. Du Bois for their hostility to the IWW and the radical labor movement.*

The MESSENGER has frequently pointed out that the editor of the Crisis, Dr. W.E.B. Du Bois, while possessing more intelligence than most Negro editors, is nevertheless comparatively ignorant of the world problems of sociological and economic significance.

In the June Crisis he enters an apology for the leading editorial in the April Crisis. The June issue's editorial, entitled "I. W. W." reads:

"An editorial in the Easter Crisis (written during the editor's absence) has been misunderstood and was, perhaps, itself partially misleading."

Note this argument, if it may be dignified by that name. The editor of the Crisis attempts to excuse his errors and misstatements on the ground that he was absent from his office. But obviously the editor had no business writing if conditions were such that he did not and could not know the facts.

In the April Crisis, Dr. Du Bois says: "Suppose we had yielded to German propaganda, suppose we had refused to shoulder arms, or had wrought mischief and confusion, patterning ourselves after the I. W. W. and the pro-Germans of this country. How should we hold up our heads?"

We take Du Bois to task here for two reasons: first, the statement of fact, and, second, his erroneous interpretation. A Negro alleged professor of sociology and economics doesn't understand the difference between the I. W. W. and pro-Germans. The I. W. W. is the only national organization of labor unions which does not discriminate against Negroes. A Negro, therefore, should be the last person to try to cast aspersion upon the I. W. W.

Again, the Negro has gotten absolutely nothing from his *shouldering arms and failing to produce mischief and confusion. He has been most loyal, but in turn, as his deserts, he is most lynched, most Jim-Crowed, most segregated, most discriminated against, most disfranchised.* The Germans were alleged to be the enemy. But Germans are not lynched, while Negroes are. Germans can ride in any part of the car in any state in the Union. The Negro is confined to the Jim-Crow car in the South. Negroes are disfranchised. Germans are not. Negroes cannot enter most places of public accommodation and amusement free and unhindered. Germans can enter any place of public accommodation and amusement in any part of the United States. (Lest we should be misunderstood, we wish to state that we do not think that any bar should be set up against the Germans. We only call attention to this discrepancy to expose the hypocrisy of the United States government on the one hand and the venality and ignorance of Negro leaders on the other.)

In the April Crisis the editorial continues, "We are not by nature traitors." This statement does not sound like the Du Bois of old. It partakes more of the old, me-too-Boss, hat-in-hand Negro generally represented by Robert Russa Moton of Tuskegee. Of all the fool-hardy claims made by the Negro, not one is so silly and asinine as "we are not by nature traitors." The vice of being traitorous depends entirely upon what one is traitorous to. *Treason of the slave to his master is a virtue. Loyalty of a slave to his master is a vice.* Liberty and justice have advanced in the world in proportion as people have been traitorous to their tyrants and oppressors. George Washington was a traitor—to British tyranny. Wendell Philips, William Lloyd Garrison, Lovejoy and Lincoln were traitors—to the slave autocracy of the United States. John Brown, upon whom the same Du Bois writes a worthless rhetorical book—was a traitor to old slave holding Virginia. The 200,000 Negroes who fought on the Union side to free themselves and their brothers from chattel slavery—were traitors to the slaveholders. It was treason beyond doubt for any slave to attempt his emancipation. But the actual character and type of the treason and the traitor depends entirely upon what that treason is to. The Russian people were largely traitors—traitors to the Czar, the proper kind of traitors. *The Negro will never gain his just rights until the great masses, 12 million strong, become thoroughly permeated, saturated and shot through with treason to the institutions of Jim-Crowism, lynching, race discrimination, segregation, disfranchisement, and to every instrument which maintains, perpetuates and fosters these pernicious institutions.*

The Crisis continues; "The Crisis did not say or intend to say that no Negroes belong to the Industrial Workers of the World, nor did it intend to condemn that organization. On the contrary, we respect it as one of the social and political movements in modern times that draws no color line. We sought to say that we do not believe that the methods of the I. W. W. are today feasible or advisable, and too, we believe the Socialist Party, wrong in its attitude toward the war, but we raise our hats silently to men like Eugene Debs, who let not even the shadow of public shame close their lips when they think themselves right."

The MESSENGER takes sharp issue with the Crisis on every one of its fundamental propositions both with respect to the questions of fact and the questions of opinion. The Crisis clearly implied that Negroes did not belong to the I. W. W. and spoke disparagingly of it as a Pro-German machine. Not only that. The Crisis representatives, like William Pickens, constantly speak of I. W. W.'s and Pro-Germans in their speeches as did William Pickens in the recent conference on "Lynching" held in New York. As to the methods of I. W. W., we state advisedly, and with sufficient reservation, that Dr. Du Bois, like most Negro professors, has no more knowledge of them than he has of the Bolsheviki. For his edification, and that of our readers who desire real information, we wish to say that the chief methods of the I. W. W. are industrial unionism. They oppose the principles of pure and simple unionism. They organize by the industry rather than by the trade. To illustrate, in a printing plant where the pressmen are on strike, by the American Federation of Labor pure and simple unionism methods, scab pressmen could be employed side by side with the union linotypers, compositors and others employed in the establishment. The principles of industrial unionism, adopted by the I. W. W. would demand that when the pressmen strike, the compositors, linotypers and all others employed in the shop should lay down their tools and cease from work until the strike is won. This method is both simple and feasible. It is advisable in every respect. Its efficiency and feasibility are shown by the fact that organized labor of the most advanced countries of Europe, Australia, Canada, and South America are rapidly adopting the One-Big-Union principle for their labor organizations. This no doubt is as new to the editor of the Crisis as it is to the average clay eating cracker of Georgia.

With respect to the Socialist Party, we endorse wholeheartedly its position on the war. History will record its position as one of the most courageous, far visioned and intelligent points of view taken by any group in the world. All wars (with exception of Revolutionary Wars like the French Revolution and the Russian Revolution) are against the interest of the people. This the Socialist Party knew and stated. That it has been against the interests of the Negroes, is hardly open to question. Lynching has increased. Race prejudice has been augmented. Discrimination is rampant. Unemployment and poverty stare the great masses of Negroes in the face, while the high prices of living continue to ascend with the rhythmic regularity of a funeral dirge. All other countries have been making slight concessions (some of them big concessions) by way of the extension of suffrage to the male and female electorates. But on account of the ignorance and spinelessness of the Negro leaders (?) not a single state has even discussed the extension of the franchise to Negroes in the South. And why should they? Why should the states think of extending to Negroes that for which no Negro leader has had the temerity, even to ask? We reiterate then, that the Negro has received nothing by virtue of his participation in the war, but has lost much—much which he will be a long time regaining, despite the Crisis' unwarranted assertion to the contrary.

The Crisis editorial for June continues: "We believe that the crushing of the monstrous pretentions of the military caste of Germany was a duty so pressing and tremendous that it called for the efforts of every thoughtful American. But we recognize that some people did not agree with us and these folks we honor for their honesty, even though we question their reasoning."

With this sentiment the MESSENGER also takes sharp issue. We were not, at any time, interested in this reactionary, militarist government of Germany. We desired to see it crushed, as crushed it would be undoubtedly with the rising tide of German Socialism and German democracy. But as monstrous a task as that was, and as imperative as it was, we did not for one moment regard it as important as crushing the southern bourbon caste system of peonage in the United States. The Huns of Georgia are far more menacing to Negroes than the Huns of Germany. The Huns of Alsace have never threatened the Negroes' life, liberty and property like the Huns of Alabama. The Huns of Lorraine are as shining angels of light compared to the Huns of Louisiana. No barbarians of Turkey could ever be compared with the howling dervish, dancing barbarians of Tennessee. The danger from the Huns of Saxony did not take rank in our minds with the Huns of Mississippi. It is only due to a sort of Negro professor's chronic short-sightedness and usual venality which could for one moment regard the danger from the alleged German Hun as greater than that from the American Hun. To illustrate more pointedly: the three class Prussian electoral system of voting was the criticism upon the German franchise. But three-fourths of the Negroes of the United States, who own more than Seven Hundred Million Dollars worth of property are deprived of the right to vote, right under the nose of the editor of the Crisis. A white man's vote in Mississippi amounts to 13 votes in Kansas. A white man's vote in Alabama is equivalent to 11 votes in Minnesota. The comparison is quite similar with any southern state. Consequently, any Negro professor of economics or sociology, who had any knowledge of political science and the honesty to proclaim it, must have known that the American political system was behind the German political system under the Kaiser. Up to 1910, the highest vote of white men in any southern state was 19 per cent. in the State of Virginia. The average vote of southern white men was less than 17 per cent., showing that there is no political democracy, even for white men, under the political caste of the United States. With respect to economic democracy, Germany had more social legislation and the best administered government of Europe, even under the Kaiser. This is a matter of common knowledge among social students and ought to be known even to an *old school Negro professor of economics and sociology like the editor of the Crisis*. With respect to race prejudice, one observation is sufficient. At all times it was possible for a Negro to attend the university of Kaiser Wilhelm, but no Negro could put his foot into President Woodrow Wilson's university—Princeton—which, by the way is in the United States. Dr. Du Bois honors those of us who disagreed with him for our honesty but he questions our reasoning. Since he has done no reasoning, we deplore his absence of reasoning, and since the facts are so overwhelmingly against his position, we question even his honesty.

The Crisis continues: "It is no credit to American Negroes if they had no conscientious objectors. It is tremendously to their credit that the vast majority of them thought straight and fought true in a mighty world crisis."

The answer to the first sentence is that there were plenty of Negro conscientious objectors and there should have been more. Every Negro who went into the army should have been a conscientious objector. He had a right to be the most conscientious, conscientious objector in the United States. Lynched, burned at stake, Jim-Crowed on street cars and railroads, barred from places of public amusement and accommodation, segregated in the army and navy itself, disparaged for his work and underrated for his services, denied an opportunity for employment, except where necessity forced it—the Negro had a right to have been the objector of objectors. A word of information too, for the Crisis. The Negroes knew nothing, as a whole, about stating their claims. But so far as their objections to fighting were concerned, they were galore. Almost every Negro with whom you talked would tell you that he wondered what we were fighting for. And as he read the periodical lynchings, almost daily, his opinions were confirmed. *It might be surprising to Dr. Du Bois to know that the masses of Negroes in the United States have no more confidence in his sincerity and judgment, than they have in that of Moton.* The mere fact that the Negro was compelled to fight, is no evidence of his desire to fight or his satisfaction with his enforced lot. It is just like the Jim-Crow car. We go into the South and we are forced to ride in it. We do it sullenly, reluctantly and under the whip of the lash, while our very soul protests against every inch of that cattle travel. We are disfranchised and can't vote. We submit to it. But where would be the manliness of any red blooded Negro who would glory in and exult in his disfranchisement merely because he was forced to submit to it.

In conclusion let us say, that the Crisis has reached its crisis. It no longer represents the opinion of the millions of Negroes of the United States who are insisting upon justice without compromise or apology. The Crisis does not voice their sentiments any more than the Tuskegee Student. The editor of the Crisis lacks (1) intelligence, (2) courage, or (3) he is controlled. In our generosity, we would say that he lacks all three, to a certain degree. He has not had modern training in economics and sociology and his knowledge of political science has not proceeded in economics beyond Adam Smith, and in sociology beyond Auguste Comte. He is essentially a classicist. His emphasis is placed upon music, Latin, Greek, French and trigonometry, to the disparagement of economics and sociology—the business of getting a living and improving the standard of living. In very truth, he lacks intelligence. We recognize, however, that Dr. Du Bois has more intelligence than the Crisis manifests, but this is subordinated to his rapidly waning courage. Third and last, he is undoubtedly controlled by the Capitalist Board of the National Association for the Advancement of Colored People. *If he lacks intelligence, he can't lead correctly. If he lacks courage, he dare not lead correctly. If he is controlled, he will not be permitted to lead Negroes, in their own interests.*

The problem of the Crisis is the problem of *intelligence, courage and control.* It is the crisis of the Crisis. The sooner its influence wanes among Negroes, the sooner will they have begun to pass their crisis. The chief problem of the American Negro today is the ridding himself of misleadership of all kinds, and especially that of so-called organs of public opinion.

# 5

## Two Editorials: "Racial Equality" and "The Failure of the Negro Church"

*In "Racial Equality" (The Messenger 2 [October 1919]: 4), Randolph outlined his commitment to racial equality in unequivocal terms; in "The Failure of the Negro Church" (The Messenger 2 [October 1919]: 5), he criticized the black church for its failure to recognize the economic and class roots of racial oppression, and for its failure to ally itself with progressive (i.e., radical) political forces.*

### Racial Equality

RACES are equal. They are equal in mind. They are equal in body. They are equal in moral and ethical standards. There is probably no bogey more pernicious or more false than the claim of racial inequality. Professor Lester F. Ward has discussed at great length the egalitarian theory of mind, both in his Dynamic and Applied Sociology. He there shows the chief differences in men to be differences in opportunity. The truth of this theory may be demonstrated to any one who will observe sufficiently carefully. Especially easy is it to examine the competition between white and colored races. In "Applied Sociology" Lester Ward, undoubtedly the ablest thinker of America and probably of the world, notes that the Japanese are the equals of any people in the world as scientists. In botany and biology they have proved their worth. In political science and economics they have held their own.

So with the Negro. He conforms to the monistic rule. Like causes produce like effects as well in the social as in the physical world. Given opportunity, the young Negro man or woman uses it about like the young white man or woman. In a large class, at a college, you will find a small percentage of bright Negroes and only a small percentage of whites in the white colleges. You will find a fair number of good speakers among the whites and only a fair number among Negroes. Those of us who see Negroes in deliberative bodies are sometimes disgusted. Attend the white deliberative bodies, and your disgust will go to the "nth" power again. You can even become nauseated in the Congress of the United States. It is hard to find a scholar in either the Senate or the House. It is most difficult to find a man in Congress who knows anything about government. Political science is a foreign subject to most men elected to Congress. They are not there to know political science and to look after the government of the people in the interests of the people. The average southern white man speaks derisively of Negroes who took part in the Government of southern states during the Reconstruction following the Civil War. But in all candor, and impartiality, we make the statement without fear of successful contradiction that the average Negro in Congress during the Reconstruction was the equal of, if not superior to, the average Congressman or United States Senator from any of the Southern states today. Indeed, it would be difficult to find a more ignorant group of men than the Southern Congressmen who infest our capital.

Physically, the races are equal. Where the living conditions are about the same, we find a similar death rate, whatever the race or color. Negroes who receive high incomes live to about the same length of time as whites who receive similar income. Where poverty prevails, whites die like flies, and Negroes die like flies. It is sometimes said that tuberculosis is a disease which especially affects Negroes. No scientist would seriously maintain such a claim. The only reason Negroes die more than others from tuberculosis is because they are in greater poverty. This means that they get less food, clothing, and shelter, and in as much as food and clothing and shelter are the chief weapons of defense against disease, tuberculosis simply claims more victims in the field which is most fertile for it.

The moral and ethical standards of Negroes are quite as high as those of whites. Their psychic traits are quite similar too. Unbounded applause in meetings is a mark of mediocre mind—not inate mind, but low mental equipment. Both white and colored people in the United States have low mental equipment. Attend any meeting where large groups are present—whether they be white or black—and you will hear them cheer almost every utterance of the speakers. Again, both Negroes and whites are too addicted to fun. The low grade mind of the average white for pleasure can be read in the fact that Charlie Chaplin is the highest paid man in the world. With Negroes the minstrel and the clown still take precedence on the stage. Both whites and blacks still place a fortune in the ground when somebody dies. They are long on inspiration and short on information. They have more heat than light.

These are just a few illustrations of what might be extended into a volume. But a careful examination will reveal the uniformity of human nature, the equality of mind among races. It is a wholesome idea also to disseminate, as it removes a great deal of racial egotism, conceit and arrogance. It makes for harmony. It destroys the boastful, super-assertiveness which works against the brotherhood of man. Racial equality is an established fact.

## The Failure of the Negro Church

YES, the Negro church has failed. It has failed in a great crisis. Its failure is patent and apparent. The only question before us then is: Why and How?

The chief cause of the failure of the Negro church is economic. That is to say, the church has been converted into a business and the ruling characteristic of a business is, that it is run primarily for profits. The interest is focused upon debits and credits, deficits and surpluses. This has been the Scylla and Charybdis of the Negro church.

To the money power in the community and the country, the church has bowed. The trustee boards of the smallest and most humble are composed of the most prosperous of the church-members who are adjudged as competent to create a surplus by organizing rallies, and by devising other means that are effective in inducing the public to release the necessary moneys. Preachers break with denominations and set up independent churches, on account of being removed from "fat charges." Collections occupy three-fourths of the time of most services. Sermons are usually selected with a view to impressing the members with the importance of the injunction that "it is more blessed to give than to receive."

Then there is that class of Negro churches that is directly dominated by white capitalists. These are the Episcopal, Congregational, Presbyterian and Methodist Episcopal. Their policies are molded and handed down from the white ecclesiastical oligarchy. This ecclesiastical oligarchy, in turn, is controlled by the "money power" of the country. It is a matter of common knowledge that Trinity church, situated at the head of Wall Street, is one of the biggest corporations in America. It controls a large number of apartment houses from which it reaps blood money in the form of extortionate rents from the working people.

Now, since the "money power" of the country which consists of the masters of the railroads, mines, factories, land, etc., receive their power from rent, interest and profits, and since the great masses of the people depend upon wages for a living, which are low when profits, rent and interest are high, and high when profits, rent and interest are low, it is plain that the interests of the people and the interests of the "money power" which dominates the church, are opposed.

Since it is beyond question that a servant will obey its master, that the power over a man's subsistence is the power over his will, one is not surprised at the church's obedience to the power that maintains it.

The church split over the issue of slavery into the North and South. The Northern church, at the behest of the industrial power, condemned it; the Southern church, upon the order of the slave owners, blessed it. Thus, the church, now as then, is using its power to defend poverty, crime, prostitution, war, ignorance and superstitution which are outgrowths of the system that allows one man to live off another's labor.

So much then for the cause of the failure. Now, how has it failed? Briefly it has failed to educate the people. Ministers are leading Negroes who are below, in intelligence, the lowest member of their church. The Negro ministry is ignorant of the modern problems of capital and labor. It is disinterested in unionism as a means of securing higher wages, shorter hours and better working conditions for Negro workers. It regards the discussion of politics in the church as sacrilegious unless some good, old Abraham Lincoln Republican desires the vote of the Negro, and is willing to pay for educational propaganda.

It has failed to use its power to rouse the Negro against disfranchisement and lynching.

No conference of Negro churches has ever gone on record as endorsing the principle of unionism.

But you ask, what constructive program do we offer?

First, the Negro Ministry must be educated. It must get the education of information instead of the education of inspiration. It needs less Bible and more economics, history, sociology and physical science.

Second, the Negro church must be put to different uses. It must become an open educational forum where problems of hygiene, labor, government, racial relationships, national and international questions are discussed by specialists.

The church might also be used as places for the beginning of co-operative stores that will enable the Negro workingman to reduce the high cost of living.

In conclusion, the world has moved a long way forward since 1914. Times have changed and institutions, if they would survive, must adjust themselves to the changed conditions. The New Negro demands a new ministry—an educated fearless and radical ministry.

The New Negro demands a new church—a church that is the center of his social, economic and political hopes and strivings. The church must become something more than a temple of prayer to a people who are lynched, disfranchised and jim-crowed. Prayer has been tried for over fifty years.

In short, the church must set its face against a philosophy of profits to a philosophy of service.

---

# 6
## The Negro Radicals

*In "The Negro Radicals" (*The Messenger *2 [October 1919]: 17–18, 20, and [December 1919]: 20–21), Randolph examined the political views and the leadership qualities of W.E.B. Du Bois and eight other African American "radical" leaders. We are including only the material from the October issue on W.E.B. Du Bois.*

Among all races there are Conservatives, Liberals and Radicals. The Negro is no exception to the rule. The term "Radical," however, is a relative term, and what may be regarded as radical among one group, may not be regarded as radical among another. Radicalism is like luxuries. It varies with time, place and circumstance. Strictly speaking, most of the men included in our survey of Negro Radicals would not be termed radicals, but if we allow a little leeway in order to group together the alleged Radical Negroes, it will be more convenient to discuss the subject.

For the purposes of this article we shall consider W.E.B. Du Bois, Kelley Miller, Archibald Grimke, William Monroe Trotter, George Frazier Miller, William Pickens, Francis Grimke, John E. Bruce, and James W. Johnson.

The best known man of this group is Dr. W.E.B. Du Bois. He secured his title to radicalism by a vigorous and militant fight against Dr. Booker T. Washington, until his death. At that time, Dr. Du Bois was opposed to disfranchisement, segregation, peonage, lynching and the Jim-crow car. He was instrumental in organizing the National Association for the Advancement of Colored People. He was the founder of the *"Crisis"* magazine, which is the organ of the N. A. A. C. P. Prior to the war, the *"Crisis,"* which is fundamentally the opinion of Dr. Du Bois, was a very vigorous proponent of Negro radicalism. By Negro radicalism we mean something different from radicalism proper. One usually thinks of a Negro radical not as one who insists upon economic or political radicalism, but as a Negro who opposes lynching, demands the vote, condemns the Jim-crow car, segregation, discrimination and general insult, while **an extreme or ultra-Negro radical means a Negro who insists on social equality.** Any student of political science, however, would readily recognize that all of these above enumerated injustices and conditions are but the results and manifestations of deeper underlying social and economic conditions. They are the inevitable consequence of hidden but powerful social forces. That Du Bois has fallen far short of recognizing the true causes of the Negro's abominable condition is evident to any scientific student who will read his books or *The Crisis* magazine which he edits. The reason, however, that Du Bois is unable to deal with scientific remedies is because he cannot diagnose his case and discover through analysis the ultimate and the immediate causes. For instance, in politics, Du Bois thinks that Negroes may select good men, here and there, who will do their bidding. Now the actual good man theory has been abandoned by real radicals for more than a half century. Have not Negroes selected their good men for Presidents ever since the Civil War? Was not Hayes one of their selected good men?—the same Hayes who compromised and sold out their rights to the South upon an old school, underhand agreement comparable only with the secret treaties which Trotsky exposed? On the economic field Du Bois is more bankrupt in sound information than he is on the political field. And the truth is that his economic ignorance is what gives rise to his political misinformation. All economists know that the economic conditions are reflected on the political field. The political organization is very little bit more than the regulative organization through which the economic forces in the background express themselves. For instance, when one man controlled a country or nation, we had monarchy as a political organization representing the king as the chief economic holder and controller of the wealth of the country. When the king was forced to include others in the control of the national resources, a few other men formed the political organization producing an oligarchy—government of the few. Later the electorate was extended to include the landed interests and industrial barons, whereupon we find our so-called republics and democracies such as France, England and the United States. These are republics and democracies, however, only in name. They represent precisely the economic forces of the United States. As President Wilson himself says: "The masters of the Government of the United States are the combined capitalists and manufacturers of the United States. They have erected upon the forms of democracy an invisible empire." This is too true. In Washington, the Government is supposed to be located. But it is not so. We have a committee which reflects the wishes of the Government in Washington. The Government of the United States is in New York and, more strictly speaking, is located in Wall Street. When the large combinations of wealth—the trusts, monopolies and cartels are broken up, and the people get the wealth which they produce, a new form of government will then spring forth just as the Soviet Government was an inevitable consequence of the breaking up of the great estates of Russia and assigning the land to the peasants, and the wealth produced in the factories to the workers. It is as impossible to have a political machine which does not reflect the economic organization of a country, as it is to make a sewing machine grind flour. A sewing machine is not made to grind flour. Neither in structure nor aim is it so designed to function.

It is a complete misunderstanding of this, to us, very elementary principle which unfits Du Bois to act as a political or economic leader for Negroes. Negroes are chiefly workers. Ninety-nine per cent of them are working people. It is not possible, therefore, to use the Republican machine, which was organized, designed and financed to represent trusts, monopolies and big business. The Negro does not own the railroads, mines, forests, water power, oil wells, mills, factories, telephone and telegraph communications. His relation to these great titanic combines is that of a consumer or a worker. As a worker the big industrial combinations are trying to work him the longest hours and give him the lowest pay. As a consumer, these same combinations are charging him the highest prices obtainable when he buys back the product which he has produced by his toil. The interests of the Republican machine, which controls the Republican Party, are diametrically opposed to the interests of the masses of Negroes who work and toil and sweat and bleed and die while engaged in the industrial warfare by which they attempt to eke out a miserable existence in these United States. This being true, it is not possible to expect that the Republican Party can represent the interests of the Negro any more than it can be expected that a sewing machine will grind flour.

Industrially, Mr. Du Bois says he opposes the I. W. W. because he does not think their methods are feasible. Here again, the doctor shows crass ignorance of economics of labor and industry. The entire modern labor movement has been tending toward the one big union principle for the last two decades. The first transition step lifted its head in the sympathetic strike. But it was found that in order to carry out unity of aim and purpose, an organization of labor must be formed which was co-extensive with the purpose. This brought forth in America the I. W. W., a group of working men who draw no race, creed or color line, not as a sentimental virtue which they dole out with hypocritical unctiousness, but because enlighted self-interest tells them that it is impossible to attain the goal at which they are aiming so long as a deadwood force of twelve million Negro workers obstructs the way as scabs, non-union men or thugs hired by the capitalists. The rise of the Triple Alliance in England including the miners, railway and transport workers again confirmed the soundness of industrial unionism. The Australian workers have adopted the same course. The Canadian workers have done the same. The United Mine Workers of America have just gone on record to combine with the railway and transport workers to form an American Triple Alliance of Labor. All of these developments are germs of the growing idea whose cosmic outlines are the One Big Union. These different alliances are embryonic. They express the trend of labor but they will not stop there. For just as a combination of the railway, mine and transport workers is more powerful than any single group standing alone—this same Triple Alliance will be greatly augmented when it includes in its force the policemen, printers, building trades and all other workers—skilled and unskilled.

The chief need of the Negro is the organization of his industrial power. It is really more important (though both are essential and must be had) than his political power. One who has neither political nor industrial radicalism can hardly be called a radical in the strictest sense of the word. But Du Bois will go on for a while yet wearing the cognomen of "radical" on the ground that he opposes lynching (and all organisms however low in the scale of animal life oppose being killed). The props, however, are fast being cut from under him by the New-Crowd Negroes who are throwing the high-powered searchlight of scientific criticism upon men once supposed to be intellectual titans.

---

# 7
**The New Negro—What Is He?**

*In "The New Negro—What Is He?" (*The Messenger *2 [August 1920]: 73–74), Randolph answers his rhetorical question by defining New Negro in economic and political terms, rather than in cultural terms.*

OUR title was the subject of an editorial in the New York Age which formed the basis of an extensive symposium. Most of the replies, however, have been vague and nebulous. THE MESSENGER, therefore, undertakes to supply the New York Age and the general public with a definite and clear portrayal of the New Negro.

It is well nigh axiomatic that the most accurate test of what a man or institution or a movement is, is first, what its aims are; second, what its methods are, or how it expects to achieve its aims; and third, its general relations to current movements.

Now, what are the aims of the New Negro? The answer to this question will fall under three general heads, namely, political, economic, and social.

In politics, the New Negro, unlike the Old Negro, cannot be lulled into a false sense of security with political spoils and patronage. A job is not the price of his vote. He will not continue to accept political promisory notes from a political debtor, who has already had the power, but who has refused to satisfy his political obligations. The New Negro demands political equality. He recognizes the necessity of selective as well as elective representation. He realizes that so long as the Negro votes for the Republican or Democratic party, he will have only the right and privilege to elect but not to select his representatives. And he who selects the representatives controls the representative. The New Negro stands for universal suffrage.

A word about the economic aims of the New Negro. Here, as a worker, he demands the full product of his toil. His immediate aim is more wages, shorter hours and better working conditions. As a consumer, he seeks to buy in the market, commodities at the lowest possible price.

The social aims of the New Negro are decidedly different from those of the Old Negro. Here he stands for absolute and unequivocal *"social equality."* He realizes that there cannot be any qualified equality. He insists that a society which is based upon justice can only be a society composed of *social equals.* He insists upon identity of social treatment. With respect to intermarriage, he maintains that it is the only logical, sound and correct aim for the Negro to entertain. He realizes that the acceptance of laws against intermarriage is tantamount to the acceptance of the stigma of inferiority. Besides, laws against intermarriage expose Negro women to sexual exploitation, and deprive their offspring, by white men, of the right to inherit the property of their father. Statistics show that there are nearly four million mulattoes in America as a result of miscegenation.

So much then for the aims of the New Negro. A word now about his methods. It is with respect to methods that the essential difference between the New and the Old Negro relates.

First, the methods by which the New Negro expects to realize his political aims are radical. He would repudiate and discard both of the old parties—Republican and Democratic. His knowledge of political science enables him to see that a political organization must have an economic foundation. A party whose money comes from working people, must and will represent working people. Now, everybody concedes that the Negro is essentially a worker. There are no big capitalists among them. There are a few petit bourgeoisie, but the process of money concentration is destined to weed them out and drop them down into the ranks of the working class. In fact, the interests of all Negroes are tied up with the workers. Therefore, the Negro should support a working class political party. He is a fool or insane, who opposes his best interests by supporting his enemy. As workers, Negroes have nothing in common with their employers. The Negro wants high wages; the employer wants to pay low wages. The Negro wants to work short hours; the employer wants to work him long hours. Since this is true, it follows as a logical corollary that the Negro should not support the party of the employing class. Now, it is a question of fact that the Republican and Democratic Parties are parties of the employing or capitalist class.

On the economic field, the New Negro advocates that the Negro join the labor unions. Wherever white unions discriminate against the Negro worker, then the only sensible thing to do is to form independent unions to fight both the white capitalists for more wages and shorter hours, on the one hand, and white labor unions for justice, on the other. It is folly for the Negro to fight labor organization because some white unions ignorantly ignore or oppose him. It is about as logical and wise as to repudiate and condemn writing on the ground that it is used by some crooks for forgery. As a consumer, he would organize cooperative societies to reduce the high cost of living.

The social methods are: education and physical action in self defense. That education must constitute the basis of all action, is beyond the realm of question. And to fight back in self defense, should be accepted as a matter of course. No one who will not fight to protect his life is fit to live. Self defense is recognized as a legitimate weapon in all civilized countries. Yet the Old Crowd Negroes have counseled the doctrine of non-resistance.

As to current movements, the Negro would accept, praise and support that which his enemies reject, condemn and oppose. He is tolerant. He would restore free speech, a free press and freedom of assemblage. He would release Debs. He would recognize the right of Russia to self determination. He is opposed to the Treaty and the League of Nations. Yet, he rejects Lodge's reservations. He knows that neither will help the people. As to Negro leaders, his object is to destroy them all and build up new ones.

Finally, the New Negro arrived upon the scene at the time of all other forward, progressive groups and movements—after the great world war. He is the product of the same world wide forces that have brought into being the great liberal and radical movements that are now seizing the reins of political, economic and social power in all of the civilized countries of the world.

His presence is inevitable in these times of economic chaos, political upheaval and social distress. Yes, there is a New Negro. And it is he who will pilot the Negro through this terrible hour of storm and stress.

# 8
## Garvey Unfairly Attacked

*In this editorial (the first of three pieces on Garvey that appeared in* The Messenger *between April and August 1922), Randolph defended Garvey from those who would dismiss his arguments solely because he was a West Indian. ("Garvey Unfairly Attacked,"* The Messenger *4 [April 1922]: 387.) On the whole, however, Randolph and* The Messenger *were very critical of Garvey and his politics.*

WE hold no brief for Marcus Garvey or the Universal Negro Improvement Association. No publication in America has given such a painstaking anaylsis of the good points and the bad points of Garvey and his movement, as the MESSENGER. The article in the September, 1921, MESSENGER, by A. Philip Randolph, is easily the masterpiece on the Garvey movement.

Nevertheless we oppose unfair tactics, such as the recent attacks upon Garvey's nativity by Roscoe Conkling Simmons in the Chicago *Defender*. The merits and demerits of Garveyism are not lessened or increased because he is a West Indian. Nor is it any sensible argument to say: "If Garvey doesn't like this country, let him go back to Jamaica, where he came from." It would be just as logical to say, If Randolph doesn't like segregation in New York, let him go back to Florida where he came from. If Du Bois doesn't like the Ku Klux Klan in New York, let him go back to Atlanta University.

If Kelly Miller doesn't like the Jim Crow Car of Maryland, let him go back to South Carolina where he came from. If Robert Bagnall doesn't like Jim-Crowing in Loew's Alhambra Theatre in New York, let him go back to Virginia. If Owen doesn't like the reluctant service in Child's Restaurant, let him go back to North Carolina. If Pickens doesn't like segregated schools in Kansas or St. Louis, let him go back to Alabama. If James Weldon Johnson is not satisfied with everything in the North and West, let him go back to Florida.

All such argument (if it can be dignified by that name) is petty, cheap, vapid, effete. A man has a right and a duty to fight to improve conditions wherever he is. He has a right to fight to improve not only his home but any other home he may be able to help. If a Negro is in Georgia and the hill billies, instigated by silk-gloved "respectable citizens," decide to lynch him, he is simply a "nigger" whether he comes from Georgia or Georgetown, British Guiana. They care nothing whether he is from Jamaica or Florida, Trinidad or Tennessee, St. Kitts or Mississippi, Barbadoes or Alabama. All Negroes, wherever they are, are born, suffer from common proscriptions, wanton narrowing of opportunities, segregation, discrimination, Jim Crow cars, laws against inter-marriage. Race and color determine the classification—not the place of birth.

It needs to be said that at times Mr. Garvey unfortunately resorts to a similar type of unfair tactics. Witness his calling Cyril Briggs a white man, and his charging the National Advancement Association with hiring persons to dismantle the machinery on his ships—both of which statements Mr. Garvey knew to be absolutely false.

Our position is that Mr. Garvey has done much good, but also much harm. His opposition to social equality is abominable. His African Empire dream is obsolete and undesirable. His *"Negro first"* policy is not defensible, is unsound in theory and in practice. His steamship line is not only impracticable, but would have no effect on the Negro problem if successfully established, *because the Negro problem is not one of transportation.*

In spite of all this, Garvey has done much good work in putting into many Negroes a backbone where for years they have had only a wishbone. He has stimulated race pride. He has instilled a feeling into Negroes that they are as good as anybody else. He has criticized the hat-in-hand Negro leadership. He has inspired an interest in Negro traditions, Negro history, Negro literature, Negro art and culture. He has *stressed the international aspect of the Negro problem.*

If we American Negroes are to attack Garveyism, do it like the MESSENGER editors. Be fair. Don't appeal to nationality—that patriotism which Dr. Johnson called "the last refuge of a scoundrel." The West Indians are among the foremost fighters in all cities for racial rights. They are assiduous workers, vigorous fighters, diligent and able students.

Let Roscoe Conkling Simmons meet Garvey on a fair field. It was Robert G. Ingersoll who once said: "I like black friends better than I do white enemies." So we like West Indian friends better than we do native Negro enemies. We have heard too much talk of anti-West Indian intolerance. We take no stock in this argument. Rather do we regard it as *"a little barrack behind which mental impotency hides when it cannot answer logic."*

---

# 9
## Marcus Garvey!

*Three months later in the editorial "Marcus Garvey!" (*The Messenger *4 [July 1922]: 437), Randolph intensified his attack on Garvey, focusing on Garvey's willingness to surrender America to whites while he pursued his African dreams.*

## Marcus Garvey! The Black Imperial Wizard Becomes
## Messenger Boy of the White Ku Klux Kleagle

A few days ago Marcus Garvey speaking at New Orleans, said:

> "This is a white man's country. He found it, he conquered it, and we can't blame him if he wants to keep it. I am not vexed with the white man of the South for Jim Crowing me because I am black.
>
> "I never built any street cars or railroads. The white man built them for his own convenience. And if I don't want to ride where he's willing to let me ride then I'd better walk."

These are the words of that self-styled, courageous, so-called "new Negro" leader who is going to free Africa of the white man's menace.

This fool talk, too, emanates from a blustering West Indian demagogue who preys upon the ignorant, unsuspecting poor West Indian working men and women who believe Garvey is some sort of Moses.

We are well acquainted with many splendid, courageous, intelligent West Indian men and women—West Indians who would suffer their right hand to be cut off before they would yield up such a servile statement.

The public men—ministers, editors and lecturers have been all too lenient with this sinister, loose talk of Garvey. Some have feared the loss of trade with his following. Others have shuddered lest they should be attacked in his paper. Still others have said: *"His members and followers are chiefly West Indians and foreigners; there are not but a handful of American Negroes among them. Why should we worry?"*

The author was probably the first to urge opposition to Garvey's preposterous schemes. His associates, thought them too absurd not to be readily seen through. But the author recalled the philosophical principle *that nothing is too absurd to be believed if only one side is presented and its opposition excluded—whether the exclusion be by force or neglect.*

We urge all ministers, editors and lecturers who have the interests of the race at heart to gird up their courage, put on new force, and proceed with might and main to drive the menace of Garveyism out of this country.

The August MESSENGER will carry a painstaking, sharp and cryptic article from the pen of the editors of the MESSENGER, exposing all of Garvey's schemes—*from his row-boatless steamship line to his voteless election to the Presidency of a non-existent nation.* The issue is joined, and we shall spare no pains to inform the American, West Indian, African, South American and Canal Zone Negroes of the emptiness of all this Garvey flapdoodle, bombast and lying about impossible and conscienceless schemes calculated not to redeem but to enslave Africa and the Negro everywhere.

*Here's notice that the MESSENGER is firing the opening gun in a campaign to drive Garvey and Garveyism in all its sinister viciousness from the American soil.*

# 10
## Reply to Marcus Garvey

*In "Reply to Marcus Garvey" (The Messenger 4 [August 1922]: 467–71), Randolph presented his most thorough and most critical attack on Garvey. He wrote this in response to a Garvey attack on* The Messenger *and on his other critics published in* Negro World, *July 8, 1922. Randolph concluded this piece with a call for blacks to drive Garvey out of the country—a demand that anticipated both W.E.B. Du Bois's 1924 recommendation, and action taken by the U.S. government in 1927.*

IN the July 8th issue of the *Negro World* under the caption "Marcus Garvey asks Malicious Negroes Who Criticize Him to Prove Their Ability," the Honorable Marcus Garvey assails the Editors of the MESSENGER, purporting to answer an editorial which appeared in the June issue, comparing the Black Star Line to the failures of the True Reformers and the Metropolitan Realty Company.

In his characteristic demagogic fashion, he proceeds to answer the above named editorial by alleging that the MESSENGER is irregularly published. Suppose it were. What has that got to do with the truth or falsity of the charge. Is the Black Star Line failure not a disgrace to Negroes similar to the True Reformers and the Metropolitan Mercantile Realty Company? That is the question. A counter charge does not answer or settle the question. Even a child can see that, to say nothing of a grown-up. Counter accusation of the accuser by the accused does not excuse or vindicate the accused.

But back to the alleged irregularly published MESSENGER. If Mr. Marcus Garvey will consult the files of the Congressional, 42nd Street, Harvard or Princeton Universities' Libraries, he will find that the monthly appearance of the MESSENGER since the United States Government ceased interference with it something over a year ago, has been as regular as the succession of day and night. It might not be amiss to say, in this connection, that the MESSENGER is the first and only Negro publication in America ever to be denied the mails. The *Negro World* was sufficiently time-serving to merit and secure the approval of the virulent Negro haters during a war period when the Negro was being called upon to sacrifice his blood and treasure for a country which was at the same time lynching and burning him. The MESSENGER, on the contrary, was militant, uncompromising and bitter in its denunciation of the hypocritical policies of the Government toward the Negro, for which it was denied second-class mailing privileges which imposed an unprecedentedly heavy burden of expense on it, entailing a cost of thousands of dollars of which the *Negro World* was free. Of course, the Garvey paper is not bothered about the lynching of Negroes in America! He wanted to deport them to Africa, hence, he had no trouble. Despite this difficult situation, however, the MESSENGER grew in power and circulation which is a verifiable question of fact and not of a piece with the inflated membership of the U.N.I.A. and the circulation of the *Negro World*.

But a word more about the subject of irregularity. How simple and stupid of Brother Garvey to conjure up this Banquo's Ghost to plague and haunt his every step! There is that joke of the maritime world—the Black Star Line. What about its irregularity? Who is there so base, so shorn of every vestige of probity and character as to jeopard his good name and interests upon the irregularity of this non-sailing, lineless ship line. If it isn't an unkind and embarrassing question for this self-elected, self-styled Provisional President of the African continent, I should like to inquire as to where that Black Star Line is, anyhow? Is it on top of, or under the water? Are the ships sailing or being assailed by the courts? Nor are these questions put in a satirical spirit; for persons of unquestioned honor give currency to the statement that the "Kanawha" is rotting away in disuse, that the "Shady-Side" is still in the shades of libels and dilapidation, and, of course, the "Phylis Wheatley" resides in the Honorable Marcus' imagination. So far as the "Yarmouth" is concerned, the *Nauticus*, a journal of shipping and investments, in its issue of Dec. 10, 1921, settles the question as to its where-abouts. It states that on December 2, the United States Marshal sold, at auction, the "Yarmouth" to Frederick Townsend, for the almost unbelieveably insignificant sum of $1,625, or for $143,375 less than what the great business genius Brother Marcus paid for it. Did you get that? Impossible? It would seem so, wouldn't it ? But not so. It's a matter of record. Consult the *Nauticus* of Dec. 10, 1921 for yourself. *This is running through the cold cash of the poor simps with a vengeance.* And yet this half-wit, low grade moron, whose insufferable presumption is only exceeded by his abyssmal ignorance, has the cheek and brass to mention the business affairs of others. If he had never attempted to do business of any kind, he would have much better grace and ground for speaking on the subject than his scandulous, disgraceful and childish business record warrants.

Far better and safer for Brother Garvey to observe the rule: "that it were better to keep silent and be considered a fool or a crook than to speak and remove all doubt." But no, the conscienceless braggart and egotist that he is, he would like the cuttlefish, muddy the waters by misrepresenting others, hide his own dirty deeds of business disgraces in order to escape detection, to foil his prosecutors.

The white Ku Klux Kleagle's Black Ku Klux Eagle thinks that by resorting to the time-worn trick of condemning others for the things he is doing himself, he will avert suspicion from himself. But that will never carry. The smoke screen is too transparent. Telling what the accused has or has not done does not prove that the defendant, the accused, is innocent of the charge. Either a charge is true or false, and it must be refuted upon a basis of fact and truth. There is no other alternative.

Does Garvey employ the direct, honest and intelligent method of meeting the indictment of the editors of the MESSENGER. Dear readers, judge for yourself. Listen to this. Says he: "Before Owen and Randolph can speak of the failure of any business and the incompetency of any individual to do business they should first prove their success and their competency to handle business." Think of such downright inanity and silly tommy-rot. In other words, a person must be a thief in order to have the right to criticise and apprehend a thief. A critic of acting or of the drama is not required necessarily to be an actor or a dramatist. A person may be the reviewer of books without being an author of books. A patient may know when his pain is relieved without being a doctor. Few economists are business men, yet they formulate the rules, laws and principles of business. Intelligent business men such as Morgan and Rockefeller employ economists to formulate, direct and guide their business policies. They don't rely upon the hit and miss method of guess, conjecture and mother-wit. That period of catch-as-catch-can economic action has passed with everybody with a grain of common sense, except the Honorable Black Kluxer. Thus, it ought to be apparent that the right to criticize work is not contingent upon the ability to do that form of work or upon the fact of having done it. Hence, it is the sheerest idle prattle and an evidence of dishonesty and guilt for Garvey to retort to persons who charge him with shamelessly mishandling the Black Star Line that they are not pilots or captains, that they have owned and operated no ship lines, and, consequently, are not justified in criticizing him! Of course, he, naturally, would wish that to be so. It is the stock and trade of crooks to call others crooks who condemn them. *It is always to the interest of a man with a false stone to impeach the knowledge and honor of a lapidary.* That is the only way he can defraud the public. By lying about Owen's and Randolph's business ability, Garvey thinks that he will be able to divert attention from his own appalling business ignorance and tricks. But he has another thought coming.

Listen to this grandiose balderdash and burlesque on business. Speaking of what he has done, with emphasis on "he," if you please—he says that he was established the greatest Negro paper—the *Negro World.* That is a lie. The *Chicago Defender* is, by long odds, the greatest Negro paper in the world. Every honest, intelligent Negro knows that. What sort of a newspaper is the *Negro World*, anyway, which devotes its front page, the news page of every modern, civilized, recognized newpaper in newspaperdom, to the wild vaporings, imbecile puerilities and arrant nonsense, of a consummate ignoramus? But what's claiming the greatest Negro newspaper in the world, or the greatest anything in the world, to this Supreme and Exalted Ruler of the Annanias fraternity?

On his erratic rampage of mendacity and bigoted, groundless braggadocio, he beats the air, waving his big, fat hands furiously, and yaps: "We find established to the credit of the Negro a line of steam ships known as the Black Star Line, which has sent out two of its ships on the high seas and has registered the Negro as a competitor in maritime affairs." Is that so? And to the credit of the Negro!

Can you beat that for unmitigated, arrogant assininity. Let us hear what Judge Jacob Panken thinks of this great miracle of business success.

Marcus Garvey, who was arraigned in the Seventh District Court upon charges of fraud, admitted that the $600,000 invested in the Black Star Line by poor, hard working Negroes had been practically wiped out, that the "Yarmouth" cost $145,000 and lost $300,000 on its first trip, that the "Maceo" was purchased for $65,000 and had lost $76,000 on its maiden voyage.

Justice Panken, in addressing his remarks to Garvey said: "It seems to me that you have been preying upon the gullibility of your own people, having kept no proper accounts of the money received for investment, being an organization of high finance in which the officers received outrageously high salaries and were permitted to have exhorbitant expense accounts for pleasure jaunts throughout the country. I advise these 'dupes' who have contributed to these organizations to go into court and ask for the appointment of a receiver. You should have taken this $600,000 and built a hospital for colored people in this city instead of purchasing a few old boats. There is a form of paronoia which manifests itself in believing oneself to be a great man."

What has happened here is not so bad from the point of view of Marcus Garvey as it is from the damage done to the confidence of colored people. The editors of the MESSENGER warned Garvey and the people that what has happened would surely come to pass.

Still the Imperial Black "Blizzard" says that the Black Star Line is a credit to the Negro. By the same token of reasoning, one may be justified in concluding that the True Reformers' collapse, the Metropolitan failure were credits to the Negro.

Would any sane white man maintain that the financial adventurers, Charles Ponzi of Boston and young Bischoff of Chicago, who wasted millions of innocent white people's money in visionary, airy schemes *not much sounder than Garvey's*, were a credit to the white people? No, not by a long shot. They pay their respects to them through the prison bars, and credit them with an involuntary vacation from the community of civilized, respectable, law-abiding citizens, such as is likely to be tendered to Garvey. Still one might well doubt whether their sins against the people are as great as Garvey's.

He says further that the ships are on the high seas. Where, may I ask? Either Brother Marcus is blind or he thinks that the public is blind. It is a matter of common knowledge that the old, rickety, rotten ships of the Black Star Line can hardly stay on top of the water in port, to say nothing about withstanding the waves of the high seas. So unseaworthy was the "Yarmouth," when it ventured out from port, bootlegging, in calm weather, that the New York white press described it as a "Booze ship," reeling and rocking as it was like a drunken old sot. This is what he styles as a competitor in maritime affairs. Indeed it is to laugh. A competitor! Think of it! A shaky "booze ship line" competing with the great British, French, Italian and American steamship lines! No doubt it is competing as the braying of a jackass competes with the roaring of a lion, as an ox-cart competes with a steam engine, as an infant competes with a man! It is competition of a sort which none but a fool would claim!

However, on he goes like a mad man making specious, foolish, irresponsible statements about what he has done.

*"We find enterprises, namely, grocery stores, restaurants, laundries, tailoring and dress making establishments* established at different points of the country in the name of the Universal Negro Improvement Association," sputters Hizzoner. Well, grant that it is true, what of it?

What good are they to the members of the U. N. I. A. or anybody else? These two-by-four, dirty, dingy, mismanaged dumps, misnamed enterprises, are a liability, instead of an asset. They are a disgrace instead of a credit. They are rat holes in which to dump money. Nobody but an idiot would mention them as an achievement. Upon seeing his inability longer to inveigle the dupes, on account of Government prosecution for fraud, to dump their dollars into the Black Star Line Sea, he got together these business jokers to serve as fly-paper to ensnare the unsuspecting, ignorant and gullible. When the well-meaning, but misguided delegates come to the convention, His Noble and Imperial Highness can point to these picayune junk shacks as the achievements of a mighty business wizard. "See what I have done; see what we have got! Down with the traitors and agitators who point out my faults! Down with all Negro leaders but me! Hurrah! for the Ku Klux Klan! Up with Kleagle Clark! Up with Marcus Garvey!" will be the effusive ejaculation of this Black Don Quixote. Add to this the ceaseless band-playing, the waving of the red, black and green flag of the African Empire, the imperial parade, the flaunting of the habiliments of the Black Cross Nurses and the Black African Legion, the Court Reception, the knighting of the "insane," and the perpetual flow of hot-air which is the supreme function of His Honor, the Black Infernal "Blizzard,"—and the mesmerized fanatics are supposed to cough up, each and every one of them, from one to a 100 bucks for the African Redemption Fund, the revival of the Black Star Line, the Factories' Corporation, the Liberian Loan, the Convention Fund, and whatever other scheme happens to crop up in his imagination which might serve to skin the people. It might be interesting to add that these so-called enterprises seldom last more than a few months before they fail like the biggest of all his schemes, the Black Star Line. But as fast as one fails, he starts a new one, ever alert to have something into which the people can waste their moneys.

But in order to justify this saturnalia of waste and reckless extravagance, he observes that: "We find this organization giving employment to thousands of Negro men and women." Yes, that's true. But are they paid? From the number of suits for wages filed in the Seventh and Third District Courts, it would appear that employment is all that he gives them. The only way he keeps work going is by getting new employees to work from week to week.

And at the climax of his grotesque and imposing claims, he settles down in a sort of satisfied imperiousness. Says he: "Now if Marcus Garvey has done these things, is Marcus Garvey a success or a failure?" Yes, Brother Marcus you have been both a success and a failure! How, you ask? Well, you have succeeded in wasting more of the Negroes' money than any other Negro. You have succeeded in beginning more impossible schemes than any other Negro. You have succeeded in making the Negro the laughing stock of the world. So much for your success. Now as to your failure: *You have failed to succeed in anything except failures!*

Now you ask what have Owen and Randolph done?

Before pointing out what Owen and Randolph have done, I shall indicate briefly what Owen and Randolph have not done.

First, they have not made away with $600,000 of the people's money on any worthless ships.

Second, they have not been indicted for defrauding the people, white or black, by the United States Government.

Third, they have not initiated any wild-cat bunco games for skinning the public, incorporating them in Delaware, a state that will incorporate anything, however fantastic.

Fourth, they have not been relieving ignorant Negroes of their hard-earned cash to establish millinery shops and grocery stores that they knew could not succeed.

Fifth, they haven't been carrying on any propaganda to divide the American and West Indian Negroes, the black and mulatto Negroes.

Sixth, they haven't conjured up any fantastic projects for conquering Africa as a means of taking in the uninitiated.

Seventh, they have never organized any non-going Black Star Lines and been compelled to suspend them because of Government indictment for fraud.

Eighth, they have never accused a Negro of being a white man to suit demagogic ends, when they knew it was a lie.

Ninth, they have never lied about men of public affairs and been compelled to retract upon pain of being locked up in jail. Everybody remembers the Assistant District Attorney Kilroe case and Marcus Garvey.

Tenth, they have never held any secret interview with the Ku Klux Klan, surrendering the rights of the Negro to a criminal, murderous gang of cutthroats and mid-night assassins. They have never advised the Negro to stop fighting those who are lynching, burning and trying to sterilize Negro men. They have never opposed and denounced as rabid race baiters all white men at one time, only to shift to the support of that most conscienceless mob of Negro phobists— the Ku Klux Klan.

Eleventh, they have never advised Negroes to go where they couldn't or didn't ever plan to go—Africa.

So much for what Owen and Randolph have not done. Not a bad record this, though negative. But I am not going to answer Mr. Garvey with mere negation.

Now about what Owen and Randolph have done.

First, they have established a great journal of scientifific opinion, fearless, able and uncompromising. Witness the survey of the United States Department of Justice in its report on radicalism in the Negro press: "The MESSENGER is by long odds the most able and the most dangerous of all the Negro publications." How is that Brother Marcus? Some publication, eh? The *Negro World* was fully considered in its report when it made this statement on the MESSENGER.

Second, we established the first publication among Negroes to advocate the principles of organized labor. Unionism gets more wages for workers. Don't you think Negroes need more wages? Ask your own underpaid employees! Wages buy food, clothing and shelter. Without wages, Negroes who are chiefly workers, cannot live. Hence, he who fights for more wages for the Negro, fights for more life for the Negro. This is no mean achievement, is it Brother Marcus? At least, *intelligent people*, white and black, think it a great achievement.

Third, Owen and Randolph have spoken to hundreds of thousands of white and black workers in the unions from Coast to Coast, insisting upon the Negro workers' right upon a basis of equality, discussing every aspect of the Negro problem to white workers who, heretofore, have been ignorant of same.

Fourth, they are the first and only Negroes to present the Negro workers' question to the European workers, radicals and liberals.

Fifth, Owen and Randolph were the first to organize the Radical Movement among Negroes in America. They organized the first Socialist Branch in a Negro community which white and black Socialists attend. The People's Educational Forum, the greatest Negro Forum in the United States, grew out of this radical work.

The Garvey Movement could only have begun in New York City where the field had been prepared by Owen and Randolph for the reception of new ideas, presented through the vehicle of radicalism. It is well known that Garvey began his propaganda in harmony with the MESSENGER's principles in order to get a hearing. He shifted his propaganda after he got a foot-hold. It is a verifiable fact that Brother Marcus got his first knowledge of the African problem from a program drawn up by the writer and presented at a conference, held at the late Madam C. J. Walker's home, Irvington-on-the-Hudson, out of which grew the "International League of Darker Peoples." Mr. Garvey was there and participated in the conference. During the pre-peace conference, Owen and Randolph were the theoretical exponents of achieving the goal of "Africa for the Africans" through the instrumentality of a league of darker peoples, re-enforced by an alliance with the white radical, liberal and labor movements of the world.

So much was this recognized that Mr. Garvey capitalized the reputation of the writer by selecting him as a representative of the U. N. I. A. to the Peace Conference. Needless to say that I never went. The money collected was used as the money has been used that was collected for the Black Star Line. It is also a matter of record, that the first big mass meeting ever held by the U. N. I. A. was held under the pretext of sending the writer to the Peace Conference. The writer didn't know then that Mr. Garvey was untrustworthy. Garvey claims to have sent some one to the conference. No legitimate reporter at the conference took note of his presence.

Seventh, Owen and Randolph organized the first Negro movement with a sound economic program—The Friends of Negro Freedom. It's founders include the ablest Negro thinkers and men of public integrity which is in striking contrast with the U. N. I. A., which does not include a single reputable scholar and honorable public figure. This is their record of achievement which I submit before the high tribunal of Negro public and world opinion. In conclusion, Mr. Garvey attempts to get an alibi for his business miscarriage by saying: "Marcus Garvey does not hold himself up to be the doer of the impossible. Marcus Garvey is not a navigator; he is not a marine engineer; he is not even a good sailor, therefore, the individual who would critcize Marcus Garvey for a ship of the Black Star Line not making a success at sea is a fool, because no head of any steamship company can guarantee what will be the action of the captain of one of his ships when he clears port." Such is his excuse for the dismal and miserable failure of the Black Star Line. If he was ignorant of the shipping business, why did he go in it?

Pointing out that he is not a captain or an engineer or a sailor is not sufficient. The owners and managers of steamship lines are not supposed to be sailors. Still they are morally and legally responsible for the business of the steam ship lines, including losses by sea and otherwise. Hedley, the president of the Subway, is not a motormon, but he is responsible for the business condition of and accidents on the Subway. This is too obvious to need debate. All honest and intelligent business men recognize and accept the responsibility of the principal for the acts of their agents.

Mr. Garvey further states in his lamentation upon the farce and mess he has made of everything he has touched: "What can Marcus Garvey do if men are employed to do their work and they prove to be dishonest and dishonorable in the performance of that work?" So Brother Marcus admits that he has failed. Very well! What about your pompous ravings on your so-called achievements? A great leader is supposed to know how to pick men. It is the chief function of a leader. But you admit that it is beyond you. Then why don't you be honest and stop misleading ignorant Negroes, wasting their money and making them the butt of ridicule and raillery? If your own stricken conscience does not lead you to stop, I assure you that the aroused and awakened, militant, intelligent Negro masses will see to it that you and all that you stand for will be driven from the American soil.

# 11
## The State of the Race

*In "The State of the Race" (*The Messenger *5 [April 1923]: 660–62), Randolph assessed the racial situation in the United States and the divisions in the black community regarding how to respond most effectively to racial prejudice in the increasingly chaotic postwar world. In this essay Randolph appeared less doctrinaire than he had been in his earlier, more radical writings. Ardent socialism seemed to be giving way to a more moderate position in Randolph's stance as a race and labor leader.*

THE state of the race, like the state of the world, is chaotic. The former mirrors the latter. They hold the relation of cause and effect. Thus, in order to understand the causes at the bottom of the existing economic, political and social debacle in the life of the Negro, it is necessary to study the causes underlying the breakdown of the economic and political mechanism of Europe, the overthrow of empires and kingdoms; the rise of revolutions and republics.

Naturally, this carries us back to the war, which is beginning to be regarded as a new epoch in human history. The passions of the Great War swept the hopes of all peoples upward. War cries and slogans rang with a promise of a "new day," a warless world; a "world upon which the gibbet's shadow does not fall; where work and worth go hand in hand"; a world without oppression of race, or class, creed or nation. Such was the dream of millions. This psychology was the handiwork of a plutocratic press, pulpit and school. It was essential to the successful prosecution of the war. But, meanwhile, ten million men were killed and thirty million wounded. A world torn and shattered by conflict; burdened with billions of debt, turned to Versailles for peace. But the Elder Statesmen of Europe and America failed to achieve peace. Their League of Nations like the Holy Alliance of Metternich holds no promise of order or justice. Following peace, in every country, the blight of unemployment, the result of over production hovered over the lands. The high wage and high price levels of war, slumped. The buying power of millions of workers, black and white, contracted as their income decreased. A world-wide panic ensued. In America, as elsewhere, this financial and industrial depression reflected itself, in the general economic, political and social life of the people. In every field of human effort visible signs of spiritual decay are manifest. Society, as a whole, seems utterly and hopelessly bankrupt of any vitalizing and recuperative powers. Not only is there little or no interest in cultural strivings; no power to heal the wounds of a bleeding world; but, far worse and far more alarming, is the absence of a "will" to salvage civilization, to reestablish ordered relationships in the affairs of mankind. In very truth, the Brahmins of the *magic cult of profits*, driven on by the inexorable forces of capitalist imperialism, have called forth monsters that now threaten to devour them. Strife and dissension, splits and disharmonies that are bitter and devastating, beset every group.

The former allies, France and England, have reached the parting of the ways over oil in Mosul. The United States is becoming, a la Coué, day by day, in every way, more estranged from her former allies over the issue of debts. Russia is outlawed and despised by those whom she helped to win the war, because of her social philosophy. Turkey, the once "sick man of Europe," is now rattling the sabre of a reborn nationalism; while Germany, her former ally, lies prostrate at the foot of a ruthless world imperialism, her very life's blood ebbing away. Thus the united front of capitalism lies in ruins, with another world war hovering in the offing.

The victorious powers can not agree on anything. Both Soviet Russia and Germany have baffled the ruling class in every conference from Versailles to Lausanne. Such is the international muddle.

Moreover, the internal conditions of the respective countries are not any more reassuring. Even the employing classes within the several countries are divided, unable to settle upon any general policy of either exploiting the workers or of opposing rival national powers. Neither premiers Bonar Law of England, Mussolini of Italy, Poincaré of France, Chancellor Cuno of Germany, President Harding of the United States of America, or Lenin of Soviet Russia can boast a united nation behind their governments. Amidst troubled times that augur grave peril to the very life of the regime of the bourgeoisie, capitalist statesmen, distressed and distracted, play at politics. The European and American diplomatists are the Neros of today, fiddling while the world burns.

One has but cursorily to observe politics in the United States to note its obvious chaos. The hardboiled, stand-pat, Lodge faction is at loggerheads with the LaFollette-Brookhart progressives, sometimes styled by the Lusk fraternity as "parlor Bolsheviks." But even the Progressives are without unanimity of thought and action on general policies. In short, the politicians like the capitalists they represent, are in bitter, ravaging feuds, incapable of evolving a common program.

And what is true of the ruling class is equally true of the subject or working class. Though division invites repression, the ranks of the workers everywhere are riven asunder. There are rights and new-rights, centers and near-centers, lefts and near-lefts. Witness the variety of proletarian political efforts, viz., the Socialist Party, the Socialist Labor Party, the Communist, the Communist Labor and the Proletarian Communist Parties. (In New York City the Workers Party is recognized as the legal expression of one wing of the Communist movement.) Then, there are the liberals, such as the Committee of 48, the Non-Partisan League, etc. What power might not be wielded by the workers, with a *united front*; still these splits serve their purpose. They are the training school of a nobler and mightier movement.

In industry, too, the workers have no less a variety of splits and splitlets. The Labor Movement of America comprises the American Federation of Labor, which constitutes the conservative wing; the I. W. W., or the left wing; and such independent organizations as the Amalgamated Clothing Workers and the Amalgamated Food Industries Unions, each of which possesses numerous wings that are ever locked in a raging war. Even during periods of strikes, the disastrous internal strife of the Labor Movement proceeds apace with redoubled fury. Doubtless such has ever been, in little measure. But this confusion and disunity in the ranks of the workers and employers are intensified and aggravated during periods of economic storm and stress—panics and the aftermath of wars.

This phenomenon of world-wide political and economic disorder was precipitated and accentuated by the world war, which world war was the outgrowth of commercial rivalry between capitalist nations; and this commercial rivalry flowed as an inevitable consequence of the existence of a socio-economic system under which the workers produce more wealth than their wages will enable them to buy back, thereby piling up a huge surplus.

By a careful study of the economic history of the United States, it will be seen that these periodic commercial and industrial crises have their roots in a system which oscillates well-nigh mechanically from overproduction to underproduction, from high wages to low wages, from high prices to low prices. The capitalist countries of the world alternate from violent business inflation to severe and drastic liquidation, expressing themselves in the closing down of factories, mines, lay-offs on railroads and steamships; widespread unemployment, bankruptcies, strikes, etc. These cycles of economic depression reappear around every decade. While wars may intensify their manifestation, wars are not essentially their cause. Our planless system of producing wealth for profits is the fundamental cause. Thus, this is not the first, and doubtless will not be the last period of industrial upheavals and maladjustments which will reflect itself in a social malaise, spiritual dry-rot, political bankruptcy and intellectual sterility. And every group, whether capitalist or worker, black or white, is a replica in microcosm of this all-encompassing world collapse. No group can escape being afflicted by this virulent bacillus of chaos because no group can escape dependence upon the existing economic order for food, clothing and shelter, the primary needs of life. And just as one loses his equilibrium when the platform upon which he stands is shaken, so does a social order reel, its ethical, religious, legal, political and cultural superstructures lose balance when once the mechanism for producing the wealth of that society is damaged, either through abuse or disuse.

Hence, the Negro race, being an integral part of the present system, will naturally and logically reflect this chaos; but, perhaps, only more acutely because of its weakness.

It is not unnatural that a group which is the last hired and the first fired, a group which works the hardest and receives the lowest pay, would show signs of moral deterioration under the stresses and strains of the present period of readjustment. Well might the race assemble in a parley to discuss its miserable plight, its apparent degeneration and the probable way out.

Our lines, defensive and offensive, have been pushed back on every sector, political, economic and social. Witness how the Dyer Anti-Lynching Bill, a supreme test of the race's virility and instinct to move forward, died because the overwhelming economic paralysis had sapped our *will* to battle for manhood rights.

Our political policies, the heritage of Civil War days, are barren of achievement. *The job-political-policy of the Old Crowd is insolvent, discredited, repudiated; still political statesmanship goes a-begging.*

In industry we have lost ground. Wages have dropped below other groups doing similar work because we lack bargaining power, which can only come with organization.

In business, our failures have been numerous and disastrous, including banks and enterprises of all kinds. Here we lack credit power, knowledge, and experience.

In the educational field the sinister monster of segregation rears its menacing head, in many cases securing our acquiescence, in others pressing us to yield through murder and threat.

Meanwhile, lynchings and riots and the indescribable depredations of the Ku Klux Klan are religiously employed to drive us back into the black night of moral slavery.

To the solution of these problems, the race has evolved many and divers schools of thought, working assiduously at cross purposes. A word about them.

The conservative, or right wing, is led, in the field of education and general social policy, by the Tuskegee-Hampton-National Urban League-Howard University group. In this group, the idea of acquiring property, knowledge of trades and professions, and of being law-abiding, thrifty, home-buying, "cast-down-your-bucket-where-you-are" citizens, rather than of the protesting, insurgent variety, is stressed. The Negro leaders of this group are largely satellites of their white benefactors, reflecting the views of conservative, imperial America.

In the center stands the National Association for the Advancement of Colored People, articulating the opinion of liberal Negro America. Through this medium, liberal white America, in alliance with liberal Negro leaders, seek to achieve civil justice for the Negro.

The radical, or left wing, is represented through the MESSENGER and Crusader groups. With this section, political and economic radicalism is the dominant note, treating race as an incident of the larger world problem of class conflict. The radical black and white leaders combine to unite black and white workers.

Finally, there is the Garvey Movement, with its "back-to-Africa" program.

The leader of this group has recently come into great disfavor on account of his interview with King Kleagle Clarke and his subsequent defense of the Ku Klux Klan. Such are, in brief, the broad streams of Negro thinking. Like their white correlatives, the Negro schools of thought are torn with dissension, giving birth to many insurgent factions in each. All are engaged in a war of bitter recriminations, tearing each other limb from limb, while the wide, long-suffering Negro masses trudge aimlessly on, victims of the vanities, foibles, indiscretions and vaulting ambitions, ignorance and dishonesty of varying leaderships.

To the foregoing picture of apparent, amazing race insanity the questions arise: whither are we trending? Is there any way out? What can be done to transform this internecine strife into constructive, co-operative effort?

First, may I observe that the Negro, like the capitalists and workers, like Nordics and Mongoloids, like various sects, cults and movements of all types, together with the great "power nations," is passing through a period of severe and relentless race dialectics, each wing, each leadership desperately striving with a sort of Machiavellian "might is right" creed, to establish a supreme mastery in leadership.

Out of this fierce competitive leadership—movement—struggle will be evolved a clearer vision, a firmer and·a more rugged morale, an unconquerable will, and a finer and more comprehensive and scientific Race policy and technique of action. The progress of the mass is indifferent to leadership—egoisms. The race will move forward even though movements of well-merited honor and distinction for service fall into the discard. For social, like organic progress, in the main, responds to material imperatives.

I am not distressed, then, as to the ultimate issue of the race in these times of world readjustment, although I am conscious of a definite summons for a orientation in race policy and method, in harmony with the trend of the economic and social forces of the age. Thus a determination of the character and tendency of these socio-economic forces is the chief desideratum, since it is obvious that the march of the Race is advanced or retarded in proportion as it is guided by the most severely tested conclusions of modern science.

In conference after conference we must search for and work out the remedy. There should be specialized conferences whose agenda is economic, political, educational. But specialized parleys do not obviate the need of an All-Race Conference.

There are myriad questions of pressing immediacy which challenge the Race for an answer, an answer which should emanate from some representative body, embodying itself in a broad reasoned policy.

What, for instance, should be the attitude of the Negro in the United States on "the conflict between labor and capital," "immigration," "a future war," "the relation of Negroes to white leadership within and without the Race," "the problem of Negro business in periods of expansion and panics," "education in white and Negro schools and colleges," "radicalism among Negroes," "unemployment," "the open and closed shops," "the problem of Africa, the West Indies, Central and South America," "Negro Culture," "lynching, race riots," "which should be the Negro's political party?—Republican, Socialist, Democratic, Workers, or a new Party," "Social Equality," "the Negro farmer," "farm tenant," "peonage," "consumers' and producers' co-operatives," "the relation of the Negro worker to the American Federation of Labor, the I. W. W., and independent unions"; "the attitude of the Negro to workers' international, economic, and political, movements."

Such is a brief sketch of problems of which Negro leadership is either ignorant or indifferent to, but which hold a vital life and death relationship to the fortunes of the race.

To this task of grappling with these riddles of the race, the Negro masses must draft their "best minds and hearts"; men and women who possess a consuming passion to build a great monument of achievement, devotion, and service to the cause of a militant constructive idealism, a free Race, a free world.

---

# 12
## Segregation in the Public Schools:
## A Promise or a Menace

*In this essay, "Segregation in the Public Schools: A Promise or a Menace" (The Messenger 6 [June 1924]: 185–88), Randolph systematically analyzed segregation in U.S. society. He then took an unequivocal stand against racial segregation, in any form, for any reason. Note that Randolph no longer limited his analysis to a narrow economic/class critique.*

IF segregation is a menace it ought to be condemned and rejected; if it is a promise, it ought to be accepted and advocated. Before accepting or rejecting it, however, it is well to inquire into its nature, cause and effects, in order to determine just what it is, and how it functions; for obviously one is unwise to accept or reject that which he does not understand.

### What Is Segregation?

The word segregation comes from the Latin word *segrego*—a compound of *se*, aside, and *grex* or *greg*, flock—to flock aside. The Latinic root derivation or the dictionary definition, however, is not adequate to explain the present meaning and significance of the term. Words, like everything else, undergo an evolution: through this process they take on new meanings. A conspicuous instance in point is: manufacture. Etymologically it means to make by hand, derived from the Latin words *manus*, hand, plus *facio*, make. It is the outgrowth of the pre-capitalist period of production when all commodities were made by hand tools in the home of the artisan. But the industrial revolution which gave the world labor-saving machinery changed the method of production, and consequently the denotation and connotation of certain words, such as the word manufacture, which today, means to make by machine. Languages, like religions, ethics, education, law, literature and art, assume transformations in meaning in consequence of basic changes in the socio-economic modes of getting a living.

Thus, in order to get at the fundamental meaning of segregation as a fact in American life, it is necessary to search the social history of the term.

## Historical Background of Segregation

From the beginning of the dawn of the systematic trade in Negro life and labor in 1517, made possible, as well as profitable, by the cultivation of sugar, tobacco, cotton, rice, etc., in the Spanish, Portuguese, English and French possessions in North, Central and South America and the West Indies, the Negro was viewed as personal property, such as an ox, a plow or clock, subject to the whims of the owner. He was naturally set aside, at the convenience of his master, just as a hog or leper. This social attitude toward people of color in these United States, intrenched and fortified by profit and privilege, persisted with legal sanction and religious justification, for approximately half a thousand years.

Now upon the abolition of our slave economy in America in 1863, the legal sanction of coercive segregation of Negroes as chattel property passed; but the economic need for cheap labor increased as a result of the demands of industrial and agricultural reconstruction. But cheap labor can be exacted only from docile, subservient human beings, beings who will not protest, organize labor unions and strike for a living wage, decent hours and conditions of work. Exploiting the labor of the newly emancipated slave, drunk with the red wine of freedom, was a big and difficult task, especially by the old slave masters, who, having recently fought to maintain slavery, were viewed as the devil incarnate. Their mental attitude toward the white ruling class was hostility personified. Such a spirit was economically unprofitable to the owners of lumber mills, turpentine stills, railroads, cotton plantations and the banking and commercial interests generally. For if Negroes didn't work, there was no production of goods; if there was no production, there was no sale; no sale, no profits. But the issue was not merely to get Negroes to work, but to get them to work cheaply. Hence the will to loaf or to demand a wage of a civilized human being must be broken upon the wheel of persecution, such as lynching, mob law, vagrancy laws, segregation and grandfather clauses. Now it was perfectly all right to maim or kill a Negro, since he was not owned by anyone, and hence would constitute no economic loss to anyone save himself. Thus to the end of perpetuating the moral and mental slavery of the Negro recently relieved from his physical chains of bondage, a hellish and vicious engine of persecution and terrorism was devised and set in motion, beside which the hateful Inquisition of the Middle Ages was a benevolent institution. In the unspeakable whirlwind of hate, rising during the period of reconstruction, thousands of Negroes succumbed, though that was incidental to the process of reducing the Negro to the status of a mental slave. For the objective of the white South was not to kill off all Negroes because that would mean the destruction of the chief source of the labor supply, which would be virtual economic suicide, but to kill his manhood, his spirit to resist economic subjugation.

One of the most effective weapons in the hands of the white owning class of the South was segregation; the business of making the "niggers" know "their place." This policy of setting the Negroes aside as a thing apart, an evil thing, an "untouchable," caused even the "white trash" to throw out its chest and look contemptuously upon the Negro as an inferior being, unfit to be admitted to the community of civilized society. The white working class assumed this arrogant attitude, despite their wretched and miserable poverty and ignorance, made possible by the same system of robbery practiced upon Negroes. Hence the barrier of race prevented the unity of class. The god of Segregation issued the commandment to both races: Thou shalt not commit the sin of *contact*, that is, in public where the equality of the races may be recognized. So insistent has been this decree of segregation that it has very largely secured the acquiescence of the victim—the Negro himself, who, in many instances, is wont to defend it as necessary and beneficent, an attitude which relieves the Lothrop Stoddards and the Ku Klux Klan of the necessity of continuing to use their time and energy in pressing segregation. In other words, the Negroes who defend segregation *ipso facto* become unconscious accessories to their own enslavement.

But this is the crux of the question. How do we know that segregation is a menace to the Negro?

## The Reason for Segregation

From our survey of the social history of segregation, it is clear that it has now assumed an invidious connotation. Always, superiors segregate their inferiors, not inferiors their superiors. In the South, we never hear of Negroes segregating white people. It is explanatory of the social law that wherever two groups are in proximity, the stronger will subjugate or segregate the weaker group. The segregating, too, is usually done for the benefit of the segregator, not the segregated. Of course, the segregating group invariably suggest segregation presumably in the interest of the segregated, and then seek, through subtle propaganda, to get the segregated to accept their lot as inevitable and just.

## The Functioning of Segregation

Let us note how segregation functions. In our social life, the criminal is segregated; not the law-abiding citizens; the insane, not the sane; the diseased, not the healthy. In very truth the entire history of segregation carries with it the idea of people of social position, culture, wealth, power and refinement, setting aside their alleged inferiors as outcasts, pariahs. I have only to mention the following instances in proof: The English segregate the Irish, not the Irish the English; the Japanese the Koreans, not the Koreans the Japanese; the white American the Indian, not the Indian the white American; the rich the poor, not the poor the rich.

## Sociology and Psychology of Segregation

The social method of segregation which results in the deliberate perpetration of palpable injustices upon the weak by the strong, upon the ignorant by the educated, upon the laborer by the capitalist, grows out of the conception that mingling of groups savors of equality. It is as unnatural for equals to segregate each other as it is natural for them to mingle together. Equals demand equal privileges and rights; unequals demand unequal privileges and rights. If John feels that he is equal to Jim, he will accept no less than Jim. But if Jim feels that he is inferior to John, he will demand and accept less than John. The former develops the superiority complex, the latter the inferiority complex.

Now, in every community, the dominant propertied group seeks to keep up the fiction of inherent, inescapable, eternal fundamental difference between, and the inferiority of the non-propertied element and themselves, by enforcing segregation. The psychology of this method is, that anything affirmed and repeated sufficiently long will come to be believed. The segregator and segregated will grow to believe and defend the principle of segregation. Generally the policy of segregation emanates from the economic masters of a community, realizing that the slaves or exploited group will revolt immediately they come to feel and think themselves the equal of the self-appointed master class, and that this belief will develop through contact, for contact tends to strip one of his self-acclaimed, god-like, superior attributes, to expose his weaknesses, his commonplaceness and similarities to the so-called common people, unless he be, indeed, intrinsically superior. Such is the reason for the hierarchical organization of monarchies and empires. The plain people are permitted only periodically, on some august, state occasion, to view the person of the King. It is ever shrouded in the halo of mystery, thereby investing the ruler with the power, authority and aspect of the supernatural. In democracies and republics, too, those who own for a living struggle to be worshipped and obeyed as little uncrowned kings by those who work for a living. In order to be so regarded, they avoid contact with the despised common herd. True is the old adage: familiarity breeds contempt. It is a fact of common knowledge to all students of the history of the slave regime, that the slave owners prevented, upon pain of severe punishment, the association of free Negroes with Negro slaves. Labor history is replete with the brutal methods, legal and illegal, employed by the capitalists in order to prevent contact between union and non-union labor. Contact invites examination. Examination dissipates unreal differences. Common people clamor for the rights and comforts of Kings when they know and realize that they are all human beings of a common mud. Sweated non-union men will fight for a union wage when they are educated through contact with their union brothers. Negroes will not continue to accept the deserts of half-men when they awake, through contact, to the fact that they are no less than white men in body and mind.

**Who Benefits from Segregation?**

It is obvious from the foregoing then that segregation never originates in the interest of the segregated, but in the interest of the segregator. For instance, it is not to the interest of criminals to be segregated. Assuming, for the sake of argument, that there are persons in society better than they, criminals undoubtedly could improve themselves through contact with the so-called "best people." Imitation in society, according to Tarde, is one of the greatest forces for modern progress. Certainly the association of criminals with their betters could not make them worse. The old saw: Show me the company you keep and I will tell you who you are, carries with it the idea that if one associates with criminals, he is a criminal; if he associates with respectable people, he is respectable. It goes further, and implies that if one is respectable and associates with bad people, he will become bad. But the reverse should also be true, viz.: that if the "no-good" associate with the good, they will become good. This principle of sociology is borne out by the entire body of literature on the subject of child psychology. Witness the institution for incorrigibles, the classes for mental defectives. No one, without a sense of humor, will contend that association between children of strong and weak minds will result in making the minds of the weak-minded children weaker, or that the insanity of the insane is accentuated by contact with the sane, or that the physically weak will be made weaker by contact with the physically strong, or that common people will be made more common by association with the kings and aristocrats, or that the ignorant will become more ignorant by contact with the educated. Now, granting that the theory of separating the bad from the good, the criminal from the law-abiding citizens, is sound, for the Negro or any other group to accept segregation is to acknowledge themselves inferiors and incompetents, and, therefore, entitled to inferior treatment. To illustrate: No one will maintain that a criminal ought to receive the same treatment of a law-abiding citizen, or that a diseased person should be allowed the same freedom of a healthy one. On the contrary, the current notion is that justice should punish the criminal in the interest of the law-abiding citizen. While this is a fallacy, it is is, nevertheless, the custom.

**Social Value**

Upon close analysis, it will be found that the philosophy of social value arises out of certain conceptions of superiority and inferiority—with respect to persons and things. This element of relative worth is reflected in every aspect of our social life, especially the economic. Note the case of a Negro caught in a wreck. He will be awarded less damages than a white man similarly injured, of similar culture. Why? Because the social estimate of a Negro is that he is less valuable than a white man, even if certain Negroes, in material possessions and culture, are obviously greater than certain white men. As a worker, a Negro will be paid less wages than a white worker, because it is assumed that his standard of living is lower; that is, that he has less wants for higher goods; not that he consumes less. This is based upon the fact that the Negro worker is recognized as being able to produce less of value. It is idle and futile to expect an inferior person to produce as much of value as a superior one. But you say that a Negro worker can produce as much of value as a white worker. Of course that's true. But the question is not what is true but what is generally believed and felt to be true. Human beings act more strongly upon belief and feeling than they do upon thought and reason. To accept the status of an inferior and then cry for being denied the recognition of a person of superior worth is as childish as it is useless. Thus the social evaluation of a people has a definite economic significance. A powerful reason for opposing any measure that affixes the stigma of inferiority to the Negro.

**Evaluation of Other Species**

Proceeding with our train of reasoning. Let us apply this principle of evaluation to other species.

A robin will not bring the price or get the treatment of a canary, because it is thought to be worth less. Nor will a common cur dog receive the attention of or fetch the price of a Newfoundland or English Bulldog, because of the conception of relative values. There is no market for a backyard cat, while a Maltese is highly prized. An ordinary cow will not secure the consideration of a Holstein or Jersey cow.

These conceptions of worth grow out of the belief that one yields a larger measure of service, of pleasure than the other. The inference is that, in proportion as one is believed to be valuable, superior, competent, or valueless, inferior, incompetent, he will be treated and recognized as such. Hence the importance of social esteem. It does not matter that one is more or less valuable than he is believed to be, he will be appraised and treated according to the prevailing social belief of his merit or demerit. Now, if the social treatment of a person or group is based upon the social estimate of his or its value, how he or the group ranks in the social scale, it logically follows that it is always to the interest of the person or group to fix, in the mind of society, the belief that he or the group is as socially valuable, and is socially the equal of any other person or group in the community. Because as a community thinks and feels, so it acts. Men and women only mob their supposed inferiors. White, Protestant, Nordic Americans mob and lynch Jews, Negroes, Catholics, foreigners and unionized workmen.

But, you say, while it is true that the social treatment of individuals and groups reflects the social estimate of them, which, in turn reacts on their ability to earn a living, still opposition to segregation is tantamount to a demand for social equality. True. We plead guilty. But what of it? If a demand for social equality is equivalent to a demand for the right to live, then there is no sensible and logical alternative to a demand for social equality. This brings us to the question: What is Social Equality? Suppose we listen to the definition of the most rabid Negro opponents. What say John Sharp Williams, Pat Harrison, Thomas Dixon and their ilk? With tongue and pen they cry out to the high heavens against the Negro aspiring to become educated, to vote, to do the most skilled work, work which they dub a "white man's job!" It is clear, then, that to the Negrophobists, political opportunity is social equality; that educational opportunity is social equality; that economic opportunity is social equality. Hence to deny that you want social equality is to admit that you don't want political, educational and economic opportunity. In other words, you admit you feel that you should apologize for living, for without the above-named opportunities, life is impossible. The logic of Cole Blease and the Ku Klux Klan is sound. You cannot educate a person or race in the same things in which you are educated and continue to convince him or it that he or it is inferior to you.

## Social Contact

But it is further argued by our friendly enemies that educational, political and economic opportunity can only be achieved through contact and contact is the essence of social equality. Here again our industrious detractors are on sound grounds. But is contact, *per se*, objected to? No, not at all. Social contact is objected to, that is contact with Negroes as ladies and gentlemen. There is contact a-plenty after dark. Witness the six million mulattoes in this country. They were not brought into being through the mystic magic of some Aladdin. Besides the results of this twilight contact have progressively increased. Note that in 1850, there were 405,751 mulattoes in these United States. In 1910, there were 2,050,686, an increase of 9.8 per cent. So much for biological contact.

Now as to the social manifestations of social equality.

It is a matter of common experience that contact between Negro bellmen, waiters, pullman porters, ushers in theatres, chauffeurs, cooks and nurses and their white employers as servants, obtains generally and daily. Contact in the capacity of a servant is not objected to. But there is objection to a Negro appearing in the same pullman coach, theatre or hotel as a guest, as a gentleman or a lady, being served as others are served. Still there is obviously less contact with the white patrons when the Negro is in a dining room, a pullman car or a theatre as a guest than when he is there, as a servant. Because as a guest he occupies his own particular seat or berth as the other white guests do; whereas a servant, he moves freely among all of the white patrons constantly. Again, the Negro may live under the same roof with the rankest Bourbon Southern Negro hater as a servant; but no Negro must buy a house beside him and live as a neighbor, as an owner. Nor is it a question of economic status here. The Negro who purchases a house in a white neighborhood would be objected to were he a millionaire doctor or a plain ash-cart driver. A white common workman who was able to buy in an exclusive neighborhood would not be objected to, however. Why? Because there is always a desire to see an evidence of inferiority on the part of the Negro, and the capacity of a menial servant is reckoned as such an evidence. But again, why? The answer is simple. If the great laboring masses of people, black and white, are kept forever snarling over the question as to who is superior or inferior, they will never combine or they will take a long time to combine for the achievement of a common benefit: more wages, a shorter work-day and better working conditions. Combination between black and white working people in the South would mean the loss of millions in profits to railroads, cotton magnates, lumber barons and bankers. White railroad workers fear the Negro as a strikebreaker, but still refuse to take him into their unions because of the social pressure that decrees that Negroes are inferior to white men, and hence should be religiously denied contact. This is an instance of a direct blow at the very life of the race as a result of the mandate of segregation.

---

# 13
## Jim Crow Niggers

*In the editorial "Jim Crow Niggers" (*The Messenger *7 [May 1925]: 196–97), Randolph continued his attack on blacks who are willing to accept any form of segregation.*

We have developed a nation of jim crow niggers. As one travels he is more impressed with the fact. He realizes that were it not for a few protesting souls, a few men who will just not "stay put," the whole nation would be threaded with jim-crow cars, dappled with jim-crow schools, disfranchised in its darker quarters, while the Negro population would be lynched without restraint.

The penalty of discrimination and segregation is that those subjected to it become used to it; becoming used to it means forming the habit. The tendency of habit is to become pleasant, and the tendency is to keep what is pleasant—happiness being the goal of life.

We are very sympathetic with the southern migrants who have come into our northern territory, but we also recognize that they are a constant menace. They have been used to disfranchisement, jim-crow schools, jim-crow railroads and street cars, discrimination in places of public accomodation and amusement. They have formulated a fool philosophy of pride in saying they don't want to be where they're not wanted. Unless the southern whites, who have come up ahead of them, are behind them, begin agitation for segregated schools, very shortly the southern Negroes themselves will lead the fight for an existence where they are "let alone." And "let alone" it is, for soon, domiciled in one district, the city lets them alone, lets their streets alone—doesn't bother about cleaning them. Lets crime alone there (allows as many bawdy houses, bootleg joints, pool rooms, dives and dens to run as physical possibilities will permit.) Leaves their schools alone; allowing the bricks to fall out, the window panes to be broken, the floors to warp and split, the plaster to crack and fall, and the general dilapidation consequent to the use of school buildings when the city fails to repair such natural wear and tear after the fashion it looks after its white schools. Lets alone is right! For here no pure food laws stop the foreign merchants from selling rotten meat, from selling fresh fish which have been on land longer than they were ever in the water.

The low level of Negro leadership is responsible for much of this mischief. As a rule the leader of the separate school drive is some ecclesiastical clown, some pusillanimous pedagogue, some pie-counter politician (more spiritous than spiritual), some real estate dealer who has risen above "the mired mass" by robbing the "mired mass," and shoving them farther in the mire, or some editor (idiotor), long on inspiration and short on information.

There is already a strong trend toward the separate school. The whites are determined to force it upon the Negroes, and the Negroes are not only acquiescent victims, but willing and anxious recipients of this bedeviled educational system. Many of these evils could be warded off were it not for a leadership of jim-crow niggers. The evils will be recognized later but as a rule, too late. It is always easier to maintain liberty than it is to secure it. Just as it is easier to retain money than it is to obtain it. Unless the trend is stopped we predict within the next ten years the segregated school in every community having a population above five thousand Negroes.

# 14

## Negroes and the Labor Movement

*The July 1925 issue of* The Messenger *was filled with articles on the labor problems of black Pullman porters and on the labor movement in general. In late June Randolph had met with a group interested in creating a union of black Pullman porters; in August he assumed the leadership of the new Brotherhood of Sleeping Car Porters. This editorial, "Negroes and the Labor Movement"* (The Messenger *7 [July 1925]: 261, 275), anticipated Randolph's new role as a labor organizer, and the new role of* The Messenger *as the organ of the Brotherhood of Sleeping Car Porters. It also reflected his continued movement away from the radical left and toward the mainstream of labor and civil rights leadership.*

It is gratifying to note that there is now considerable interest manifest in the organization of the Negro workers. Doubtless the real reason is that the white unions are slowly but surely awakening to the serious necessity of unionizing the Negro worker in self defense. They are beginning to realize that Negro labor is playing an increasingly larger and more significant role in American industry. Especially is this true in the East, West and North, where large numbers of Negro workers have migrated and are competing in the labor market with organized labor. It is this competition which has jolted the organized white workers out of their state of chronic indifference, apathy and unconcern. Of course, even now nothing definite has been done in the interest of Negro labor by the organized labor movement. Some of its leaders such as Hugh Frayne, Thomas J. Curtis and Ernest Bohm, are members of the Trade Union Committee for Organizing Negro Workers, but it is not apparent that this committee has anything as yet save the moral good will of some of the local unions of New York City. In order for it to succeed in its organization work, however, it must be financed by the white organized workers. So far its financial backing has come from the American Fund for Public Service. It has made possible the employment of Frank R. Crosswaith as Secretary. This Committee was started under the aegis of the National Urban League led by Mrs. Walzer and Mr. Holden. Of course, this work is not new or original. THE MESSENGER has been the pioneer in the field advocating the organization of Negro labor. Now the *Crisis* is belatedly taking up the fight for the next three years, and the Negro press generally has become sympathetic and active in advising Negroes to organize into labor unions wherever their white brothers will accept them. We are glad to note that Negro editors are learning their economic lessons slowly but surely. Let no Negro fail in his duty of advancing the cause of Negro labor without let or hindrance. The time is rotten ripe. Immigration from Europe has been materially cut, which means that the yearly supply of labor is much less than it formerly was. This gives the organized workers an advantage, greater bargaining power by virtue of this limited supply. It also gives the Negro worker a strategic position. It gives him power to exact a higher wage from capitalists, on the one hand, and to compel organized labor to let down the bars of discrimination against him, on the other. Thus it benefits him in two ways. And the Negro workers cannot rely upon anything but the force of necessity, the self-interests of the white unions, and the fear of Negro workers' competition, to give them a union card. Another potent force in the organization of Negro labor is education and agitation. A certain course of action may be to a group's interest to take but if it doesn't realize it it is not likely to act upon it. Thus the Negro press and the enlightened white labor press have a big task before them. But the task of Negro workers consists in more than merely deciding to organize. They must guard against being lured up labor blind alleys by irresponsible labor talkers who present them all sorts of wild, impossible dreams such as are advocated by the Communists. No labor movement in America among white or black workers can solve the industrial problems of the American workers, white or black, whose seat of control is outside of the country. This ought to be too obvious to require argument. The Communist movement in America is a menace to the American labor movement. It is a menace to the Negro workers. While healthy, intelligent, constructive criticism is valuable and necessary to the American labor movement, criticism which starts from the premise that the existing organized labor movement should be disrupted and destroyed must be resolutely opposed. This has been ably done by Abram Cahan, Vladeck of the Jewish Daily Forward; Geleibeter and Baskin, President and Secretary, respectively, of the Workmen's Circle; Sigman and Baroff, of the International Ladies' Garment Workers; Kaufman and Wieneiss, of the Furriers; Hillman and Schlossberg, of the Amalgamated Clothing Workers, etc. It ought to be patent now that the social history and psychology of the American workers will not yield to Communists' methods and tactics. Thus instead of advancing, the Communists have set back and retarded the cause of labor in America. If such is true of the white worker it is as equally true of the Negro worker.

# 15
## The Negro and Economic Radicalism

*Randolph published the article "The Negro and Economic Radicalism" (Opportunity 38 [February 1926]: 62–64) in the monthly magazine of the Urban*

*League, an organization he had labeled as "conservative, or right wing" only
three years earlier (see "The State of the Race" above). In this article he placed
black economic radicalism, which he defined in terms of class consciousness and
labor organization, in the tradition of Booker T. Washington. As he moved
toward the mainstream as a labor leader, Randolph turned his back on the
bolshevism he had once so admired.*

THE term radicalism is a bugbear in these United States of America. So adroitly
has it been manipulated in the press that in the mind of the average man it
connotes something sinister, terrible. Merely to mention the word makes our
so-called respectable gentry feel creepy. Before them lurid visions arise of wild-
eyed, hairy men and women, with red bandana handkerchiefs around their necks,
daggers between their teeth and flaming torches in hand, stealthily prowling
amidst banks, factories and homes, bent upon the destruction of private property.
Even common wife-beaters and murderers, from the viewpoint of the 100 per-
centers, are shining angels of light to the radicals. As the behaviorists would say,
this is the result of their language organization or language habit.

But, of course, it is all pure fiction. It does not mean any such thing of the
kind. Radicals are not lawless. They are not such ungodly humans. They merely
have the courage of their convictions, seeking ever not only to point out social
wrongs, but also to indicate the cause and prescribe a remedy. They are seekers
after truth. As the word implies, they want to get at the roots of our social
problems. It is for this only that they are damned and spat upon, for the nonce.

Now, there are different shades, types and schools of radicals, differing
largely in forms of tactics, of methodology, in trying to right our social maladjustments. But all represent a revolt against the old ways of thinking and doing
things. Of course, any one who breathes the slightest social, political or economic protest, such as Roosevelt, Woodrow Wilson, Jane Addams or La Follette,
is forthwith labelled a radical.

During and since the World War the outcry for economic citizenship, for
industrial democracy, has become more insistent and passionate.

Doubtless the war, the dynastic and political revolutions in Russia, Germany
and the Balkans, contributed to the growth of radical movements working for the
relief of the masses from economic stresses and social injustices.

And out of different social situations have emerged varying forms of radical-
ism. In India, China, Egypt and Ireland it is nationalistic; in England, France,
Germany and Italy, economic; in Russia, politico-economic; among Negroes in
America and South Africa, politico-economic and racial.

In these United States of America, among Negroes, the radical form has taken
precedence, since the obvious incidence of oppression was racial. The elder race
radicals, such as Frederick Douglas, Bishops Daniel A. Payne and Henry
McNeal Turner, Monroe Trotter, Kelly Miller, W.E.B. DuBois, James Weldon

Johnson, the Grimkes, T. Thomas Fortune, etc., struck out against the race's detractors of the ilk of former Confederate slave masters, Thomas Dixon, Vardaman and Blease, instead of against the race's exploiters, such as the pawnbrokers, loan sharks, turpentine still and plantation owners who foster peonage and tenant-farming; and the lumber mill and railroad barons who overwork and underpay the black proletariat. This attitude of mind was doubtless due to the fact that they stood under the shadows of the old slave regime and the aftermath, which through vagrancy laws, corrupt court practices, grandfather clauses, the subtle nullification of the 13th, 14th and 15th amendments to the Constitution, and segregation, well-nigh effectually re-enslaved the Negro. Hence theirs was not an unmerited fight.

Out of this revolt the Niagara Movement, the National Association for the Advancement of Colored People and the Equal Rights League, were formed. They proclaimed a civil rights program. They wanted political citizenship. Of the outstanding Negro leaders, only Archibald and J. Francis Grimke, James Weldon Johnson, W.E.B. DuBois and George E. Haynes seem to have sensed, though lightly and seldom stressing it, that there were other factors in the so-called race problem equation save race; that there was the "nickel under the foot," an economic basis to the conflict of races in America.

Of organizations, in the last two or three conventions, the National Association for the Advancement of Colored People has been definitely adopting a program in the interest of the organization of black workers. The National Urban League, too, in a less militant way, more in the form of surveys and securing new industrial opportunities, has turned its attention to the question of improving the lot of the Negro workers. In the main, the old crowd leadership damned the detractors and blessed the exploiters of the race, because the former criticized and the latter subsidized the Negro industrial schools and colleges. The elder race radicals, in their heyday, while they did not bless the exploiters of the race, they did not oppose them. They simply thought that the struggle for civil rights was more important. Kelly Miller is a peculiar exception. Though a consistent fighter in the interest of civil rights, he fawns before the altar of big business and glorifies the so-called capitalists' benefactions to the race, apparently unmindful of the service which black labor is to white capitalists.

Only since the war has economic radicalism within the race emerged. Its chief mouthpiece is the *Messenger* magazine, which is more philosophically and less dogmatically radical. It is more pronouncedly labor unionistic. During the hot days of the war and immediately thereafter the outstanding Negro economic radicals were Chandler Owen, Otto Houiswond, Frank R. Crosswaith, Ross D. Brown, Helen Holman, Eugene Moore, W.A. Domingo, Lovett Fort-Whiteman, Hubert H. Harrison and the writer. They were Socialists. The Communists' schism, which grew out of the Russian revolution, split them just as it did the white Socialists everywhere. Today the Negro radicals, like the whites, are few in number and weak in influence. Their movements were well-nigh liquidated by the frenzied persecution under Burleson, Palmer, Daugherty and Sweet, during and after the war. The movement represented by the American Negro Labor Congress is perhaps the strongest, which is not saying anything for it, but a whole lot against it.

However, the Negro radicals have not wrought in vain. It was theirs definitely to shape a working class economic perspective in Negro thought. Booker T. Washington had very masterly stressed the bourgeois side. Negro workers had been viewed as the flotsam and jetsam of the race; for had not even the white workers in the South been dubbed reproachfully as poor trash, while the rich white people were regarded as the Negroes' benefactors?

Booker T. Washington had sought to prepare Negro workers for new industrial and agricultural tasks which grew out of the rapid industrialization of the South, whereas the burden today is securing an adequate reward for the performance of those tasks. This raises the question of the how and wherefore.

It is out of this latter economic concept that the trend of Negro workers into economic organization grows.

Perhaps the most significant manifestation of this trend is the movement to organize the Pullman porters. Of course, this movement is not radical, except in the sense that the whole trade union movement is fundamentally radical. It is not backed by Moscow, nor has it any Communistic connections, as has been falsely charged. It is a simple labor union seeking a living wage and better working conditions. It also has spiritual aims, such as the abolition of professional mendicancy, which is the result of relying upon tips for the means of life—a demoralizing practice. The porters also want a voice in the determination of the conditions under which they work, the abolition of the Pullman feudalistic paternalism, a relic of the old master and servant relationship. They want to maintain their manhood, their self-respect. This can only be secured through organization of, by and for themselves, because organization is the only basis of power. The Brotherhood will not injure the Pullman company; it will help it. It does not counsel insubordination, but efficient discipline.

Specifically, the porters want to raise their wages from $67.50 a month to a point which will enable them to command commodities and services essential to a decent American standard of living, as budgeted by such accredited economic agencies as the U.S. Bureau of Labor Statistics.

They also want pay for preparatory time, or the time from which a porter reports for duty and the train departs. For example, a porter leaving for Washington from New York at 12:30 midnight, any night, reports for duty at 7:30 P. M., works until 12:30 making ready his car and receiving passengers, but his time does not begin until the train leaves the terminal station. In other words, he has given the Pullman Company five hours of his labor for absolutely nothing. On the basis of his monthly wage, $67.50, he receives 25 cents an hour. Five hours of work put in as preparatory time represents $1.25. This the porter is deprived of every night he makes the trip. He makes the trip twelve times a month, which means that he loses in labor values $15 every month, or $180 a year; not an inconsiderable item, this, for a worker whose yearly wage is only $810. There are thousands of porters in the service who thus work without pay, so that, over a period of a year, it would be conservative to estimate the exploitation to trench hard upon a million and a half dollars.

But this is not the only palpable injustice practiced upon the porters.

There are what is known as "in charge" porters, or those that do the conductor's and porter's work combined. But they only receive a porter's pay, plus $10 additional monthly. Since the minimum conductor's pay is $155 a month, the company saves $145 on every porter who runs "in charge." One of the demands of the Brotherhood is: Conductor's pay for conductor's work. The company will not even flatter the porter with the title of conductor. He is titled "in charge."

Perhaps the most unreasonable condition of the porter's work is the requirement that he make 11,000 miles a month, which is nearly 400 hours' work, an inhuman exaction. Upon such a mileage basis, if a porter's train were five or six hours late every trip, he would not get a cent for it, because the time sheet requires that his delayed arrivals be put in the accumulated mileage column, which renders it practically impossible for a porter to make overtime unless he has an extraordinarily long run. The demand of the porters is for 240 *hours or less in regular assignment* as a monthly basis of pay. This is not a revolutionary demand, since the other railroad workers have it, including the Pullman conductors.

It is practically because of these just demands, already possessed by all other railroad workers, that the Pullman company has waged a vicious and relentless war upon the men organizing. Through threats and intimidations it has attempted to force the men to vote for its company union, euphemistically called the Employee Representation Plan, a plan initiated, dominated and controlled by the company and which was designed to impress the men and the public with the idea that the porters have an organization. Under the plan the Assistant District Superintendent, who has the power to recommend the discharge of a porter, sits in the Local Grievance Committee and passes on all cases involving disputes between the porters and the company or porters and passengers. In other words, the local management of the company acts as prosecutor, judge and jury.

In order to prevent the porters from achieving their objective, the company has employed Mr. Perry W. Howard, Negro Special Assistant to the United States Attorney General, and smothered the criticism of several Negro newspapers by placing advertisements with them. Be it said to the credit of the Eastern Negro press that they refused to be bought.

But the company, in utter desperation, did not stop at trying to throttle the Negro press. It reached out for the Negro leaders, and it has not entirely failed.

The conference of fifty Negro leaders recently held in Washington, presumably to discuss matters of segregation, actually engaged only in condemning the movement to organize the Pullman porters. I do not charge, however, that every person in that conference knew that he was being used as a tool to prevent the porters from getting a living wage. But it is difficult to understand their silence after they learned of the corruption of the conference. It is quite significant that a conference called to discuss segregation did not invite the National Association for the Advancement of Colored People, the organization which has most consistently fought the evil. But, of course, the reason was that the N. A. A. C. P. had already officially endorsed the Brotherhood of Sleeping Car Porters, and its speakers, James Weldon Johnson, William Pickens and Robert W. Bagnall, have spoken for the movement throughout the country.

One need not be a prophet to realize that the beneficent consequences of this movement to the Negro are immeasurable. It will awaken the Negro workers everywhere to a sense of their power and rights, and the methods to adopt in order to secure them. It will develop more spirit, manhood and independence in the race. It is a promise of economic and spiritual liberation.

---

# 16
## The New Pullman Porter

*In the essay "The New Pullman Porter" (*The Messenger *8 [April 1926]: 109), Randolph defines the class consciousness of the unionized Pullman porter in terms similar to, but far less radical than, the terms he used to define the New Negro in 1920. This essay also reflects the status of* The Messenger *as the official organ of the Brotherhood of Sleeping Car Porters.*

A new Pullman porter is born. He breathes a new spirit. He has caught a new vision. His creed is independence without insolence; courtesy without fawning; service without servility. His slogan is: "Opportunity not alms." For a fair day's work, he demands a fair day's wage. He reasons that if it is just and fair and advantageous for the Pullman Company to organize in order to sell service to the traveling public, that it is also just and fair and advantageous for the porters to organize in order to sell their service to the Pullman Company; that if it is to the best interests of the Pullman Conductors to form an organization of, by and for themselves, it is to the best interests of the Pullman porters to form an organization of, by and for themselves. He has learnt from experience that the Company Union sugar-coated the Employee Representation Plan cannot and will not serve his interests any more than it can or will serve the interests of the Pullman conductors, the engineers, switchmen, firemen, train conductors or trainmen. He has common sense enough to sense the fact that the Plan is the darling creature of the Company, hatched and nourished for the benefit of the Company, not the porter; that he can no more get justice at its hands than could a rat get justice before a jury of cats. His doctrine is that the best kind of help is self-help expressed through organized action.

The new Pullman porter is a rebel against all that the "Uncle Tom idea suggests. The former possesses the psychology of let well enough alone." The latter that of progressive improvement. The former relies upon charity and pity; the latter upon his intelligence, initiative and thrift. The old time porter is afflicted with an inferiority complex; the new porter logically takes the position that a man's worth in society is not the result of race, color, creed or nationality; but that a man's worth is based upon the quality of his service to society.

The old time porter assumed that a clownal grin or a "buck and wing" was a necessary part of the service in order to extract a dime tip from an amused and ofttimes a disgusted passenger; whereas, the new porter believes that intelligence and dignity and industry are the chief factors in service of quality and value. As a service agent, the new porter seeks to anticipate the desires of his passengers with a view to making their travel ideal. He realizes that his service is a representative form of salesmanship for the Company to the public, and for himself to the Company and the public. His work is not alone regulated by the mechanical requirements of the service, but out of his rich and full experience, he is ever formulating new and higher forms of service. Many constructive and practical ideas lie in the heads of porters who are reluctant to reveal them because they feel that they neither get the proper appreciation or reward from the Company for them. A just wage stimulates the employees to give their best to their employer; it develops a larger interest in the job and a joy in performing a high type of workmanship.

The new porter is not amenable to the old slave-driving methods, his best service is secured through an appeal to his intelligence. Just as he demands fairer treatment than the old time porter, for the same reason, he gives a higher type of service. Just as he rejects charity and pity on the grounds that he is a man, and doesn't need such, so he refuses to make excuses, but performs his duties in accordance with the requirements of efficient service.

His object is not only to get more wages, better hours of work and improved working conditions, but to do his bit in order to raise and progressively improve the standard of Pullman service. The new Pullman porter takes the position that his ability to render the Company increased productive efficiency can only result from his increased physical, moral and mental efficiency, which rest directly upon a higher standard of living, which in turn, can only be secured by a higher, regular income. His insistence upon a regular, living wage is based upon the fact that not only is the tipping system morally unjustifiable, but because tips fluctuate violently in amounts, from month to month, and a porter is for ever uncertain as to how to regulate his household affairs, since he cannot definitely plan on how much money he can spend above his meager wage of $67.50 a month, on his wife's clothing, furniture for his home, or his children's education. No other group of workers are required to work under such distracting uncertainty. Of course, the reason is that they are organized.

The new Pullman porter believes in organization and is wont to convince the Company and the traveling public that the Brotherhood will be a distinct asset to the Pullman industry in the practical and efficient handling of service and personel problems. He is cognizant of the fact that the security and well-fare of the porters are bound up with the steady, continued and sustained progress of the Pullman industry. He is confident that his experience in the service equips, adapts and furnishes him with a peculiar and unique type of training and knowledge which no other employee possesses, and, therefore, renders him highly capable of giving constructive cooperation to the Company which will reflect itself in better service, and, hence better business.

The new porter is not a Communist, but a simple trade unionist, seeking only to become a better and a more useful citizen by securing a higher standard of living and preserving his manhood.

The new porter is not a slacker either on the job or in his organization. He is not content to consume the fruits that the hands of others produce. He is willing and ready to shoulder his share of the responsibility in making conditions better for the porters in particular and the race in general. Nor does he assign his ills to the sinfullness of the officials of the Pullman Company but to his own failure to sense his rights, duties and power to right them.

The new porter recognizes the necessity of cooperating with the Pullman conductor, since both are workers for the same employer whose policy is to pit one against the other in order to keep them at logger-heads. Each can get more through cooperation; both will be exploited the more should they permit themselves to be deceived by the Company into believing that their interests are opposed. Though they accidentally belong to different races, they belong to the same class.

The new porter is not flattered by the claim that he has a monopoly on a job which does not yield him a decent living. He maintains that a fuller consideration of the relation of wages to production costs will show wage rates accompanied efficient management, lower production costs, higher production efficiency and a higher type of workmanship. Higher production efficiency is reflected in lower selling prices which makes possible service to a larger group of consumers, and a consequent larger volume of trade. The new Pullman porter contends that low wages encourages indolence, irresponsibility and dishonesty, and hence it is not an economical wage.

The new porter thinks hard but says little.

# 17
## The Negro Faces the Future

*The following essay was originally presented as an address at the opening cere-
monies of the Sesquicentennial Exposition in Philadelphia. The invitation to
speak on this occasion indicated Randolph's growing reputation as a major
African American leader, and also how completely he had shed his earlier reputation as a radical. The honor bestowed on Randolph recalled the honor shown
Booker T. Washington when he was asked to speak at the opening of the Atlanta
Exposition in 1895. The address was published as "The Negro Faces the Future"* (The Messenger *8 [July 1926]: 201–03).*

*The following is the address of A. Phillip Randolph, General Organizer of The
Brotherhood of Sleeping Car Porters and editor of* THE MESSENGER, *delivered
at the opening of the Sesqui-Centennial Exposition at Philadelphia, May 31,
1926, before an audience of 60,000 persons. Because of the historical importance of this speech it is herein reprinted in full. Mr. Randolph was one of three
speakers, the other two being Secretary of State Kellogg and Secretary of Commerce Hoover, and represented on that occasion the Negro race of the world.—*
THE EDITORS.

*Honorable Chairman, Ladies and Gentlemen, and Fellow Citizens:*

It is eminently fitting and timely that a great people should pause, a brief while,
in their busy life, in their onward conquering march in the acquisition of power
to take inventory of their material, technical, intellectual and spiritual stock, that
they may not face the future distressingly unwitting of their way.

The signs of the times would seem to indicate that the world we live in has
moved into a cycle of political uncertainty, economic unsettlement and social
maladjustment, consequent, largely upon the Great World War, and its immediate aftermath.

### Problems

In this period there are three great, outstanding problems: the problem of peace
between nations, the problem of peace between races and the problem of peace
between labor and capital. Upon the rational and permanent solution of these
problems will rest the continuance of modern civilization.

In our own country, these problems are ever present, ever pressing, ever insistent upon a solution. In our own country, too, one hundred and fifty years ago, the Founding Fathers gave eloquent expression in one of the world's immortal documents, the Declaration of Independence, to a formula which may serve as the solvent key to our perplexing problems.

This formula reads: We hold these truths to be self evident; that all men are created equal, that they are endowed by their Creator with certain inalienable rights; that among these are life, liberty and the pursuit of happiness. That to secure these rights, governments are instituted among men, deriving their just powers from the consent of the governed.

To Aframericans, the embodiment of this formula of practical, righteous idealism into the warp and woof of American life, its laws, its customs, its institutions, its practices, its traditions, in politics, in industry, in education and religion, is a consummation devoutly to be wished; for no people on God's green earth have suffered as poignantly as the Negro peoples of the world, on account of the failure of the world to achieve higher reaches of humanity. Thus, no group of people in America can have a greater and a more genuine concern in the commemoration and perpetuation of the spirit of the Declaration of Independence on this Sesqui-Centenary than the Negro.

But if there are those, either because of ignorance or malice who would challenge the right of Aframericans to share in the glories and achievements of our country, my answer is that of all the Americans, the Negro is, doubtless, the most typically American. He is the incarnation of America. His every pore breathing its vital spirit, without absorbing its crass materialism.

If early contact with and long residence in a land are a price of security and equal opportunity, the Negro has grounds for double reassurance of a square deal. No white man can boast of longer habitation in America than can the Negro. He was a pioneer in the Western world. Garcia de Montalvo published in 1510 a Spanish romance which spoke of the presence of black people in an island called California. That the Negro had visited America before the coming of Columbus is again strongly established by the fact that the Negro countenance, clear and unmistakable, occurs repeatedly in Indian carvings, among the relics of the Mound Builders and in Mexican temples, according to Professor Wiener of Harvard, in his book Africa and the Discovery of America. In religious worship and mound building, the influence of Negro customs is evident. There is accumulating ethnological authority to give weight to the belief that African pomberiros or Negro traders were present in America before Columbus because of the discovery of the use in trading of an alloy of gold called guanin. Guanin is a Mandingo word and the very alloy is of African origin. Wiener again observes that the presence of Negroes with their trading master in America before Columbus is proved by the representations of Negroes in American sculpture and design and by the occurrence of a black nation at Darian early in the sixteenth century, but more specifically by Columbus' emphatic reference to Negro traders from Guinea, who trafficked in a gold alloy, guanin, of precisely the same composition and bearing the same name as is frequently referred to by early writers in Africa.

Some ethnographers maintain that tobacco, cotton, sweet potatoes and peanuts are of African origin and were introduced to the Indians by the Negro. The historian Helps, speaks of the presence of the Negro in the very early history of the American continent. They were with Columbus, Balboa, De Soto and Cortes.

But the claim of the Negro to an honorable place in America does not rest alone upon the fact that the Negro was one among the first peoples to set his feet upon American soil.

**The Gift of Black Labor**

He has given the meed of service to the building of this great nation. He gave his brain and brawn to fell the forests, till the soil and make America the most powerful and prosperous country in the world. Yes, the chief reason for his presence in this country was the call for labor to cultivate tobacco, cotton, rice and sugar. His was the original labor force of the new world. Upon it rests the first great commercial cities of our times. His hard physical labor transformed forbidding wildernesses into habitable centers. Withal, it was the means of releasing for other employment, thousands of white men, and thus advanced the economic development of America with an astonishing acceleration. Verily, black labor established modern world commerce, which began with the systematic trade in black labor, Negro slaves. A strange paradox this; black labor was commodity as well as the producer of commodities, for the world market.

With pertinent discernment, Dr. DuBois, remarks that "The Negro worked as farm hand and peasant proprietor, as laborer, artisan and inventor, and as servant in the house and without him, America as we know it, would have been impossible." The economic value of the Negro in America was attested by the enormous growth in their population. It is estimated that one million Negroes came in the sixteenth century, three million in the seventeenth century and seven million in the eighteenth and four million in the nineteenth or some fifteen million in all. This meant sixty million or more killed and stolen in Africa because of the methods of capture and the horrors of the middle passage. Thus, the early foundations of America's material greatness rests upon a labor force which cost Africa nearly one hundred million souls.

It is a matter of common place history that New York, Massachusetts, Rhode Island, Connecticut and New Hampshire built up a lucrative commerce based largely upon the results of Negro labor in the South and the West Indies, and this commerce supported local agriculture and manufacture.

The growth of the great slave crops shows the increasing economic value of Negro labor. In 1619, 20,000 pounds of tobacco were shipped from Virginia to England. Just before the Revolutionary War, 1,000 million pounds a year were being sent, and at the beginning of the twentieth century, 800 millions were raised in the United States alone. The production of cane sugar jumped from one million in the middle of the nineteenth century to three millions in 1900. And cotton, the chief commodity of the South, rose in production from 13,000 or more bales sent to England in 1781, to a production of 3,366,000 in 1860. The United States raised 6,000,000 bales in 1880, and 11 millions at the beginning of the twentieth century. Such was the basis of modern American commerce. It was hard, manual labor, the gift of black men. If there are those who would sneer at the service of manual labor, let me observe that the problem of America in the fifteenth and sixteenth centuries was the problem of manual labor. It was met by importing white bond servants from Europe who, too, were virtual slaves, and servants from Africa.

The full significance of the Negro as a labor source was sharply emphasized during the sudden transformations of the World War. In a few short months, 500,000 black laborers came North in answer to the call of industry, brought about by the cessations of immigration from Europe and the absorption of white men into new phases of industry. It is quite likely that the Negro worker will continue to be the great labor reservoir of America. Nor is it all manual. On many of the large plantations during the slave regime, in the towns and villages, Negroes did the chief mechanical work. Advertisements of runaway slaves are instances in proof. At one time, Negroes were said to comprise all of the mechanics New Orleans possessed.

Moreover, not only were there skilled Negro workers during the slave regime, but a large number possessed the ingenuity for invention. Etiene de Bore, a colored San Dominican, discovered the process of granulating sugar, which saved Louisiana from economic ruin. There is a strong claim that the credit for the invention of the cotton gin is due to a Negro on a plantation where Eli Whitney worked. In the United States patent office, there are 1,500 inventions made by Negroes. In 1846, Nobert Rillieux, a colored man of Louisiana, invented and patented a vacuum pan which revolutionized the methods for refining sugar. Jan E. Matzeliger invented a machine for lasting shoes, the patent of which was bought by Sydney W. Winslow, upon which was built the great United Shoe Machinery Company. Hundred of dollars' worth of business flow from this invention. Then there is Elijah McCoy, a pioneer inventor of automatic lubricators for machinery, and Granville T. Woods who patented more than fifty devices relating to electricity, many of which were assigned to the General Electric Company of New York, the Westinghouse Company of Pennsylvania, the Bell Telephone Company of Boston and the American Engineering Company of New York. Today, Negro men and women are engaged in practically every field of industry, and in all of the professions.

Such is the contribution of black labor to America. In South Africa, Neigeria, the Sudan, Brazil, the West Indies and the United States, the Negro worker has been and is the manual labor backbone of industry. This belies the Nordic charge of laziness as a racial characteristic of Negroes. And as to African thrift, well does Herbert J. Seligman, in his book, "The Negro Faces America" observe: "To cut down a tree with stone hatchets, and then to make a canoe from the trunk by burning out the core, is no task for the indolent or the man of unsteady purpose."

## In Wars

More and more the judgment of mankind is registering its decisions against wars as the cure for the ills of the world. Wars according to our historical experience, breed and beget wars. They engender and foster hatreds and enmities. They do not lead to peace. But since deeds of heroism are regarded generally as forms of measurement of the value of a group's service and worth to a nation, in a certain sense, I shall here briefly set forth the Negro's record in America.

In every war in which America has been involved, the Negro has taken his part, Chrispus Attuck, a Negro, being the first to fall on Boston Commons in defense of American Independence. In the War of 1812, Negroes distinguished themselves for bravery under Perry, Jackson and McDonnough. And Abraham Lincoln fully realized that success in the prosecution of the Civil War was dependent entirely upon the unlimited employment of Negro soldiers. But for the 200,000 black soldiers who answered the call of Lincoln, the cause of the Union, the chief reason for the war would have perished.

In subsequent conflicts, from El Caney, in the Spanish American War to Carrizal in Mexico and Flanders Field in Europe, the valor and fighting spirit of the Negro are notable and outstanding, challenging the admiration and praise of the most critical and prejudiced.

Despite his struggle and supreme sacrifice in these memorable conflicts the freedom he won he has seldom enjoyed. This is the bitter tragedy of it all.

## Democracy

Can the victims of slavery be the carriers and preservers of democracy? In no small measure, the Negroes' status in America has been a test of America's democracy, of America's Christianity. The insistent cry for freedom on the part of the Negro has kept the American people face to face with the fact that a democracy has not fulfilled its highest mission so long as there are people in the country, black or white who cannot participate in the affairs of government, industry or society generally as free, intelligent human beings.

## The Reconstruction Regime

Despite the cynicism of certain political historians on the reconstruction period of Negro history, an unbiased examination will reveal that the black freedom gave to the South the first glimpse of democratic institutions. The Reconstruction constitutions of 1868 in both South Carolina and Mississippi not only forbade distinctions on account of color, but abolished all qualifications for jury service and property and educational qualifications for suffrage. They began free public schools and adopted considerable social legislation in harmony with the trend of social and political progress.

These reconstruction governments carried on under these respective constitutions for twenty-seven and twenty-two years, without any essential change. Moreover, in Mississippi, the reconstruction constitution was the only constitution of the State which had ever been submitted to popular approval at the polls. And what of the spirit of the Black American?

## Folk Songs

One of those gifts which will ever live in the hearts of the white Americans and the world, making them aware of the presence of the creative souls of their black brothers, is the "Folk Songs" accredited by most musical critics as the only American music. They are the distillation of the sorrows of an oppressed people. The rythmic cry of the slave. Says James Weldon Johnson, "In the spirituals, or slave songs, the Negro has given America not only its only folk songs, but a mass of noble music." " 'Go Down Moses' is considered as one of the strongest themes in the whole musical literature of the world," he continues.

## Art and Literature

It is not unnatural too, that the tragic story of Negro oppression would seek its embodiment in forms of art and literature. Through training and experience, a deft and practised hand in workmanship is rapidly developing. In the broad stream of American literature have come the offerings of Phyllis Wheatley, the black poetess of the latter part of the eighteenth century. She was easily the peer of her best American contemporaries. Dunbar holds a place of envious distinction in American literature. He sings with an intensely tragic charm. In the contributions of Dr. Du Bois, Booker T. Washington, James Weldon Johnson, Kelly Miller, Chestnut, The Grimke's Braithwaite, Carter G. Woodson, Brawley, and the ever developing newer school of Negro writers, America is the recipient of as fine a body of writings as has ever blossomed in a country from the pen of any white American. They represent the highest reaches of literary American genius and talent.

As outstanding luminaries of Negro creative genius, too, are S. Coleridge Taylor, perhaps England's most noted musical composer, Alexander Pushkin, Russia's premier poet, Alexander Dumas, one of France's most prolific and distinguished writers of historical romance, H.C. Tanner, America's greatest living painter, whose works hang in the Luxemborg Gallery, Roland Hayes, doubtless America's leading concert singer, Harry T. Burleigh, America's incomparable song writer, and Rene Moran, winner of the De Gouncourt court prize and many others of growing merit and promise.

## Education

Steadily are the Negro youth swelling the tide of trained workers of hand and brain, drinking at the fountain of arts, science and letters of America's leading colleges and universities, achieving bachelors of art, masters of art and doctors of philosophy. This is irrefutable testimony of the fallacy of Gobineau, Madison Grant and Lathrop Stoddard, the high priests of the Nordic Creed, whose racial hierarchy is implicit with social dangers since it postulates the existence of inferior races, despite the verdict of modern anthropology that so-called race characteristics, dolechochepalic and bracyephatic cerebral formations are not correlated with intellectual excellence or achievement, but that environment as attested by the psychology of Bahaviorism, is mainly responsible for achievement. Black and white boys under similar circumstances react similarly.

What now of America's debt to black men. By the enactment of the Clayton Anti-trust act, the establishment of the Federal Trade Commission and the Interstate Commerce Commission, the government indicated that it sensed the necessity of watching the exercise of vast economic power by gigantic combinations of capital, lest the interests of the people be invaded. Repeated manifestations of the abuse of this power have arrested the attention of the American people.

But who are chief victims of the misuse of economic power by the powerful corporations. The answer is the plain people, those who work for a living. In that category fall the large majority of Aframericans.

From the beginning of the systematic trade in men up to the present moment, the Negro is the one outstanding unpaid worker of the modern world. To allow any man to work and produce and deny him the benefits and protection of the society he makes possible is an inexcusable form of exploitation of which the Negro is a hapless example. He is the last to be hired, the first to be fired, the longest worked and the lowest paid of modern workmen in the Western world.

To the end of correcting this evil, the Negro's next gift to America will be in economic democracy, demonstrating the virtue of the principle of collective bargaining in rational, mutual cooperation around the conference board with a view to effecting a constructive settlement of disputes between employers and employees. To this big task of achieving modern industrial peace upon a democratic basis, in the spirit of brotherhood, the Negro will bring a sympathetic spirit, a genial character and a radiant soul, unimbittered or revengeful. Experience and necessity are teaching him of the value of labor organization, that he can only face the future with head erect and soul undaunted, if he possess power which rests upon economic, political and social organization. This will rescue him from the stigma of being regarded by organized white labor as the classic scab of America.

## The Watson-Parker Bill Enlightened

Black workers are more and more realizing that they cannot hope to go forward so long as they permit themselves to serve as strike breakers to break down the eight hour day and a decent American standard of living built up by the organized white workers of America. That such a policy will flare forth into economic race riots, such as East St. Louis of some years ago, is evident.

And with the possession of this new power on the part of the Negro worker through organization, will come also new obligations, duties and responsibilities. Black workers as well as white, have a joint interest with capital in the expansion and development of industry. Their object shall be not to cripple and paralyze industry, but to help it. The organized Negro worker will not expect the union to protect inefficiency, incompetency and irresponsibility.

In the future, the Negro workers shall expect and demand and organize to secure a fair day's wages for a fair day's work, equality of reward for equality of service; increased wages with increased production, a higher measure of dignity, manhood and independence.

Upon organized labor too, the Negro workers will insist upon the right to work wherever his ability warrants. To capital, he offers increased productive efficiency, initiative, intelligence and responsibility. He is ever in quest for the training to fulfill this end. To society, he pledges his spirit to work, for industrial peace with justice, and to supply a high quality of workmanship in the production of commodities for the satisfaction of human wants.

In politics, the Negro demands political equality, the right to be voted for as well as to vote, a place in the responsible agencies of the nation. But, more than that, the Negro today, would have his suffrage be the means of securing the adoption of social legislation as will reflect itself in more and better schools, better housing, improved community sanitation, larger and modern recreational opportunities and facilities for the children of the community in which they live, as well as a more pronounced, even-handed justice before the courts.

In American social relations, the Negro insists upon equality, upon being recognized as the social equals of any man regardless of color, which will result in the abolition of disfranchisement, segregation and the abolition of the jim crow car.

In the modern world, no people can live beside another and remain as separate as the fingers. Mutual understanding which can only come with the meeting of minds, is a condition to world progress.

But to achieve these objectives, we need men. The world needs men, for men are the agents of the social forces; and the problem of the modern world is the organization and direction of the social forces into constructive channels in order that conflicts between nations, races, creeds and classes may be obviated.

# 18
## The Need of a Labor Background

*In this editorial, "The Need of a Labor Background" (*The Messenger *8 [August 1927]: 256), Randolph suggested that the key to combating racial problems in the United States was the development of a "labor background" among all African Americans and the organization of black workers into black-controlled unions.*

FOLLOWING the Civil War, the Negro workers showed considerable interest in organization. The fact that they had been suddenly transformed from a chattel to a wage slave, threw them into the labor market to compete with the white workers. The fires of race bitterness were burning fiercely, and the helpless freedmen were the victims of this bitterness. To offset this disadvantage, Negro workers banded themselves together into unions of their own as well as sought to join with their white brothers. Isaac Myers, according to Charles H. Wesley, in his Negro Labor in the United States, perhaps, the first Negro labor leader, was the leading spirit in the early Negro labor movements.

It is interesting to note, and it was natural, that the Negro labor unions were largely concerned with securing work, new industrial opportunities, rather than increased wages, although they wanted more pay.

Negroes, like the white workers of post-Civil War period, were distressingly unwitting of their way. But the rapidly developing industrial life of the country, the rise of higher forms of business organization, drove the American workers to build up their own organizations to fight for decent wages and working conditions. They also fought for certain civil and social legislation. Negroes, especially, were fighting hard to consolidate their civil status.

The National Labor Union, the first broad, national attempt of Negro workers to get together, was unfortunately turned from its economic program to politics. This doubtless was due to the failure of the efforts of labor, white and black, to get results.

Here and there, the Negro workers have cast their lot with organized labor, when permitted. They have developed but little organized labor psychology, due largely to the fact that they have not had the privilege of actually leading the workers in labor struggles. They are just beginning to experience what it means to face a formidable foe, to close their ranks and fight unflinchingly, under fire. While Negro workers have fought nobly in the ranks of white workers in long industrial struggles, they have not known what it means to have the responsibility for the moral and financial maintenance of a struggle. The Brotherhood of Sleeping Car Porters is supplying this first experience.

Upon this spirit and work must be built a broad Negro Labor movement, which, of course, will be a part, a conscious and articulate part of the American Labor Movement.

Not alone must Negro workers develop a labor union background, but the Negro public, too, must come to know what it means to suffer and sacrifice for a group of black workers fighting for industrial justice.

Such a labor background can best be developed through a definite systematic Negro labor movement, and experience shows that such a movement must be built up by Negroes themselves. This must be done despite jurisdictional or any other question. Practically, all conditions hindering the economic advancement of Negro workers will vanish before the enlightened organization of Negro workers. Necessity will demonstrate the potency of this fact to white workers. Necessity will also demonstrate the fact that Negro workers must be self-organized. White workers cannot and will not organize them. The history of the Jewish, Italian and Irish workers shows that various groups of workers must organize themselves. In the process of self-organization and self-struggle, Negro workers will develop the necessary labor view-point sense of responsibility, a labor union morale and technique.

The economic self-organization of Negro workers, is most fundamental for the economic emancipation of the race. It also marks the beginning of the period when the Negro earnestly begins to help himself instead of merely looking for his friends to help him.

---

# 19
## Hating All White People

*In the editorial "Hating All White People" (*The Messenger *9 [September 1927]: 280), Randolph argued against stereotyping all whites as enemies of African Americans. This theme was consistent throughout Randolph's career.*

"ALL coons look alike to me"—was once the title of a popular song which expressed the homely philosophy of a multitude of white people on the Negro. It typified their spiritual attitude toward the Negro as well as his physical effect upon their sense of right.

This opinion had economic consequences, too. Insurance companies made this a pretext or excuse for not insuring colored people, saying one Negro would die for another, and they could not, therefore, protect themselves against fraud.

(Finger printing had probably not reached its present stage of accuracy in identi-
fication!)

Moreover, the theory had social consequences. When a crime was committed
by one Negro, instead of taking pains to detect and to apprehend the real culprit,
punishment meted out to "just any Negro" was regarded as sufficient. It was
commonplace for a mob to lynch an innocent Negro, then later admit that a
mistake had been made, while after the Chinese cynic's philosophy its members
would soothe their slippery consciences with the consolation, "well, they are all
bad fellows anyway!"

In physics there is a law which reads, Reaction is equal to action in the
opposite direction. Which is also true of social physics—human psychology.
Thus Negroes concluded that the way to fight fire is with fire. "All white
people are alike," countered the Negro to the whites saying, "All coons look
alike." Negroes grew to hate or distrust most white people. They acted trustfully
in their presence, it is true, after that well known histrionic ability of weaker
peoples, yet all the while they had reservations just as they believed and still
believe that white people have reservations as to them. Abraham Lincoln gives a
rather nice and succinct illustration of this principle in his Douglas debates. Said
he, "When our fathers wrote in the Declaration of Independence 'all men are
created equal,' they whispered behind their backs, 'all *white* men are created
equal.' "

That both the white and the Negro opinion was and is erroneous is easy to
expose by analysis, but more difficult to dispel by logic. In their sober moments
most Negroes were always willing to admit that John Brown—who gave not
only his own life, but the lives of his sons for Negro freedom—was not like all
the Negro-hating whites. Today they accord to Clarence Darrow the high place
of true friend, despite his being a Democrat and an agnostic—both of which are
normally anathema to the Negro mind.

We are not, however, thrown for proof upon such isolated examples as John
Brown, Lincoln, Sumner, Lovejoy, Greeley, Lowell, Beecher, Stowe, Garrison,
and Darrow. For thinking colored people are well acquainted with Blaine's
history of the Ku Klux Klan in the reconstruction period, wherein he points
out how that notorious organization murdered over fifty thousand white union
soldiers and Yankee teachers who went South to protect and instruct the freedom
during those hectic and hazardous days. Likewise all Negroes, who have so-
journed or been educated in the South, recall the splendid New England white
teachers of Hampton, Howard, Fisk, Virginia Union, Atlanta, and other schools
—remember with what industry they labored, with what devotion they toiled,
with what unselfishness they chose to do a work for which there was little
compensation except ostracism as "nigger-lovers," outside of the joy which one
gleans from doing good deeds for others and performing what he considers his
duty.

Chicago Negroes today would readily recall Darrow and Rosenwald, the late

Victor F. Lawson, and Patrick O'Donnell, Mary McDowell and Jane Addams, and many others whose lives impress them as refuting the absurd principle that "all white people are alike."

A more powerful example as proof that homogeneity of opinion on the race question does not exist among all white people is to be found in a comparison of Negro treatment in different states. For instance, Mississippi has about 950,000 Negroes, and 800,000 whites. South Carolina, 900,000 Negroes, and 800,000 whites. New York has about 250,000 Negroes and 12,000,000 whites; Illinois 200,000 Negroes and 7,000,000 whites.

Mississippi and South Carolina, however, have Jim Crow cars, disfranchisement, discrimination in places of public accommodation and amusement, segregation in education and recreation, notwithstanding their racial populations are about equal numerically. Nevertheless, New York with a population of forty-eight whites to one Negro, and Illinois with thirty-five whites to one Negro, could, more easily than Mississippi and South Carolina adopt Jim Crow cars, disfranchise Negroes, discriminate again them in public accommodation and amusement, segregate in education and recreation. That they do not do so is based upon a difference of opinion among the white populations of those respective states.

In other words, all white peoples are no more alike than all Negroes. The person who asserts such rot writes himself down as either an ignorant or prejudiced bigot, whether he be white or black.

---

# 20
## Negro Congressmen

*In the editorial "Negro Congressmen" (*The Messenger *10 [March 1928]: 60–61), Randolph argued for the development of a strategy of ethnic politics. The principal short-term political goal for African Americans would be the election of black congressmen from those urban districts in the North and Midwest that had black majorities.*

THE time has come for Negroes to secure representation in Congress. It is obviously a disgrace that one-tenth of the population of the great American Republic has not a single representative in either house of Congress. The Jews, Irish, Italians, Catholics, Klu Kluxers, Prohibitionists, Wets, Women and practically every other group in America which has a corporal's guard, can point to somebody in Congress which definitely and directly represents them. They can do that only because the representative is one of them.

Nothing can be raised in Congress against the Jews or Catholics, or Wets or Drys, or Women, which will not be challenged by a representative of that group. It is unreasonable to expect that a Jew will look out for the interest of Catholics, or a Catholic for Negroes. While Jews may not oppose Catholics in Congress, still they have so many problems of their own that they cannot devote the proper time to study the problems of the Catholics in order to champion their cause successfully.

Every group in America which has special problems has shown the good sense to elect one of their group to work for the solution of their problems in Congress. No, it is not correct to say every group has done this, because the Negro has not. He alone stands out, as perhaps the largest, single racial or nationality group in the country which can point to no representative in the nation's greatest legislative body. It is true that there are white representatives from Negro districts, in New York, St. Louis and Chicago. But those white congressmen think of the Negro only to the extent that it is found to be good politics.

In all three of these centers, Negroes should select and elect their own representatives. Of course they will eventually. But that is not enough for intelligent people to set forth as a reason for their political recreancy now. Perhaps the most outstanding contestant for Congress among colored people is Chandler Owen of Chicago. He can and will win, if Negroes will vote for him and see to it that his votes are counted.

Not until Negroes can point to a Negro in Congress will the race get any considerable political dignity or win any definite measure of political respect. The assumption by the white and black public is that since there are no Negroes in Congress, they have no right to be there. But we want more than a Negro in Congress. We want a fearless, brilliant and honorable representative Negro sent there. A man who does not think white; but one who thinks right; one who is without the taint of a slave psychology, but who knows the mechanics and technique of modern social psychology; one who is not the typical politician, but who has a broad, sound fundamental understanding of national political problems in particular, and world problems in general; one who is not a wild erratic gesture-maker and kaleidoscopic sensation-monger, but a serious, dignified student and fighter. Owen fits this bill for Chicago, and the task is for Negroes to find someone who will measure up to the fight in New York and St. Louis. We hope this can be done. We want a Negro congressman who will not alone be interested in the Negro problem but in all the problems of America.

# 21
## Consumers' Co-operation

*In the editorial "Consumers' Co-operation" (*The Messenger *10 [May–June 1928]: 108), Randolph introduced a new strategy. Acknowledging the overall failure of efforts to strengthen black business, he urged black workers to take advantage of the persistence of segregation and establish consumers' cooperatives. In taking this position Randolph anticipated the call for black cooperatives that would appear during the Great Depression.*

*The May–June 1928 number was the last issue of* The Messenger *ever published. Inadequate funding had plagued the journal from its inception. By 1928 the demands of the Brotherhood of Sleeping Car Porters, which also suffered setbacks, left Randolph with insufficient time or resources to keep* The Messenger *going.*

FOR the past eight or ten years considerable emphasis has been laid by Negro leaders on the possibility of solving the problem of the Negro in America by the building up of Negro business. It has been held that since the Negro is hanging precariously on the fringes of national industry and commerce, the only way to save the race economically is to establish a little Negro economy inside the larger national economy. While *The Messenger* has long recognized the precarious situation confronting the Negro worker who must attempt to maintain an American standard of living with a grossly inadequate income with which to do it, we cannot see that building up a little jim crow group economy along capitalistic lines would greatly benefit him, even if it were possible.

But it isn't possible. Hampered by lack of capital confronted by trusts, chains, syndicates and cartels Negro business is rapidly losing ground except in the field of insurance and cosmetics. This condition is not due to color but due to the fact that Negro business is small business, and the day of small business is doomed. The only way small businesses can survive nowadays is by organizing themselves into combines with other small businesses. In other words, the only way a small business can succeed for long in the United States today is by becoming a part of a large business. But since big business has not proved beneficial to the masses of workers at large, how can we expect Negro big business to become beneficial to the masses of Negro workers? After 100 years of intensive industrial expansion and accumulation of wealth, over three-quarters of the population in this country today owns no more than five per cent of the national wealth. White workers are still being paid, in the main, starvation wages, the need for charity is greater than ever and workers are being thrown on the scrap heap at earlier and earlier ages.

*The Messenger* has been very fair to Negro business. For the past 18 months it has carried a department of accurate information as to its activities and progress. It has carried a score of articles on every phase of Negro business from farming to manufacture. Two entire issues have been devoted to telling just what Negro business is doing or was doing at the time. No other publication in the United States has given as much attention to the economic life of the race, and this was done because we realized eleven years ago that all other phases of the so-called race problem was predicated upon it.

But we have not been unaware that Negro business has sharp limitations, being large[ly] restricted to the lines of endeavor mentioned above for the reasons set forth. So far as the Negro worker is concerned, the only way he can extricate himself from his present dilemma is through consumers' cooperative enterprises such as have proved so successful abroad. Living largely in segregated areas, proscribed because of color, forced into a group solidarity, the Negro is admirably suited to this form of economic organization. With the requisite brains and determination, the Aframerican can solve his economic problem in this matter. It is a democratic method and has the added value of benefiting all of the Negroes rather than a few. Organized for service rather than profit, it can flourish alongside capitalist organizations without fear of their competition becoming ruinous. It behooves Negroes to bestir themselves and investigate the merits and methods of consumers' co-operation. The Co-operative League of America, 167 West 12th Street, New York City, will gladly furnish information.

---

# 22
## The Economic Crisis of the Negro

*In "The Economic Crisis of the Negro" (*Opportunity *9 [May 1931]: 145–49), Randolph offered his analysis of the economic crisis confronting the western world in general and African Americans in particular. While calling for a shorter work week and additional social legislation, he argued that the long-term solution would be found in increased organization of labor, long-range economic planning, and the development of effective consumers' and producers' cooperatives. (The footnote that originally appeared with this article has been placed in the text in parentheses.)*

*A. Philip Randolph is the General Organizer of the Brotherhood of Sleeping Car Porters. For a number of years he has been one of the leaders in the fight to*

*organize Negro workers. He was one of the founders and co-editor of the* MES-
SENGER *Magazine during the period of its publication.*—THE EDITOR

WE are in the grip of an intensive and extensive economic crisis. It is severe. It is
stubborn. It is baffling. It involves the business man, the worker, the doctor, the
lawyer, the teacher, the preacher and the farmer, the buyer, the seller, the tenant,
the landlord—all.

It is not local. It is not national. It is not racial. It is not creedal. It is world-
wide in scope. Different from and worse than a scourge or pestilence such as the
Black Death of the Middle Ages in Europe or an earthquake anywhere, it is a
blight on all lands and afflicts all peoples.

In its devastating path, stalk the menacing and unsightly figures of hunger and
want, crime and corruption, crashes and conflicts of labor and capital, increased
bankruptcies, mergers, mob violence, lynching, racketeers, bribery, blackmail,
political and intellectual hijacking, moral malaise, misery and suffering of men
and women, aged and children.

Unemployment, the most serious aspect of this crisis is guessed at, in the
absence of an index gauge in the United States of America, to range from 3 to 8
millions. In England where more accurate figures obtain, the jobless are estimated at some 2,500,000; in Germany about, 3,000,000; in Italy 800,000; in
Japan 500,000; and now even France of a small estate, peasant class population,
hitherto relatively free from unemployment is swinging into the vicious cycle.

Estimated bank failings, another aspect of the crisis, for 1930 up to December
are 981 with deposits of $312,000,000; fifty-one closing their doors in the South
in one day, according to the Literary Digest of December 27th, 1930. The record
year for bank suspensions was 1926 with 956 involving $270,000,000 in depos-
its. Nineteen thirty, when the smoke clears, is expected to record 1000 failures
with well-nigh three quarters of a billion deposits. The collapse of the Bank of
United States in December with some $200,000,000 deposits and 400,000 depos-
itors with 59 branches, together with the Chelsea Exchange Bank with 7
branches in New York, involving $23,000,000 in deposits, will quite consider-
ably swell the sum. In this financial debacle, Negro banks and their general
business have been hit hard. Probably the strongest bank ever organized among
Negroes, the Binga State Bank of Chicago and the First Standard Savings, the
American Mutual Savings of Louisville and the Peoples Savings Banks in Nash-
ville, closed their doors.

In the last decade, according to the Comptroller of Currency, 5640 banks
failed with deposits of $1,721,000,000. And the mortality among wholesale and
retail merchants, foreclosures on homes and farms, is frightful and staggering.
Commercial failures exclusive of banks numbered 26,335 with total liabilities of
$668,283,842. There is no way of estimating its tremendous extent, and the
social and economic losses entailed.

Suppose we say that an average of 5 millions of workers have been unemployed during the year 1930 which is probably more nearly right than wrong and that the average wage-salary loss is $3.00 per worker per day, the total wage-salary income loss is five billion four hundred million dollars.

Now, it is estimated that the Negro working class population, as of the U.S. Census of 1920, represents 11.6 per cent of the general working class population of the country. Thus, considering the fact that the Negro is regarded as the marginal worker, "first fired and last hired," there are surely not less than 500,000 unemployed. Says the National Urban League, in a recent survey of unemployment in 25 industrial centers among Negroes, by T. Arnold Hill and Ira De A. Reid: "Unemployment statistics of twenty-five cities for the period January 1st to September 30th, 1930, show a decrease of 34.5 per cent in number of available jobs for Negroes and an increase of 39.9 per cent in number of applicants over same period for 1929. But the average wage-salary income per Negro worker is not as high as the general average for the country. Let us say that it is roughly $2.00 per day per worker, this would represent a minimum wage-salary income loss for the race for 1930 of some 360 million dollars or about a million dollars a day.

This economic loss reflects itself in increased physical deterioration, sickness, moral degeneration, family difficulties, reduced patronage of doctors and non-payment of bills, less and poorer food and clothing, lapses of insurance policies, longer bread lines and the giving of the "dole."

According to the survey of the National Urban League: "In almost every city Negroes constitute a larger part of the beneficiaries of charitable agencies than they do of the population. This is because they receive a smaller share of the work."

Such are the plight and ills of the Negro.

What of the remedy? This may be more obvious after we seek the causes that appear to be many and varied. It is quite possible, too, that there is no absolute cure for unemployment under the present competitive economic system. But some fundamental remedies are applicable when the behavior of phenomena making for unemployment is adequately known.

As to the nature of the types of unemployment, there are residual, seasonal, cyclical, and technological.

Residual unemployment, like the poor, is always with us. The Committee on Elimination of Waste in Industry of the Federated Engineering Societies in its report, "Waste in Industry," published in 1921, states: In the best years, even the phenomenal years of 1917 and 1918 at the climax of war-time industrial activities, when plants were working to capacity and when unemployment reached its lowest point in twenty years, there was a margin of unemployment amounting to more than a million men. This margin is fairly permanent; seemingly one or more wage earners out of every forty are always out of work" (Hearings before the Committee on Education and Labor, Unemployment in the U.S., p. 491). And it is difficult to visualize the non-existence of some lag of unemployment, though short, less vexatious and burdensome, to be sure, even under a socialized and more highly coordinated economy.

## Seasonal Unemployment

Seasonal unemployment has long since beset the heels of the worker. It is probably putting it conservatively to say that practically every industry is in a measure seasonal. Hoover engineers showed that workers in the building trades were employed on the average but 63 per cent of the year. Investigation discloses that factories in the men's clothing industry are running on the average of about 69 per cent of the possible working time, according to Dr. Harry W. Laidler, Director of the League for Industrial Democracy. Here again, seasonal unemployment seems to be indigenous and chronic to our Manchester *laissez faire* economy.

But probably the type of unemployment which occasions greatest fear and hardship among the workers is cyclical in its character. In the last 120 years in America about fifteen periods of industrial depression and prosperity, appearing with a sort of rhythmic regularity, have given us pause.

## Technological Unemployment

But cyclical unemployment is not the most baffling aspect of the depression, for its average duration, says the Cambridge Associates of Boston, is slightly over 18 months. Whereas, there is no apparent end to technological unemployment, that is, unemployment created by the machine, labor-saving devices, efficiency methods and industrial and commercial consolidations.

Note this picture. The automatic elevator in apartments and office buildings has eliminated men. "Seven men now do the work which formerly required 60 to perform in casting pig iron; 2 men do the work which formerly required 128 to perform in loading pig iron! One man replaces 42 in operating open-hearth furnaces. A brick-making machine in Chicago makes 40,000 bricks in one hour. It formerly took one man 8 hours to make 450. In New York from 1914 to 1925 the number of workers in the paper box industry decreased 32 per cent while the output per wage earner increased 121 per cent."

It is estimated that some 15,000 or 25,000 extras in the motion picture industry are unfavorably affected by the "talkies" and that "canned" music in the movie theatres has destroyed the skill and rendered jobless thousands of musicians. According to the Federal Reserve Board, the output per man in manufacturing is 45 per cent greater in 1929 than in 1919, although there was a decrease in workers in manufacturing of 10 per cent, even before the depression of 1929. In mining, the output per person increased from 40 to 45 per cent, but the numbers employed dropped approximately 7 per cent. In the last decade, the efficiency of the railroad workers measured in ton-miles greatly increased, and rail employees lost jobs to the extent of 300,000 more or less. As a result of tractors, corn huskers, binders in the wheat fields and other machinery, the output per farm worker increased 25 per cent, and, according to the Department of Agriculture, about 3,800,000 left the farms for the cities, white and colored. In mining, railroading, manufacturing and farming, workers decreased in the last 10 years by about 2,800,000, observes Prof. S.H. Schlicter of Cornell.

Former Secretary of Labor James J. Davis points out "that a puddler and one helper, in the old days could turn out from 2,500 to 3,000 pounds of puddled iron a day. With a machine and the new process, an engineer has produced 2,000 tons in ten hours. The corn husker does the work of 5 men. Binders in the wheat fields in Kansas with 10,000 men will do what 30,000 men formerly did. One hundred men in the Bureau of Labor Statistics with the adding machine can do the work of 500 brain workers. There is a machine in the Census Bureau that with 1,000 employees does the work of 10,000." "Wherever you turn," he continued, "drills, machinery, conveyors, processes and chemicals are doing the work—Track-layers and the railroad section hands find rails laid by mechanical devices, riveted by acetylene welders, and the dirt tramped around the ties with mechanical trampers. Longshoremen find ships loaded by mechanical devices and the freight laid upon conveyors that carry it from the ship's hold into the storage warehouse on the dock. The hod carrier finds the brick and mortar dumped into boxes automatically pulled by a chain into an elevator and scooted up to the top of the building without his assistance. The concrete mixer finds the mix poured into a great cylinder which is a part of an automobile truck and is mixed by the same power that propels the car from the material yard to the place where the concrete is to be used."

This is but a glimpse into the amazing technological revolution going on around us. It touches the Negro worker, skilled and unskilled, as farm laborers, longshoremen, hod carrier, rail employee, etc. And whether Negro workers are employed in an industry directly affected by technological changes or not, they are hit indirectly, since when the skill of a group of white workers is liquidated by an invention, they fall into the category of unskilled workers or competitors of Negro workers, unless, they (the white workers) are vocationally restrained, which is not yet the rule. Already in the South, the influence of the mechanization of the farms and the march of mass production are creating a surplus of white workers who are becoming absorbed easily into menial forms of work formerly considered "Negro jobs," such as teamsters, ice delivery men, scavengers, street cleaners, ash-cart drivers, road making, etc.

Domestic work, too, is rapidly becoming mechanized, thereby requiring less and less personal servants. Besides, there is going on a process of hotelization and apartmentalization which tend to make for the centralization of personal service work where it is being subjected to the process of mass production, which, in turn, will result in more work done with less workers. While this may not be an immediate exigency, it is a rather certain future contingency, according to our present industrial trends.

## Some Remedies

The machine is a challenge to the nation, not only to black and white workers, and this challenge cannot be met by charity, unemployment surveys and temporary jobs, however, important they may be for the *nonce*. No amount of charity is a remedy. Its a palliative. To feed the hungry and shelter the homeless is necessary but this should not obscure the fundamental problem.

The fact is the workers have worked themselves out of work and will repeat the process in the next five or six years. They have produced more goods and services than they can buy back with the wages they receive. The depression is not so much the result of over production as of under consumption. The people have a physical desire for goods they have no economic power to command.

## High Wages

Obviously if the wage earners, the large majority of the population, cannot buy back what they produce which results in piling up large inventories, one remedy will consist in increasing the purchasing power by raising the wage scale. A word about this problem. In the decade from 1919 to 1929, the numbers of workers engaged in manufacturing decreased 449,775. Wages paid in 1929 showed an increase of $809,229,749 over 1919. Whereas the increase in the total value added by manufacture was $6,286,762,484. Put in another way, the employer was able to add $7.70 to the value of his goods for every dollar he gave to his employees in increased wages. The increase in the cost of raw materials in 1929 amounted to only $124,928,718 above the figures for 1919. Thus the value added by manufacture increased $5,352,604,017 more than the increase in raw materials and wages combined.

In 1914, the average wage in American manufacturing establishments was $589, the value added by manufacture per worker was $1,407. Five years later, in 1919, owing largely to the World War, wages had gone up to $1,162, but the value added by manufacture had increased to $2,756. In other words, the workers had received $573 more for creating $1,349 of additional value. Eight years later, in 1927, the average wage was $1,299 and value added by manufacture had gone up to $3,303. The worker was receiving $137 more wages than in 1919 but his production had increased $547 in value. Finally in 1929, the average wage was $1,318, and the value added by manufacture was $3,636. Here we find the workers' wages had increased $19 in two years and the value of his output had gone up $333. Herein lies the basic cause of recurring depressions. The problem can only be solved by the most scientific industrial statesmanship and social visions.

High wages (real wages) are most significant as a remedy because wage earners are the most important and largest group of consumers in the country. Roughly, with their families, they represent 70 per cent of the population and receive an income of something more than 32 billion dollars a year or 36 per cent of the national income; with the earnings of the salaried workers, who represent about 13 per cent of the population, the two groups, while constituting 83 per cent or more of the population, receive only 57 per cent of the nation's income. And they purchase a great deal more than 57 per cent of the nation's consumer goods. On the other hand, the bond and share-holders and property owners, though representing 17 per cent or less of the population, receive about 43 per cent of the nation's income, and most of this income is reinvested in producers' capital, which is, in turn, a source of the production of more commodities the workers cannot buy, thereby, creating huge inventories and commodity congestion or industrial paralysis.

## Shorter Work Day and Week

But high wages alone will not solve the problem of depressions. This fact is clearly recognized by the American Federation of Labor which is fighting for a 5-day week and by the Big Four Railroad Brotherhood Unions that have inaugurated a crusade for the 6-hour day. The 6-hour day may absorb nearly a quarter of a million idle rail workers. The progress of productive machinery, too, may eventually render the 4-hour day and the 4-day week practicable. How else will the surplus workers be employed?

## Labor Unions

Obviously neither high wages nor the shorter work day or week will come without the struggle of those who will benefit from them. All history attests that every social, economic, political and religious reform has only been won through the utmost struggle, sacrifice and suffering. "Verily, there is no remission of sin except through blood."

Thus, labor organization is the primary and most effective factor in the solution of the problem of seasonal cyclical and technological unemployment, for it is only through the exercise of power, attainable through the organization of wage earners is it possible increasingly to exact higher wages and shorter hours of work. Labor alone will make the necessary struggle, sacrifice and undergo the suffering to stop its own exploitation. But the workers must be organized. Out of 41 million—only 5 million are organized and benefit from fairly high wages and shorter work hours.

## Social Legislation

But labor may be helped. Old Age Pensions are essential to those who have paid their price to society in industry in blood, sweat, tears and toil and are no longer able to keep the pace. And while the aged should be pensioned, the deadline against the men of 45 in industry should be removed.

Employment could also be provided by raising the compulsory school age and the adoption of a Federal Child Labor Law which would affect over a million child laborers who are competitors of their fathers in the labor market.

Unemployment insurance, too, like sick, accident, death and fire insurance, should be formulated and enacted as a national measure by Congress. Private charities are far too inadequate. If unemployment, like sickness and death are unavoidable, insurance against it is indispensable.

Of course, free national employment exchanges and government works, planned over a long period, will help, but usually the political red tape incidental to developing public works, prevents the works from beginning until after the depression ends.

**Twenty-five Year Plan**

Beside the above-mentioned measures is the broad field of self-help by the people. In this field may be listed consumers and producers, cooperatives and workers' credit unions, to mobolize small units of capital into large volumes, for economic strength and protection.

Among Negroes as among farmers and economically weak groups, the Appian Way of private capitalism is difficult if not impossible to trod, especially, in view of the increasing concentration and centralization of financial and industrial power into fewer and fewer hands.

Through a process of interlocking directorships, about 1,000 corporations dominate American business, and at the top of these stand J.P. Morgan and Co., the Bankers Trust and Guarantee Companies, the First National, the National City and Chase National Banks, who have under their control over $74,000,000,000, of corporate assets, equal to more than one-quarter of all the corporate assets of the United States. They practically dominate the business life of the United States, Central and South Americas and exercise a tremendous control in all Europe, Asia and Africa. This amazing empire of capital is more powerful than any political empire or monarchy the world has even seen.

In this regime, the individual, black or white, is helpless. Negroes can only survive modern science and industrialism through consumers' and producers' cooperatives and labor organizations and through the support of labor and social legislation and political action in sympathy with the collective ownership, control and operation of the social productive and distributive instrumentalities in our industrial society. This, however, requires scientific intelligence and a new type of character which can only come through systematic and methodical planning to eventuate through a period of a quarter of a ceutury, much of a piece in principle, with the Russian 5-Year Plan. Much time is needed for the tragedy of it all is that there are but few, either among the leadership or followship, who are aware of what is happening to our modern, industrial life.

Major factors in the plan should be workers' and adult education, and a leadership of courage, education and integrity and a will to sacrifice for the economic well-being of the masses.

To the development of such a plan the "best minds" of the race should be called to form a sort of Supreme Economic Council through which such a plan might be formulated and executed. No existing Negro organization can do it. It should embrace the "best brains" in all of the Negro movements, somewhat of the nature of Kelly Miller's Sanhedrin, but smaller. Probably more nearly like the League of Nations which assembles the worlds greatest experts to grapple with world problems such as the Young Plan. No single Negro organization is now strong enough to withstand the economic stress and strain of the coming years. United, scientific, courageous, honest and sacrificial endeavor alone can save the race. Have the leaders of church, school, press, politics, social service and race movements, the will and the spirit and world vision to meet this challenge? Either we accept the challenge, unite and rise or remain as we are and go down and perish. For, forsooth the old order passeth.

# Index

# About the Editor

**Cary D. Wintz** is currently Professor of History at Texas Southern University. He is the author of *Black Culture and the Harlem Renaissance* (1988) and coeditor of *Black Dixie: Afro-Texan History and Culture in Houston* (1992). His research interests include African American history, ethnic and immigration history, social history, and research methodology.